GUIDE TO GENEALOGICAL SOURCES AT THE PENNSYLVANIA STATE ARCHIVES

Robert M. Dructor

Associate Archivist

Second Edition

Commonwealth of Pennsylvania
Pennsylvania Historical and Museum Commission
Harrisburg, 1998

Cover photo:
A portrait of John and Luisa Gaskins Ball and their
family (MG 467), Pennsylvania State Archives.

CONTENTS

INTRODUCTION

T his guide describes the records of genealogical interest that are currently available for research in the Division of Archives and Manuscripts (Pennsylvania State Archives) of the Pennsylvania Historical and Museum Commission. The Pennsylvania State Archives was established in 1903 as an administrative unit of the State Library, and was combined in 1945 with the State Museum and the Pennsylvania Historical Commission to form the Pennsylvania Historical and Museum Commission. The primary function of the State Archives is to acquire, preserve, and make available for study the permanently valuable public records of the Commonwealth, with particular attention to be given to the records of state government. In fulfilling its general responsibility for the preservation of historic documents, the State Archives also acquires and preserves private papers relevant to Pennsylvania history.

The records are arranged by series under broad topical headings. Since the holdings of the State Archives are divided into record groups (RGs) and manuscript groups (MGs), each series description includes a reference to the particular group to which it has been assigned. Those records created or received by agencies or officers of the Commonwealth and its political subdivisions are maintained in record groups based on the agency of origin. Personal papers, non-governmental records, and historical manuscripts are placed in Manuscript Groups. Included in the manuscript groups are the records and papers of prominent individuals and families, business enterprises, and social, cultural, political and military organizations. To assist users of this guide an appendix is included listing all of the record and manuscript groups cited in this volume. Researchers desiring a more comprehensive overview of the holdings of the State Archives, information about search room hours, reprographic capabilities, and staff services should cosult the Commission's web site at www.phmc.state.pa.us or write to the reference staff at Division of Archives and Manuscripts. Post Office Box 1026, Harrisburg, PA 17108-1026. Though the web site information includes a summary list of all government records series and manuscript collections readily available for public inspection, researchers may want to clarify their research needs and interests prior to visiting the State Archives. The Archives is located at the corner of Third and Forster Streets in Harrisburg adjacent to The State Museum of Pennsylvania.

Researchers seeking genealogical information, family histories, or newspapers should first contact the Genealogical/Local History Section of the State Library of Pennsylvania, Post Office Box 1601, Harrisburg, PA 17105. This section will also supply, upon request, the names of professional genealogists who may be employed for research. On-line information is available at www.cas.psu.edu/do cs/pde/lib1.html.

The original *Guide to Genealogical Sources at the Pennsylvania State Archives* was published back in 1980. As a rookie archivist I was asked to compile a revised handout that would alert genealogists to our resources. After examining the holdings of the Archives floor by floor, however, the handout grew in size to become a guide. Genealogists, or family historians as they are popularly called today, are now the most significant users of the State Archives (approximately 70 percent of all visitors). As an older if not wiser archivist who was concluding his service with the State Archives, it was satisfying to revisit the stacks once again, complete the circle, and describe the PHMC's latest acquisitions.

As with the original enterprise, the production of this revised edition required the cooperation and assistance of numerous persons. Approval was given by the members of the Pennsylvania Historical and Museum Commission and its Executive Director, Brent D. Glass. Harry E. Whipkey, who recently retired as Director of the State Archives and Frank M. Suran, the current State Archivist and Director of the Bureau of Archives and History, gave support and encouragement. To them I am grateful. I particularly wish to thank Jonathan Stayer and John Shelly for generously sharing both their in-depth knowledge of the records and their genealogical expertise with me. The constructive comments, suggestions, and relevant source materials that they identified appear throughout this guide. I also am indebted to Donna Williams, Director of the Bureau of Historic Sites and Museums, for temporarily loaning my services back to the State Archives, being patient, and allowing the new edition to be completed in a thorough fashion. James Arnold assisted in the reworking of several record series, most notably the land records. Likewise, Jan Kinzer meticulously updated the list of microfilmed county records. The core of the original manuscript that was published many years ago was patiently typed by Deborah Miller and Angie Orsini. As a result of the efforts of Harry Parker and Cindy Bendroth their manual work, through the wonders of electronic scanning, became part of this new manuscript. The staff of the PHMC's Division of Publications, including Division Chief Diane Reed, editor Harold Myers, and graphic designer Kimberly Krammes handled design, production and publication. Thanks to all of you.

ROBERT M. DRUCTOR
Associate Archivist

PASSENGER LISTS
(2 Cubic Feet)

The State Archives has custody of the official SHIPS LISTS OF GERMAN PASSENGERS, 1727-1744, 1746-1756, 1761, 1763-1775, 1785-1808 (RG-26), that record the arrival of passengers at the Port of Philadelphia. The lists are arranged chronologically by the date that the vessel arrived at Philadelphia, with an entry usually giving the name of the passenger, the date of arrival, the port of embarkation, and the name of the vessel and its captain. In a few rare instances the passenger's age and famil ial relationships (name of wife, child, etc.) are indicated. From the 1790's onward the occupation and nativity of the individual is also frequently noted, and after 1805 a physical description of the traveler sometimes appears. The lists dating before the Revolution pertain to immigrants from the continent of Europe only (chiefly German, Dutch, Swiss and French), and they do not cover British subjects whose status remained unchanged by their removal from one part of the King's dominion to another.

These lists of immigrants have been published completely in *Pennsylvania German Pioneers* (Norristown, Pa.: Pennsylvania German Society, 1934; reprinted by Picton Press) by Ralph Beaver Strassburger and William John Hinke. Volume III of this three volume set contains a name index and volume II carries facsimiles of all signatures appearing on the original lists.

A HEALTH OFFICER'S REGISTER OF PASSENGERS' NAMES (RG-41) may be utilized to obtain additional information about persons arriving at Philadelphia by sea from October 25, 1792, to May 3, 1794. In addition to listing the vessel's name, master, port of departure and date of arrival, the register records the name of each passenger and oftentimes indicates said person's race and whether a wife or child accompanied him on the trip. (See example on page 2.) The register is arranged chronologically according to the date that the vessel arrived at Philadelphia.

All passenger lists have been microfilmed, and copies of the film may be purchased from the State Archives.

1793   Amount Brought forward ----- 548

April 26th In the Ship Fabius Walter
Kerr Commander from Bristol

James Stobin, & James Butler & Eliza ----- 3

In the Ship Manchester George
Clay Commander from Liverpool

Mr. John Cocks & Mrs. Marrow ----- 2
John Reel & Wm. Elliot ----- 2
Mary Hewet ----- 1
                               ----- 5

In the Brig Chester from Halifax
Richd. Oneil Commander

Thomas Hunt & Wife ----- 2
A negro wench named Sally ----- 1
                               ----- 3

29 In the Sloop Supply Nath.
James Commander from Bermuda

Mr. Eston ----- 1

30 Passengers in the Ship Roebuck
Freedore Bliss Command from Bristol

John Atkinson & Wife ----- 2
Wm. Atkinson & Saml. Battersby ----- 2
John Mansell ----- 1
                               5

                     Carred forward   565

A page from the HEALTH OFFICER'S REGISTER OF PASSENGERS' NAMES, 1792-1794 (RG-41), Pennsylvania State Archives (PSA).

RECORDS OF NATURALIZATION
(61 Cubic Feet)

From the colonial period to the present, the British government, and then the federal, struggled with the problem of attracting desirable settlers to its lands while concurrently attempting to screen such immigrants so that a responsible citizenry would be fostered. The Commonwealth's courts, particularly the Supreme Court of Pennsylvania and the courts of common pleas were the local agencies charged with implementing a national citizenship policy in a liberal but orderly fashion. The naturalization records that are in the custody of the Pennsylvania State Archives were the administrative instruments by which the process was to be uniformly carried out.

Basically, researchers will find three types of documents among our naturalization records. (See examples on pages 4 and 5.) Naturalization lists are precisely what the name implies, chronological listings of individuals who appeared before the courts and were granted denizenship. Declarations of intention and naturalization petitions, on the other hand, are representative of the effort made to achieve greater control over the citizenship process. The declaration of intention was a preliminary form filed by the alien. In this document the immigrant renounced forever all allegiance and fidelity to any foreign ruler or state while declaring his bona fide intention of becoming a United States citizen. The naturalization petition was the last form to be filed by the immigrant. In this document the petitioner reiterated the desire of becoming a United States citizen, declared attachment to the principles of the Constitution, relinquished any title or order of nobility, demonstrated good moral character (by duly sworn vouchers), and proved that the residency requirement had been fulfilled. When all the data provided were sufficient, the petitioner was issued a naturalization certificate, which concluded the citizenship process.

The type of information to be found for each immigrant, along with the dates and geographical areas covered by the naturalization materials, is indicated in the series descriptions that follow.

Naturalization List, 1798, NATURALIZATION PAPERS, Eastern District of the Supreme Court of Pennsylvania, 1794-1868 (RG-33), PSA

Declaration of Intention, 1849, NATURALIZATION PAPERS, Eastern District of the Supreme Court of Pennsylvania, 1794-1868 (RG-33), PSA.

To the Honorable the Judges of the Supreme Court for the Western District, in the Commonwealth of Pennsylvania.

The petition of *Moses Thompson* of *Allegheny bets*
HUMBLY SHEWETH, That your petitioner is a native of *Scotland* —
and was heretofore a subject of *Queen of Great Britain*
——————— and that he has resided within the limits and under the jurisdiction
of the United States of America for *Five* years, and within the state of Pennsylvania
one year; and that *Two* years prior to this application, that is to say, on the *Tenth*
day of *September A.D. 1838* — at a ~~Court~~ *Mayors Court*
in of for the City of Pittsburg ———————
your petitioner declared his intention of becoming a citizen of the United States, in the
manner required by law, as in and by *said Declaration* ———————
——————————————— ~~appears, that he will support the Constitution~~
of the United States, and that he doth absolutely and entirely renounce, and forever abjure all allegiance and fidelity to any foreign prince, potentate, and sovereignty whatever,
and particularly to *Queen of Great Britain* — whereof he was here-
tofore a subject. Your petitioner, therefore, prays that he may be admitted to become a
citizen of the United States of America.

Moses Thompson

I, *Moses Thompson* do swear, that the facts set forth in this my petition, are
true, and that I will support the **Constitution of the United States**; and that
I do absolutely and entirely renounce, and abjure forever, all allegiance and fidelity to any
foreign prince, potentate, and sovereignty whatever; and, particularly, do absolutely and
entirely renounce and abjure forever all allegiance and fidelity to *Queen of*
Great Britain ——————— whereof I was heretofore a subject.

SWORN AND SUBSCRIBED IN OPEN COURT,
THIS *10th Sept A.D. 1840*

N.B. Cuthard *Moses Thompson*
Proth.

we, *John Fox* ——————— of *Pittsburgh*
and Commonwealth of Pennsylvania, do swear, that the petitioner, *Moses*
Thompson — has resided within the limits, and under the jurisdiction of the
United States of America *Five* years, and within the State of Pennsylvania one year;
that is to say, he, the said *Moses Thompson* resided

all which places are within and under the Constitution of the United States;—and that
during his residence within the United States, he has behaved as a man of good moral
character, attached to the Constitution of the United States, and well disposed to the good
order and happiness of the same.

John Fox

SWORN AND SUBSCRIBED IN OPEN COURT,
THIS *10th Sept A.D. 1840*

N.B. Cuthard
Proth.

Naturalization Petition, 1840, NATURALIZATION PAPERS, Western District of the Supreme Court of Pennsylvania, 1831-1867 (not inclusive) (RG-33), PSA.

NATURALIZATION RECORDS OF THE SUPREME COURT OF PENNSYLVANIA

NATURALIZATION LISTS OF THE SUPREME COURT AND COURTS OF NISI PRIUS, 1740-1773 (RG-21). A naturalization record generated during the proprietary period. The documents are arranged chronologically and usually give the alien's name, county of residence, date of affirmation or of taking the Anglican Church's sacrament, and date of certification. These lists are available in printed form, in *Pennsylvania Archives*, Second Series, Volume II, which was published with an index as *Persons Naturalized in the Province of Pennsylvania, 1740-1773* (Clearfield County, 1995). An older but somewhat less complete publication that represents records held in England, Montague Spencer Giuseppi's *Naturalization of Foreign Protestants in the American and West Indian Colonies (Pursuant to Statute 13, George II, c.7)*, published as Volume XXIV of the *Publications of the Huguenot Society of London* (London, 1921) can also be consulted in many libraries.

NATURALIZATION PAPERS, the Eastern District, 1794-1868 (not inclusive) (RG-33). The papers are organized chronologically by the date that the petition was filed and from 1842 onward are also assigned file numbers. Two types of documents, naturalization petitions and declarations of intention, are contained in the record. Data entered vary with the forms utilized and the actual dates of the documents, but usually petitions for naturalization show the person's name, signature, native land and prior sovereign; the date of the petition; the date and place of the declaration of intention (from 1815 onward); the approximate years of residence in the Commonwealth and the U.S.; and the name of at least one voucher. From 1842 to 1863 the petitions frequently indicate if the migrant was under eighteen years of age when he or she arrived in the United States. Moreover, during certain time periods information about the migrant's date (1808-1815, 1824-1842) and port of arrival (1863-1867) is also listed. Declarations of intention are interfiled with the naturalization petitions except in those cases where the individual might have been under eighteen years of age upon arrival in America, an honorably discharged Civil War veteran, or a U.S. resident between June 18, 1798, and

April 14, 1802. Normally, these declarations record the native country of the individual, the port of entry or the place of residence, and the name of the sovereign being renounced. At times, however, the documents also make reference to the foreigner's age, occupation and date of arrival in America, and occasionally even record the names of the migrant's parents. Researchers should also note that the record contains several lists of persons naturalized or making declarations of intention before the Court during the 1790's. Information provided on these lists may include the name and occupation of the alien, the place of nativity, the sovereign to whom he or she had been subject, and the date and place of the naturalization or declaration of intention. For those interested the lists cover these counties and time periods:

Allegheny County, May of 1798 and 1799, at a court held in Pittsburgh Chester County, October 23, 1798
Cumberland County, April and October of 1798, at a court held in Carlisle
Dauphin County, October of 1798, at a court held in Harrisburg
Fayette County, May of 1798 and April 30, 1799, at a court held in Uniontown
Lancaster County, April of 1798, at a court held in Lancaster
Northumberland County, May and October of 1798, at a court held in Sunbury
Philadelphia County, January 9, 1792, and December 15, 1798, at a court held in Philadelphia
Somerset County, April of 1798, at a court held in Somerset
Washington County, May of 1798 and 1799, and July 12, 1798, at a court held in Washington
Westmoreland County, May of 1798, at a court held in Greensburg
Miscellaneous Alphabetical Lists, 1798, with no regions designated.

An INDEX TO THE NATURALIZATION PAPERS OF THE EASTERN DISTRICT OF THE SUPREME COURT OF PENNSYLVANIA, 1794-1824, 1842-1868 (RG-33); the WORK PROJECTS ADMINISTRATION (WPA) INDEX TO PHILADELPHIA NATURALIZATION RECORDS, 1794-1880 (RG-13) (microfilm); and P. William Filby's published *Philadelphia Naturalization Records: An Index to Records of Aliens' Declarations of Intentions and/or Oaths of Allegiance, 1789-1880* (Detroit, 1982) may be consulted in the search room of the State Archives for retrieval purposes. It must be emphasized, however, that the WPA Index and the Filby work list the names of the individuals who not only applied to the state supreme court for citizenship but also to the courts of common pleas, the court of quarter sessions, and the U.S. circuit and district courts. *The Archives' holdings include records only for those persons listed as having filed their petitions with the Eastern District of the Supreme Court of Pennsylvania.*

NATURALIZATION PAPERS OF THE CHAMBERSBURG (SOUTHERN) DISTRICT, 1815-1829 (RG-33). The papers are arranged according to the date that each was filed, and contain diverse data which vary with the time period. During the 1820's, entries usually show the person's name, residence, birthplace and port of arrival. On the other hand, prior to 1820 the name, age, occupation and previous sovereign of the immigrant are often mentioned along with the date of arrival in the country.

NATURALIZATION PAPERS, the Western District, 1831, 1840, 1841, 1844-1856 (also a few petitions from 1862 and 1867) (RG-33). The documents are grouped by years and thereafter arranged alphabetically by petitioner's surname. As in the Eastern District two types of documents, petitions of naturalization and declarations of intention, are found. The naturalization petitions generally contain the name, country or city of origin, previous sovereign, and length of residence in the United States of the alien; the names of any vouchers; and the place and date where the person's declaration of intention was filed. As a rule those declarations of intention that were submitted in Allegheny County give only the immigrant's name and country of origin, the name of the sovereign who was being renounced, and the date and place where the declaration was being made. Declarations made in other western counties, however, sometimes also record the birth date and birthplace of the petitioner.

NATURALIZATION DOCKET, the Western District, 1812-1867 (RG-33). Listings in the docket are grouped alphabetically by petitioner's surname and show the name and nativity of the immigrant, the name of the voucher, the date of the declaration of intention, and, where appropriate, the date of naturalization. Although entries regarding the declarations of intention date from as early as September 12, 1812, to as late as November 2, 1867, and the dates recorded for the naturalization petitions cover the period September 12, 1818, to November 27, 1856, the majority of the listings are from 1830 to 1855.

DECLARATIONS OF INTENTION, the Eastern District, 1832-1870, 1873-1875, 1881-1906 (RG-33). The documents are contained in bound volumes and for the most part are arranged by the date of the declaration. There are indices to the declarations made from September 24, 1832, to June 4, 1840, and from October 4, 1867, to September 24, 1906, but they appear to be unreliable. Normally from 1839 to 1882, the declarations list the alien's name, nativity and age. Prior to 1839 they also indicate the person's place of birth and embarkation, the date and port of arrival in the United States, and the intended place of residence.

OATHS OF ALLEGIANCE AND COUNTY NATURALIZATION RECORDS

LISTS OF PERSONS WHO TOOK THE OATH OF ALLEGIANCE, 1789-1794 (RG-26) and OATHS OF ALLEGIANCE, 1777-1790 (RG-27). Many of these documents are loyalty oaths rather than naturalization papers. The emphasis of the record is on the Philadelphia environs, with individual items arranged by the date of the oath. While the oaths recorded from 1777 to 1786 usually only give the person's name and residence, those dating after 1786 also provide the person's occupation. From 1789 to 1794 the foreigner's name, occupation, birthplace, age and date of arrival in America are frequently mentioned and in some instances the name, occupation and residence of the alien's parents are noted. (See also: COMMISSION BOOK [No. 1], 1777-1800, RG-17, for persons taking the oath before Philadelphia city aldermen from June 2, 1789 to July 24, 1794.) Some of the oaths have been printed in the *Pennsylvania Archives*, Second Series, Volume III, and as in the case of all published records. staff will not search documents for specific details.

NATURALIZATION MATERIALS, 1911-1932 (MG-307). A record generated at Laporte, Pennsylvania (Sullivan County) while Albert F. Heess was prothonotary for the court of common pleas. The materials are arranged by filing date. Three types of government forms found in the file from 1916 to 1929 can be of particular value to genealogists.

Applications for a Certificate of Arrival. The dated and ascribed documents contain the following categories of information: applicant's name, marital status, and immigrant identification card number; mother's maiden name; date and port of arrival; name and nationality of the vessel arrived on; method of arrival (i.e., as passenger, stowaway, seaman, etc.); place where the ticket was purchased; name of the person to whom coming; location of the immigration office where examined; names of other passengers with whom the trip was made; dates and places of residency in the United States; name of sovereign being renounced; name and address of any employer for five years past; and in the case of a woman, maiden name. Questions are also answered on the forms concerning whether the alien ever took up arms in defense of the U.S., claimed an exemption from the draft, believed in anarchy, practiced polygamy, lived on public charity, or had been an inmate in an insane asylum.

Facts for Petition for Naturalization. The forms are dated and usually record such information as the name, postal address, occupation, physical description (height, complexion, color of eyes and hair), marital status, date of birth and place of birth (city or town, country) of the migrant; the date and place of the declaration of intention; date and port of embarkation; date and port of arrival; original destination (city or town); name of the ship or railroad vessel on which he or she arrived; names of persons with whom the trip was made; place of last foreign residence (city or town); sovereign being renounced; dates and places (state, territory or district) of continuous residence in the United States; names, occupations, and residences of two witnesses; and where suitable the names, birth dates, birthplaces, and places of residency of spouse and children. The document is signed by the petitioner.

Notices of Final Hearing on Petitions for Naturalization. Entries simply give the name and petition number of the immigrant, the date of posting and notice, and the approximate date of final hearing.

Preliminary Forms for Petition for Naturalization. Contains virtually all data provided in the "application for a certificate of arrival" and "facts for petition for naturalization" forms with the exception of a physical description of the petitioner. The form also records who purchased the passage ticket for the person.

Request for Certificate of Arrival. Has the same information entered on the "facts for petition for naturalization" forms, but in those cases where the foreigner was a woman the document also lists the date of her marriage and whether her husband was a native or naturalized (with date of naturalization) citizen.

A Certificate of Citizenship was given to the naturalized person as the final step in the process of becoming an American. The document shown above was issued by the Court of Common Pleas of Luzerne County to Harry Stofik, a coal miner who had emigrated from the town of Snine in what was to become Czechoslovakia. It remained in his possession as a prized memento until his death in 1955.

No. 9086

UNITED STATES OF AMERICA

DECLARATION OF INTENTION
(Invalid for all purposes seven years after the date hereof)

State of Pennsylvania

County of Erie

In the **Common Pleas** *Court*

of **Erie County** *at* **Erie, Pa.**

I, **Mary Kondzielska** now residing at **226 E. 4th St., Erie, Erie County, Pa.** occupation **Housewife**, aged **55** years, do declare on oath that my personal description is: Sex **Female**, color **White**, complexion **Ruddy**, color of eyes **Lt.Green** color of hair **Gray**, height **5** feet **no** inches; weight **170** pounds; visible distinctive marks **None**

race **Polish**; nationality **Polish** I was born in **Nacreek, Bigurn, Poland** on **Sept. 8, 1881** I am **married**. The name of my wife or husband is **Alexander** we were married on **Oct. 20, 1914**, at **Detroit, Mich.**; she or he was born at **Bojewo, Poland**, on **Sept 16, 1885** entered the United States at **New York, N.Y.**, on **1905**, for permanent residence therein, and now resides at **Erie, Pa.** I have **8** children, and the name, date and place of birth, and place of residence of each of said children are as follows **Wladyslawa 6-6-06 inPoland, now in Youngstown, Ohio., Wanda 6-22-08 in Oil City,Pa.,now in Oil City, John 10-27-12 in O. City, Thaddeus 7-29-14 in Detroit,Mich, Helen 1-2-17 in O.City Frances 2-21-20 in O.City, Josephine 6-11-23 in O. City, Mary 6-3-25 in O. City. All the rest reside in Erie, Pa.**

I have **not** heretofore made a declaration of intention: Number _____, on _____ at _____ my last foreign residence was **Tamusa, Lubelski, Poland** I emigrated to the United States of America from **Bremen, Germany** my lawful entry for permanent residence in the United States was at **Baltimore, Md.** under the name of **Maryanna Grabowska**, on **July 27, 1907** on the vessel **SS Hannover**

I will, before being admitted to citizenship, renounce forever all allegiance and fidelity to any foreign prince, potentate, state, or sovereignty, and particularly, by name, to the prince, potentate, state, or sovereignty of which I may be at the time of admission a citizen or subject; I am not an anarchist; I am not a polygamist nor a believer in the practice of polygamy; and it is my intention in good faith to become a citizen of the United States of America and to reside permanently therein; and I certify that the photograph affixed to the duplicate and triplicate hereof is a likeness of me: So HELP ME GOD.

Mary Kondzielska

Subscribed and sworn to before me in the office of the Clerk of said Court, at **Erie, Pa.**, this **10th** day of **May** anno Domini 19**37**. Certification No. **5-70671** from the Commissioner of Immigration and Naturalization showing the lawful entry of the declarant for permanent residence on the date stated above, has been received by me. The photograph affixed to the duplicate and triplicate hereof is a likeness of the declarant.

LAWRENCE A. TAYLOR

[SEAL]

Clerk of the **Common Pleas** *Court.*

By *Arthur M. Lung*, *Deputy Clerk.*

Form 2202-L-A

U. S. DEPARTMENT OF LABOR
IMMIGRATION AND NATURALIZATION SERVICE

Nº 65941

Declaration of Intention, 1937, filed by Mary Kondzielska. NATURALIZATION PAPERS FOR ERIE COUNTY, 1801, 1819-1820, 1823-1940 (RG-47), PSA.

NATURALIZATION PAPERS FOR ERIE COUNTY, 1801, 1819-1820, 1823-1940 (RG-47). Indexed. Declarations of intention and naturalization petitions filed with the Court of Common Pleas of Erie County located in Erie, Pa. Most of the papers found prior to 1906 are declarations of intention. The type of form utilized (handwritten or printed) varies with the time period, but with the exception of where the documents are being filed, the information closely resembles that submitted by petitioners to the Supreme Court of Pennsylvania. After 1906, the petitions for naturalization consist of standardized forms received from the United States Bureau of Immigration and Naturalization. Data recorded include the petitioner's full name, residence (dwelling number, street, city or town, and state), occupation, date of birth, place of birth and marital status; the date and place of emigration; the date and port of arrival in the United States; the name of the vessel, and if appropriate, the character of conveyance or the name of the transportation company; the place, date, and court where the person declared his or her intention of becoming a U.S. citizen; if married, the spouse's name, birth place, and residence; the name, birth date, place of birth, and residence of any children; and the names, occupations, and places of residence of two witnesses. The document, which is signed, dated, and sworn to by both the applicant and witnesses further declares that the petitioner is neither an anarchist nor polygamist; reiterates that he or she renounces allegiance and fidelity to any other sovereign; and states that the person can speak English and has continuously resided in the United States for at least five years (gives exact date) and in the state of Pennsylvania for one year. The reverse side of the petition is dated and signed by a judge and indicates whether the request is accepted and or denied; gives the reason for any denial; and has a completed oath of allegiance for successful applicants. As needed, after October, 1910, sections captioned "memorandum of continuances" and "names of substitute witnesses" are available on the forms for handling special circumstances or situations. The declarations of intention filed for this period also are standardized federal forms and contain most of the information listed on the naturalization petitions plus a personal description of the alien (color of skin, hair, and eyes; type of complexion; height; weight; and distinctive marks). The earlier forms, however, do not provide data regarding spouses or children. The more modern declarations, that is, those from the late 1930s, mention the names, birth dates, and residences of family members. They make note of the immigrant's sex, race, and date of marriage as well. As can be seen from the sample declaration appearing on page 12, photographs of the person might be attached to these forms. Prior to 1906 the naturalization papers are arranged in chronological order by date of declaration or petition. The pages of each document are numbered for microfilm retrieval purposes. After 1906, the naturalization papers are in numerical order by petition numbers. The Erie Society for Genealogical Research, Inc. prepared an index to these records which was published under the title of *Erie County, Pennsylvania, Naturalizations, 1825-1906* (Marceline, 1983).

NATURALIZATION RECORDS FOR INDIANA COUNTY, 1806-1941 (RG-47). The file contains naturalization petitions, 1806-1906, declarations of intention, 1815-1906, certificates of naturalization, 1807-1811, and alien registration receipt stubs, 1911-1941, created by or submitted to the Court of Common Pleas of Indiana County at Indiana, Pa. by county residents seeking citizenship. The naturalization petitions and declarations of intention record information similar to that described as being filed with the state supreme court. The certificate of naturalization consists of a form printed by the county that certifies that the person listed had exhibited a petition to become a United States citizen (court and date noted); renounced allegiance to his or her previous sovereign; chose to support the Constitution; resided in the United States before January 29, 1795, and met the two year Pennsylvania residency requirement; was of good moral character; and, as a result, had been admitted by the court to become a citizen. The registration receipt stub is signed by the alien and records the person's name, postal address, and age; the date of the admission order; the name of the court that issued the naturalization certificate and the date; and the naturalization petition and certificate numbers. Receipts issued from 1911 to the 1930's also have space for providing the names, ages, and places of residence of the spouse and any children. All of the stubs are numbered. The naturalization records are arranged in chronological order by petition dates and thereinafter numbered. A typed alphabetical index can be used for reference purposes. The receipt stubs are in chronological order by date certificate was issued. There also is a separate file folder of declarations of intention, 1904-1906, which is in alphabetical order by name of immigrant.

NATURALIZATION PAPERS FOR JEFFERSON COUNTY, 1835-1910 (RG-47). A variety of declarations of intention and naturalization petitions filed by immigrants seeking citizenship status from the Court of Common Pleas of Jefferson County. Many of the declarations originate from other regions, however, including neighboring courts from the northern tier such as Elk County, and the more distant mayor's court for the city of Philadelphia. The amount of information found in a particular document varies greatly, sometimes even during a relatively short time span. For example, the declaration of intention can be a simple dated and signed form from the county prothonotary that records the alien's name, native country, and the name of the sovereign ruler being renounced (apparently used from 1855 to 1891). It might also include the immigrant's age and place of birth (1890's); the number of continuous years residency in the United States and the state of Pennsylvania; and the port of arrival and approximate date of entry (Ca. 1830's and 1840's). Naturalization petitions found through the 1890's are similar in content to those described under the Supreme Court of Pennsylvania. (See example on page 5.) During the early 1900's, however, the petitioner's age, date of birth, date of landing, place of landing, and business or occupation are included. The declaration and naturalization forms received from the United States Bureau of Immigration and Naturalization (prevalent from 1907 to1910) contain the same type of data described for Erie County. The documents are numbered and thereafter arranged in chronological order court term.

NATURALIZATION RECORDS FOR LAWRENCE COUNTY, 1850-1858, 1861-1939, 1950 (RG-47). While the records focus on the Court of Common Pleas of Lawrence County the file provides excellent examples of the various types of documents that were developed and used throughout the Commonwealth to grant or deny citizenship to aliens from foreign countries. The naturalization petitions and declarations of intention (some as enclosures, dating back to 1843) filed by immigrants for the 1850 to 1905 period are representative of the those identified and already described under the holdings of the state supreme court and of Jefferson County. Likewise, with the exception of some records that deal with court cases involving disputes over residency and qualifications for citizenship (1935-1939, 1950), the forms and petitions utilized from 1906 to 1935 are for the most part identical to those listed under Erie and Sullivan Counties. Additional documents found, however, and that have not been described previously include:

Facts for Declaration of Intention. An undated form that was filled out by the alien in order that the issuance of the declaration of intention would be expedited and the possibility of error obviated. It contains the same information recorded on the declarations of intention for the 1906-1915 time frame.

Preliminary Form for Declaration of Intention. The forms are undated and were used as both a guide in preparing the declaration of intention and as a tool for verifying the accuracy of the information reported by the immigrant. It has the usual information recorded on declarations regarding allegiances as well as the person's name, age, occupation, residence, date of birth, place of birth, physical description (color, complexion, height, weight, distinctive marks, eye and hair color), spouse (place of birth, residence, and maiden name if a woman), origin (port and vessel), and values (not an anarchist, polygamist, etc.). In addition, the form contains much of the data that was later incorporated into the "applications for a certificate of arrival," that is, questions regarding the place where the ship ticket was purchased; the method of passage (1st, 2nd, 3rd cabin or stowaway, seaman, member of the crew) the names of some persons who traveled with the alien; and the dates and places in the United States where he or she resided and had been examined by an immigration office. Other questions posed included whether the person had ever used another name and why; the maiden name of the mother; the name of the steamship line used; was a head tax paid; and what kind of papers were used to travel in the United States (an immigration visa, a passport, a permit). The form is found among the naturalization records filed from 1927 to 1930.

Statement of Facts to be Used in Filing My Petition for Citizenship. Another undated form that was used to complete the processing of the petition for naturalization from 1929 to 1935. As such it contains all of the information mentioned as characteristic of naturalization petitions filed in Erie County after 1906. The form, however, also has space for allowing the person to list a name change, if so desired. Entries appearing here, usually reflect an English translation of the alien's foreign name.

Notice to Take Depositions under the Fourth Subdivision of Section 4, Act June 29, 1906, As Amended and Interrogatories in Depositions of Witnesses. Forms utilized in cases where citizenship was rejected and the immigrant sought redress. The notice shows the names of the court and the branch of the Immigration Service involved in the case; the alien's name, address and signature; the number and filing date of the naturalization petition; the names, occupations, and addresses of the two citizens to be questioned; the county, state, and date that the depositions are to be made. The depositions are signed, dated, and subscribed by the witnesses and record their names, addresses, occupations, ages, and birthplaces; the years of residence in the county where they knew the petitioner; and if naturalized citizens, the dates, places, and courts where they were naturalized. The name of the state and county where the depositions were taken appear at the top of the document and the following facts about the petitioner solicited from the witness: the circumstances under which he/she met the person in the United States; the length of time the immigrant continuously resided in the United States; the county and state of residency; frequency of contact with the alien; any time absent from the United States; date that the individual moved from the county and state; his or her moral character; knowledge of the petitioner ever being arrested, engaging in any unlawful occupation, practicing polygamy, believing in anarchy; and commitment to the principles of the Constitution.

NOTICES OF APPLICATION FOR ADMISSION TO CITIZENSHIP, CARBON COUNTY,1916-1920 (RG-47). A record that was to be posted in a conspicuous place of all aliens who submitted petitions to the court of naturalization held at Mauch Chunk, Pa. from February, 1916, to April, 1920. Data appearing in columns include the petitioner's name, place of birth, and residence; the place of arrival; the date of arrival in the United States; the date of filing petition; date of posting notice; approximate date of final hearing; and the name and residence of witnesses. Entries appear on the notices by date of posting.

Facilities are available at the State Archives for producing either xerographic (for loose documents) or photostatic (for documents in bound volume) copies of these records for patrons. To obtain information about naturalization records not in our custody, researchers can write to the U.S. Immigration and Naturalization Service in Washington, D.C. 20536. That agency has duplicate records of all naturalizations that occurred after September 26, 1906. The National Archives (Washington 20408) also has natural- ization proceedings for the District of Columbia courts, 1802-1926, and photocopies and indices of naturalization documents, 1787- 1906, filed by courts in Maine, Massachusetts, New Hampshire and Rhode Island. Persons desiring data about all other citizen- ships granted prior to September 27, 1906, should send their requests to the clerk of the federal, state or other court that issued the naturalization certificate.

VITAL STATISTICS
(44 Cubic Feet)

P rior to 1906, Pennsylvania births, marriages and deaths were officially recorded by the Commonwealth in only a few exceptional cases. For the most part, therefore, genealogists must rely upon county records or unofficial sources such as newspaper files, church registers, entries made in family Bibles, and gravestone inscriptions in order to obtain data for the earlier years. There are, however, a few official marriage records that have been preserved and that are now in the Archives' care. Among these are·

GOVERNOR'S ACCOUNTS, 1742-1752, 1759-1763 (RG-21). The accounts include lists of marriages (December, 1742-July, 1752, November, 1759-January, 1762) that are arranged by the date that the licensing fee was paid. Normally, entries provide the date that the fee was received, the amount of the fee, the name of the husband, and sometimes the name of his wife.

MARRIAGE BONDS, PHILADELPHIA COUNTY, 1784-1786 (RG-27). Listings are in alphabetical order according to the surname of the groom. Entries usually give the name and residence of the married couple, the date and amount of bond paid, and the name of any co-bonder. The Marriage Bonds have been microfilmed as part of the Records of Pennsylvania's Revolutionary Governments and are also printed in the *Pennsylvania Archives*, Sixth Series, Volume VI.

Inquiries regarding marriages performed in Pennsylvania after September 30, 1885, and births and deaths occurring between 1893 and 1906 should be directed to the Clerk of the Orphans' Court for the appropriate county. The Archives' staff, however, can provide patrons who visit the search room with a RECORD OF MARRIAGES (RG-14) that covers all existent counties and dates from October 1, 1885, to September 20, 1891. Consisting of three sets of volumes kept by the state Board of Health and Vital Statistics, one set is arranged in alphabetical groups by surname of husband, and another is grouped alphabetically by maiden name of wife. A third set, covering the period April 1, 1889 to September 20, 1891, includes both males and females in one volume. In addition to the couples' names, the volumes usually record each person's residence (county or township), place of birth (county, state or country if a foreigner), age, color (white or black), and occupation; the county where the license was procured; and the date of the marriage. If one of the parties was divorced, the individual was expected to state the cause for it.

For interested researchers, information about the dissolution of marriage contracts can be found in the DIVORCE PAPERS of the Eastern District of the Supreme Court of Pennsylvania (RG-33). Covering the period 1786 to 1815, the cases are organized alphabetically by surname and often mention diverse data about the estranged couples. Likewise, the Division has a GENERAL MOTION AND DIVORCE DOCKET, 1750-1837 (RG-33), for this Court, which contains data about divorce cases for the period 1800-1805. Usually entries in the docket give the names and residences of the married couple; the date of the marriage; the occupation of the husband; the reason for the divorce; the date, place, and court where the petition for divorce was filed; and the date that the marriage bond was nullified. At times, particulars such as the name of the individual who married them, the wife's maiden name, and the names and residences of the couple's parents are also entered. Entries are arranged by the date that the individual appeared at court and filed the petition.

The Archives also has Coroner's Inquisitions and Escheats for the Eastern District of the state supreme court. The materials are arranged by the date of the inquiry and contain the following information:

CORONER'S INQUISITION PAPERS, 1751, 1768-1790, 1792-1796 (RG-33). The documents (see example on page 23) are signed by the coroner and witnesses and give, when possible, the name of the victim, the approximate date and manner of death, the date and place of the inquiry, and the location of the body. The occupation, age, and race of the deceased person sometimes appear, and in the case of a slave, the name of his or her master is provided.

ESCHEAT PAPERS, 1796-1822 (RG-33). A record of persons whose possessions passed into the custody of the Commonwealth because they died intestate without heirs or known kindred. Besides listing the deceased individual's name, residency, approximate

County of Philadelphia, *to wit.*

AN Inquest indented and taken this *28th* Day of *Febuary* in the Year of our Lord 1775 before me *John Knight* Coroner for our Sovereign Lord the King, for the *city & * County of *Philadelphia*, on View of the Body of *a negro Man Named Harry belonging to Adam Baker* then and there lying dead in the *Township of Chillingham* and County aforesaid, on the Oaths

of *Rudolph Neff Michell Baker Richard Statherford Joseph Miah Conrad Bear Jacob Lesher Peter Long Joseph Scull John Turner and George Falkes and Solemn Affirmation of Thos Roberts and James Tyson*

lawful Men of the County, sworn and affirmed to en-
quire how, and after what Manner the aforesaid *Negro man* came by *his* Death, who, upon their Qualifications, respectively do say, That the aforesaid *Negro Man Harry was found hanging by a with on a limb of a white Oak Tree supposed to have wilfully hung himself*

so doth say the Jurors, as well as the Coroner, that the aforesaid *Negro Man* came by *his* Death in Manner aforesaid,
In Witness whereof, we have hereunto set our Hands and Seals the Day and Year above written.

John Knight Coroner

Peter Long   *Rudolf Neff*

Joseph Scull   *Richard Baker*

John Turner   *Richd Stettaford*

George his X Father mark   *Joseph Miah*

Thos Roberts   *Conrad Bar*

James Tyson   *Jacob Lesher*

*An example of the type of document found in the CORONER'S INQUISI-
TIONS, 1751, 1768-1790, 1792-1796, for the Supreme Court of
Pennsylvania, Eastern District (RG-33), PSA.*

date of death, and personal possessions, the documents record the date of the inquest and the name of the official conducting it. In at least one instance a marriage certificate is also found.

As a result of the Act of May 1, 1905, which implemented a state system of registering vital statistics at a central depository, births and deaths occurring in Pennsylvania during 1906 and beyond are normally on file with the Division of Vital Statistics. Because of inconsistencies in conforming to the act, however, particularly on the part of midwives, researchers may have some difficulty in obtaining data about persons being born or dying prior to 1920. Official copies of those birth and death certificates held by the Division of Vital Statistics (P.O. Box 1528, New Castle, Pennsylvania 16103) may be secured upon application and payment of a nominal fee.

During the years 1852 to 1854 the register of wills for each county was required by law to keep a RECORD AND INDEXES OF BIRTHS, DEATHS AND MARRIAGES (RG-26), and to semi-annually submit a duplicate copy to the secretary of the Commonwealth in Harrisburg. For forty-nine of the sixty-four existent counties (i.e., no returns for Blair, Clarion, Clinton, Crawford, Erie, Fayette, Forest, Fulton, Jefferson, Lebanon, Philadelphia, Pike, Potter, Sullivan and Wyoming Counties) these duplicate records and their indices are now in the custody of the State Archives. It must be understood, however, that these returns are not inclusive. Hence, while there are complete marriage, birth and death registration tabulations for thirteen counties (Adams, Allegheny, Bucks, Chester, Cumberland, Delaware, Luzerne, Mercer, Montgomery, Perry, Schuylkill, Tioga and Westmoreland) from 1852-1854, there are no birth records for at least ten other counties (Centre, Clearfield, Columbia, Franklin, Green, Juniata, Lawrence, Montour, Union and Warren) during this period. The kinds of information usually entered on these indexed returns are as follows:

Registration of Births. Listings show the name, sex, color, place of birth (town or township, county), and date of birth (hour, month and year) of the child; the name and occupation of the father; the maiden name of the mother; the name and residence of the physician or other person signing the birth certificate; the date of the certificate; the date and county where registered; and the signature of the register or his deputy.

Registration of Deaths. The returns are signed and dated by the county register or his deputy and list the name, color, sex, age (years, months, and days), occupation, place of birth, and residence of the deceased person; the date, place, and cause of death; the name and place of interment; the date of the death certificate; and where fitting, the names of parents, spouse, and children.

Registration of Marriages. Entries record the names and race of the couple; the names of their fathers and mothers; the occupation, residence, and birthplace of the husband; the date and place of the marriage; the type of ceremony; the name and residence of the person performing the marriage; the name of the individual signing the certificate; and the date of registration. As in the case of other registration returns, the listings are signed by the county registers or their deputies.

As part of its day-to-day function of furnishing citizens with diverse services and programs, government creates official records that often cover a wide range of activities and topics rather than just one subject. Because the titles of such records are often nondescript, researchers are likely to overlook them. Records of this type include these:

HOUSE FILE, 1790-1903 (RG-7). Primarily documents topics, such as road and bridge construction, public transportation, taxation, labor relations, immigration, consumer safety, and other similar issues that generated strong grass roots interest and, therefore, were a high priority on the legislative agenda. In addition to petitions, reports, and drafts of bills relating to these subjects, however, are memorials seeking pensions for military service; papers relating to estates and guardians; petitions asking that marriages be annulled (see page 25); and requests praying that laws be passed to enable the children of persons who died intestate to have property titles perfected. The documents are not indexed but arranged by house sessions.

To the honorable the Senate and house of Representatives of the Common=
=wealth of Pennsylvania in general assembly

The Petition of Catharine Lippincott Respectfully Sheweth
that on the 17th of April 1823 She was Joined in lawfull wedlock with
Joseph Lippencott now of Mountpleasant Westmoreland County

Your Petitioner further States that at the time of her intermarriage
with sd Joseph She was an orphan not seventeen years of age destitute of the ad=
vice & guardianship of a Father left to the premature & rash counsel of her own inex=
perienced understanding She therefore prays your honorable bodies to compassionate
her youth & her misfortunes and release her from obligations contracted in her mi=
nority which seem to procure her nothing but trouble & misery

Your Petitioner further represents that she is entitled by the Will of her
Father John Stouffer late of Fayette County Decd to a considerable sum of money
and your Petitioner firmly believes that his only motives in marrying was her
money At one time saying it never should do her any good that he intended living
a gentleman &c After your Petitioners marriage with sd Joseph instead of experiencing
from him the kindness & protection due from a husband he treats her with the most perfect
indifference and after some cold & brief interviews alienated himself from your Petitioner
and has never provided for her any home or residence Your Petitioner further states
that her sd husband has not only declined to live with her & extend to her the protection
of a husband but from some cause never claimed from her the interesting & peculiar
offices of a wife Under the affliction of mind produced by the early dissolution of her hopes
your Petitioner throws herself upon the mercy of your honorable bodies Her husband refused
to provide a home or maintenance for her and has declined all the offices & duties of a husband
And whilst the cold & unnatural connexion exists your Petitioner cannot obtain even from
the fund provided for her by her fathers kindness

Your Petitioner therefore prays your honorable bodies to annul her marriage
and divorce her from the bonds of matrimony and she will pray &c

Catharine Lippincott

This October 9, 1824, petition of Catharine Lippincott of Westmoreland
County for a divorce from her husband Joseph is found in the HOUSE FILE,
49th Session, 1824-1825 (RG-7), PSA.

MISCELLANEOUS SUPREME COURT RECORDS, Ca. 1786-1800 (RG-33). This series contains sundry court records found in the basement of the State House building in Philadelphia and given to the Genealogical Society of Pennsylvania in 1895 for safekeeping. Volume 45, pages 187-211, contains lists of marriage licenses issued that normally show the names of males paying the license fees, their residences, the fees paid, and the names of the officials making the returns. Returns for the following counties are present: Lancaster, 1780-1782 (not inclusive); Northampton, August 7, 1780-September 11, 1780; Philadelphia (also city), April 10, 1780-November 7, 1782; and York, March 20-September 21, 1780. The volume is indexed. Similar returns are located in ESTREAT OF FINES, 1780-1783, of the Supreme Court of Pennsylvania, Eastern District (RG-33). Counties represented include Lancaster, May 22-September 20, 1780, August 18, 1781-March 20, 1782; Northampton, September-December, 1780; Philadelphia (also city), April 10-September 25, 1780, September 24, 1781-November 7, 1782; and York, June 8, 1779-May 18, 1780. There are returns for Bedford County from October 3, 1781 to January 14, 1783, but the statement "no licenses issued" appears. Many of the these estreat listings also give names of the women being wedd (see example on next page). The documents are in no discernible order.

Researchers must also be aware of the fact that some rather unlikely sources also contain vital statistics data. Business records are a good example of such records. The PINE GROVE FURNACE COLLECTION (MG-175), contains DIARIES, 1880, 1882-1884, and TIME BOOKS, 1812-1845, 1864-1872, that not only list the names and jobs of the workers but also mention noteworthy occurrences such as the marriages and deaths of employees and employers (example on page 28). Likewise, similar information is found in the TIME BOOKS, 1836-1843 (Reading Furnace) and 1853-1869 (Robeson, Brooke & Company) of the CHARMING FORGE COLLECTION (in MG-262); in the TIME BOOK, 1809-1810, of the BIRDSBORO FORGE RECORDS (MG-258); and in the DAY BOOKS, 1815-1828, 1855-1864, and TIME AND PAYROLL BOOKS, 1840-1852, 1857-1866, 1877-1913, of the CURTIN IRON WORKS RECORDS (MG-155). As might be expected, there are no indexes for these unofficial records and many hours must be spent perusing the pages of these books in order to obtain pertinent data.

In addition to these records the Division of Archives and Manuscripts has original or microfilmed copies of the following municipal records:

BIRTH RECORDS for the city of Johnstown, February 15, 1891-December 30, 1912 (RG-48). Microfilmed volumes that provide the name (usually only surname), sex, color, date of birth, and place of birth of the child; the names and residence (also election ward in later returns) of the parents; the occupation of the father; the certificate number; and the name of the person signing the certificate. Miscellaneous birth records and affidavits regarding births that occurred from as early as 1878 and which had been destroyed in the May, 1889 flood are also included. The records are arranged in numerical order by certificate numbers.

BOARD OF HEALTH MINUTE BOOKS for the borough of Yorkville, 1894-1907, and the city of Pottsville, 1872-1874, 1893-1923 (RG-48). Although these microfilmed minutes are not indexed, they contain, in chronological order, data about deaths in these two communities. Generally entries provide the name, age, and residence of the deceased person; the date of the certificate of death; the cause of death; and the surname of the official making the report. Similar data about persons who contracted contagious diseases appear in the minute books as well.

DEATHS AND INTERMENTS in the city of Reading, July 15, 1873-December 31, 1905 (RG-48). Prior to 1901 the microfilmed volumes have two sections, one consisting of a physician's certificate and the other an undertaker's certificate. Besides giving the name and residence (from June, 1883 onward) of the physician, the physician's section records the name, color, sex, age, marital status (married or single), residence (street, number, and from June, 1883, ward), place of birth, date of death, and cause of death of the deceased person. The undertaker's certificate usually provides the occupation of the deceased and the names of his or her parents; the date and place of burial; the burial permit number; and the undertaker's name and residence (from June, 1883 onward). In addition to this information, the volume created from 1901 to 1905 has space for listing the dead person's date of birth, conjugal condition (married, divorced, widowed, single), the birthplace of each parent, the duration of last sickness and any contributing causes of death, and the place of death. Entries are numbered and for the most part arranged in chronological order by date of death.

DEATH RECORDS for the city of Johnstown, August 18, 1895-February 2, 1912, (RG-48). Indexed. From 1895 to 1898 the bound records normally show the names, sex, color, age, marital status, nationality, occupation, date of death, and cause of death of the deceased; the date of the death certificate; the place of interment; and the name and residence of the physician who pronounced the person dead. After December 28, 1898, the form is divided into two sections, a "physician's certificate" and an "undertaker's certificate in relation to deceased." Additional data recorded includes the deceased person's address (also ward), place of birth, and if a minor, parents' names; the date of burial; and the name and address of the funeral director. The certificates are numbered, but not in sequence from one volume to another.

INDEX TO BIRTH CERTIFICATES for Johnstown, Pa., 1891-1932 (RG-48). The microfilmed volumes are grouped in alphabetical order by first letter of surname and then arranged in chronological order by month and thereunder by year. Information shown includes the certificate number; the child's name (usually surname) and date of birth; the name (first and last) of the father or mother; and the address of the family. The indexes from 1891 to 1909 also gives a birth record volume and page number.

INDEX TO DEATH CERTIFICATES for Johnstown, Pa., 1891-1931 (RG-48). The bound volumes are grouped in alphabetical order by first letter of surname and then arranged in chronological order by month and thereunder by year. Information appearing includes the certificate number and the deceased person's name, age, date of death, place of death, and interment. The index for 1891 to 1909 also gives a death record page number and the dead person's race.

INDEX TO REGISTRATION OF DEATHS, CITY OF PHILADELPHIA, 1803-1860 (RG-13). The microfilmed transcript is in alphabetical order by surname and shows the deceased individual's name, age, date of death, and cause of death; the name of the doctor who pronounced the person dead; and the name of the cemetery where he or she was buried. Although there is a column for indicating the person's race, it is normally left blank for Caucasians. The code "Blk." is used for African Americans.

MARRIAGE RECORDS for the city of Johnstown, October 11, 1892- December 18, 1914 (RG-48). Provides the following information: the name, occupation, residence, birthplace, and age at marriage of the husband; the residence, age at marriage, birthplace, and name of the wife (previous to marriage or if a widow maiden name); the date of marriage; the type of ceremony employed; and the color of the parties. The records are in chronological order by date of marriage.

MAYOR'S RECORD BOOK, February 3, 1852- February 10, 1863 (RG-48). The microfilmed book provides particulars about marriages performed by Lancaster city mayors Thomas H. Burrowes and George Sanderson from February 13, 1858, to February 28, 1861. The listings are arranged chronologically and give the names and residences (township and county) of the couple, the date of their union, and the name of the person performing the ceremony.

RECORD OF BIRTHS for the city of Altoona, January 31, 1886, April 1, 1886- May 31, 1905 (RG-48). The microfilmed volumes are grouped in loose chronological order by month of birth. Data shown include the child's name (often left blank in the early volumes), sex, color (white or black), and date of birth; the names and address of the parents; the ward of residence; and occupation of the father. The early registers also note the name of the physician or individual assisting with the birth. Entries are for the most part in chronological order by date of birth.

RECORD OF BIRTHS for the city of Williamsport, 1869-1917 (RG-48). The microfilmed record is arranged alphabetically by parents' surname. Researchers may expect to find the following categories

A list of couples applying for marriage licenses in York County, 1780. Note that the last entry pertains to Sam Bevis and Catharine Johnston, a slave couple. The document is located in the ESTREAT OF FINES PAPERS, 1780-1783, of the Supreme Court of Pennsylvania, Eastern District (RG-33), PSA.

of information: the name, nationality, and residence (usually ward) of each parent; the child's name, sex, color, and date of birth; and the attending physician's name.

RECORD OF BIRTHS, DEATHS, AND BURIALS for the boroughs of Easton, 1888-1907, and South Easton, 1893-1898 (RG-48). The microfilmed volumes are arranged by the date of the event and contain these categories of data:

Record of Births for Easton, January 1, 1888- June 28, 1907, and South Easton, October 8, 1893- October 1, 1898. Indexed. Entries give the child's name, sex, and color; the date and place of birth; the father's name, country of birth, age, and occupation; the mother's maiden name, country of birth, and age; the number of children born in the marriage and the number still living; and the attending physician's name and address.

Record of Burials for Easton, January 10, 1888- August 1, 1905, and South Easton, November 8, 1893- December 31, 1895. Information usually provided includes the name, residence, and place of birth (only during 1888) of the deceased person; the name and residence of the undertaker; the date and place of burial; and in the case of a minor the name of his or her father. Occasionally the occupation of the departed (until 1893 for Easton) person in also listed.

Record of Deaths for Easton, January 11, 1888- May 31, 1907, and South Easton, October 27, 1893- August 25, 1898. Data appearing include the deceased person's name, residence, color, sex, age, and marital status; the date and cause of death; and the attending physician's name and residence.

RECORD OF BIRTHS IN THE CITY OF MEADVILLE RETURNED TO THE BOARD OF HEALTH, April 1, 1880- December 31, 1926 (RG-48). Entries in the microfilmed volume show the child's name, sex, color, residence (street and number), and date of birth; the name of the father and his occupation; the name of the mother; the name and address of the person signing the birth certificate; and the dates of the certificate and registration. Several entries appear at the end of the book for births in 1864, 1869, 1870,

1874, and 1876. The volumes are in chronological order by date of registration.

RECORD OF DEATHS for the city of Pottsville, February 24, 1897-February 7, 1907 (RG-48). Indexed. Microfilmed entries show the deceased individual's name, age, sex, color, birthplace, residence, and occupation; and the date, place, and cause of death.

RECORD OF PHYSICIANS' AND UNDERTAKERS' RETURNS OF DEATHS in the city of Titusville, April 10, 1879- January 13, 1918 (RG-48) A record kept by the city's Board of Health. Each entry of the microfilmed volume has space for recording the name, color, sex, marital status, occupation, residence (street, number, and ward), birthplace, age, date of death, and cause of death of the deceased individual; the name of his or her parents; the period of residency in Titusville (rarely filled in); place of previous residence (usually blank); the date and place of interment; the name of the physician registering the person as dead; and the name of the undertaker or informant. The entries are numbered and arranged in chronological order by date of death.

REGISTER OF BIRTHS for the city of Harrisburg, 1875-1879, 1883-1886 (RG-48). A record kept by the Health Department that shows the color, sex, and date of birth of each child born; the names and residences of the parents; and the name of the attending physician. Information regarding the birth of the child, that is, whether it was living, stillborn, a twin, or premature is also found. The microfilmed register is arranged by birth date.

REGISTER OF DEATHS for the city of Harrisburg, May 3, 1883-August 28, 1886, May 1-October 28, 1892 (RG-48). The microfilmed register was created by the Health Department with a listing generally giving the deceased person's name, color, sex, age, marital status, and street address; the date and cause of death; and the attending physician's name. Entries are arranged and numbered in chronological order by date of death.

RETURN OF BIRTHS in the city of Reading, July 1, 1876-December 31, 1905 (RG-48). A microfilmed set of volumes that shows the name (sometimes blank), sex, color, date of birth, and place of birth (street and number) of the child; the names of the parents; the occupation of the father; and the name and address of the attending physician. Space is available for recording the date of the birth certificate and the date of registration, but these columns are blank. Written remarks noting that a baptismal certificate, etc. was used to obtain the information sometimes appear. Entries are numbered and for the most part thereinafter arranged in chronological order by date of birth.

RETURN OF MARRIAGES in the city of Reading, July 1, 1876- December 31, 1909 (RG-48). Microfilmed volumes that list the names, ages, places of birth, and residences of the married couple; the date of marriage; the occupation of the husband and the race of the wife; the name and address of the person performing the ceremony; and the type of ceremony employed (alderman, Lutheran, Reformed, Catholic, etc.). Entries are numbered and for the most part thereinafter arranged in chronological order by date of marriage.

JUSTICE OF THE PEACE DOCKET BOOKS, LEBANON COUNTY, 1811-1905 (MG-4). Records of marriages performed by the justice of the peace are interspersed in the three volumes.

For the convenience of the researcher, a select list of vital statistic legislation affecting Pennsylvania residents, 1676-1975, appears in the appendices to this book.

MILITARY AND WAR RECORDS
(4,583 Cubic Feet)

The Division of Archives and Manuscripts holds voluminous records providing evidence of enrollment or service with Pennsylvania military units during the period 1775-1985. Unfortunately, most of the records of military service created prior to 1861 contain scant genealogical or descriptive data. Among those military service and war records that offer genealogical potential are the following:

THE FRENCH AND INDIAN WAR

Coverage of service by Pennsylvanians in the French and Indian War is limited when it comes to original documentation. There are about twenty muster rolls and military returns filed among the PAPERS OF THE PROVINCIAL COUNCIL, 1682-1775 (RG-21). (See sample on page 34.) In most cases the dated returns and rolls simply list the name and rank of the soldier, the military unit or station to which he was attached, and the officer under whom he was serving. At times, the person's date and place of enlistment may appear as well. All of these records are published in the *Pennsylvania Archives*, Fifth Series, Volume 1. (Original items that were in the custody of the Archives at the time of publication have a "c" in parentheses after the document's title.) A scattering of historical records pertaining to the war also can be found in the MILITARY MANUSCRIPTS COLLECTION, 1758-Present (MG-7), the PENNSYLVANIA COLLECTION, 1626-Present (MG-8), the SEQUESTERED BAYNTON, WHARTON, AND MORGAN PAPERS, 1725-1827 (MG-19), the BURD-SHIPPEN FAMILY COLLECTION, 1715-1834 (MG-30), THE EDWARD SHIPPEN THOMPSON COLLECTION, 1684 (1746-1904)-1941 (MG-125), the FORT PITT MUSEUM COLLECTION, 1747-1785, 1896 (MG-193), and the BUCHER-HUMMEL FAMILY COLLECTION, 1763-1963 (MG-382).

Capt. John Bull's Return Of Recruits, Pennsylvania Regiment, July 1, 1758, *EXECUTIVE CORRESPONDENCE, 1682-1775 (RG-21)*. Note: Most military returns for the French and Indian War do not include such extensive details about the soldiers.

THE REVOLUTIONARY WAR

AMERICAN LOYALIST CLAIMS, Ca. 1783-1788 (in MG-262). Microfilmed documents preserved as records of the Exchequer and Audit Department, in the British Public Records Office. Each case follows a standard presentation, that is, it starts with the petition being addressed to the commission appointed by Parliament to inquire into the losses and services of American loyalists; provides the name, occupation or title, and late residence of the memorialist; states that the petitioner has always been a loyal subject of the King; and then describes his or her treatment by the Americans, and in some cases the British military. An estimate of the financial losses incurred from damaged or seized property, goods, and or services usually follows. Many of the narrative descriptions are detailed personal histories that depict how the claimant served British interests in a military, commercial or political capacity. The person's story usually includes facts concerning when and why the loyalist came to America (if a new arrival, particularly merchants, sea captains and the like) and the exact date that he or she left the colonies. Supporting letters providing background information about the petitioner and/or indicating commercial or family connections are normally presented as part of the claim review process as well. The microfilm in the possession of the State Archives covers Pennsylvania loyalists. A few claimants from New York and Delaware, however, are included. Indices appear before each set of claims.

APPLICATIONS FOR PASSES, 1775-1787 (RG-27). Consists of applications submitted to the Supreme Executive Council by persons requesting permission to pass through enemy lines. The type of information recorded differs with each document. Most applications are dated and only mention the person's name and reason for having to cross over to enemy-held territory. On some occasions, however, the applications give the individual's name and place of birth and particulars about children or the death of a spouse. The applications are in alphabetical order by applicant's surname and have been microfilmed as part of the Records of Pennsylvania's Revolutionary Governments, 1775-1790.

APPOINTMENTS FILE (MILITARY), 1775-1790 (RG-27). Petitions filed by persons seeking a military commission. Among the data which may be found are the petitioner's name, residence, rank, and the position sought. Information concerning the individual's experience or past military service is frequently included as well. The petitions are arranged alphabetically by petitioner's surname.

CLAIMANTS FOR DONATION LANDS, Ca. 1792-1799 (RG-17). Contains several lists, the largest segment of which dates from 1792-1796 and is grouped alphabetically by first letter of surname. Entries normally record the claimant's name, rank, and regiment; the applicant's name (widow, heir, etc.); and the date of the application. Other entries include information pertaining to soldiers who were casualties, either during the war or afterwards, 1779-1799; and data regarding the number of acres drawn, 1788-1796.

COMMISSARY ACCOUNTS, 1775-1792 (RG-4). In addition to documenting routine expenditures for military supplies, equipment, and services, the accounts include numerous lists of wages paid to Hessian soldiers for labor performed at Lancaster, Pa. during the American Revolution. The documents are arranged in chronological order.

COPIES OF INVENTORY SHEETS FOR TORY SYMPATHIZERS, 1778-1779 (RG-33). Thirty-five certified copies of inventories describing the real estate holdings and/or household goods seized from the homes and businesses of attainted loyalists in Pennsylvania. Normally the inventories have an introductory statement that mentions where the person lived (county, city, estate, or street), the date that the property was inventoried, and the name of the agent conducting it. This is followed by a detailed inventory which lists the appraised value of the real estate, goods, and chattel. The documents are signed, sealed, and sworn to be accurate by the both the appraisers and the agent representing the state. Familial relationships are at times included, generally to either justify seizures that might not otherwise be evident or to explain why no punitive action was taken. The materials are part of an AUTOGRAPH FILE that is found in the records of the Supreme Court of Pennsylvania, Eastern District. The documents are not in any discernible order but an alphabetical name listing is available for perusal.

DEPRECIATION CERTIFICATE ACCOUNTS, 1781-1792 (RG-4). Contains dated depreciation interest certificates, 1782-1787, that normally list the name and rank of the soldier, the military organization to which he was attached, and the amount of the interest. The certificates are grouped according to military units and are thereunder arranged alphabetically by surname. A published account of the record appears in *Pennsylvania Archives*, Fifth Series, Volume IV.

DEPRECIATION LANDS [REGISTER], Undated (RG-17). The Depreciation Lands were located just north of Pittsburgh within a "V" formed by the confluence of the Allegheny and Ohio rivers. Sale of these lands represented an attempt by the Commonwealth to raise sufficient funds to redeem or underwrite depreciation certificates that had been given to Revolutionary soldiers. The certificates were issued to make up for lost pay caused by the depreciation of Continental currency. The register includes three parts. The first part is arranged by survey districts (1st-5th) and shows the name of the surveyor in whose district the land was situated; the district number; the map page where the land was recorded; the name of the patentee; the number of acres and perches; the date of patent (1785-1934, not inclusive); and the patent and survey book, volume, and page number were recorded. This section is followed by an index to the patentees (inscribed "depreciation certificates patented") that lists the person's name, the survey district, the lot number, and the page in the register where the data were found. A final section consists of "depreciation tickets," an alphabetical list that is grouped by first letter of surnames and which gives the names of purchasers of depreciation tickets; the warrant dates (1785-1822); and the ticket, lot, and surveyor district numbers. See also: DEPRECIATION LAND MAPS, 1785-1789 (RG-17), which were constructed from the original surveys and often include a description of each lot, the acreage, and data regarding the soil quality of the tract.

DONATION LANDS [REGISTER], Undated (RG-17). The Donation Lands program was set up in March, 1780, to entice veteran soldier's who were fighting in the Revolutionary War to remain in the army. Each Pennsylvania Line soldier or officer that served until the end of the conflict and who was attached to the Continental Army was granted tracts of land in northwestern Pennsylvania, the size and location of which were based upon rank and a lottery. This register, which appears to be of nineteenth century vintage, is described on the first page as containing the following parts:

A List of the Donation or Military Tracts of Land Granted to the Officers and Soldiers of the Pennsylvania Line in the Revolutionary Army Arranged by Districts (pages 2-84). Entries record the name of the deputy surveyor, the district (Nos.1-8, 10), the map page where the data are recorded, the name and rank of the patentee, the acres and perches, the return date (1785-1953), and the patent and or survey book and page number. Information pertaining to heirs, assignees, or the fact that a patentee was a widow of the soldier also appears.

Index to Patentees (pages 85-128). The index references pages 2-84 of the register and lists the name of the patentee, the district number, and the register page number. The names of assignees, devisees, widows, etc. are noted as well.

Names, Regiment, Rank, Number of Acres if Drawn, etc. of the Pennsylvania Line Entitled to Donation Land (pages 129-173). Entries are grouped in alphabetical order by first letter of surname. Besides the data enumerated in the title, remarks are written that note if the person had been killed in action or was a deranged prisoner; received land as a foreign officer, a supernumerary officer, or because of resolution by the General Assembly; and whether a surname might have alternate spellings.

Names, Rank, Regiment, etc. of the Pennsylvania Line, Donation District No. 10, Who Drew Lots Which Were Found to be Wholly in the State of New York (pages 174-177). Consists of 140 lots with the names of the patentees grouped alphabetically by first letter of surname. In addition to the information listed above, entries record the old and new district where land was drawn; the acres and perches; the return date (1792-1794, 1797, 1804); and the names of any pertinent assignees, attorneys or interested parties.

Lots Which Fell Partly in Pennsylvania and Partly in New York with Lots Afterwards Drawn in their Places in the Other Districts, etc. (page 178). Contains twenty-one names in no discernible order for lots situated in District 10. The information is identical to that on pages 174-177.

Lots Drawn for the Widows and Children of the Pennsylvania Line (page 179). Data shown includes the name and rank of the veteran, the number of the district and the lot, the date of return (1794-1795), and the name of the heir and his or her relationship to the original patentee (son of, daughter of, widow of, etc.). Fourteen widows or children are reported as claiming fifteen lots.

List of the Officers and Men of the Pennsylvania Line Entitled to Donation Land for Whom There Appears to be No Numbers in the (Lottery) Wheel (pages 180-185). Entries are grouped in alphabetical order by first letter of surname and show the number of acres that the person was entitled to and on occasion his rank. There are 406 names listed.

An Account of Fees Received from Sundry Persons by James Trimble in Pursuance of an Act of 6th April 1792 (pages 186-188). Data listed includes the tract's district and lot numbers, the name and rank of the veteran, the acres, the date of the return (1792-1801), and the name by whom drawn (assignee, son, in trust, etc.). The twenty-four names appearing are not in any discernible order.

Explanations (page 200). Provides information regarding irregularities in patenting or data recorded for seven lots.

For graphic information about these tracts including Surveyor General John Luken's official certification of the surveys see:

DONATION LAND MAPS, 1785-1786 (RG-17). DONATION LAND BOOK, 1791-1808 (RG-17). The volume contains copies of some of the pertinent legislation relating to the bounty program and a list that shows the name of the patentee, his assignee, or heir; the

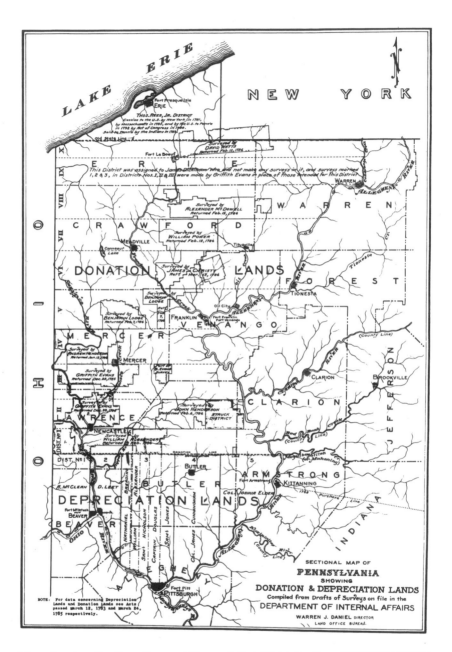

Map showing the Donation and Depreciation Districts. See: DEPRECIATION LANDS [REGISTER], Undated and DONATION LANDS [REGISTER], Undated (RG-17), PSA.

date; the soldier's army rank; the number of his lot; the quantity of the land received; and the donation district. From 1801 to 1808 the information presented is in a short narrative format. Entries are chronological.

DONATION LANDS GRANTED PENNSYLVANIA LINE, Ca. 1780-1830 (RG-17). The volume is grouped in alphabetical order by first letter of surname and includes the name, rank, and regiment of the soldier; the number of acres; the lot number; and the donation district. Notations, some as late as 1830, regarding heirs and assignees who claimed the land appear as well.

DONATION LANDS - PENNSYLVANIA LINE, 1813 (RG-17). Indexed. The volume is inscribed as "Surveyor Generals Office Harrisburg 26th April 1813 - This book contains a list of the Donation, or Military tracts of land granted to the officers and soldiers of the Pennsylvania Line in the Revolutionary Army arranged as follows, viz.: District no., number (lot), quantity of acres, name of Patentee, and return of patenting (date)."

DONATION LOTS LYING IN NEW YORK, 1792-1796 (RG-17). The book is inscribed as a "List of numbers of lot of Donation Land out of which the persons whose lands have been found to lie in the State of New York" and gives the date; the name of the soldier, his heir, or assignee; his army rank; the lot number; and the acres. Entries are in chronological order for the most part and relate to Donation District 10. See also: the actual DONATION PATENTS, 1792-1804, not inclusive (RG-17) which were returned to the Land Office in exchange for land in other districts.

FORFEITED ESTATES FILE, 1777-1790 (RG-27). A record of persons whose estates were seized because of their allegiance to the British cause during the Revolutionary War. Information usually shown includes the name and residence of the attainted individual, a description of the estate that he owned, an inventory of the property seized (with the date), and a record of the estate's disbursement. At times the occupation of the individual is also noted. The file is available on microfilm and is arranged alphabetically according to attainted person's surname and by county when more than several names appear. For those researchers interested, the names of attainted loyalists and particulars about the property they owned can be found in the FORFEITED ESTATES ACCOUNTS, 1777-1809 (RG-4). A published account of the Forfeited Estates File is contained in the *Pennsylvania Archives*, Sixth Series, Volumes XII-XIII.

MILITIA FINE EXONERATIONS, 1777-1793 (RG-4). Statements filed by Pennsylvania residents to demonstrate that they or their kin should be exempt from fines being imposed for not serving militia duty. The data appearing differ from document to document. While some statements only list the person's name, residence, and reasons for seeking an exemption, others indicate the individual's age, occupation and parents' names. The exonerations are grouped by county and are not indexed.

PAPERS OF ATTAINDER, Ca. 1778-1793 (RG-33). Consists of lists of persons who were attainted for their loyalty to the British cause during the Revolutionary War. The lists, which are not indexed, give the name, residence and, occasionally, occupation of the individual.

PENNSYLVANIA LINE ENTITLED TO DONATION LAND AS REPORTED BY THE LATE COMPTROLLER GENERAL, Ca. 1780-1794 (RG-17). Entries record the name, rank, and regiment of the soldier; the number of acres; and whether a lot was drawn. Comments noting that the person was killed in action are found as well. The book is grouped in alphabetical order by first letter of surname.

REGISTER OF DONATIONS, 1786-1796 (RG-17). The book is arranged by donation districts and gives the date and name of the person paying the patent fee, the lot number and acres (denomination), the name and rank of the soldier by whom the land was drawn, and the amount credited or debited.

RETURN OF OFFICERS AND SOLDIERS TO WHOM PATENTS WERE NOT ISSUED, Undated (RG-4). The entries are grouped alphabetically by soldier's surname. Little information is actually entered in the volume other than the name of the individual, the lot number, and the number of acres drawn. The rank of the soldier is sporadically supplied as well.

RETURN OF PENNSYLVANIA LINE ENTITLED TO DONATION LANDS, Undated (RG-4). Indexed. Entries normally record the name, rank, and corps of the soldier and the number of acres drawn. Remarks concerning whether the person was killed in action or was a foreign officer are often included.

REVOLUTIONARY WAR ASSOCIATORS, LINE, MILITIA AND NAVY ACCOUNTS, AND MISCELLANEOUS RECORDS RELATING TO MILITARY SERVICE, 1775-1809 (RG-4). Indexed by the REVOLUTIONARY WAR MILITARY ABSTRACT CARD FILE, Undated (RG-13). Includes the following materials:

Associators Accounts, 1775-1777. Consists of receipts, accounts, returns, payrolls and muster rolls for associators in Bedford, Berks, Bucks, Cumberland, Lancaster, Northampton, Northumberland, Philadelphia, Westmoreland and York counties. While the accounts and returns usually only list the soldier's name, rank and military unit, the pay and muster rolls may also record the associator's residence, commanding officer, and dates of entering and leaving service. The documents are arranged by county and thereunder chronologically.

Line Accounts, 1775-1809. Contains pay and muster rolls that may show the name, rank, regiment, company, and pay rate of the soldier; the name of his commanding officer; and the dates and locations of the musters. At times the dates that the soldier enlisted, deserted, or was discharged are also noted. In a few instances enlistment papers are to be found. The materials are arranged by regiment and thereunder alphabetically by surname.

Militia Accounts, 1777-1794. Has militia receipts, returns, operations documents, and lists of white males between ages eighteen and fifty-three for Allegheny, Bedford, Berks, Bucks, Chester, Cumberland, Dauphin, Delaware, Fayette, Franklin, Huntingdon, Lancaster, Luzerne, Montgomery, Northampton, Northumberland, Philadelphia, Washington, Westmoreland, and York counties. The information entered varies with each type of document. Returns of absentees are dated and normally list the name and company (or battalion) of the soldier, the officer to whom he was attached, the number of days that he mustered, and the number of days that he was absent. In addition, some operation accounts also mention the dates that the militia members were ordered into and released from service. The items are arranged by county and thereafter by company and battalion.

Navy Accounts, 1775-1794. Contains muster and pay rolls that usually give the name, rank, station, and pay rate of the sailor; the time of his service; and the dates of his entry, discharge, or desertion. The age of the individual is periodically recorded as well. The documents are arranged chronologically and grouped according to stations of duty. There is an alphabetical list of vessels (stations of duty) for reference purposes.

Most of the returns comprising this series have been printed in the fifth and sixth editions of the *Pennsylvania Archives.*

REVOLUTIONARY WAR MILITARY ABSTRACT CARD FILE, Undated (RG-13). Consists of 4 X 6 inch cards compiled by the Division of Archives and Manuscripts from original muster rolls, payrolls, military accounts, depreciation certificates, militia loans, and delinquent lists, 1775-1783, in its custody. Information contained on the cards differs for each individual. While some entries may only give the person's name and county of service, others may also list his rank and dates of service; the name of the officer under whom he served; and the military unit to which he was attached. In a few instances father-and-son relationships are also indicated. The cards are arranged alphabetically by surname.

REVOLUTIONARY WAR PENSION FILE, 1809-1893 (RG-2). (See reproduction on page 46.) Contains letters acknowledging the receipt of pensions, affidavits, certifications from the county courts, and statements of need and service filed by claimants seeking Revolutionary War service pensions. The dated documents may have any of the following written on them: the name, rank, and military unit of the veteran; the name of the officer to whom he was attached; the dates of his service; and the residence of the applicant at the time of petitioning. Facts regarding the soldier's military service and particulars about his destitute state are also sometimes noted. The file is organized alphabetically by pensioner's surname.

REVOLUTIONARY WAR PENSION FILE AND RELATED ACCOUNTS, 1785 -1809 (RG-4). Includes the following materials:

Pension File, 1785-1809. Consists mainly of certifications prepared by the Orphans' Court or the state supreme court entitling Revolutionary War veterans or their wives to obtain compensation such as that provided for in the Act of September 22, 1785. Information shown varies with each document. While some certifications only list the soldier's name, residence and military unit, others also mention the wounds suffered by the veteran and his rank, age, and dates of enlistment. In those cases where the pension was to be received by a patriot's widow (see example on page 47), it is not unusual to find diverse familial data and the date of husband's death noted. The petitions are in alphabetical order by pensioner's surname.

Pension Index, Book A, 1790-1791. Contains short statements that mention the pensioner's name, the basis of service, the unit or company to which he was attached, the amount of pension granted, and the date that the pension was allowed.

Pension Ledger, Book 1, 1785-1789. Indexed. An incomplete record of disabled soldiers, line and militia, granted pensions under the Act of September 22,1785. Entries usually give the name, age, rank, and corps of the soldier; the period of the pension; and the amount of pension received. A brief statement of how, when, and where the disability occurred is included. An alphabetical name listing has been compiled for reference purposes.

Pension Ledger, Book B, 1790-1793. Indexed. A record of warrants for payments made to line and militia veterans or their dependents under the Act of March 11, 1790. Entries usually provide the name of the pensioner, his or her relationship to the veteran, and the date and the amount of the warrant drawn. Quite often the veteran's military unit is listed, and at times particulars about his

Lycoming County ſſ.

At a stated Orphans Court held at Williams-
Port for the County of Lycoming the on the thirty first Day of
August in the Year of our Lord one thousand seven hundred and
ninety six, before the Honorable

William Hepburn
John Adlum   } Esquires, Judges of the same
James Davidson   Court &c.

On the Petition and Application of
Robert Ritchie and Rovanna his Wife late Rosanna Saltzman,
Widow and Relict of Anthony Saltzman deceased

George Saltzman
Mary Saltzman, intermarried with Lewis Keeth
Anthony Saltzman
John Saltzman &
William Saltzman, Children of Anthony Saltzman
deceased; and it appearing to the said Court on due proof that the said
Anthony Saltzman was a Serjeant in Captain Thomas Wilson's Company
in the fourth Battalion of Northumberland County Militia from the math
of August in the Year one thousand seven hundred and seventy seven, untill
the Beginning of January, One thousand seven hundred and seventy eight –
and that at the Time of the said Anthony Saltzman's being called into service
he was resident within the State, having lived on the Frontiers of Northumberland County with his Wife and Family – and it also appearing to the
said Court that the said Anthony was on the second Day of January
One thousand seven hundred and seventy eight actually tomahawked and
scalped by the Indians a Party of hostile Indians in the Neighbourhood
of a Garrison on the South Side of the West Branch of Susquehanna, com
manded by Col. Cookson Long, when he the said Anthony was in the actual
service of this State — And it appearing further to the said Court
on due Proof, that the said Anthony left a Widow named Rovanna, &
four small Children to survive him, the youngest of whom was at the
Breast – which said Children upon due and sufficient Proof made to the
said

The document shown on these two pages illustrates just how detailed
pension requests filed on the behalf of a slain revolutionary soldier's family
could be.

said Court were born at the following Times, to wit,

George Saltzman born the 23rd Day of September M.DCC.LXVII.

Mary Saltzman since intermarried with Lewis Heath
     born the 25th Day of September M.DCC.LXX.

Anthony Saltzman born the 21st Day of September M.DCC.LXXII.

John Saltzman born the 26th Day of January M.DCC.LXXVI. &

William Saltzman born the 22d Day of November M.DCC.LXXVII.

        And that the said Rosanna intermarried with Robert Ritchie about one Year after her said Husband's Death:

        The Orphans Court therefore, the Premises being considered, do adjudge and determine that the Widow and Children of the said Anthony Saltzman are entitled to receive a Pension amounting to the half Pay which the said Anthony was entitled to at the Time of his Death, which said Pension to commence from the Time of the Death of the said Anthony to wit on the second Day of January 1778, and to continue untill the Youngest Child of the said Anthony arrived at the Age of fourteen Years — Which said Pension is to be distributed as follows, to wit;

        To the Widow of the said Anthony the full Amount of half Pay from 2d January 1778 to 2d January 1779 at which Time She was intermarried with Robert Ritchie

        To the five Children of Anthony Saltzman, the full Amount of half Pay untill the eldest became of the Age of fourteen Years to be equally divided between them —

        To the remaining four Children of Anthony Saltzman the full Amount of half Pay from thence untill the second Child became of the Age of fourteen Years, to be equally divided between them —

        To the remaining three Children of Anthony Saltzman the full Amount of half Pay from thence untill the third Child became of the Age of fourteen Years, to be equally divided between them —

        To the remaining two Children of Anthony Saltzman the full Amount of half Pay from thence untill the fourth Child became of the Age of fourteen Years, to be equally divided between them — — — — — — And

Orphan's court certificate of Rosanna (Saltzman) Ritchie and family, 1796, *REVOLUTIONARY WAR PENSION FILE AND RELATED ACCOUNTS, 1785-1809 (RG-4).*

death (where, when, and how) are recorded. In a few instances such information as the date that the soldier's widow remarried and the name of the individual that she married appears.

Pension Ledger, Book C, 1794-1804. Indexed. A record of warrants for payments made to line and militia veterans or their dependents under the Act of March 11,1790. The listings normally record the name of the pensioner, the name and military organization to which the soldier was attached, the period of pension, and the amount of pension received. In those instances where the pension-er is the veteran himself a short statement about how and when the disability was suffered appears.

REVOLUTIONARY WAR PENSION LIST BOOK, 1834-1837 (RG-28). A record of revolutionary veterans or their wives who applied for compensation as provided for in the Pension Act of April 14,1834. Entries record the name of the pensioner, the date that the annu-ity was due, and the amount of the annuity. The volume is arranged by county, with names thereafter appearing in alphabeti-cal order.

REVOLUTIONARY WAR ROLLS 1775-1783 (in MG-262). Micro-filmed muster rolls and returns relating to Pennsylvania units that served in the Revolution, the originals of which are in the custody of the National Archives. The rolls do not appear to be in any dis-cernible order but are identified by microfilm targets which indi-cate the name of the military unit and its commanding officer. Many of the rolls only provided the name, rank, and period of ser-vice for each officer and soldier. Others, however, are more descriptive. For example, typical monthly returns indicate how many officers (field, commissioned, staff, and non-commissioned) and rank and file soldiers were fit for duty; the number of men needed to complete the detachment; and the alterations (prisoners of war, dead, deserted, discharged, invalid, and promoted) since the last returns. These statistics are usually followed by a listing according to rank that shows the names of any members who were killed; might have deserted; became sick; were wounded; were taken prisoner; or might have resigned or been promoted. The dates of such events and particulars regarding what happened usually appear as well. The last roll of microfilm contains a RECEIPT BOOK FOR PIERCE'S CERTIFICATES (Numbers 67529-84425), Undated.

REVOLUTIONARY WAR SOLDIERS' CLAIMS AND RELATED PAPERS. 1786-1789 (RG-33). Consists of petitions submitted before the State Supreme Court, Eastern District. The type of data found varies with each petition. Some documents show the soldier's name, rank and corps, and at times even indicate the petitioner's occupation, age, and residence. Short statements concerning the person's service and the type of wound received appear, and in a few cases the soldier's commission or enlistment papers are included. The petitions are arranged alphabetically by soldier's surname.

As part of an automation initiative from 1989-1993, a computerized index to Revolutionary War pension records was prepared by the staff and volunteers of the State Archives. This index can be used by visitors to the search room in either an on-line or hard copy format.

THE WAR OF 1812

WAR OF 1812 INDEX OF SOLDIERS (RG-2). An undated list of soldiers who served during the War of 1812 that is arranged alphabetically by soldier's surname. Data include the name of the soldier, the term of his service, and the name of the officer commanding his company. Written remarks concerning desertion are entered, and the name of the battalion in which the soldier served is noted.

WAR OF 1812 MILITIA ACCOUNTS AND RECORDS OF FINAL SETTLEMENT WITH THE UNITED STATES, 1812-1838 (RG-2). Contains general accounts and orders, receipts, pay vouchers, musters, and payrolls for Pennsylvania militia on active duty during the War of 1812. The documents are grouped according to military detachments and districts and thereunder according to military units. Although the documents normally contain only the name, rank, and regiment of the soldier, in those instances where muster rolls are found such data as the dates of enlistment, discharge, promotion or death also appear. There is an index of final settlements with the United States that gives the names of officers who served during the war.

WAR OF 1812 PENSION FILE, 1866 (1866-1879)-1896 (RG-2). A record created as a result of the legislative Act of April 30, 1866 (with subsequent supplemental acts) that granted annuities, gratuities, or pensions to Pennsylvania soldiers (or their widows) who had served at least two months duty, or who had been wounded or otherwise disabled during the war. The file usually contains either of the following two types of notarized documents:

Applications of Soldiers. Submitted by the veteran himself, the form shows his name, signature, residence, rank, regiment, and military unit; the name of the officer under whom he served; the period of service; and the approximate dates of his enlistment and honorable discharge.

Applications of Widows. Filled out by the deceased veteran's wife, the signed document contains the same information found on the soldier's application. From the 1870's onward, however, the dates of the marriage and of the husband's death are frequently recorded. Some applications mention not only the widow's age but even her spouse's age and place of death.

The file is in alphabetical order by pensioner's surname and an alphabetical name listing has been prepared for reference purposes.

Published muster rolls and payrolls for the War of 1812 appear in the *Pennsylvania Archives*, Sixth Series, Volumes 7-10, and Second Series, Volume 12. A list of medallists also can be found in the Fourth Series, Volume 4.

THE MEXICAN WAR

As the first step in researching whether an ancestor served in the Mexican War, 1846-1848, family historians should check the alphabetical listing contained in the *Pennsylvania Archives*, Sixth Series, Volume 10. Original materials include these files:

DISCHARGE MUSTER ROLL, COMPANY G, 2ND REGIMENT, PENNSYLVANIA VOLUNTEERS, JULY 20, 1848 (MG-318). Part of the Edward C. Williams Family Collection, 1848-1923. The company was organized by E.C. Williams in Harrisburg, Pa. in December, 1846; rendezvoused in Pittsburgh on January 2, 1847; and was in action near Mexico City by October, 1847. The discharge roll shows the name, rank, and age of each member of the company; date, place, and by whom enrolled ; date, place, and by whom mustered into service; date last paid and by whom; number of travel miles from place of discharge to home; the value of horses and equipment received; and as needed, date of promotion, desertion, discharge, transfer, or death. Written remarks about the death or injury of a soldier usually include the place where the battle occurred and the exact date that he was wounded or killed.

GENERAL CORRESPONDENCE OF THE ADJUTANT GENERAL, 1793-1935 (RG-19). Chiefly correspondence regarding the returns of election of officers; requisitions for arms and military stores; copies of general orders; papers concerning the formation of military companies; and materials relating to the setting up of monuments at Vicksburg,1905-1906, at Gettysburg,1909-1935, and at Antietam and Monocacy,1932-1935. A few items concerning efforts to preserve regimental flags from the Civil War period, 1914- 1928, and celebrations in honor of the battle of Saratoga, 1927, also are present. Of primary interest, however, are the rolls of Pennsylvania volunteer units tendering service to prosecute the war against the Republic of Mexico. In response to the May 13th, 1846, request of the president for six regiments, the Commonwealth recruited ninety companies or enough for nine regiments (7,475 men). Rolls, providing the name of the volunteer unit, its county of origin, and the names, ranks, and township residences of its members appear for the following units in June and July, 1846:

(Units marked with an asterisks (*) have the ages of their members written on the rolls while those with a plus (+) do not appear on the Adjutant General's July 15, 1846, list of available volunteer companies. The rolls are grouped by months.)

American Highlanders of Cambria County
Artillery Corps of Philadelphia Grays, Philadelphia County +
Beaver County Guards of Beaver County +
Big Spring Adamantine Guards of Cumberland County +

51

Birmingham Guards of Allegheny County
Bloomfield Light Infantry of Perry County
Carlisle Light Infantry Company of Cumberland County
Centre Guards of Centre County
Citizen Blues of Allegheny County +
City Guards, Philadelphia, Pa., Philadelphia County
Conemaugh Guards of Cambria County
Dauphin Guards of Harrisburg, Pa., Dauphin County *
Doylestown Grays of Bucks County
Duquesne Grays of Pittsburg, Pa., Allegheny County
Easton Fencibles of Lehigh County +
Fayette Riflemen of Fayette County
First Northumberland Troop (Cavalry) of Northumberland
    County * +
Frankford Artillery of Philadelphia County
Franklin Blues of Westmoreland County *
German Grays of Pittsburg, Pa., Allegheny County +
Germantown Blues of Philadelphia County *
Harrisburg Rifle of Dauphin County
Harrison Blues of Philadelphia City and County *
Hibernia Jackson Guards of Schuylkill County *
Independent Grays of Bedford, Pa., Bedford County *
Independent Guards, Philadelphia, Pa., Philadelphia County
Irish Volunteers of Philadelphia City and County
Jackson Infantry of Union County *
Jefferson Grays of Washington County *
Junior Artillerists of Philadelphia City and County *
Lancaster Fencibles of Lancaster City, Lancaster County
Lancaster Guards of Perry County +
Lewistown Artillerists of Mifflin County
Lewistown Guards of Mifflin County
Mechanics' Rifle Company of Philadelphia City, Philadelphia
    County
Mercer Volunteers of Mercer County *
Mercersburg Artillerists of Franklin County
Monroe Guards of Philadelphia County
Montgomery Grays Alexandria +
Montgomery Guards of Philadelphia City and County *

National Artillery of Philadelphia City and County *
National Guards of Delaware County *
National Grays of Oxford Borough, Chester County
National Grays, City of Philadelphia, Philadelphia County
National Grays of Reading, Pa., Berks County
National Light Infantry of Schuylkill County *
Newport Guards of Perry County +
Nittany Riflemen of Centre County * +
Northumberland Infantry of Northumberland County *
One Hundred and Ninety-Sixth Regiment of Pennsylvania
    Militia * +
Pennsylvania Riflemen +
Philadelphia Light Guards of Philadelphia County
Philadelphia Repeal Volunteers of Philadelphia County *
Pittsburg Irish Guard of Allegheny County +
Schellsburg Artillerists of Bedford County *
Scott Artillerist of Cumberland County +
Sewickley Artillery Volunteers of Westmoreland County
Springfield Light Infantry of Cumberland County +
Swatara Light Infantry of Dauphin County
Ten Mile Independent Blues of Washington and Greene Counties +
Tyler Guards of Philadelphia County *
Union Guards of Bucks County
Union Volunteer Company of Fayette County
Warrior's Mark Fencibles of Huntingdon County
Washington and Marion Rifle Company of Pottsville, Pa.,
    Schuylkill County * +
Washington Artillery Company of Schuylkill County *
Washington Blues of Philadelphia, Pa., Philadelphia County
Washington County Guards of Washington County *
Washington Guards of Pittsburg, Pa., Allegheny County +
Washington National Guards of Philadelphia County *
Washington Patriots of Fayette County
Washington Rifle Blues of Reading, Pa., Berks County +
Washington Rifle Company of Pittsburg, Pa., Allegheny County +
Washington Riflemen of Lebanon, Pa., Lebanon County
Waynes Light Artillery of Cumberland County +
Waynesburg Blues of Greene County

Westmoreland Guards of Greensburgh, Pa., Westmoreland
County *
Williamsburg Blues of Blair County
Youghiogheny Blues of Fayette County

REGISTER OF RECRUITS, 1ST AND 2ND REGIMENTS, PENNSYL-
VANIA VOLUNTEERS, 1847-1848 (RG-2). The register records the
name, age, and regiment of the soldier; the date and place where
he was enrolled and mustered in, and the names of the person
who enrolled and mustered him in. Data about whether the recruit
was rejected or deserted and the place and date of his discharge
are entered at times. Many of the names have been printed in
Pennsylvania Archives, Sixth Series, Volume X.

MEXICAN WAR ACCOUNTS AND RELATED PAPERS, 1846-1880
(RG-2). Contains muster rolls for the 1st and 2nd regiments of the
Pennsylvania Volunteers, arranged by company, and claims for
state pay that are filed by regiment and company and thereunder
alphabetically soldier's surname. The muster rolls generally show
the name, age, and rank of the soldier; the date and place where
he was mustered in; the name of the person who mustered him in;
and the unit, regiment, company, and the commanding officer to
which he was assigned. Particulars regarding the death (cause,
place, and date) or desertion (date and place) of a recruit are frequently noted as well. Information appearing in the claims for
state pay differs with each document. While some claims simply
list the veteran's name, unit of service, and reason for claim, others also give the soldier's residence, date of enlistment, term of
service, wounds suffered, date of discharge, and pension received.
An alphabetical listing of soldiers attached to the 1st (companies
A-K) and 2nd (companies A-M) regiment has been prepared to
facilitate the retrieval of documents for researchers.

MEXICAN WAR SERVICE INDEX, 1846-1848 (RG-19). A record of
soldiers attached to the 1st Pennsylvania Volunteers. Information
appearing includes the name of the volunteer; the dates that he
was mustered in and discharged; and the regiment, company, and
commanding officer to which he was assigned. Remarks regarding
the soldier's rank and whether he deserted, died or was discharged
are regularly recorded.

To his Excellency the Governor, Commander-in-Chief
of the Militia of Pennsylvania;

The undersigned, officers and members of the Schellsburg
Artillerists, an organized volunteer Artillery company, in
the county of Bedford, tender our service, through you,
to the President of the United States, to serve as infantry volunteers, in accordance with the provisions of the act of Congress
of the 13th May, 1846, entitled "An Act providing for the
prosecution of the existing war between the United States and
the Republic of Mexico.

Names	Towp. Bor.	Age		Names	Towp. Bor.	Age
			7	James Dull	Napier	28
Capt. Robert Fry	Schellbg	40	8	James Hankisson	Harrison	22
1st Lieu. John C. Statler	Napier	23	9	Frederick Mowry	"	22
2d Lieu. Joseph S. Reed	Schellbg	32	10	Frederick Hilligas	"	23
Sergeants 1st Samuel C. Statler	"	20	11	Joseph Mitchell	Napier	25
2d John M. Davis	"	26	12	Michael Dull	"	22
3d Samuel McMullen	Napier	22	13	Abraham Hull	"	24
4th David Miller	"	22	14	Luther Davis	St Clair	23
Corporals 1st Nathaniel Horn	"	26	15	Daniel Metzgar	Harrison	29
2d George Culp	"	30	16	Jacob Corley	"	26
3d Wm McMullen	"	26	17	Lewis M. Statler	Som. C. Shade	26
4th Daniel Crouse	"	24	18	Samuel Taylor	Harrison	22
Musicians			19	Adam Smolle	Schellbg	23
Michael A. Reed	"	20	20	Rudolf Statler	Harrison	21
Joseph F. Fry	"	19	21	George Rock	"	20
Privates			22	William Mahoney	"	25
1 William Culp	"	20	23	Joseph S. Philson	"	20
2 Jackson Galbraith	"	20	24	John D. Salom	"	24
3 Joseph Burkhart	Harrison	28	25	Joseph W. Hoart	"	25
4 Reuben Davis	St Clair	28	26	Wm Frazier	Napier	23
5 Andrew Dull	Napier	28	27	Daniel Hicke	"	25
6 Peter Ellenberger	"	26	28	William Darr	"	22

Bedford County volunteers who joined the Schellsburg Artillerists in 1846 to fight against the Mexican Republic. A muster roll in the GENERAL CORRESPONDENCE OF THE ADJUTANT GENERAL, 1793-1935 (RG-19), PSA.

THE CIVIL WAR

CASUALTY LIST, 42ND REGIMENT ("BUCKTAILS"), PENNSYLVA-
NIA VOLUNTEERS, Undated (MG-234). The list gives the name of
soldier and the engagement in which he was killed or wounded.

CIVIL WAR MUSTER ROLLS AND RELATED RECORDS, 1861-
1866 (RG-19). The materials are arranged by regiment and thereinafter according to company. Included in the record are the following types of muster roles:

Muster-in Rolls. Entries usually list the name, age, rank, unit, regiment, and company of the soldier; the date and place where he
was enrolled; the name of the person who mustered him in; the
term of enlistment; the date of mustering in; and the name of his
commanding officer. Remarks concerning promotions and assignments are sometimes recorded.

Muster-out Rolls. The dated lists ordinarily give the soldier's name,
age, rank, unit, regiment, and company; the name of his commanding officer; the date, place, and person by whom he was
mustered in; the period of enlistment; the date last paid and by
whom; the number of miles to and place of rendezvous; the
amount of clothing in hand and or money advanced; the bounty
paid and due; and remarks concerning pay earned, promotions,
capture by the enemy and the like.

Muster and Descriptive Rolls. Generally the rolls show the name,
age, place of birth (town, county, state or country), previous occupation, description (complexion, height, color of eyes and hair),
and rank of the soldier; the unit, regiment, company, and commanding officer to which he was assigned; and the amount of
money received for pay, bounties, and clothing. Rolls for unassigned U.S. black troops are included in this group.

Alphabetical Rolls. The rolls are arranged alphabetically by the soldier's surname. Entries usually indicate the name, age, rank, previous occupation, and residence of the soldier; the unit, regiment,
company, and commanding officer to which he was assigned; and
the date and place where the roll was taken. Particulars about
sickness or injury suffered by the soldier are sometimes noted.

Descriptive Lists of Deserters. Lists that indicate the name, age, place of birth, description (height, color of hair and eyes), previous occupation, and rank of the deserter; the unit, regiment, and company to which he was assigned; and the date and place where the person absconded.

The data found on the documents in this series were used to create the Civil War Veterans' Card File noted as follows.

CIVIL WAR SERVICE AND PENSION ACCOUNTS, 1861-1873 (RG-2). Includes a Civil War pension file, 1861-1864, that contains sixteen applications that were submitted by the widows or orphans of Civil War veterans. The type of information recorded varies with each dossier. In compliance with the stipulation of the Pension act of May 15, 1861, and the Act of April 11, 1862, the applications usually list the name of the veteran and his widow, the date of their marriage, the names of their children, the time of service of the soldier, and the date of his death. Oftentimes, the birth dates of the veteran's children and particulars about his service and death are also enumerated. The applications are organized by application number with these soldiers represented: William A. Callahan (Clinton County), James Confer (Clinton County), Thomas M. Covert (Luzerne County), John Gibson (Adams County), John S. Grubb (Butler County), Rudy Haverstick (Berks County), Irwin R. Long (Jefferson County), John J. Martin (Chester County), George W. Myers (Lancaster County), James Nicholson (Jefferson County), Charles Reem (Blair County), James Reilly (Schuylkill County), Solomon W. Smith (Lawrence County), Joseph S. Stine (Jefferson County), Oscar C. Wagner (Berks County), and Henry Wunder (Berks County).

CIVIL WAR VETERANS' CARD FILE, 1861-1866 (RG-19). Consists of 3 X 5 inch cards initially prepared to serve as an index to Samuel Penniman Bates's *History of Pennsylvania Volunteers, 1861-65*, (Harrisburg, 1869-1871). The Office of Adjutant General later expanded the scope of the listing by transcribing data found on the original documents to the cards. Among the information that might appear on the cards is the soldier's name, military unit, age at enrollment, description (complexion, height, color of hair and eyes), residence, and birthplace; the date and place where he was enrolled; the date and place where he was mustered in; and the date of discharge. The cards are arranged alphabetically according to soldier's surname. The listing is not inclusive.

CONSCIENTIOUS OBJECTOR DEPOSITIONS, 1862 (RG-19). The file is comprised of stylized forms that state why the person refused to take up arms in defense of the country. Little information is actually found on the forms other than the individual's name and residence (county) along with the date that the statement was ascribed and sworn to (or affirmed). The documents are signed by the Commissioners to Superintend Drafting and are arranged by county. The microfilmed REGISTER OF ALIENS AND PERSONS HAVING CONSCIENTIOUS SCRUPLES AGAINST BEARING ARMS, 1862 (in MG-262) serves as an index to this file.

CORRESPONDENCE RELEVANT TO THE SURGEON GENERAL'S OFFICE, 1861-1866 (RG-19). The documents are arranged in chronological order. Topics covered in the correspondence includes the following: individuals requesting appointments as regimental surgeons; families requesting information from hospitals pertaining to wounded soldiers following battles; requests for furloughs from injured soldiers or from their families; correspondence from vendors offering supplies and equipment for sale; recommendations for filling regimental surgeon vacancies; medical conditions in the field; soldiers seeking medical discharges; surgeons' oaths; election returns; permits for examination of surgeons; and telegraph messages relating to acquiring regimental surgeons, transfers, supplies and the like.

DESCRIPTIVE BOOKS (REGIMENTAL AND COMPANY), 1861-1864 (RG-19). A record of soldiers attached to the 48th Regiment of Pennsylvania Volunteers, Companies A-K (1861); the 1st Artillery, 43rd Regiment, Pennsylvania Reserve Volunteer Corps, Batteries A-H (1861-1864); Battery M of the 5th Artillery (1861); the 122nd Regiment of Pennsylvania Volunteers, Infantry, Company K (1862-1863); the 46th Infantry Regiment, Company K, Pennsylvania Volunteer Emergency Militia (1863); and the 1st Battalion of the 22nd Regiment, U.S. Cavalry, Companies A-D (1863). A typical entry for non-commissioned officers might show the soldier's name, age, height, complexion, birthplace, previous occupation, and eye and hair color; the date, place, and term of enlistment; the person who enlisted him; and the regiment and company to which he was attached. Information concerning the death, desertion, discharge, promotion, rank, or transfer of a soldier is also frequently recorded. Entries are arranged according to regiment and thereunder by company or battery.

DESCRIPTIVE BOOK, COMPANY A, 127TH REGIMENT, PENNSYL-
VANIA VOLUNTEERS (FIRST CITY ZOUAVES), July 22, 1862.-
August 1, 1862 (MG-16). The book is in chronological order according to the enlistment date of the volunteer. Entries in most instances give the name, age, physical description (height, complexion, eye and hair color), place of birth (county and state, or country), and occupation of the soldier; the term of his enlistment; and when, where, and by whom he was enlisted. Registers of men discharged (October 23, 1862-April 10, 1863) and of deserters (August 2, 1862-December 29, 1862) which list the name, rank, and place of discharge or desertion of the individual are also contained in this book. For interested researchers, the signature of the volunteer can be found in the COMPANY CLOTHING BOOK, 1862 (MG-16).

DESCRIPTIVE BOOK OF THE 47TH REGIMENT, COMPANY H, PENNSYLVANIA VETERAN VOLUNTEERS, February 10, 1865 (MG-55). Contains the same type of data found in the preceding series description plus information concerning equipage and clothing given to the soldiers.

DESCRIPTIVE BOOK, COMPANY "H", 127TH REGIMENT, PENN-
SYLVANIA VOLUNTEERS, 1862-1863 (MG-272). The book is divided under the following headings:

List of Officers, 1862-1863. Shows the officer's name, rank, place of birth, date of birth, and date of appointment. Data also appear concerning the person's military service, for example, battles participated in and the dates of promotion, transfer or resignation. Where appropriate, the officer's date and place of death or of being wounded are also noted.

List of Non-Commissioned Officers, 1862. Simply gives the individual's name, rank, and date of appointment.

Register of Men Discharged, 1862-1863. Records the name and rank of the soldier, the date and place of discharge, and by whose order he was discharged.

Register of Deaths, 1862-1863. Lists the name and rank of the deceased soldier, the date and place of his death, and the cause of his demise.

Register of Deserters, 1862. Mentions the name and rank of the deserter, and the date and place that he absconded.

Descriptive Roll, 1862-1863. The listings are for privates and are in alphabetical order by surname. Normally an entry indicates the name, age, physical description (height, complexion, eye and hair colors), place of birth, and occupation of the soldier; the date, place, and by whom he was enlisted; the term of his enlistment; and the date and place of discharge. Remarks are also entered that note which battles he served in; what types of wounds he may have received; and where appropriate the dates of his promotion, transfer, and death. In those instances where a soldier was taken as a prisoner, facts about his capture and release are found too.

DESCRIPTIVE BOOKS OF THE GRAND ARMY OF THE REPUBLIC (G.A.R.), 1866-1933 (MG-60 and MG-272). The books are arranged numerically by post. A listing usually indicates the name, age, rank, birthplace, residence, and occupation of the member; the dates of his entry and discharge from the service; the length of his service; the cause of his discharge; the nature of any wounds that he received; the company and regiment to which he was attached (on entry and discharge); the date of his muster into the G.A.R.; and where applicable the dates when he was honorably discharged, suspended, dropped, dismissed, or reinstated. Books for Philadelphia Posts 5, 7, 8, 18, 21, 94, and 363, as well as Posts 22 (Danville), 23 (Pottsville), 76 (Reading), 78 (Middletown), 99 (Hanover), 102 (Union City), 104 (Connellsville), 116 (Harrisburg), 118 (Columbia), 132 (Oxford), 170 (Catawissa), 176 (Lewistown), 178 (Belle Vernon), 197 (Lemont), 201 (Carlisle), 203 (Pine Grove),

207 (Homestead), 219 (Marion Centre), 347 (Smethport), 404 (Prospect), 424 (Harmonsburg), 429 (Pleasantville), 450 (Mount Morris), 475 (Shippenville), 527 (Bethlehem), 583 (East Springfield), 591 (Bryn Mawr), 600 (Saulsburg), 608 (Jennerstown), 609 (Hazen), 613 (Strongstown), 614 (Jermyn-Mayfield), 620 (Harford), 624 (unknown but probably Cambria County), 625 (Homestead), 628 (West Finley), 631 (Worrelville), and 639 (Norwood) are included.

DESCRIPTIVE BOOK OF THE 72ND REGIMENT, PENNSYLVANIA VOLUNTEERS, 1861-1862 (MG-235). The book is grouped by company and in some instances thereinafter arranged alphabetically by soldier's surname. Data found are the same as those described for the other regimental descriptive books. Information about members of companies A through I, K through N, P and R is contained in the volume.

DESCRIPTIVE ROLLS OF COMPANY C, 11TH REGIMENT, PENNSYLVANIA VOLUNTEERS, 1861-1864 (MG-253). Besides recording the volunteer's company and regiment, the rolls give the name, rank, nativity, age, occupation, and physical description of the soldier; and when, where, and by whom he was enlisted. The rolls are in chronological order and thereafter grouped according to rank. Entries for privates are arranged alphabetically according to their surnames.

DESCRIPTIVE ROLL OF OFFICERS AND MEN, BATTERY B, 1ST PENNSYLVANIA LIGHT ARTILLERY, 1861-1865 (MG-18). The roll is arranged by rank with the listing for privates in alphabetical order according to surname. Normally entries list the name, rank, postal address, occupation, and date of enlistment of the soldier. Information such as the dates of death, dismissal, and discharge is frequently recorded as well.

DIARY OF JAMES W. EBERHART, 1864-1865 (in MG-262). Sergeant Eberhart was a member of the 8th Pennsylvania Reserve Corps and the 191st Regiment of Pennsylvania Volunteers and his diary contains a record of his experiences as a prisoner of war (August 19,1864-February 22,1865) at Castle Thunder, Libby, Belle Island and Salisbury, N.C. Included in the diary is a list of members of Company G, 191st Regiment, that were captured on August 19, 1864. Besides giving the name and rank of each soldier, the account mentions whether the person might have escaped or died in captivity. The names of those troops not captured also is recorded. Likewise, a similar roll for Company G of the 8th Pennsylvania Reserve,1865, appears. Remarks here, however, note if the soldier, was discharged, wounded, killed, or died during the war.

DISCHARGE ORDERS AND LETTERS OF NOTICE OF ALIEN STATUS OF INDIVIDUALS SERVING IN THE MILITARY, 1862-1863 (RG-19). Consists of petitions submitted by foreigners to qualify for an exemption from military service. The documents are grouped by county and thereinafter arranged by filing dates. Entries usually give the alien's name, county or township where drafted, and native country. Occasionally, the age of the person and the length of time he was in the United States are mentioned.

INVENTORY OF EFFECTS, BATTERY B, 1ST PENNSYLVANIA LIGHT ARTILLERY, 1864-1865 (MG-18). The inventories are filed alphabetically by the deceased person's surname. Information varies with each document. While some inventories give only the name, company, regiment, date of death, place of death, and cause of death of the soldier, others also record the person's age, occupation, physical description, place of enrollment, date of enlistment, and term of service.

LEDGER, LT. D. H. WILSON POST NO. 134, G.A.R., 1879-1892 (in MG-262). The ledger contains an alphabetical name listing that records the dates of death for some members.

LIST OF MEN IN COMPANY A, 15TH REGIMENT, PENNSYLVANIA VOLUNTEERS, 1861-1862 (MG-97). The list records the name, rank, date of birth, place of birth, residence, marital status, and occupation of the soldier and the date and place of his enlistment. A brief medical history of the person appears and for an individual of foreign birth, the number of years that he had lived in America is mentioned.

LIST OF PENNSYLVANIA SOLDIERS BURIED AT ANDERSON-
VILLE, GEORGIA, July 1,1865 (in MG-7). A record of Pennsylvania
soldiers who died in the Andersonville Military Prison in Georgia
from February 26,1864 to March 24,1865. Entries usually give the
name, rank, company, regiment, date of death, and grave number
of the deceased soldier, and the cause of his demise. The printed
list is in alphabetical order by soldier's surname.

LIST OF PENNSYLVANIA TROOPS BURIED AT ANDERSONVILLE,
GEORGIA, Undated (in MG-7). A handwritten list of approximately
1,720 Pennsylvania soldiers who died as captives at the Confed-
erate military prison in Andersonville, Georgia from March 1, 1864
to August 19, 1865. The list has the same information described
in the preceding series description but was apparently compiled or
preserved by the Surgeon General's Department.

LISTS OF SICK AND WOUNDED SOLDIERS, PENNSYLVANIA VOL-
UNTEERS, 1861-1864 (RG-19). Entries are dated and usually
only record the name, company, and regiment of the soldier; the
disease or casualty that he suffered; and the place where he was
hospitalized. In some cases, however, the person's residence is
mentioned along with facts regarding his dates of discharge, transfer, or death. The lists are grouped by hospitalization locations and
thereunder arranged by admittance date.

MILITARY CLAIMS FILE AND CLAIMS REGISTER AND INDEX,
1862-1905 (RG-2). A record created in response to the Acts of
April 16, 1862, and April 22, 1863, providing for the adjutant general, the quartermaster, and the commissary general to act as a
board to adjudicate and settle claims for pay of all Pennsylvania
Volunteers and persons acting in the capacity of officers. The following materials are included:

Military Claims File, 1862-1905. Contains various affidavits, certifications and declarations that indicate the name, signature, rank,
company, regiment, unit, and county of residence of the soldier;
the date that the warrant was issued; the amount of pay that was
received; the time of service that was paid for; and the place where
the claim was made. In those cases where a declaration (voucher
no. 1 form) was submitted to the board by the claimant, the

researcher may also find the claimant's postal address and the date and place of being mustered in. An alphabetical name listing has been prepared for all claims settled from 1862 to 1905. The listing shows the name, rank, company, and regiment of the claimant; the date the claim was settled; and the claim number (except for the period 1875-1888).

Register of Claims Submitted Under Act of April 16, 1862, September 9, 1863-July 5, 1905. The register is arranged by claim number and shows the name, rank, company, and regiment of the claimant; the time claimed; the pay rate per month; the dates when the claim was received and paid; the amount claimed and paid; and the nature of the claim.

Index to Register of Military Claims, 1863-1905. Lists the full names of the claimants and their claim numbers.

MILITARY COMMISSION BOOKS, 1800-1944 (RG-26). Includes commissions to Pennsylvania Volunteers in Service of U.S., 1861-1865. The commissions issued from 1864 to 1865 are indexed while those granted from 1861 to 1864 are arranged according to regiment. Information appearing about the officers includes name, county of residence, rank, date of taking rank, military unit, regiment, company, and the date of the order or commission. Data about whether the person was discharged, transferred, or killed are also recorded.

MILITARY ORDER OF THE LOYAL LEGION, PENNSYLVANIA COM-MANDERY RECORDS, 1865-1935 (in MG-262). The order was founded in 1865 with members drawn primarily from officers who served in the Civil War or their eldest male descendants. The microfilmed records consist of membership rolls and biographical data obtained from newspaper clippings and memorial announcements.

MISCELLANEOUS DISCHARGE CERTIFICATES, 1861-1866 (RG-19). Contains approximately thirty discharge certificates for recruits who served with federal (Army, Navy, and Marine Corps) or state (Pennsylvania Militia or National Guard) military units. Generally the documents give the name, rank, birthplace, age (at enlistment), occupation, race, height, and hair and eye color of the person; the dates and places where he was enlisted and discharged; the reason that he was discharged; the term of enlistment; and the branch of service and unit to which he was attached. The certificates are grouped by years.

MISCELLANEOUS REGISTERS, ROSTERS AND LISTS, 1859-1872 (RG-19). Includes the following materials:

Alphabetical Roll of Men Mustered into the Pennsylvania Reserve Volunteer Corps, 1861. A record of men mustered into military service by the Commonwealth under the Act of May 15, 1861. Entries are arranged by regiment and company and thereunder alphabetically by surname. Among the information often recorded is the soldier's name, age, rank, residence, and previous occupation; the place and date that he was mustered in; and his muster number. Incidental remarks regarding discharges, refusals to take the oath of U.S. service, promotions and the like also regularly appear.

Muster Roll Book, 1863-1865. A record of commissioned officers kept by the Adjutant General's Office. Entries normally show the officer's name and rank, the date of joining, the bounty received, the date when the bounty was claimed, the commencement time, the date and place of enlistment, and the name of the person who enlisted him. The amount of pay received by the officer and particulars concerning dismissals, promotions, or the mustering-in process are also periodically noted. The volume is arranged according to regiment and thereunder by company.

Roster of Commissioned Officers of Pennsylvania Volunteers, 1861-1865. The listing is arranged alphabetically by officer's surname. Information usually posted includes the person's name, rank, company, and regiment.

Volunteer Register of Capt. S. G. Simmons, U.S.A. Mustering Officer for Three Month Troops, 1861. Entries are arranged by company and regiment and thereunder alphabetically by soldier's surname. The amount of information provided varies with each entry. While some listings only mention the person's name, number, rank, regiment, and company, others also indicate his age, occupation, and residence.

Volunteer Register of Men Mustered into U.S. Service for Three Years or Duration of War, 1861. A record of men joining the 26th to 29th regiments of Pennsylvania Volunteers of Philadelphia County from May 27 to July 9, 1861. The names of the soldiers are arranged alphabetically by company and regiment. Normally entries record the volunteer's name, rank, age, company, and regiment; the date and place where he was mustered in; and the name of his commanding officer.

MUSTER AND DESCRIPTIVE ROLLS OF COMPANY C, 201ST REGIMENT, PENNSYLVANIA VOLUNTEERS, 1864-1865 (MG-333). Found in the GEORGE WASHINGTON FENN COLLECTION, 1829, 1861-1927. Information found on the rolls is identical to that described in the preceding series description. Also included in the collection are the commission of George Washington Fenn as Captain of the Regiment, October, 24, 1864; his discharge certificate, June 23, 1865; and soldiers memorials (company rosters) for Company C, of the 201st Regiment, and Company D, of the 11th Regiment of Pennsylvania Volunteers.

MUSTER ROLL, COMPANY H, 47TH REGIMENT, PENNSYLVANIA VETERAN VOLUNTEERS, June 30, 1865 (MG-55). Contains the information listed in the series description for the muster-out rolls.

MUSTER ROLL, COMPANY I, 7TH PENNSYLVANIA CAVALRY, ca. 1865 (in MG-8). Found among the Keith Family Papers, 1861-1906. The roll has the name, rank, and age of each soldier; date, place, and by whom enlisted; date, place, and by whom mustered into service; date last paid and by whom; and remarks about whether the person was a veteran or volunteer and/or the date that rank commenced from. Discharges and copies of a special order and property settlement returns relating to Isaac S. Keith, 1861, 1865-1866, are included among the papers.

MUSTER ROLL, COMPANY K, 42ND REGIMENT ("BUCKTAILS"), PENNSYLVANIA VOLUNTEERS, August, 1862- December, 1863 (MG-234). Contains the same type of information found in the preceding muster-out rolls.

MUSTER ROLL, COMPANY A, 72ND REGIMENT, PENNSYLVANIA VOLUNTEERS, 1862 (MG-235). The roll shows the soldier's name, rank, company, and regiment; and when, where, and by whom he was enlisted. Entries are grouped by rank, with the names of privates listed in alphabetical order.

A photograph of George Washington Fenn (1845-1866), a resident of Harrisburg, Pa. who saw action at Manassas Gap, Virginia, and other places while serving with the 127th Regiment, 181st Regiment, and 201st Regiment of Pennsylvania Volunteers. From the GEORGE WASHINGTON FENN COLLECTION, 1829, 1861-1927 (MG-333), PSA.

MUSTER AND PAY ROLLS OF COMPANY C, 11TH REGIMENT, PENNSYLVANIA VOLUNTEERS, 1861-1864 (MG-253). A typical roll mentions the name and rank of the soldier; when, where, and by whom he was enlisted; the date that he was last paid; and the reason why the volunteer may have been absent. The rolls are in chronological order by the date of the muster or pay.

POPULATION RECORD BOOKS OF THE PENNSYLVANIA SOLDIERS' AND SAILORS' HOME, 1864-1883 (RG-19). Includes the following volumes:

Roster of Admissions, April 12, 1864- May 21, 1872. Entries list the veteran's name, age, place of birth, number, date of admittance, disease, and the result of treatment. Particulars concerning the date that a patient was released or died are frequently recorded, and from time to time data about operations or amputations performed on the individual are noted. The entries are arranged by admittance dates.

Descriptive List, Soldiers' Home, Philadelphia, June 1, 1866- March 12, 1867. The list is arranged according to the date that the statement was made. A house register can be used as an index. Generally a listing shows the veteran's name, age, marital status, nativity, number of children if any, previous occupation, rank, regiment, company, and residence prior to enlistment; the place and date of enlistment; the place where he was wounded; the place and date of his military discharge; the nature of the disability suffered; the amount of pension received; and the reason he was unable to support himself. Additional information contained on the entries includes the date that admission to the home was approved, the date and the reason why the person was discharged from the home, the ward and bed number of the patient, and data about whether the veteran's parents were alive or dead. The statement is signed or marked by the patient and lists the names of two vouchers and their postal addresses.

House Register, Soldiers' Home, Philadelphia, December 13, 1864- March 28, 1872. The entries are grouped alphabetically by patient's surname. Data appearing include the person's name, his ward and bed numbers, the dates of his admission and discharge, and the descriptive list page number.

Muster Roll of Pennsylvania Soldiers Admitted to the National Home for Disabled Volunteer Soldiers, Central Branch, Dayton, Ohio, November 12, 1880. A record of Pennsylvania soldiers admitted to the home from 1867 to 1880. Entries list the veteran's name, number, company, regiment, disability, barracks number, amount of pension received per month, and the date of death or discharge from the home. The muster roll is arranged alphabetically by soldier's surname.

RECORD BOOK OF CANDIDATES EXAMINED BY THE PENNSYL-VANIA STATE MEDICAL BOARDS FOR APPOINTMENTS AS SUR-GEONS AND ASSISTANT SURGEONS, 1861-1865 (RG-19). Indexed. Normally, entries show the candidate's name, postal address, county of residence, and age; the institution from which he graduated; the date that he was examined; and the standard. Remarks concerning where the person was assigned or whether he resigned also appear.

RECORD BOOK OF CANDIDATES EXAMINED BY THE STATE MEDICAL BOARD, July 28- August 1, 1862 (RG-19). A record kept by Dr. Henry H. Smith while surgeon general of Pennsylvania. The listings are numbered and grouped chronologically by date of examination. The record contains the same information described in the preceding series.

RECORD BOOK OF CLAIMS FOR ARREARS OF PAY AND BOUN-TY, June 6, 1864- August 24, 1869 (RG-19). Indexed. Entries usu-ally indicate the soldier's name, rank, company, and regiment; the date and place of death; the claim number; the date of the certifi-cate and of filing; the monetary amount received; and the appli-cant's name, postal address, and relationship to the soldier. Remarks which record the reasons why a claim was rejected, for example, because the soldier was drafted or was a substitute also appear.

RECORD BOOK OF GOWEN POST 23, G.A.R. (POTTSVILLE, PA.), 1894-1925 (MG-60). Gives the names and residences of Civil War veterans; the companies and regiments in which they served; and the names and numbers of the posts that they were members of. A handwritten list is found at the end of of the book that records information regarding the deaths and burials of Post 23 veterans from 1906 to 1909. Entries appear to be grouped in chronological order, perhaps by dates of meetings or reunions.

RECORD BOOK OF ZOUAVE CADETS OF PENN YAN, 1861-1865 (MG-48). Contains the names, ages, and residences of the founding members. Notes about whether the cadet enlisted into the regular service, died, or left town appear as well. The book is organized according to the date of the meeting.

RECORD OF BURIAL, G.A.R. POST 78 (MIDDLETOWN, PA.), 1862-1931 (in MG-272). Entries usually give the name, rank, company, regiment (or other unit), year of birth, and year of death of the veteran; the name of the cemetery where he was interred; and the lot and block where he was buried. The names are not arranged in any discernible order.

RECORDS OF APPLICATIONS FOR MILITARY POSITIONS, VACANCIES, APPOINTMENTS AND RESIGNATIONS, AND COMMISSIONS ISSUED, 1861-1865 (RG-19). Contains lists of vacancies and appointments. Information found on the lists usually includes the person's name, rank, company, and regiment. Remarks about whether the soldier was mustered out, resigned, or died are regularly recorded, and at times the individual's county of residence is indicated. The lists are arranged by corps and thereinafter chronologically.

RECORDS OF COMPANY G, 211TH REGIMENT, PENNSYLVANIA VOLUNTEERS, 1864-1865, 1868, 1877,1890. (in MG-7). Approximately 150 documents consisting of musters and payrolls; records of clothing, quartermaster's stores, camp, and equipage; transportation accounts; hospital and sick leave forms; and post war correspondence concerning pension applications. Information shown on the muster and payrolls, 1864-1865, includes the soldier's name, rank, unit, regiment and company; the name of commanding officer; the date, place, and by whom mustered into service; the period of enlistment; the date last paid, for what period, and the name of the paymaster; and remarks regarding dates appointed, sick, and so forth. Each soldier signed or marked the roll. The muster and descriptive rolls, 1864, and the muster-out rolls, 1864-1865, are identical to those described under CIVIL WAR MUSTER ROLLS AND RELATED RECORDS, 1861-1866. The hospital and sick leave forms, 1864-1865, are signed by a doctor or an assistant and inform the commanding officer of the company that in compliance with a particular order, and for the these reasons, the following named soldiers are being mustered out.

RECORDS OF DRAFTED MEN AND SUBSTITUTES, INCLUDING COUNTY AND TOWNSHIP DRAFT LISTS, MUSTER AND DESCRIPTIVE ROLLS, AND LISTS OF DESERTERS AND CONSCIENTIOUS OBJECTORS, 1862 (RG-19). The materials are arranged by county. Information found varies with each item. While some documents are dated and merely list the name, township, and county of the draftee, others record more diverse information. Of particular interest to researchers are the following materials:

Adams County, Copy of Draft, 1862. Entries are numbered and show the name, occupation, and age of the drafted person; the name of the township; and at times the name, age, and occupation of the substitute.

Bedford County, List of Drafted Men, October 16, 1862. Contains the name and age of the drafted person; the reason for an exemption; and where apropos the name, age, and regiment of his substitute. The names are grouped by township.

Chester County, Roll of Drafted Men, 1862. Shows the name, township, and occupation of each drafted man.

Clarion County, Roll of Drafted Men, 1862. The entries are numbered and give the drafted person's name, age, occupation, and township of residence.

Cumberland County, Roll of Drafted Militia, 1862. The roll is numbered and mentions the name, occupation, and township of residence of the drafted militiaman. Where appropriate the names of substitutes and the units in which they enlisted are also noted.

Dauphin County, Draft List, October 16, 1862. The list is numbered and indicates the name, occupation, and township of residence for each drafted person.

Elk County, List of Men Drafted, September 25, 1862. Consists of a numbered list that gives the individual's name, age, and township of residence.

Greene County, Roll of Men Drafted, October 16, 1862. Records the name, age, occupation, and township of residence of each person.

Lebanon County, List of Drafted Men, 1862. A typical entry shows the name, age, occupation, and township of residence of the drafted man and, when appropriate, the reason for the exemption and the name and military unit of the substitute.

Lehigh County, Listed of Drafted Men, 1862. The list is arranged alphabetically by draftee's surname and thereunder numbered. Entries record the name, age, occupation, and residence of the individual and at times also contain data about whether the person was rejected or mustered in.

Lycoming County, List of Militia Drafted, October 16, 1862. Shows the name, number, age, occupation, and township of each drafted man.

Monroe County, List of Volunteers and Drafted Men, 1862. The list is numbered and mentions the name, age, occupation, and township of residence of the person.

Montgomery County, Draft, 1862. Records the name, number, age, occupation, and township of the draftee and, where apt, the substitute's name.

Tioga County, Roll of Drafted Men, 1862. The roll is numbered and records the name, age, occupation, and township of residence of the drafted individual.

Venango County, List of Men Drafted, October 16, 1862. Lists the name, age, and occupation of the draftee.

Washington County, Roll of Drafted Men, August 4, 1862. Indicates the name, age, occupation, and township of residence of the drafted person.

York County, List of Drafted Men, 1862. The list is numbered and records the draftee's name, age, occupation, and township of residence; the reason why an exemption may have been granted; and the name of his substitute.

Philadelphia City, Militia Draft, 1862. Gives the name, number, age, occupation, and residence (street address, city ward, precinct) of the drafted individual.

RECORDS OF THE 172ND REGIMENT AND 210TH REGIMENT, PENNSYLVANIA VOLUNTEERS, 1862-1865 (MG-337). Part of the SOLOMON BOWERMAN PAPERS, 1823-1922. Chiefly muster rolls, monthly returns, special and general orders, clothing returns, ordinance stores returns, and quartermaster stores returns for Company A of the 172nd Regiment (1862-1863) and Company A of the 210th Regiment (1864-1865) of Pennsylvania Volunteers during the Civil War. Also found are ninety enlistment papers and hospital records for eight members of the 210th Regiment. The muster rolls contain the same type of information described previously under CIVIL WAR MUSTER ROLLS AND RELATED RECORDS. The clothing, camp, garrison equipage returns, 1862-65, are for non-commissioned officers, artificers, musicians, and privates and provide the name and rank of the each soldier; the date that the clothing or supplies were issued; and use a check mark within a column to indicate what materials were received (for example, in the case of clothing hats, feathers, badges, stockings, jackets, etc.). As part of an audit-receipt process, the names of witnesses appear on the returns as do the signature or mark of each soldier. Other returns unique to this collection include:

Volunteer Enlistment Papers, 1864. Sworn and subscribed statements in which the recruit in the presence of witnesses declares his allegiance to the United States of America; promises to obey the orders of the president and officers appointed over him ; states that he knows of no impediment to his serving honestly and faithfully as a soldier; and agrees to serve in the United States Army for a period of one year. In addition to the date of enlistment, the document records the person's name, height, age, birthplace, and occupation; the state and town of his residence; and the color of his eyes, hair, and complexion. Notations sometimes state what township, county, and congressional district should receive credit for the enlistment. An examining physician and recruiting officer further certify that they have examined and inspected the volunteer and that they are of the opinion that the individual is of lawful age; free from all bodily defects and mental infirmity; and qualified to perform the duties of an able-bodied soldier. In cases were the recruit was a minor, a consent form section was signed and dated by the parent or guardian. The enlistments are not arranged in any type of order.

Inventory of the Effects, 1864-1865. Two printed and standardized forms used by the military to record the death of a soldier at a hospital facility. The first form issued originates from a surgeon in charge of a hospital and is a form letter addressed to the dead soldier's commanding officer. An official notification of death, it is endorsed "inventory of effects" and gives the soldier's name, company, regiment, and military unit; the date and cause of death; and the hospital facility where he died. A list of accouterments is then checked off to signify what government issued clothing and supplies (caps, boots, blankets, haversacks, cartridge box, etc.) were in the possession of the soldier when he died. At the end of this list a space is available for recording the presence of personal items, such as pocketbooks, pins, and the like. The second form is endorsed in the same fashion as the first. Instead of the hospital site, however, it records the town or battlefield where the soldier died. The reverse side of the document repeats all of the information provided on the front and then enumerates what the person's rank was; the name of the Captain (Solomon B. Bowerman) of the unit; the date and place of being mustered into service; the period of enlistment; the county and state where born; age and occupation at enlistment; height; color of eyes, hair, and complexion; place of death (facility and geographic area); and cause of death. An inventory of articles (caps, flannel shirts, etc.), personal effects, and money (specie and notes) found on the deceased follows along with a dated certification by the commanding officer that it is complete and properly being disposed of through the Council of Administration.

Final Statement, 1865. Provides all of the information recorded in the "inventory of effects" plus particulars about when the deceased soldier was last paid (amount and time period) and what amounts should be deducted from pay for clothing received on entering service or stoppages. Since this form was used for discharges in general, there also is a section which covers expenses for transportation, the laundress, and sutler. The documents are signed and dated by the commander of the company and record the place where the statement was prepared.

REGISTER OF ALIENS AND PERSONS HAVING CONSCIENTIOUS SCRUPLES AGAINST BEARING ARMS, 1862 (MG-262). Microfilmed Civil War documents from the records of the Provost Marshal General's Bureau preserved by the National Archives. Arranged by counties. Normally, each entry is numbered and simply lists the name and residence (township and county) of the conscientious objector. For some counties, the person's nativity, and dates of application and discharge also are noted.

REGISTER OF APPLICATIONS FOR PENSIONS, ca.1864-1868 (RG-19). Indexed. The listings generally mention the name, rank, company, and regiment of the soldier; the date when and the place where he was wounded or killed; the name of the applicant; the relationship of the applicant to the soldier; the postal address of the applicant; and the date that the certificate was filed. Remarks appear that indicate the date on which payment was to commence.

REGISTER OF SICK AND WOUNDED SOLDIERS, PENNSYLVANIA VOLUNTEERS, ca. 1861-1865 (RG-19). Entries are grouped alphabetically by person's surname and usually give the name, residence, company, and regiment of the soldier; the disease or impairment that he suffered; and the hospital where he was being treated.

RECORDS RELATING TO COMPANY I, 149TH REGIMENT, PENNSYLVANIA VOLUNTEERS,1862-1865 (in MG-7). Records relate to the military career of Second Lieutenant David Neely and include a muster-in roll dated August 26, 1862; fifteen muster rolls from October 31, 1862- April 30, 1865; a muster-out roll for June 26, 1864; a descriptive list of two recruits dated March, 21, 1864;

twenty-six monthly returns dating from March, 1863 to May, 1865; and a diary covering the Wilderness-Petersburg Campaign of 1864. The documents are grouped by genre and thereafter arranged in chronological order.

REGISTERS OF PENNSYLVANIA VOLUNTEERS, 1861-1865 (RG-19). Listings are arranged by regiment and thereunder by company. The names of the soldiers are usually posted alphabetically. Information ordinarily recorded includes the soldier's name, age, rank, regiment, and company; the term of his service; and the date, place, and name of the person who mustered in and enrolled him. Written remarks regarding the promotion, desertion, death or discharge of the volunteer are frequently entered as well.

RETURNS OF MEDICAL OFFICERS CONNECTED WITH PENNSYLVANIA REGIMENTS, 1861-1864 (RG-19). The dated returns are grouped by regiments and show the name, rank, regiment, and unit of the surgeon or assistant surgeon; the dates that he was appointed and mustered in; and where applicable, from and to which regiment he was promoted. Notations that mention the reasons for and the dates of dismissals, resignations, and transfers are also found.

ROLLS, COMPANIES A-I, 42ND REGIMENT ("BUCKTAILS"), PENNSYLVANIA VOLUNTEERS, 1861-1864 (MG-234). The rolls are grouped by companies and thereunder arranged alphabetically by soldier's surname. A typical entry lists the name, rank, company, and regiment of the volunteer; the date, place, and reason for his discharge; the date that he was transferred; and where appropriate, the date and place where he was wounded or killed.

STOYSTOWN (SOMERSET COUNTY) VOLUNTEER ENLISTMENT CERTIFICATES COLLECTION, September 7, 1864 (in MG-7). The certificates are arranged alphabetically by the person's surname and usually show the name, residence, place of birth (county and state), age, and occupation of the volunteer; the date that he enlisted; and his signature. Only a dozen items are contained in the collection.

Harewood General Hospital,

WASHINGTON, D. C.

Dec. 19 : 1864

Partial Descriptive List and Account of Pay and Clothing of _Prvt._

Daniel Shultz _____ 210° Regiment _Pa_

Vol., Co. _A_, while at this Hospital.

Admitted into Hospital. Oct. 30 / 64

He was _not_ paid on the rolls of this Hospital for the months of Sep & Oct. /64.

Muster & not paid for. not due

Returned to duty Feb. 20th 16-

Dr. h. U.S.Gov. f. c. 24/100 Transportation

Total amount of Clothing drawn, ... $ 20.85

I certify that the above is a correct transcript from the records of this Hospital.

R. B. Bontecou

Surgeon U. S. V.
In charge of Hospital.

Partial descriptive list, pay and clothing account, while in Harewood Hospital, of Private Daniel Shultz, 1864. Found in the hospital records, 1864-1865, of the SOLOMON B. BOWERMAN PAPERS, 1823-1922 (MG-337), PSA.

SUBSTITUTES' DEPOSITIONS, 1862 (RG-19). The depositions are grouped by county and show the substitute's name, signature, township, and county; the date; and the name of the person for whom he was acting as a surrogate.

VOLUNTEER ENLISTMENTS, BATTERY B, 1ST PENNSYLVANIA LIGHT ARTILLERY, 1863-1864 (MG-18). The enlistment papers are filed in alphabetical order by volunteer's surname. Information usually entered on the documents includes the name, signature, residence (state and town), place of birth, age, occupation, and physical description (height, eye and hair color) of the soldier; the date and place of enlistment; the term of enlistment; the date and place where he was mustered in; the name of the unit to which he was attached; and the name of the officer who recruited him.

Other collections that provide information about individual Civil War soldiers or the context in which an ancestor's military unit may have served in the conflict include the following: the HIRAM C. ALLEMAN PAPERS (127th Regiment, Pennsylvania Volunteers), 1856-1926 (MG-15); the L.M. ANDERSON COLLECTION (Company F, 211th Regiment, Pennsylvania Volunteers), 1860-1865 (MG-225); the PAPERS OF WILLIAM WATSON ANDERSON (2nd Pennsylvania Cavalry), 1857-1866 (in MG-147); an ANONYMOUS DIARY (Company I, 187th Infantry Regiment, Pennsylvania Volunteers, MG-262); the WILLIAM C. ARMOR COLLECTION (28th Regiment, Pennsylvania Volunteers), 1862-1930 (MG-228); the BRADY FAMILY PAPERS (Company B, 12th Pennsylvania Volunteer Infantry), 1814-1964 (MG-249); the CIVIL WAR DIARY OF FRANCIS L. BRUBAKER (97th Regiment, Pennsylvania Volunteers), 1862 (in MG-262); the DIARIES OF JOHN JOYCE CARTER, 1861-1916 (in MG-262); the GENERAL RICHARD COULTER PAPERS (11th Regiment, Pennsylvania Volunteers), 1786-1908 (MG-176); the RECORDS OF THE FIRST CITY ZOUAVES; COMPANY A, 127TH PENNSYLVANIA VOLUNTEER INFANTRY; HARRISBURG CITY GRAYS; AND COMPANY D, 8TH REGIMENT, N.G.P., 1862-1917 (MG-246); the RECOLLECTIONS OF JOHN FLEMING (28th Regiment, New York State Militia), 1861-1864 (in MG-262); the DIARIES OF ASA FOSTER, 1837-1869 (in MG-262); the SOLOMON FOX COLLECTION (Company G, 93rd Regiment,

Pennsylvania Volunteers), 1862-1879 (MG-227); the JOHN S. GARRETT COLLECTION (Company A, 46th Regiment, Pennsylvania Volunteers), 1861-1863 (MG-224); the CHRISTIAN GEISEL COLLECTION (Company H, 6th Pennsylvania Cavalry, 70th Regiment of Pennsylvania Volunteers), 1862-1868 (MG-226); the SAMUEL P. GLASS COLLECTION (Company B, 21st Pennsylvania Cavalry, 182nd Regiment of Pennsylvania Volunteers), 1861-1865 (MG-221); the WILMER C. HALL PAPERS (Company G, 1st Pennsylvania Cavalry), 1860-1879 (MG-65); the JOHN F. HARTRANFT PAPERS, 1853-1897 (MG-144) the JACOB R. HILL COLLECTION (Company F, 56th Regiment of Pennsylvania Volunteers), 1864-1889 (MG-231); the JOURNAL AND REMINIS- CENCES OF WILLIAM DRAYTON HOUGHTELIN (77th Regiment of Pennsylvania Volunteers), 1861-1865 (in MG-262); the PAPERS OF SAMUEL HOUSTON (Company B, 4th Pennsylvania Cavalry), 1861-1864 (in MG-262); the DAVID W. HOWARD COLLECTION (Company D, 18th Pennsylvania Cavalry, 163rd Regiment of Pennsylvania Volunteers), 1863-1889 (MG-230); the LETTERS OF DANIEL LEASURE ("Roundheads" or 100th Regiment, Pennsyl- vania Volunteers), 1861-1864 (in MG-262); the McCORMICK FAMI- LY PAPERS (7th Regiment, Pennsylvania Cavalry), 1818-1881 (MG- 83); the HUGH W. McNEIL COLLECTION ("Bucktails" or 1st Rifle Regiment, Pennsylvania Reserve Volunteer Corps), 1855-1916 (MG-87); the DIARY OF JAMES H. MONTGOMERY (Signal Corps, U.S. Army, Department of Pennsylvania), 1864-1865 (in MG-262); the DANIEL MUSSER COLLECTION (various units), 1861-1865 (MG-95); the WILLIAM JACKSON PALMER PAPERS (15th Pennsyl- vania Cavalry, 160th Regiment of Pennsylvania Volunteers), 1822- 1948 (in MG-262); the R.W. PENN COLLECTION (Company K, 11th Regiment, Pennsylvania Volunteers), 1863-1865 (MG-229); the DIARY OF GEORGE L. PRESTON (Company B, 100th Regiment, Pennsylvania Volunteers), 1864 (in MG-262); the FRANCIS W. REED COLLECTION (Company L, 7th Pennsylvania Cavalry, 80th Regiment of Pennsylvania Volunteers), 1861-1865 (MG-223); the JEREMIAH ROHRER COLLECTION (127th Regiment, Pennsylvania Volunteers), 1852-1863 (MG-243); the REMINISCENCES OF LIV- INGSTON SAYLOR (Company H, 20th Pennsylvania Cavalry), 1864-1865 (in MG-262); the SCHAFFNER FAMILY COLLECTION

(Company I, 87th Regiment, Pennsylvania Volunteers), 1859-1866 (MG-232); the PAPERS OF EDWARD SCHILLING (4th Regiment, Maryland Volunteers), 1862-1874 (in MG-262); the OSCAR SHARPLESS PAPERS (93rd Regiment, Pennsylvania Volunteers), 1861-1865 (MG-448); the CORRESPONDENCE OF JOSEPH A. SHAW (12th Regiment, Maine Volunteers), 1862-1864 (in MG-262); the JACOB SIGMUND COLLECTION (Company E, 7th Pennsylvania Cavalry, 80th Regiment of Pennsylvania Volunteers), 1863-1865 (MG-222); the ROBERT TAGGERT PAPERS (9th Regiment of Pennsylvania Reserves or the 38th Regiment of the Line), 1861-1864 (MG-124); PHOTOGRAPH COLLECTION OF WILLIAM M. TAYLOR (Company M, 22nd Regiment of Pennsylvania Cavalry), 1864-1870 (in MG-446); the DIARIES OF JOSEPH FRANKLIN P. TREZIYULNY (Company E, 5th Pennsylvania Infantry Reserves), 1857-1861 (in MG-128); and the PAPERS OF JAMES HARRISON WILSON, 1865-1920 (in MG-262).

THE SPANISH-AMERICAN WAR

In addition to the original records which follow any research work involving service during the Spanish-American War should start with an examination of the published *Record of Pennsylvania Volunteers in the Spanish-American War, 1898* (Harrisburg, 1901) by Thomas J. Stewart, Adjutant General.

MILITARY COMMISSION BOOKS, 1800-1944 (RG-26). Includes an indexed volume called Commissions to Pennsylvania Volunteers in Service of U.S., 1898. Information appearing about the officer includes his name, county of residence, rank, and date of taking rank; the regiment and company to which he was attached; and the date of the order or commission. Data concerning whether the soldier was discharged, transferred, or killed are also noted.

SPANISH-AMERICAN WAR MUSTER ROLLS AND RELATED RECORDS, 1898 (RG-19). The materials are arranged by regiment and thereinafter according to company. The record includes the following types of muster rolls:

Muster-in Rolls. Entries usually list the name, age, place of birth (town or county, state or country), previous occupation, residence, description (height, complexion, eye and hair color), marital status, and rank of soldier; the unit, regiment, and company to which he was attached; the date and place where he was mustered in and enrolled; the period of enlistment; the location of the station of general rendezvous; the number of miles traveled to reach the rendezvous; and the date and location of the muster. Data regarding the physical disabilities of recruits and the names and addresses of parents or guardians of single soldiers are routinely included.

Muster-out Rolls. The dated lists generally give the name, rank, and residence of the soldier; the military unit, regiment, and commanding officer to which he was attached; the date and place where he was enrolled; the name of the enroller; the period of enlistment; the date of last pay; the date and place of the muster; and the place where discharged. Remarks concerning the physical disabilities of the person or changes in the soldier's rank are oftentimes mentioned too.

SPANISH-AMERICAN WAR VETERANS' CARD FILE (RG-19). Consists of 4 X 6 inch cards created from information taken from official records of the United States War Department between 1940 and 1941. Data appearing on the cards usually include the name, race, age, birthplace, residence, and rank of the veteran; the date and place where he was enlisted; the dates and places of service; and the military organization (infantry, regiment, company or the like) to which he was attached. Remarks concerning the date and place of discharge and information about prior military service are oftentimes noted.

SPANISH-AMERICAN WAR VETERANS' COMPENSATION FILE (RG-19). The file was created by the state Adjutant General's Office in 1934, and covers men who served in the Spanish-American War and in the occupation of the Philippines from 1898 to 1904. Included in the file are the following types of documents:

Veterans' Compensation Applications. Normally, entries indicate the name, rank, address, date of birth, and place of birth of the veteran; the date and place of enlistment; the dates of service and the regiment to which he was attached; his legal address at the time of entry; and the date and place of discharge. Information regarding engagements participated in, wounds suffered, the dates of over-seas service, and the names and addresses of dependents is also included.

Verification of Service and Bonus Payments. Consists of forms that normally show the soldier's name, rank, company, and regiment; the dates that he was mustered in and out; the date of enrollment; and the application number.

The file is in alphabetical order by soldier's surname.

MEXICAN BORDER CAMPAIGN

DESCRIPTIVE LISTS OF COMPANIES, B AND C, 2ND INFANTRY, AND BATTERY D, 2ND ARTILLERY OF THE PENNSYLVANIA NATIONAL GUARD, 1917 (RG-19). Consists of forms that record the name, rank, residence, age, place of birth, occupation, physical description (complexion, height, color of hair and eyes, scars), marital status, and military organization of the serviceman; the dates of his enlistment, rendezvous, and mobilization; and the date that he was mustered into U.S. service. The forms list the name, residence, and relationship of a person to notify in case of emergency and are filed alphabetically by soldier's surname.

MEXICAN BORDER CAMPAIGN MUSTER ROLLS AND RELATED PAPERS. 1916-1917 (RG-19). Includes muster-in rolls of Pennsylvania National Guardsmen that show the name, signature, rank, occupation, marital status, place of birth, description (height, complexion, eye and hair color), age, and residence of the soldier; the military unit, station, and commander to which he was assigned; the date of commission or enlistment; and the date of the muster. The name, address, and relationship of a person to be notified in case of an emergency are listed for each guardsman, and remarks regarding whether the soldier was discharged or transferred are regularly included.

MEXICAN BORDER CAMPAIGN VETERANS' CARD FILE, 1916-1917 (RG-19). Consists of 4 X 6 inch cards that have "Mexican Emergency, Call of President, June 18, 1916," printed on them. Information shown includes the name, rank, regiment, company, age, place of birth, occupation, marital status, physical description

To all Whom it May Concern:

Know ye, That _Ray E. Miner_, a _Corporal_ of _Company C_, of the _15th_ Regiment of _Pennsylvania_ Volunteers, who was enrolled on the _seventh_ day of _— May —_, one thousand eight hundred and ninety-_eight_, to serve _- two years -_, or during the war, is hereby DISCHARGED from the service of the UNITED STATES, by reason of _— Muster-Out —_

* NO OBJECTION TO HIS REENLISTMENT IS KNOWN TO EXIST.

The said _Corporal Ray E Miner_ was born in _Baraboo_, in the State of _Wisconsin_ and when enrolled was _20_ years of age, _5_ feet _8_ inches high, _Fair_ complexion, _Grey_ eyes, _Blonde_ hair, and by occupation a _Printer_.

GIVEN at _Athens, Ga.,_ this _Thirty-first_ day of _January_, 189_9_

Wallace Printer
Captain 15th Pa. Vol. Infty.
Commanding the _Company_.

Countersigned.

Edward Howe
Captain 17th Infantry.
Mustering Officer.

* To be erased should there be anything in the conduct or physical condition of the soldier rendering him unfit for the Army.

3—1276

A discharge certificate of Corporal Ray E. Miner, a veteran of the Spanish-American War. Filed among the VETERAN'S MILITARY SERVICE DIS-CHARGE PAPERS, 1899-1937 (RG-19), PSA.

(height, complexion, hair and eye color), and residence of the veteran; the date of his commission or enlistment into the service; his home station; the date of rendezvous; and his date of acceptance into U.S. service. Written remarks also are entered that indicate the date that the soldier's enlistment was to expire and the name and address of a person to contact in case of an emergency. The cards are in alphabetical order by veteran's surname.

WORLD WAR I

CARD RECORDS OF NATIONAL NAVAL VOLUNTEERS, 1917 (RG-19). Composed of 3 x 5 inch cards originally filed in the Office of the State Adjutant General. The cards indicate the name, rating, and residence (town and state) of the volunteer; the date and place where he was enrolled into service; and the battalion or division to which he was assigned. The cards are arranged alphabetically by surname.

DRAFT BOARD RECORDS, CONSISTING PRIMARILY OF LISTS OF PERSONS WHOSE REGISTRATION CARDS ARE IN THE POSSESSION OF THEIR LOCAL BOARD, Ca. 1917-1918 (RG-19). Contains registration and induction lists that are arranged by regions and thereunder according to draft board numbers. Information usually appearing on the lists includes the draftee's name, postal address, and age. At times the occupation of the person is also recorded.

GENERAL FILE, PENNSYLVANIA WAR HISTORY COMMISSION, 1915-20, 1928 (RG-19). Chiefly histories of military units that served in World War I and copies or transcripts of monthly rosters; casualty lists and statistics; field messages; military orders; correspondence; daily, weekly, and monthly returns; and diaries and letters pertaining to individual soldiers. The casualty lists generally note the name, serial number, rank, cause, and date of death of each fatality. In some instances original documents are interfiled with the reproductions. Also included are diverse group and portrait photographs of the troops and a file folder captioned "Register of Commissioned and Warrant Officers of the U.S. Navy and Marine Corps, January 1, 1916." The file is arranged by military units.

EDWARD MARTIN PAPERS, 1866 (1894-1966)-1967 (MG-156). Among the records of this former state auditor general (1925-1929), adjutant general (1939-1943), governor (1943-1947), and U.S. senator (1947-1958) there is a manuscript draft of his book *The Twenty-Eight Division, Pennsylvania's Guard in the World War* (Pittsburgh, 1923). A five volume published version also is available for search room use. Besides containing a history of each unit's (company, battery, etc.) activities and contributions, the books are filled with group photographs and individual portraits. Data that accompany the photographs usually includes the soldier's name, unit, rank, and information about when he was wounded, discharged, or reported missing.

SELECTIVE SERVICE ROSTERS FOR INDUCTEES IN PENNSYL-VANIA, 1917-1918 (RG-19). A record of men inducted into the army, navy, and marine corps by the selective service system in Pennsylvania. A typed and bound manuscript, it was compiled by Major William G. Murdock, state draft executive, for Brigadier General Frank D. Beary, Adjutant General of Pennsylvania. The eleven volumes are arranged in alphabetical order by name of county and thereunder in numerical order by draft board number and draft order number. Only Allegheny through Perry Counties are covered by the records. Each "Final Induction Report" includes the draft order number; name of registrant; date of induction; call number; the post, station or camp; date of acceptance or rejection; and, if needed, date of discharge for cases in which the registrant was discharged after having been accepted at camp.

UNDELIVERED DISCHARGE CERTIFICATES, 1918-1919 (RG-19). Consists of several discharges for soldiers attached to the U.S. Army. Entries on the certificates give the name, rank, serial number, military unit, birthplace, age (at enlistment), occupation, physical description (height, complexion, eye and hair color), physical condition, and marital status of the soldier; the dates and places where he was enlisted and discharged; the reason for his discharge; and the name of the person processing the discharge. Particulars about wounds received in service, battles participated in, and vocational knowledge possessed are also noted. The certificates are arranged alphabetically according to the surname of the discharged individual.

"Members of the American Expeditionary Forces World War I." A photograph
from *PHOTOGRAPHS OF THE AMERICAN EXPEDITIONARY FORCES,
28TH DIVISION, IN FRANCE, 1918-1919 (RG-19), PSA.*

WORLD WAR I MUSTER ROLLS, 1917 (RG-19). Consists of muster rolls for the Pennsylvania National Guard. Information shown includes the name and rank of the guardsman; his residence; the date of his enlistment; and the regiment, company, troop, or battery to which he was attached. Data about whether the person was in the U.S. service or discharged are oftentimes noted as well. The muster rolls are grouped according to military units.

WORLD WAR I VETERANS' SERVICE AND COMPENSATION FILE (RG-19). The items are arranged by service branch (Army, Navy, and Marines) and thereunder alphabetically by the veteran's surname. An "out-of-state" category also exists for persons who applied to the Commonwealth for a bonus, but were unable to substantiate Pennsylvania residency. Any of the following may be found:

Service Statement Cards. Entries may show the name, rank, serial number, race, birthplace, age (sometimes date of birth), and residence of the soldier; the military organization or unit to which he was attached; the dates of assignments and transfers; the engagements served in; the date of any wounds received; and the dates of overseas service and discharge.

Compensation Applications. Contains information such as the name, rank, serial number, race, date of birth, and place of birth of the veteran; his legal residence at the time of application and enlistment; the place and date where he was enrolled and discharged; and the period for which he served. Data concerning engagements involved in, wounds suffered, the dates of serving overseas, and the names and addresses of dependents are also included. The documents are signed and dated by the applicant.

War Service Record of Soldiers, Sailors and Marines. Consists of survey questionnaires filled out by World War I veterans in 1920 for the Pennsylvania War History Commission. Normally the questionnaire gives the name, postal address, and county of residence of the person; his age at entry into the service; the date of entry into the service; and the military unit, regiment, and company with which he served. Data about the veteran's next of kin (their address and relationship to him) and particulars regarding the dates and places of his residency since beginning service are also provided.

WORLD WAR II

RECORDS OF PENNSYLVANIA NATIONAL GUARDSMEN MUS-TERED INTO WORLD WAR II, 1940-1941 (RG-19). The file, which is organized by military units, contains rosters of troops and officers, individual enlistment records, and reports of physical examination upon induction.

Rosters. List the name and rank of the soldier; the organization and station (city and state); and the date. The documents are signed by the person preparing them.

Enlistment Record, National Guard of the State of Pennsylvania. Consists of a basic enlistment section, a declaration of the applicant, a physical examination, an oath and certificate of enlistment, and a designation of beneficiary and person to notify in case of emergency. The first part of the enlistment form records the soldier's name, serial number, race, home address, and grade; the location and date of enlistment; the name and rank of the individual who did the enlistment; the company, regiment, and arm of service; the length of enlistment; date and place of birth; and a chronological statement of any prior military service. A dated, signed and witnessed "Declaration Of Applicant" provides information regarding the guardsman's place of birth; race; citizenship status; education; civilian trade or occupation (years and weekly wage); special military qualifications; marital state; dependents; criminal background; and medical history. Data found on the "Physical Examination" section includes the height, weight, chest girth (at expiration and inspiration), complexion, hair and eye color of the applicant. This is followed by a description of the person's general examination (physique, skin, head, chest abdomen, extremities); general surgical conditions (hernia, hemorrhoids, varicose veins, and state of abdominal wall and viscera); organs of locomotion (bones, joints, muscles, and tendons); genito-urinary system (functioning of kidneys); vision; hearing; ear, nose, and throat; teeth; mouth and gums; cardiovascular system (heart, pulse rate, condition of arteries); lungs; neuropsychiatric examination; and immunizations. The date of examination, place of examination (city and state), and the accuracy of the recorded results are certified by a member of the medical corps. Also found on the enlistment form are fingerprints of the recruit's right hand; an oath of allegiance to the United States of America and the state of Pennsylvania; and a designation of beneficiaries and a person to notify in case of an emergency (names, relationships, and addresses).

Reports of Physical Examination of the Enlisted Man on Induction. Provide the date of the president's call order; the name of the military organization or unit; the home station; and the name, army serial number, race, grade, occupation, permanent address, mother tongue, birthplace, and birth date of the person to be examined for induction. Examination entries include the presence of any eye, ear, nose, throat, mouth, and gum abnormalities; the condition of the individual's teeth and skin; and the existence of varicose veins, a hernia, or hemorrhoids. Additional examination subjects include feet, muscular-skeletal defects, abdominal viscera, the cardiovascular system, lungs, the nervous system, endocrine disturbances, results of laboratory examinations, a summary of defects in order of importance, physical fitness, vision, hearing, height, weight, chest girth, posture, frame, hair color, eye color, complexion, pulse, blood pressure, and urinalysis. The examination is certified by the Physical Examination Board.

REPORTS, CORRESPONDENCE, AND RESEARCH FILE RELATING TO THE WAR HISTORY PROGRAM, 1938-1947 (RG-13). Contains the following two items covering military casualties from Pennsylvania:

State Summary of War Casualties [Pa.], U.S. Navy, 1946. The volume is arranged alphabetically by surname of service man and usually gives his rank, home address, and data about family relationships (name of parents if not married, name of wife, etc.).

World War II, Honor List of Dead and Missing, State of Pennsylvania, June, 1946. Compiled by the U.S. War Department, the volume is arranged by county and thereinafter by name of serviceman. Data listed include the person's name, serial number, rank, and a code indicating the cause of the casualty (that is, "DNB" for died in non-battle, "DOI" for died of injuries, "DOW" for died of wounds, "FOD" for finding of death, "KIA" for killed in action, and "M" for missing.

WORLD WAR II APPLICATIONS FOR VETERANS' COMPENSATION, 1950 (RG-19). A record of veterans who applied for the World War II bonus provided for by the Act of June 1, 1947. Information contained on the applications includes the name, signature, residence, birth date, place of birth, sex, and serial number of the individual; the dates of domestic and foreign service rendered; the branch of the service enlisted in; the dates and places where the applicant entered and left active service; the person's residence at the time of his enlistment; the name and location of the applicant's draft board; the dates that the application was received and processed; the amount of compensation awarded; and the names and residences of the veteran's beneficiaries, living parents, and dependents. The application, which is notarized and dated, also records the ages of all dependents, whether the person was still on active duty in the armed forces (at the time of filing the application), and whether he had ever received sea duty pay or a bonus. The applications are arranged alphabetically according to the surname of the veteran.

THE KOREAN AND VIETNAM WARS

The bonus applications for Korean veterans from Pennsylvania were lost in the Agnes Flood of 1972. As a result, few records for either this conflict or the more recently concluded Vietnam War are part of the current holdings of the State Archives. Materials that are available include these series:

CASUALTY LISTS OF PENNSYLVANIA MILITARY PERSONNEL FROM THE KOREAN AND VIETNAM WARS, UNDATED (MG-7). Computer listings generated from machine-readable records that are part of RG 330, Records of the Office of the Secretary of Defense at the National Archives. Each list is arranged alphabetically by home state, then name. The following data appears:

U.S. Military Personnel Who Died from Hostile Action (Including Missing and Captured) in the Korean War, 1950-1957. Provides the name, rank/grade, branch of service, home (city, town or county), and state of the serviceman; the date of casualty; and the category of casualty (died while missing, killed in action; died while captured, etc.). A total of 2,333 names appear.

U.S. Military Personnel Who Died (Including Missing and Captured Declared Dead) in the Vietnam War, 1957-1986. Depicts all of the data shown on the Korean list plus the country of casualty and the person's date of birth. Categories of casualties include hostile, died-missing; hostile, killed; hostile, died-wounds; hostile, died-missing BNR; hostile, died-capture, BNR; non-hostile, died-other; non-hostile, died-missing; non-hostile, died-ill. There are 3,139 names enumerated.

ROSTERS OF TROOPS INDUCTED INTO KOREAN SERVICE, 1949-1952 (RG-19). A record of Pennsylvania National Guard units inducted into federal service during the Korean War. In addition to the rosters there is a folder of delay orders dated 1951, and an alphabetical listing of inductees that was prepared on May 1,1952, and which gives the name, serial number, rank, and date of enlistment for each person. The rosters are dated and show the name of the National Guard unit; the station (city and state); the reason for submission (essentially ordered into active military service per a specific order); and the rank, organization, and name of the individual submitting the roster. Entries on the roster normally provide the name, grade (rank), serial number, race, and year of birth (sometimes date) of each enlisted man; the military component (National Guard or National Guard of the United States) attached to; and his principal duty (for officers) or military specialty (for enlisted men). At times, the date of current commission or enlistment is also included. The rosters are arranged by military units.

VIETNAM BONUS RECIPIENTS RECORD, September 11, 1984 (RG-11). A record of military personnel from Pennsylvania who received a bonus for fighting for their country in the Vietnam War. The computer listing which was generated for use by the Vietnam Veterans Herbicides Information Commission, provides the name, address (city, state and zip code), and social security number of the veteran; a county code; and a code indicating military branch. The file is arranged in numerical order by social security number.

SERVICE RECORDS OF THE NATIONAL GUARD OF PENNSYLVANIA

COMPANY RECORD BOOKS, 1890-1916 (RG-19). Each book usually contains company rolls; records of drills, parades, and marksmanship; company, regimental, brigade, division, and headquarter orders, both general and special; and enlistment and descriptive books. After 1901 returns of state property and state property issued, annual allowance accounts, and armory rent records (post 1908) are included as well. Of particular interest to family historians are the enlistment and descriptive sections covering the 3rd, 4th, 6th, 8th, 11th, 17th, 19th, 20th, and 21st regiments and Divisions B and A of the 1st and 2nd Naval Battalions of the National Guard, respectively. Entries have the name, signature, age, residence, date of birth, place of birth, occupation, and physical description (height and color of complexion, eyes, and hair) of each recruit; dates of enlistment and discharge; and the reason for discharge. Name indexes are in the fronts of the descriptive book sections created during the 1890's.

DIRECTORY OF THE PENNSYLVANIA NATIONAL GUARD AND ROSTER OF THE COMMISSIONED OFFICERS, August 5, 1917 (MG-242). The directory is grouped by unit and gives the name, rank, and address of the officer; the date of present commission; and the date on which that rank was assumed.

ENLISTMENT RECORDS, 1867-1945 (RG-19). The data vary with the type of form utilized. Among the information likely to appear are the name, signature, age, date of birth, place of birth, race, occupation, marital status, education, and residence of the recruit; the date of his enlistment or application; and the name and address of his nearest relative. A brief medical history and physical description (weight, height, eye and hair color) of the person is usually included, and a married guardsman listed the number of children that he had. Some of the older applications also record the nationality of the individual. The enlistment papers are arranged alphabetically according to surname.

FIELD TRAINING MUSTER AND PAY ROLLS, 1873-1912 (RG-19). The materials are arranged by regiment and company and thereunder alphabetically according to the guardsman's surname. Data contained on the rolls include the name, signature, rank, age, height, and residence of the individual; the regiment, company, brigade, station, and commanding officer to which he was assigned; and the date of enlistment. Particulars about the amount of pay earned and received are recorded, and data regarding whether the person was absent or present for roll calls are frequently noted.

MILITARY ORGANIZATION AND COMMISSION BOOKS, 1866-1929 (RG-19). Indexed. Entries list the name and residence of the person, the date of the commission, the date from which rank was to be held, and the brigade to which he was assigned. Remarks regarding transfers, termination of commissions, and the like are included.

MUSTER ROLLS AND RELATED PAPERS, Ca. 1867-1917, 1920- 1924, 1927 (RG-19). The materials are arranged according to military unit and thereafter by the date of the document. The following types of muster rolls are found:

Abstract of Daily Roll Call and Muster and Pay Roll. The rolls are dated and normally show the name, rank, signature, age, height, occupation, and residence of the guardsman; the company, organization (infantry, artillery and the like), and brigade to which he was attached; the date of his present enlistment; and his total number of enlistments. Particulars concerning the amount of pay earned and received by the person and remarks about whether he took the federal oath or had been discharged are regularly entered.

Applications for Company Organization. Usually an application records what type of company (infantry, artillery, and the like) permission was sought to form, the county where the company was being organized, the name of the person forwarding the application, and the date on which the application was filled out and received. The documents are signed by each volunteer and list his name, residence, and place of nativity.

Inspection Rolls. The rolls are dated and give the name, rank, age, height, residence, and occupation of the guardsman; the regiment, brigade, company, station, and commanding officer to which he was assigned; the date of his enlistment; and the number of drills and parades that he attended. Comments about whether the individual might have been absent without leave are included.

Muster Rolls. Entries usually show the name, rank, description (height, complexion, color of eyes and hair), age, birthplace, marital status, occupation, residence, and signature of each member of the company; the date and period of enlistment; the name of his commanding officer; and the station, regiment, or unit to which he was attached. Data about whether the person was discharged or transferred are noted, and at times even the fact that a recruit might not have been naturalized is recorded.

NATIONAL GUARD VETERANS' CARD FILE, Ca. 1867-1921 (RG-19). Consists of 4 X 6 inch cards originally maintained by the state Adjutant General's Office. Generally the cards show the name, rank, age, physical description (height, complexion, hair and eye color), occupation, and residence of the guardsman; the date and place of his enlistment; the date and reason for discharge; and the unit (company, regiment and the like) to which he was assigned. Information about federal service rendered by the individual or the date of his death or first appearance in the military records also routinely appears. The cards are arranged alphabetically by veteran's surname.

OFFICERS MASTER FILE, NATIONAL GUARD SERVICE, 1941-1960 (RG-19). Two sets of index cards (3 X 5 inch) that are labeled "officers From 1946" and "PNG-NGUS." The first group of cards simply lists the name of the officer with the phrase "active PARNG." The date that the person separated from service is then noted. The second set consists of printed cards that have the officer's name typed on them and one of the following lines checked off: Active National Guard, Inactive National Guard, Assigned National Guard Service, Unassigned National Guard Reserve, Supernumerary List, or Retired List. In some cases "separated from National Guard" is typed in. Both sets of cards are arranged in alphabetical order by surname of officer.

RECORDS OF THE 2ND REGIMENT OF THE NATIONAL GUARD OF PENNSYLVANIA, 108TH FIELD ARTILLERY AND PREDECESSOR ORGANIZATIONS, 1840-1948 (MG-436). The parent unit was constituted and organized on December 11, 1840, at Philadelphia as the National Guards, a volunteer militia company assigned to the 1st Volunteer Infantry Regiment of Pennsylvania. Before being reorganized on October 23, 1916, as the 2nd Field Artillery Regiment, the unit was known as the Infantry Corps of National Guards of the City of Philadelphia in 1856; as the 2nd Infantry Regiment in 1860; as the 19th Pennsylvania Infantry Regiment in 1861; as the 90th Pennsylvania Volunteer Infantry Regiment in 1862; as the 2nd Infantry Regiment (National Guards) in 1867; as the 2nd Pennsylvania Volunteer Infantry Regiment in 1898; and as the 2nd Infantry Regiment, Pennsylvania National Guard, in 1899. These records are noteworthy:

Constitution and Enlistment Book, National Guards, 1840-1878. Covers enlistments from the organization of the unit on December 11, 1840 to September 9, 1878. The data is set up in a column format and gives the date of enlistment and the guardsman's name, residence (from the 1860s onward), height, age, and color of hair, eyes, and complexion. There are occasional notations regarding death dates and the enlisted person's occupation normally appears in the 1870's. Entries are arranged in chronological order.

Roll Book, National Guards, 1854-1882. For the most part simply lists the last name of each guardsman, his rank, and the dates that he was present for drills, parades, and roll calls. Musicians also are identified as well as dates of resignation and or death.

Minute Books of "Old Guard," 1910, 1916-1948. A record of roll calls, orders drawn to pay bills, the election of officers, and resignations. A list of members interred in the Old Guard lot in Mount Moriah Cemetery, West Philadelphia, 1924-1925, 1948, showing their names and dates of death is included as are "page dedications" to deceased comrades. The books are in chronological order by date of meeting.

Membership Book and Personal Record, 1858-1911. Indexed. Contains lists of "lifetime memberships" and "dues paying members." The lifetime members are in alphabetical order and have the dates that they were admitted and died (if appropriate) written after their names. The dues paying members appear in a debit-credit ledger format with admittance information noted on the top and death or suspension data on the bottom of each page.

Company Record Books, 1893-1916. The record books for 1893-1899, have indexes in them. Each volume usually contains the company roll; record of drills, parades, and marksmanship; company, regimental, brigade, division, and headquarters orders; and enlistment and descriptive books. Returns for state property issued, annual allowance accounts, and rifle practice commutations are included after 1901 as well. The enlistment and descriptive books have columns that provide space to enter the following data regarding members: name, age, residence, where born, when born, date of enlistment, number of order admitting to membership, date when uniformed, height, complexion, eyes, hair, occupation, date of discharge, signature of recruit, and remarks. Companies A, 1894-1897, 1899-1916; B, 1893-1916; C, 1893-1903, 1906-1916; D, 1893-1916; E, 1893-1895, 1899-1916; F, 1893-1906; G, 1893-1916; H, 1898-1913; I, 1893-1907, 1913-1916; K,1893-1906, 1908-1914; L, 1900-1904, 1906-1916; M, 1900-1916; and band, 1903-1910, of the 2nd Regiment and Companies A, 1898-1899, and C, 1899, of the 19th Regiment are represented in the books.

RECORDS OF THE STATE FENCIBLES, 1813-1956 (MG-379). Significant materials of the State Fencibles, the oldest infantry Command in Pennsylvania, include:

State Fencibles Roll of Active Members, 1871-1874. Records the member's name, residence, occupation, and date of enlistment. An age column is not filled in. Entries are grouped alphabetically by surnames.

Roster of the State Fencibles Battalion, 1st Brigade, National Guard of Pennsylvania, 1871 (1886-1896)-1896. Entries are grouped alphabetically in a column format and provide the name, residence, and occupation of the member; the company attached to; the color of his eyes, hair, and complexion; his height; the dates of enlistment and discharge; and the reason for separation (business engagement, neglect of duty, deceased).

Company Enlistment and Descriptive Books, Battalion State Fencibles, Companies A-D, 1878-1891. Five books covering Company A, 1878-1890 (enlistments from 1871-1890); Company B, 1885-1892, 1894 (enlistment from 1871-1886); Company C, 1878-1886, 1889-1893 (enlistments from 1871-1893); and Company D, 1887-1891 (enlistments from 1871-1891). Each book is arranged in chronological order by dates of enlistment. Information provided includes the name, age, residence, occupation, and height of the soldier; the color of his eyes, hair, and complexion; and the dates of enlistment and discharge. A remarks column is used to indicate the reason for discharge or to record dates of death.

Officer's Rosters of State Fencibles Battalion, 1880-1898. The volumes are arranged by companies and provide each officer's name, rank, and residence; the date rank was from; the date of commission, and as needed, the date of resignation and sometimes death. There is no index.

Roll Book (Honorary and Lifetime Membership), 1884-1890. Entries are grouped alphabetically by name of member and show the date dues were received, the years paid for, the person's address, and as appropriate, his date of death.

Record of Company Regiment, National Guard of Pennsylvania, 1890-1908. Indexed. The volume is arranged by enlistment numbers and contains general and special orders from 1890-1908 as well as an enlistment and descriptive book of Companies A-D, February 13, 1901-June 15, 1908. Column entries list the enlistment number, name, age, residence, and occupation of the soldier; his dates of enlistment and discharge; color of eyes and complexion (dark, light, and fair); and height. There is a space for providing the person's place and date of birth but it is not filled in. Remarks, however, do appear that record information regarding dates of promotion, or the fact that the person might be a musician, or was discharged for neglect of duty.

Record of Medical Department, State Fencibles Battalion, 1st Brigade, National Guard of Pennsylvania, 1893-1898. Contains form No. 18 A.G.O, re-enlistment papers. Each enlistment form consists of two parts. The first section provides standard personal

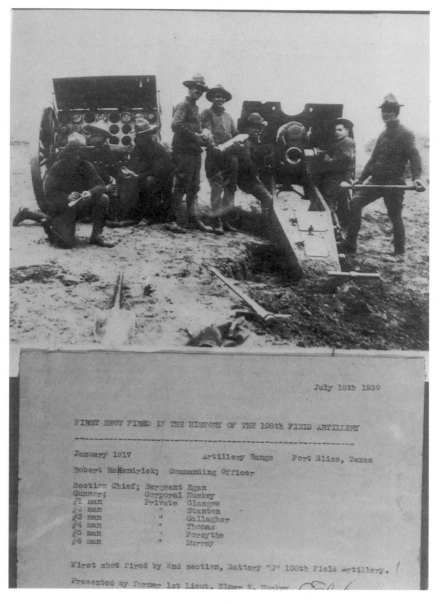

Photograph documenting the first shot fired by members of Battery "D," at Fort Bliss, Texas in 1917. From RECORDS OF THE 2ND REGIMENT OF THE NATIONAL GUARD OF PENNSYLVANIA, 108TH FIELD ARTILLERY AND PREDECESSOR ORGANIZATIONS, 1840-1948 (MG-436), PSA.

and background information about the guardsman, that is, his name, place of birth, age, residence, height, complexion, color of eyes and hair, occupation, date of enlistment, and the company enlisted in. A dated, sworn, and subscribed statement then follows in which the member declares that he will support the Constitution of the United States and Pennsylvania and that he will faithfully discharge the duties of a soldier in the National Guard. The second part of the form is a medical examination that is dated, certified, and signed by a medical officer. Questions addressed include the condition of the person's nervous and vascular systems; girth of chest under normal circumstances and at expiration and inspiration; circumference of abdomen; and the presence of hernia, varicocele or varicose veins. The two volumes are arranged by dates of enlistment and there is no index.

RECORDS OF TROOP A, 52ND MACHINE GUN SQUADRON, PENNSYLVANIA NATIONAL GUARD, 1924-1930 (in MG-272). The WILLIAM McALEVY COLLECTION contains the following items:

Enlistment Records, 1924-1930. The form is signed by the recruiting officer and has five sections. The first section gives the guardsman's name, race, and home address; the name and address of the nearest relative; the date and place of enlistment; the length of enlistment; the company, regiment, and branch of service attached to; and if appropriate a chronology of past service and the soldier's army serial number. The "physical examination before enlistment" section is dated, signed and certified by a physician and describes the person's physical features, that is, the color of his eyes, hair, and complexion; his height, weight, and girth of chest; the appearance of his physique, skin, head, chest, abdomen, and extremities (usually normal); the status of his vision and hearing; and the condition of his eyes, ears, nose, mouth, gums, teeth, throat, lungs, heart, cardio-vascular, and genito-urinary systems. Remarks also appear concerning whether the person had flat feet; showed any signs of a neuropsychiatric condition or had been vaccinated (typhoid and smallpox). Part three of the form, a "record of inoculation at enlistment," was utilized to document when and by whom vaccinations were administered; and if not, why. The reverse side of the enlistment record consists of a "declaration of applicant," in which the recruit lists his place and date of birth; the number of years spent in grammar school, high school, and college; and his occupation and years of experience. These facts are then followed by a series of statements, for example, that he is a citizen of the United States or has made a legal declaration of intention to be so; that he is not married, has no children, or persons dependent upon him; that he has never been convicted of a felony or imprisoned in a reformatory, jail or penitentiary; that he was not a member of the military or naval services of the United States at the time of enlistment or before; that he was not a member of the Officer's Reserve Corps, Enlisted Reserve Corps, or National Guard Reserve; that he had not previously applied for enlistment and been rejected; that he believed that he was physically qualified to perform the duties of an able-bodied soldier; that he was free from illness, did not have convulsions, spit up blood, wet the bed, and so forth.

An *"Oath of Enlistment" and a "Certificate of Inspection and Enlistment"* signed by the soldier and recruiting officer, respectively, complete the form. The former gives details regarding what military unit the recruit enlisted in, the date of enlistment, and for how many years. The latter certificate is a sworn statement that all legal requirements had been met and that the soldier seemed sober and in full possession of his mental capacities. The documents are arranged in alphabetical order by surnames.

Extract from Service Record, 1924-30. At times, form no. 29A is present instead of an enlistment record. While the form is rather lengthy, the only information filled out for this troop is the name of the soldier; the date and place where accepted for enlistment; the enlistment period; and the name and address of a person to notify in case of emergency.

Roll Book, Machine Gun Troop, 103rd Cavalry, 1925-1930. Contains an alphabetical list of enlisted men that shows their names, street addresses, and the dates that enlistments expired. Summary statements at the end of each quarters roll call also are used to indicate significant events, such as the death of a current or past troop member. Such remarks usually include the cause of death, the date of death or internment, and squad members in attendance at the burial service. The roll calls, which merely report who was present each month, are arranged in chronological order.

RECORDS RELATING TO COMPANY K OF THE 6TH INFANTRY REGIMENT, 4TH BRIGADE, PENNSYLVANIA NATIONAL GUARD, 1906-1918 (RG-19). The file is arranged randomly by type of record and contains diverse muster, pay, and inspection rolls, 1906-1913; enlistment papers, 1917; descriptive lists, 1913-1916; quarterly returns, 1912-1917; sick reports, 1917; reports of examination, 1917; service records, 1917; financial reports of armory rent, 1906-1907; account allowances and rifle practice commutations, 1906; debit and credit slips, United States service, 1916-1917; statements of state property, 1912-1913; vaccination registers, 1916-1917; personal equipment accounts, 1917; clothing records, 1916; requisitions for bulk clothing, 1916-1917; individual clothing slips, 1916-1917; and general and special orders, 1904-1918. Of these records the following are worth highlighting for their content:

Abstracts of Daily Roll Call and Pay Roll, 1913-1917. Records the name, grade or rank, age, height, residence and occupation of the soldier; the number of drills attended since last inspection; the date of present enlistment; the number of enlistments; and the dates of each full enlistment. Rolls prepared prior to 1916 also have a "casualties since last annual encampment" section on them. Data found includes the name and rank of the soldier being dropped from the roll; the date of present enlistment; the date of discharge, transfer or promotion; and the cause (expiration of enlistment, transferred, died, etc.). While there is space available on the rolls for recording the total amount paid to the unit, this information is not always filled in. The pay per muster, that is, the rate of pay per day; total days of attendance; service allowances; balances due for mess, company dues and the like; and the total amount due each soldier are recorded, however.

Descriptive Lists, 1913-1916. Arranged in alphabetical order by names of soldiers. The forms (twelve pages) contain four information sections. The first page gives personal information and a physical description of the soldier, that is, the presence of any scars or physical defects; his name, rank, residence, age, place of birth, occupation, marital status, height, and color of eyes, hair, and complexion; the date and place of enlistment; the military organization enlisted in; and the name, residence, relationship, and address of a person to notify in case of an emergency. Page two and three have a "military record" section on them which addresses both prior and current service. Questions to be answered include the following: experience as a noncommissioned officer, marksmanship or gunnery, horsemanship; furloughs; battles; wounds or other injuries received in action; medals of honor (actions, with data thereof, for which granted); certificates of merit; physical condition; vaccinated (place, date, and result); thyphoid immunization completed (date); general character; character of service; and convictions by court martial or dates of pay forfeitures. This section is followed by a "statement of accounts" which gives particulars concerning when the soldier was last paid, by whom, and the date. The remainder of the form deals with "clothing accounts," that is, the value of clothing drawn when enlisted; the amounts due the government for ordinances, quartermaster supplies, or other stoppages; dates and money values of gratuitous issues of clothing; and clothing settlements (date of, allowance, money value of clothing drawn, balance due the United States, and balance due soldier). The end of the list has remarks that mention the dates and places of rendezvous, musters, and/or discharge. The forms are dated and certified as to completeness and accuracy by the commanding officer of the company.

Enlistment Papers, 1917. Four page documents that are arranged in alphabetical order by surnames. Page one gives the name of the enlisted man; the date and place of enlistment; the name, rank and military unit of the person by whom enlisted; the organization or arm of service enlisted in; and an enumeration of any prior military service. Page two consists of a "declaration by the applicant" that he is enlisting in the National Guard of Pennsylvania for three years; that he is of legal age, and physically fit to perform the duties of an able-bodied soldier; that he is of good habits and character in all respects and has never been discharged from the military service because of disability or through sentence of either civil or military court; that he is, or that it is his intention to become a U.S. citizen; and that he is not married nor is anyone solely dependent on him. The declaration is dated and signed by both the applicant and a witness. Page three contains an "oath of enlistment" which records the date and place of enlistment (state, and city or military post); the name, age (years and months), and occupation of the recruit; and the date that the oath of allegiance was subscribed and duly sworn to. The oath is signed by the soldier and a recruiting officer. A "certificate of inspection and enlistment" follows. This certificate states that the recruit was minutely examined and that he was found to be sober and fit to enlist in the Guard. The place of inspection (city and state); the date of inspection; the name and rank of the inspecting officer; and a physical description (height, complexion, and color of eyes and hair) of the enlisted person are found on this section of the form. The last page mentions where the soldier resides and the name, relationship, and address of a person to call in case of an emergency. An "endorsement of U.S. mustering officer" section is not completed on any of the documents.

Inspection Rolls, July 13, 1905- April 8, 1913. Dated and subscribed rolls submitted by the captain of the company to the commanding officer. In addition to giving the name of the company, regiment, and brigade, the roll records the headquarters and location of the unit during the inspection. Information provided about each soldier includes his name, rank, height, age, residence, occupation, and date of enlistment; the number of drills attended since the last inspection; and, if appropriate, years of continuous enlistment. The back of the roll contains a recapitulation, indicating the company's troop strength by grades; and the number of soldiers who were uniformed, sick, enlisted, promoted, transferred, discharged, died, and/or deserted.

Muster and Pay Rolls, 1906, 1912. Dated and subscribed rolls submitted by the captain of the company to the commanding officer. Besides recording the total amount paid to the military unit the roll indicates who was present and absent; the number of soldiers in each grade (captain, lieutenants, sergeants, corporals, musicians, cooks, artificers, and privates); the name, rank, and residence of each soldier; the date of enlistment; number of days pay due; pay per day; amount of pay; service allowance; and the total amount due. The names of privates are in alphabetical order. Each soldier's signature appears on the roll.

ROSTER, PHILADELPHIA CITY CAVALRY, 2ND TROOP, 1898-1915 (MG-242). Shows the name and rank of the guardsman, the date and the officer to whom he was attached. In a few instances the postal address of the soldier is also noted.

UNDELIVERED DISCHARGE CERTIFICATES, 1894-1895, 1900, 1903-1917 (RG-19). Includes the following papers:

Discharge Certificates from the National Guard of Pennsylvania, 1894, 1895, 1900, 1903-1916. Most of the certificates are for members of the 1st Infantry Regiment, Company I. Several discharges for individuals serving in the 2nd and 6th Infantry Regiments are also found. Information listed includes the name, rank, birthplace, age (at enlistment), description (height, complexion, color of eyes and hair), and occupation of the guardsman; the company, regiment, brigade, and commanding officer to which he was assigned; the reason for the discharge; the date and place of discharge; and the name of the person who approved the discharge. The certificates are arranged alphabetically according to the discharged person's surname.

Discharge Certificates from the National Guard of the United States and the State of Pennsylvania, 1917. All the discharges are dated August 4 or 5, 1917, and were issued because the individuals were drafted into federal military service. Entries on the certificates record the person's name, age (at enlistment), birthplace, occupation, physical description (height, complexion, eye and hair color), and marital status; the date and place where he enlisted; and the date and place where he was discharged. Additional information such as whether the person received any wounds in service, participated in any battles, or had any knowledge of a vocation is entered too.

UNIT PERSONNEL RECORDS AND ORGANIZATIONAL FILE OF THE PENNSYLVANIA NATIONAL GUARD, Undated (RG-19). Index cards and forms on a tissue type paper (3 X 5 inches) that appear to cover Guard unit history from approximately the late 1920s to the early 1960s. The file is arranged by military units with the initial card listing the name of the unit, where it was stationed, and the dates that federal recognition was granted and or withdrawn. Significant general orders that influenced the status of the unit, for example, its troop strength or organization, are also enumerated. This organizational card is followed by a series of forms issued by the National Guard Bureau, which reflect any changes made in unit assignments. Generally the forms record the name of the person; his rank, organization, and status (promoted, inactive, terminated, died, retired); and the dates of the personnel actions.

RECORDS OF THE PENNSYLVANIA RESERVE MILITIA

ALPHABETICAL LIST OF MEMBERS (RG-19). An undated list that gives the militiaman's name, company, and regiment.

MUSTER ROLLS, 1918-1921 (RG-19). The materials are arranged by military units and thereunder according to the date of the document. The following types of rolls are found:

Abstract of Daily Roll Call and Muster and Pay Roll. For particulars concerning the data found, see similar entry in the National Guard section of this guide.

Muster-in Roll. Entries record the name, rank, physical description (height, complexion, eye and hair color), age, birthplace, occupation, marital status, and residence of the militia member; the military unit, station, and commanding officer to which he was assigned; and service enrollment date. Written remarks such as whether the person was absent because of sickness and so forth also appear.

Muster-out Rolls. The list give the name, rank, and military unit of the reservist; the name of the commander to whom he was assigned; the dates of his enlistment and discharge; and the type of discharge received.

MISCELLANEOUS MILITARY SERVICE RECORDS

LIST OF MEMBERS, PHILADELPHIA CITY CAVALRY, SECOND TROOP, 1910-1914 (MG-237). The list is in chronological order and thereunder by soldier's surname. The name, rank, and postal address of the trooper is found on it.

MILITARY PENSION ACCOUNTS AND RELATED RECORDS, Ca. 1789-1883 (RG-2). The record is comprised of various pension books and lists that are indexed or grouped alphabetically by pensioner's surname. Most of the accounts consist of pensions granted by special legislative acts and usually mention the pensioner's name and county of residence, the date that pension payments were due or made, the amount of money paid, and the act governing the allotment. At times the claimant's approximate date of death is also recorded. Of particular interest to researchers are the following items:

Pension Warrant Book Index, 1866-1880. Entries show the name, rank, and service (military organization attached to) of the War of 1812 veteran; the dates and places of his enlistment and discharge; the certificate number; and the applicant's name, county of residence and, where appropriate, the relationship to the soldier. The name of the soldier's company, regiment or brigade commander is frequently provided, and in some instances the number of persons making up the company or regiment is noted. The names are grouped alphabetically by pensioner's surname.

Census of Pensioners for Revolutionary and Military Service as Returned under the Act for Taking the Sixth Census, 1840. Listings in this printed volume are arranged by county and political subdivision, and ordinarily give the name and age of the pensioner and the name of the head of family with whom he resided on June 1,1840.

MILITIA ABSENTEE RETURNS, PHILADELPHIA CITY, 1777-1791 (RG-4). A record of fines paid by militiamen. Typical information that might be entered includes the name, rank, and regiment of the militia member; the fines extracted; and the name of the officer in charge. The returns are grouped by battalion or company and are thereinafter arranged chronologically.

MILITIA ACCOUNTS, 1793-1809 (RG-4). Contains rolls, receipts, accounts, and returns of absentees and exempts for militiamen from Allegheny, Berks, Bucks, Bedford, Chester, Cumberland, Dauphin, Delaware, Fayette, Franklin, Huntingdon, Lancaster, Luzerne, Mifflin, Montgomery, Northampton, Northumberland, Philadelphia, Washington, Wayne, Westmoreland, and York Counties. In most instances returns simply give the name, rank, and military unit of the soldier; the name of his commanding officer; the date of the returns; and the county of origin of the organization. At times details concerning the militia member's residence (township), date of service, and pay earned and received are also entered on the returns. The record is arranged according to division and thereunder by brigade, regiment, and company.

MILITIA ACCOUNTS, 1809-1864, (RG-2). The accounts are grouped according to military unit and consist basically of documents relating to the paying of fines by militia members or the exonerations from such. In most instances the materials are dated and only give the soldier's name and military unit. In some cases, however, the militiaman's rank, residence (county or township), and officer to whom attached are also recorded.

MILITIA ENROLLMENT BOOKS, PHILADELPHIA CITY, 1867-1868, 1870-1872 (RG-19). The books are arranged by wards and years and thereunder numerically by assigned enrollment numbers. Normally the books show the name, enrollment number, postal address, and occupation of the militia member. During 1867 the ages of the volunteers are sometimes recorded (for wards 2, 5, 9, 11, 12, 16, 20, and 23), and in 1868 remarks about whether the person changed his address or was crippled appear.

MILITIA ENROLLMENT LISTS AND RELATED RECORDS FOR PHILADELPHIA CITY AND COUNTY, 1870-1872 (RG-2). Contains lists that are grouped alphabetically according to militia member's surname. Entries usually give the individual's name, residence, age, and occupation.

MUSTER ROLLS OF THE PENNSYLVANIA RESERVE DEFENSE CORPS AUXILIARY, 1942-1945 (RG-19). The P.R.D.C. Auxiliary was created by executive order of Governor Arthur H. James on

July 14, 1942. Organized as secondary and stationary armed force units under the control of the Pennsylvania Reserve Defense Corps, their mission was to guard vital installations such as water works, electric light plants, telegraph and telephone exchanges, bridges, airports, airfields, railroads, traffic control centers, gas works, defense plants, and governmental agencies within the boundaries of their county. The muster rolls are dated and signed by an accepting officer and record the name of the county, the date of the subscription, and the volunteer's name and address. The rolls are arranged by counties. A typed list of "Appointments" also is found in the file. Data shown includes the name, grade, address of the member; the county; the date that rank was from; and the date that certificate was issued. Remarks in the margins note dates of resignation, promotion, and at times, death. The documents are arranged in chronological order by date certificate was issued.

ROSTER, 15TH U.S. ENGINEER REGIMENT, Ca. 1939-1941 (MG-236). The rosters are arranged alphabetically by soldier's surname and list the name, company, and address of the regiment member.

Access to the Archives' military service records for World War II and beyond is subject to some restrictions because of confidentiality. Requests for information from such records will be honored only if the inquiry comes from the veteran himself, his immediate family, or from official government sources.

OCCUPATIONAL RECORDS
(687 Cubic Feet)

The Division of Archives and Manuscripts has many records that contain information about the occupations of Pennsylvania residents. Spanning the decades and the vocational gamut, these series can provide the researcher with the opportunity of uncovering data either about an ancestor who was an eighteenth-century Indian trader or a relative who was a twentieth-century optometrist. The following records may be of particular interest to genealogists:

ACCIDENT RECORDS, 1916-1930 (in MG-2). A record kept by the Standard Steel Works Company of Burnham (Mifflin County), Pennsylvania. From 1924 to 1930 the listings give the name, postal address, and extent of injury of the employee; the capacity in which he was employed; the cause and date of the injury; the names of any witnesses observing the accident; and the name of the place where the injured party was sent for aid along with the initials of the person who treated him. The entries are in chronological order by accident date.

ADDRESS BOOK OF BRANCH OFFICES ISSUED LICENSES, 1915-1963 (RG-22). An account of undertakers who were issued branch-office licenses to practice in Pennsylvania. The majority of the listings pertain to persons licensed from 1915 to 1936. Entries show the name, address, and license number of the mortician; the certificate number; and the date that it was issued. Information about the changing status of funeral directors, for instance, whether they retired, died, or had their licenses revoked, is periodically indicated as well. The book is arranged alphabetically by surname.

ADMISSION BOOK, 1896-1947 (RG-41). A record of men admitted to the Pennsylvania Nautical School and Pennsylvania Maritime Academy from May 28, 1896, to February 13, 1947. Ordinarily a listing provides the name, age (at entry), birthplace, birth date, and physical description (height, weight, and sometimes chest measurement) of the trainee; the date of entry; and the name and address of his parent or guardian. Written remarks are also entered in the book that specify the date that the individual graduated, deserted, or was dropped from the rolls of the school. The entries are arranged and numbered chronologically according to the date of the student's admission.

ADMISSION OF ATTORNEYS DOCKETS AND PAPERS, 1742-1970 (RG-33). A record of lawyers admitted to practice law before the bar of the Supreme Court of Pennsylvania, Eastern District. Included are the following materials:

Admission Dockets, 1742-1935. From 1742 to 1902 the dockets list the name of the attorney, the date, and usually the name of the motioner. After 1902 the place and date of admittance to practice law is also provided. The names of the lawyers appearing in the dockets are grouped alphabetically.

Admission Papers, 1885-1970. Consists of lists, motions for admissions, and certificates. The lists which cover the period 1742-1809 simply give the name of the attorney and the date that he was admitted to the bar. Motions for admission typically show the attorney's name, county of residence, date of filing, and signature of the sponsor. Prior to 1904 the documents indicate where and for how long the applicant worked as a clerk in a law office and as a lawyer before the courts of common pleas. After 1904, the motions are normally accompanied by certificates of the state Board of Law Examiners attesting to the candidate's good moral character and passing of the bar examination, and urging his or her admission. Additional information found on these certificates includes the date of certification, certificate number, the seal of the state Board of Law Examiners, and the signatures of the board's secretary and chairman. The papers are grouped according to year from 1885 to 1903, and from 1904 to 1970 are arranged by year and thereunder alphabetically by surname. There is a name index for certificates filed between 1903 and 1935.

ADMISSION OF ATTORNEYS PAPERS, 1886-1980 (RG-33). Contains motions, certificates and applications relating to the admittance of individuals to practice law before the Supreme Court of Pennsylvania, Western District. Information usually recorded on the motion includes the name and county residence of the attorney and the dates that the document was issued, mailed, and filed. Prior to 1903 the admission request is signed by vouchers and mentions the experience the applicant had as a law office clerk and as a lawyer practicing before the courts of common pleas. The judicial district where the counselor practiced law is listed from 1893 to 1903, and after 1925, the postal address and telephone number of the barrister is recorded as well. From 1903 to 1965, the motion is normally accompanied by a signed and sealed certificate from the state Board of Law Examiners that recommends the candidate's admission to the bar and which attests that the person is of good moral character; has satisfactorily passed the examination; and has complied with the conditions prescribed by the rules of the court. Beginning in 1971, instead of separate motions document, an application for admission was filed with the certificate. The application lists the name and address of the lawyer followed by a motion for admission and oath of admission. The application form utilized from 1975-1979 consists of a certified personal statement submitted by the applicant, a statement of two sponsors supporting the application and giving their home and business addresses, a motion for admittance made by one of the sponsors, and a subscribed oath of admission by the applicant. The personal statement section records the applicant's name, social security number, place of birth, date of birth, and address (residential and business); lists the names of both parents, including the mother's maiden name; and describes the legal education and work experience of the person. After 1979, the application form does not include a personal statement or sponsors statement. It does give the lawyer's address and telephone number (residential in 1980 and business in 1982), however. Other documentation found in the file include admissions in absentia, 1941-1971. Used by military personnel, the form has an oath section that was signed and administered by a officer at a military camp or base, a certificate of authority, and a certificate of absence, that record the following: name and rank of the enlisted person seeking admittance, the location of his station, and the unit that he was attached to. Although the certificates are numbered, the documents are grouped by years and thereunder arranged in alphabetical order by surname.

ADMISSION OF ATTORNEYS PAPERS, 1895-1971 (RG-38). The record is comprised of these materials that were filed in the Middle District of the Superior Court of Pennsylvania:

Admissions, 1895-1971. The documents are arranged by court term and thereunder alphabetically by lawyer's surname. Normally the dated lists mention the name and county residence of the attorney, and the name of the person making the motion for admittance. The lists include admittances made before the Superior Court at Harrisburg, 1895-1930, 1951-1952; Pittsburgh, 1895-1960; and Philadelphia (some listings for the Scranton District are also found), 1931-1960.

Motion for Admittance, 1896-1971. A typical entry on the dated documents shows the lawyer's name and county of residence, the signature of the person making the motion for admittance, the term and county where the applicant practiced as an attorney before the courts of common pleas, the term and place where the individual served as a law office clerk, and the date when the motion was filed. The documents are arranged chronologically by court term.

AFFIDAVITS OF REGISTERED PHYSICIANS, June 30, 1881-March 25, 1898 (RG-47). A record of individuals who registered as practitioners of medicine and surgery with the prothonotary of Carbon County. The affidavits are signed and subscribed by both the applicant and the prothonotary and show the name, place of nativity, and residence of the physician; the name of the institution which conferred the medical degree; the date that the degree was received; and place or locations of continuous medical practice in Pennsylvania since 1871. Space also is available for recording information about other degrees held by the doctor and for indicating if the person died or had his license removed. The registers were created to comply with the Act of June 8, 1881. Similar data for other counties appears in the REGISTER OF MEDICAL LICENSES and in the MEDICAL REGISTERS. The documents are arranged in alphabetical order by surnames.

APPLICATIONS FOR ADMISSION TO THE BAR OF THE COURT OF
COMMON PLEAS AND CERTIFICATES OF THE ALLEGHENY
COUNTY BAR ASSOCIATION, 1879-1880, 1883-1911, 1932-1980
(RG-47). The records are arranged in numerical order by applica-
tion numbers. Depending on the time period any of the following
types of documents are present:

Student's Certificate of Registration, 1879-1880, 1883-1887. A
signed, sealed, and dated form from the prothonotary of the court
of common pleas that records the name and age of the law student; the name of the preceptor who's law office he was registered
in; and the date of registration. This certificate usually is accompanied by a voucher from the preceptor that the person diligently
studied law for over two years in his law office; and by an oath of
publication of notice that stated that the law student's intent to
apply for admission to the Allegheny County Bar had been published in a newspaper. The documents are numbered.

Certificate of Registration, 1886-1911. Consists of a certified and
dated statement from a Board of Examiners Committee to the prothonotary of the court of common pleas that the applicant underwent examination and was found to be suitably prepared and of
satisfactory moral character to commence the study of law. This
statement is followed by a preceptor's request to have the person
registered as a student in his law office. Besides giving the names
of all the parties concerned, the certificate lists the age and nativity (usually city, county, and state) of the applicant. The certificates
are numbered.

Application for Admission and Certificate of Committee, 1932-1980.
Typically the dated application gives the name, age, place of birth,
and address of the applicant; the location, and name of law office
where registered as a student; the date of registration; and the
names of character witnesses (prior to 1960). A signed certificate
by the chairman and secretary of the Board of Examiners recommending that the applicant be admitted to the bar appears on the
bottom of the application. The applications are numbered according to date filed.

APPLICATIONS FOR CERTIFIED PUBLIC ACCOUNTANT CERTIFI-CATES, 1899-1900 (RG-22). Consists of applications submitted to the state Board of Exam-iners of Public Accountants from May 22, 1899, to April 13, 1900. Data appearing on the applications include the name, date of birth, and place of birth of the applicant; the education received; the number of years in the accounting practice; and the names, occupations, and places of business of persons acting as vouchers for the individual. The applications are arranged numerically by application number.

APPLICATIONS FOR PILOT LICENSES, 1908-1925 (RG-41). A record of persons who applied for pilot licenses at the Port of Philadelphia. The documents, which are arranged chronologically by the dates that the applications were filled out, are signed by the applicant and generally give the person's name, residence, age, and birthplace.

APPLICATIONS FOR TEACHING CERTIFICATES, 1866-1922 (RG-22). Contains application forms for permanent, provisional, tempo-rary, special, and temporary special continuation certificates sub-mitted to the superintendent of public instruction. The type of data listed varies with the forms utilized. Application forms for provisional college certification contain the name, age, address, county residence, and college of the candidate; the college courses that he or she studied; the date that the diploma was issued; and the dates that the application was received and the certificate granted. Application forms for permanent certification, on the other hand, usually only indicate the name, address, semesters of teaching experience, and school district of the applicant; the date that the application was received; and the date that certification was granted. The applications are in alphabetical order by teacher's surname.

APPLICATIONS OF VETERANS FOR PEDDLERS' LICENSES (DAUPHIN COUNTY), 1867-1905 (RG-47). A record created in accordance with the Act of April 8, 1867, permitting disabled sol-diers to peddle by procuring a license without charge. Whether the application consists of handwritten affidavits or printed forms (from 1887), as a norm the documents provide the name, residence, rank, company, and regiment of the veteran; a description of the disability or infirmity; and the date that the license was filed and approved. The affidavits and or certifications are signed by the veteran, the county prothonotary, and an examining physician or surgeon. Also included in the file is a "list of licenses granted under the act" which contains the names of 320 disabled veterans authorized to peddle or hawk goods in Dauphin County.

APPOINTMENTS FILE (CIVIL OFFICERS), 1790-1947 (RG-26). A record of correspondence sent by or in behalf of applicants seeking political appointments. Information found differs with each document. While most of the letters only mention the person's name, residence, and position desired, others may also indicate the applicant's race and familial relationships. From 1790 to 1947 the materials are arranged by gubernatorial administration and thereunder chronologically by county and appointment category. Prior to 1790 the file is arranged alphabetically by surname and is microfilmed. Researchers should consult the *Guide to the Microfilm of the Records of Pennsylvania's Revolutionary Governments, 1755-1790, in the Pennsylvania State Archives*, compiled and edited by Roland M. Baumann (Harrisburg, 1978), in order to ascertain the names of those applicants who applied for positions from 1775 to 1790.

CHECK ROLLS AND WORK RECEIPTS, 1826-1860 (RG-17). Primarily work receipts for either constructing or repairing parts of the Pennsylvania canal system. The check rolls consist of work charts that show the names of each worker, the job or service that they performed (laborer, foreman, engineer, rigger, wood hauler, etc.), the county and canal site where employed, the number of days worked, the rate of pay per day, and the amount earned. In most cases the signature of the worker also appears, as a receipt for payment. (An example of such a check roll appears on the next page.) Work receipts can vary as to both content and form. Handwritten and dated lists often are present that simply give the names of individuals, the services performed, and the amount that they were paid. Printed forms utilized to pay one person for carrying out grubbing and clearing, puddling, and or for excavating services, are found as well. Records for the Beaver, Delaware,

An example of the payroll information shown on a check roll, May 1-July 31, 1849, for the Allegheny Portage Railway. CHECK ROLLS AND WORK RECEIPTS, 1826-1860 in the RECORDS OF THE BOARD OF CANAL COMMISSIONERS (RG-17), PSA.

Eastern, French Creek, Juniata, North Branch, Susquehanna, West Branch, and Western divisions of the Pennsylvania Canal; the Allegheny Portage Railway; the Columbia and Philadelphia Railroad; the Erie Extension Canal; the Gettysburg Railroad Extension; the Harrisburg and Pittsburgh Railroad; and the Wiconisco Canal are included.

COMMISSION BOOK, April 14, 1840- January 31, 1862 (RG-47). Copies of commissions issued by the governor to candidates that were elected to offices such as justices of the peace, notaries public, and alderman in Dauphin County. Besides recording the date of the commission and the office to which appointed, entries normally show the name and residence of the public official along with the length of term. A copy of the oath of office which was sworn and subscribed before the recorder of deeds appears at the bottom of each record. The commissions are arranged in chronological order by the date recorded.

COMMISSION BOOK, ALLEGHENY COUNTY, 1891-1905 (RG-47). Entries are grouped alphabetically by first letter of surname and show the name of the notary public, alderman, or justice of the peace; the office involved and its location; and the commission's beginning and expiration dates. At times, remarks mention the date that the individual resigned or passed away.

CORNWALL ORE BANK COMPANY (CORNWALL MINES) RECORDS, 1802-1935, 1954 (MG-339). The company was organized in 1864 to improve mining operations and increase profits at the furnace and ore bank facilities in Cornwall, Lebanon County. By 1920 most of the ore rights had been sold to the Bethlehem Steel Company. The archives of the company, consisting of minutes, reports, accounting records, general correspondence, payrolls, production statements, letter press books, and legal papers, were placed at the State Archives in 1980 with a twenty-year restriction. The following records are representative of the type information and documents found in the collection:

Legal Papers, 1859-1929. Consists of agreements, deeds, releases, wills, leases, powers of attorney, and accident reports. A number of releases represent settlements negotiated with the widows or parents of workers killed or maimed while in the employ of the company. Usually such releases are signed by the next of kin and describe the person's relationship to the victim; give the place of residence of the family; record the amount of compensation being paid; and absolve the company of any blame or liability. Reports that often accompany the releases attempt to explain in great detail how, when, and why the accident occurred. The wills, deeds and powers of attorney found in the file primarily relate to the owners, the Grubb and Coleman families, and guardians, and heirs of the Cornwall mines and its assets. The accident reports, 1911-1915, can be as formal as the "standard schedule for accident reports" submitted to the Pennsylvania Department of Labor, Division of Accident Reports, to letters, or mere notes describing how the incident happened. With the exception of data relating to witnesses and the names of attending physicians, the "standard schedule" form contains the same information described below under reports relating to state workmen's compensation cases, 1916. One pension application, that of Henry L. Deemer, who worked as a powder magazine man from 1899 to 1923, also ended up in the legal papers. The documents are numbered and a descriptive listing is available for reference purposes.

Letters Received and Sent, 1886-1921. Part of the company's business records, the file contains a folder of materials relating to state workmen's compensation cases for the year 1916. In addition to final and draft copies of reports describing the accidents, listings are present that can be used as indices to the file. The lists show the name of each accident victim, the accident number, the date of the accident, the amount paid to the doctor, and the amount received by the injured party or his next of kin. The reports describe how the accident occurred and give the name, address, sex, age, marital status, nationality, and race of the employee; the company's name and address; the date, time (day of week, hour and minute) and location of the accident; the name and residence of the attending doctor; the occupation and department of the victim when injured; if not his regular job, the individuals normal occupation; time or piece worker; the name of any witnesses; if accident was not fatal, the number of days of work lost; and the amount of compensation paid. Written draft reports often include notes regarding the competence and experience of the worker, whether he could speak English and follow directions, and transcripts about what witnesses saw. Two folders of correspondence with the Aetna Accident And Liability Company, 1916, relate to the same accidents and provide excellent details regarding the backgrounds of the injured parties, even to the point of describing familial relationships back in Europe.

Minute Book, 1864-1911. Chiefly reports, motions, statements, and discussions dealing with administrative matters, finances, and legal issues. Reports presented by the general superintendent reviewing the working operations of the mines, however, provide details about the types of accidents that injured or killed workers; the repercussions of such events on the employees and their families; and the company's policy regarding compensation.

Old Relief Plan Account Book, May 1, 1917- January 1, 1919. Indexed. Records the name of the member; the dates dues were paid and the amounts contributed; and as needed, the dates that the person died or left employment.

Receipt Book, April 11,1823- April 3, 1829. Has some entries relating to monies paid out regarding estate transactions.

Time Book,1828-1835. Has an occasional note about the laborers boarding at Cordorus Forge and the death or burial of workers. Most of the remaining time books from 1864-1935, however, simply record the employee's name and days of work.

COUNTY OFFICERS' ACCOUNTS, 1809-1879 (RG-2). A record of financial returns submitted by various county officers to the state auditor general. Many of the materials relate to the collection of licensing fees from tavern keepers, wine retailers, innkeepers, and dealers of foreign merchandise. The returns are grouped by years and usually only record the name and residence of the dealer, the date that the fee was collected, and the amount of the fee received.

COUNTY OFFICERS' ACCOUNTS, LICENSE RETURNS FOR PHILADELPHIA COUNTY, 1820-1838 (RG-2). A microfilmed record that contains license returns for peddlers and hawkers of tinware, clocks, and foreign merchandise. The returns were submitted to the state auditor general by officers of the Court of Common Pleas, the Court of Quarter Sessions, the Mayor's Court, and the city treasurer of Philadelphia. Besides recording the amounts of fees received, the documents usually mention the name and residence of the dealer, the type of license applied for, and the date that he or she was licensed. The items are arranged according to the date that the statement was received at the Auditor General's Office.

DECEASED OSTEOPATH FILE, Ca. 1909-1954 (RG-22). Consists of the application records submitted to the Pennsylvania Board of Osteopathic Examiners by osteopaths who are now classified as deceased. Data shown on the application include the osteopath's name, date of birth, legal address, educational credentials, and application (license) number. From 1910 onward, a photograph of the individual is also filed. The applications are arranged by application (license) number.

DENTAL REGISTER, 1883-1897. Indexed. A record generated to comply with the supplemental Act of June 30, 1883, providing for the registration of dentists and the Act of April 17, 1876, regulating the practice of dentistry. The register contains copies of diplomas from dental schools that were granted to individuals who wished to practice dentistry in Allegheny County. Information shown includes the dentist's name and date of graduation; the course of study (or department) and degree earned; the name of the college or university granting the degree; the date that the diploma was recorded; and the names of all of the school officials conferring the degree. Entries appear in chronological sequence by date recorded. For identical records see also: DENTAL REGISTER, 1883-1897, for Dauphin County.

DENTAL REGISTER, 1883-1899 (RG-47). Indexed. A record spawned by the supplemental Act of June 30, 1883, providing for the registration of dentists and the Act of April 17, 1876, regulating the practice of dentistry. Entries in the register are in the form of either affidavits made before the prothonotary of Bedford County or transcripts of diplomas filed with the county recorder of deeds. The affidavits give the name, residence, and training of the applicant; the time and places of continuous practice in Pennsylvania; and the dates that the statement was subscribed before the prothonotary and recorded in the office for the recording of deeds. The copied diplomas have the dentist's name and date of graduation; the course of study (or department) and degree earned; the name of the college or university granting the degree; and the date that the candidate was approved and endorsed for registration by the Pennsylvania Board of Dentistry. The names of all of the school officials conferring the degree as well as the secretary of the dental board and the recorder of deeds also appear. Entries in the register are in chronological order by date recorded.

DENTAL REGISTER, January 24, 1899- September 12, 1955 (RG-47). Indexed. A record of individuals who obtained dental licenses from December 20, 1898, to September 2, 1955, and applied for the right to practice in Schuylkill County. Entries normally give the name, place of nativity and residence of the applicant; the degree held (usually Doctor of Dental Surgery); the date that the degree was received and the name of the institution granting it; the date licensed by the Pennsylvania Dental Council; and as required, the dates and places of continuous practice in Pennsylvania. Space also is provided for recording information about other degrees held by the dentist. The register was created to comply with the Act of July 9, 1897, establishing a Dental Council and state Board of Dental Examiners. Other identical records available include DENTAL REGISTER, September 1, 1898- April 26, 1934, for Dauphin County; and June 7, 1899-December 3, 1953, for Franklin County. The dated and signed entries are in chronological order.

DENTAL REGISTER AND INDEX TO SOLDIERS' DISCHARGE BOOKS (ERIE COUNTY), 1883-1896 (RG-47). The dental records were created in accordance with the supplemental Act of June 30, 1883, providing for the registration of dentists and the Act of April 17, 1876, regulating the practice of dentistry in Pennsylvania. The register consists of affidavits that show the name, residence, and training of the applicant; the time and places of continuous practice in Pennsylvania; and the date that the statement was subscribed before a notary, an alderman, or other qualified county official, and recorded in the office for the recorder of deeds. Other records found in the register include copies of medical licenses issued by the Bureau of Professional Licensing; affidavits regarding births, that in the case of Luther R. Kent involves a family record; and affidavits as to marriages. The index to soldier's discharges is grouped in alphabetical order by first letter of surname and gives the name of the soldier and either a page or certificate number.

DENTAL REGISTERS, September, 13, 1883- February 12, 1896, July 15, 1898- September 14, 1956 (not inclusive) (RG-47). Indexed. A record of individuals who appeared before the prothonotary of Bradford County to register as dentists. The first register was created to comply with the Act of April 17, 1876 providing for the regulation of the practice of dentistry. The second register was kept to conform with the stipulations included in the Act of July 9, 1897 which established a Dental Council and state Board of Dental Examiners (to become the state Dental Council and Examining Board per Act of June 7, 1923). Information in the first volume is in the form of affidavits. The dated and signed statement provides the applicant's name and residence along with the number of years that he had continuously practiced dentistry in the Commonwealth. Data in the second register consists of forms with an affidavit at the bottom. Entries give the name, place of nativity, and residence of the applicant; the degree held (usually Doctor of Dental Surgery); the date that the degree was received and the name of the institution granting it; the date licensed by the Pennsylvania Dental Council; and as required, the dates and places of continuous practice in Pennsylvania. Space also is provided for recording information about other degrees held by the dentist. The forms are dated and signed by the applicant and the prothonotary. Entries are in chronological order. Identical records can be found in DENTAL REGISTERS, August 31, 1883- October 22, 1941, for McKean County.

DESCRIPTIVE BOOK OF TROOPERS, 1906-1939 (RG-30). Indexed. A record of persons employed as state troopers by the Commonwealth. Entries list the person's name, identification number, age, birthplace, race, height, color of hair and eyes, and occupation previous to enlistment.

DOCKETS (includes LANCASTER AND CHAMBERSBURG DIS-
TRICT DOCKETS), 1800-1961 (RG-33). Includes a docket for registration of law students, June 22, 1905- September 30, 1936, a
record of law students who registered with the Supreme Court of
Pennsylvania, Middle District. Entries are arranged alphabetically
according to the surname of the student. Data appearing in the
docket include the name, age, postal address, and county residence of the law student; the date of the prothonotary's certificate;
the date of registration; and the name of the law school at which
he or she was enrolled.

GOVERNOR'S ACCOUNTS, 1742-1752, 1759-1763 (RG-21).
Includes data on the following subjects.

License Fees Paid by Indian Traders, 1744-1746. A record of
Indian traders and the dates and amounts of license fees that they
paid. Listings are arranged by the date that the fee was paid.

License Fees Paid by Peddlers, 1743-1752, 1759-1760. Entries are
arranged by the date that the fee was paid and show the name of
the peddler and the amount of the fee paid. Occasionally the place
of business is also noted.

*License Fees Paid by Taverns, July, 1746-1752, November 1759-
December 1761.* The listings are arranged by the date that the fee
was paid, and usually record the name of the proprietor, the location of the tavern, and the amount of the fee paid.

INDEX OF LICENSED PHYSICAL THERAPISTS [LIST OF LICENS-
ES ISSUED TO PRACTITIONERS OF MASSAGE AND ALLIED
BRANCHES], 1915-1980 (RG-26). The names are grouped in
alphabetical order by first letter of surname. Entries list the person's name and address, the college or university attended, the
date of examination (and state if not in Pennsylvania), the date of
issue, and the license number.

INDEX OF LICENSED PRACTITIONERS OF DENTISTRY IN PENN-
SYLVANIA, 1897-1978 (RG-22). Entries are grouped alphabetically
by first letter of surname and provide the following information:
name of dentist, date of license, license number, name of college
attended, the year of attendance, and if relevant, date of death.

INDEX OF LICENSED PRACTITIONERS OF MEDICINE IN PENN-SYLVANIA, 1894-1981 (RG-26). The names in the volume are grouped alphabetically by first letter of surname. Information recorded includes the physician's name; the date and number of his or her medical license; the name of the college where trained; the school of medicine; and as required, the date of the physician's death.

INDIAN TRADER LICENSES, June 20, 1765- December 28, 1771 (RG-21). Entries are arranged chronologically and list the date of the license and the trader's name and residence.

JOURNALS OF EDWARD STOVER, 1864-1866, 1873-1874 (MG-320). While most of information found in the accounts relates to wages paid for work done at the Stoverdale Farms in Dauphin County, some entries also mention the nationality and or race of the worker. Representative jobs performed include sawing wood, planting trees, post setting, moving rocks, ditch digging, and so forth. The entries are somewhat chronological in order but at times data are recorded in a random fashion.

JUSTICES AND JUDGES OF THE COURTS OF PENNSYLVANIA FILE, 1943, 1953, 1961-1984 (RG-26). A record created and filed with the Bureau of Elections, Department of State. While most of the file consists of copies of certifications issued to individuals elected to the positions of Justices of the Supreme Court, Judges of the Superior Court, Judges of the Commonwealth Court, and Judges of the Court of Common Pleas, the following records are found to comply with Article V, Section 16(b) of the Pennsylvania constitution which requires members of the judiciary to retire at age seventy:

Birth Date Certifications. For the most part dated and signed form letters that give the name, date of birth, judicial district, county, and court of each justice or judge holding office at various inter-vals between 1970 and 1978. Occasionally, copies of birth certifi-cates are present.

Birthdays of Judges. Lists that give the name of the court, the judicial district, county, last name, and date of birth of each justice or judge. One listing apparently is from 1970; another represents a 1978 update. This latter list also records the year that the term of the judge expired.

The file is not in any type of discernible order. Subject titles with inclusive dates do appear on the folders, however.

LAW STUDENT REGISTRATION DOCKET, 1905-1971 (RG-33). Indexed. A record of persons registered as law students with the Supreme Court of Pennsylvania, Western District. The dockets are organized according to the date that the registration certificate was filed, and give the name, address, and age of the applicant, the name and address of the student's preceptor; the name of the law school that was to be attended; the registration certificate number and filing date; the application number; and the number and date of the prothonotary's certificate. The date of the registrant's admission to law school is sporadically entered until 1911, and from 1932 onward an applicant number is also assigned.

LEHIGH COAL AND NAVIGATION COMPANY INACTIVE PERSONNEL FILE, Ca. 1913-1965 (MG-311). The file consists of 5 X 8 inch cards that are arranged alphabetically by surname. Entries may show the name, address, date of birth, marital status (number of children where appropriate), nationality, and social security number of the employee; the department, position, and salary of the person; the date of service; and the date and reason for the termination of employment. Particulars (names and addresses of employers and the positions held) about the individual's previous employment are also routinely recorded. Access to the information contained on these cards may be subject to some restrictions.

LEHIGH VALLEY RAILROAD COMPANY RECORDS, 1844-1970 (MG-274). A major freight and passenger carrier in northeastern Pennsylvania, parts of New York and New Jersey, the following corporate records contain information about employees and or residents living near the company's rail lines:

Annual Reports of the Board of Managers, 1855-1864, and Board of Directors, 1865-1969. Arranged in chronological order by fiscal years. Published reports to the stockholders that usually provide information regarding the financial status of the railroad but from time to time also contain biographical data relating to the retirement or passing away of significant company officials.

Employee Payrolls of the Maintenance Equipment Department, Superintendent of Motive Power, 1918-1951. The documents are semi-processed and for the most part arranged in chronological order. Two types of forms covering the period 1920-1951, shed light about the occupations and pay rates of employees.

Application for Changes of Pay or Force. Shows the names, occupations, work location, and social security numbers of workers; the current and proposed rates of pay; and the reasons for requesting a change (position abolished, promotion, transfer, etc.). Signatures and/or the names and titles of company officials recommending and approving the personnel actions are included. Approximately two cubic feet of applications for both the maintenance of equipment department as well as other employees working for the superintendent of motive power, 1945-49, also have been preserved as a separate series.

Department Payrolls. Give the names, job titles, work locations, and monthly salaries of employees; the time periods worked; the amounts earned; and deductions from pay (insurance, railroad retirement, federal income tax, war bonds). Administrative data concerning where checks should be sent (place and company official) appears in a remarks column.

Employment Files of the Superintendant of Motive Power, 1937-1970. Apparently a sampling of personnel records primarily dealing with employees who left company service from 1940 to 1960 and who worked for the maintenance of equipment department at the Sayre, Pa., system shops. The files are arranged alphabetically by name of employee. While the amount of information varies with each case file, normally these documents should be present:

Application for Employment. The forms are signed and dated by the employing officer and contain the following categories of information: date and place where the application was submitted; full name, age, marital status, date and place of birth, nationality or race, citizenship status, and physical description (weight, height, color of eyes and hair), address, and social security number of the applicant; status of applicant's eyesight and hearing; name and address of spouse; names and ages of children; names, residence, and nationalities of parents and or nearest living relative; names, ages, and relationship of any dependents; person to be notified in case of serious illness or injury (name, relationship and complete address); education, that is, names, locations (city and state) and years of attendance in grade school, high school, college, or business school; subjects studied in business and or night school, relatives employed in the service of the company (names, occupations, work locations, and relationship to the applicant); and employment record (names and addresses of previous employers, occupations, dates of entering and leaving service, reasons for leaving, and names of supervisors). Diverse questions such as whether the potential employee was ever injured, used intoxicating liquors, or was involved in litigation with any railroad company also appear on the four-page application. The documents are signed by the applicant and two witnesses and conclude with a section stating when and where the person started work (date and time), the job title, and hourly pay rate.

Employment Record. Index cards that provide summary data about the work history of an employee. The cards show the name, place of birth, date of birth, marital status, and social security number of the worker; the titles, places (both geographic and the division or railroad), and date spans (month, day, and year) of positions held in the company; and as needed, a discipline record. A remarks column is utilized to indicate any breaks in service, for example, to note that the person was furloughed, transferred, displaced, or that the position was abolished. Later editions of the cards (post 1940s) also record the employee's residential address and the hourly pay rate received for each job performed.

Notice of Suspension, Dismissal, Resignation, Retirement, or Death. Data recorded includes the name and occupation of the worker; the location of the work site (city and state); the date of entering service; the type of personnel action being reported; the effective date; and the reason for the suspension, resignation, or dismissal. The notice is signed or initialed by a company officer. In some cases a memo or letter of resignation is utilized in lieu of this form.

Physical Examination for Employment Form. Completed and signed by physicians employed by the surgical department, the examination reports show the names, age, address, height, weight, color (race), marital status, and nationality of the candidates; provide answers to questions about whether they had ever been injured, had a surgical operation, had been declined by a life insurance company, had any physical defects (congenital or acquired), had a hernia, or had fits, convulsion or epilepsy; and describe features of the prospective employees using categories such as general appearance (deformities, skin eruptions, mentality, reflexes), head and neck (shape, scars on face, goiters, condition of teeth, color of hair, etc.), eyes and hearing (color perception, iris reflexes, color of eyes, condition of corneas, and results of vision, reading and hearing tests), trunk (any deformities, chest expansion, status of heart and lungs), arms and legs (any loss of members or functions, varicose ulcers, condition of joints, muscles and veins), and lower torso (venereal disease, etc.). The bottom of the examination forms contain the physicians' evaluation of whether the applicants are suitable for the positions applied for (first class, average, defective, or rejected); give the names of the jobs and divisions where employment was sought; and have brief statements signed by the candidates that they agree with the findings.

Other optional forms that may be found include:

Employee's Selective Service Questionnaire. A survey form used by the railroad to prepare an inventory of essential man power and to justify employee deferments during World War II. Information requested included the name, occupation, gender, race (white, colored, other), marital status (single, married, divorced, separated, widower), and social security number of the employee; the department and division employed in; the location of the job site (city and state); month and year employed by the railroad; month and year entering the present occupation; if married, the date of marriage; number of dependent children under eighteen years old and ages of each; date of birth of youngest dependent child; current selective service classification and date that it expires; selective service order number and local board number and location (county, city and state).

Consent to Employment of Minor. The dated and certified (sealed) releases are signed by the parents or guardians of minors and two witnesses. Each form usually records the name and birth date of the minor, the residence of the parents or guardians, the position hired for, the start date, and the name of the work site.

Report of Apprentices Starting, Discontinuing, or Completing Apprenticeships. A typical report is dated and gives the name, address, class, and craft of the apprentice; the shop submitting the form; the type of personnel action taking place (started or completed apprenticeship, resigned, dismissed, disposed, transferred, furloughed, etc.); the effective date for the change; and the name and title of the officer in charge.

Minute Books of the Board of Pensions, 1944-1963. A record of supplemental pensions granted to workers from June 1,1944 to August 16, 1962 (276 applications). Entries routinely give the name, age (years and at times also months), job title, and years of service of the employee; the date that the pension was to become effective and the amount to be paid monthly; and the application number. Many of the citations also mention where the person worked. The minutes are arranged in chronological order by dates of board meetings and thereunder by application number. The first volume contains a list of pension applicants from 1944 to 1954 along with their ages and titles at retirement, the effective dates of the annuities, the application numbers (1-94), monthly salaries at retirement, and the amounts of the pension and railroad retirement annuity. As relevant, the dates that pensioners died were added to the record.

Minutes of the Board of Directors 1850-1962. Although the minutes chiefly relate to corporate decisions and reports regarding earnings, expenditures and administrative matters, the volumes from

1855 to 1892 contain a surprising amount of data submitted by the superintendent of engineering relating to railroad accidents. Typical information found in these reports includes the date,location, and cause of the accident; the name, occupation, and/or relationship of the victim to the railroad (passenger, child playing near the track, etc.); the extent of injuries sustained; and where appropriate, the date that the person died. Occasionally, the race, age, and nationality of the injured person is noted along with the amount of compensation granted. The minutes, as might be expected, also record eulogies or memorials for prominent company officers who passed away or retired. The volumes are in chronological order by dates of board meetings. There is no discrete index for identifying accident victims.

Relief Fund Books, 1884-1893. Financial accounts created to record contributions and expenditures involving workers enrolled in the the relief fund established by the railroad. The first section of each volume contains columns for listing the contributor's name, occupation, place of employment, relief fund number, and amount collected through payroll deductions. While the occupation (fireman, conductor, engineer, etc.) and place of employment (Wyoming Division, Lehigh Division, H.W. Co., etc.) columns are often blank, a remarks column was routinely used for describing injuries sustained by members and the dates that they were injured, killed, or died. Data appearing in the second part of the books includes the name of the person to whom a relief payment was made, the relief fund number, the amount paid, the date of payment, and the names of the individuals who signed the voucher. The books are organized by the dates (month and year) that calls for contributions were made. The relief fund number was assigned in the order that contributions were collected. The expenditure section is arranged in chronological order by date of payment.

Rent Rolls of the Real Estate Department, 1894-1909. Grouped by railroad lines or subsidiary companies and thereunder numerically by street or house numbers. Entries in the volumes provide the names of the tenants; the house or building numbers; the annual rent rates; the dates rents were to commence; the amounts of rent paid or owed; and a description of the properties (number of acres) being rented. Occasionally, a remarks column is used to note that the tenant was a widow and no rent was to be charged.

LIQUOR LICENSE DOCKET, 1895-1924 (RG-47). A record of individuals from Dauphin County who applied for licenses to sell liquor as distillers, brewers, bottlers, wholesalers, tavern owners, or retailers. The dockets are organized by geographic areas (city, ward, township, etc.) and thereunder by number on license list. Typically entries list the name and occupation of the applicant, the number of the applicant on the license list, the attorney's name, and the decree (approved or refused).

LIST OF APPLICATIONS FOR RETAIL, WHOLESALE, BOTTLING AND BREWING LICENSES, 1921-1932 (RG-47). A record of residents from Schuylkill County who applied for licenses to sell liquor. Entries in the volumes are grouped by geographic areas (cities, towns, wards, etc.) and show the name and residence of the applicant; the type of business and its location; the date of filing; the name of the petitioner's lawyer; whether the business (stand) was a new or old one; a disposition code ("SG" for substitute application granted; "CG" for continuance of application granted); and the license's date of issue. At times, notations are present that indicate the date that the application was withdrawn or that someone else was applying for the license.

LIST OF ATTORNEYS AND LAW STUDENTS, 1788-1981 (RG-47). Indexed. A record of persons allowed to enter the practice of law in Allegheny County. The books list the name, residence, and age of the candidate (after June 17, 1933, date of birth); the date of the certificate (blank during the early 1800s); the date registered (up until 1933); the date admitted to practice; and the name of the sponsoring preceptor. A remarks column is used sometimes to also record the date of death of the attorney. After 1971, the date of registration, date of certification, and preceptor's name do not appear. Entries in the volumes are arranged in chronological order by date of admittance and thereunder numbered.

LIST OF LICENSES ISSUED TO CHIROPODISTS, 1914-1956 (RG-22). A record of chiropodists issued licenses by the state Board of Chiropody Examiners between May 12, 1914, and March 15, 1956. Entries give the name, address, and license number of the practitioner and the date that the license was issued. Information such as whether the individual died or had a name change is sometimes noted too. The names on the list are grouped alphabetically.

LIST OF LICENSES ISSUED TO DRUGLESS THERAPISTS, 1914-1951 (RG-22). Entries are grouped alphabetically by first letter of surname and record the name, address (post office), and county of residence of the therapist and the date that the license was issued. Written remarks are present well into the 1960s that also give the date that the person died or note that the license was canceled.

MARY SACHS INC. EMPLOYEES' PENSION PLAN LISTS, 1961 (MG-297). The lists are arranged alphabetically by surname and record the name, age, sex, and date of birth of the employee; the year or projected date of retirement; the value of the person's pension and funeral plans (as of 1961); and when apropos, the amount of money paid out for funeral expenses.

MEDICAL DIPLOMAS, 1881-1897 (RG-47). The Act of June 8, 1881, which provided for the registration of practitioners of medicine and surgery with the county prothonotary, allowed applicants to either submit affidavits depicting their medical experience or exhibit their medical diplomas for recording. These records for Carbon County are representative of the latter option. The transcribed diplomas have the physician's name and date of graduation; the course of study (or department) and degree earned; the name of the college or university conferring the degree; and the signatures of relevant college faculty and administrators. In cases where the applicant was an immigrant, a statement describing his training, date of arrival, and even date of birth may also appear. The diplomas are arranged in alphabetical order by surnames. See also: AFFIDAVITS OF REGISTERED PHYSICIANS, 1881-1898.

MEDICAL REGISTERS, June 20, 1881- September 7, 1915 (RG-47). Indexed. A record of Dauphin County practitioners of medicine and surgery. A typical listing shows the name, signature, place of birth, date of birth (until March 12, 1883), and residence of the physician; the date that he received his medical degree; the name of the institution from which he graduated; and the date that he registered. Particulars concerning the person's medical experience are sometimes provided as well.

MEDICAL REGISTERS, June 27, 1881-September 21, 1934 (RG-47). Indexed. A record of individuals who registered as physicians with the prothonotary of Lehigh County. There are two volumes, the first of which was created to comply with the June 8, 1881 act passed to provide for the registration of all practitioners of medicine and surgery. The second book was kept to be in compliance with the May 18, 1893 act that established a Medical Council and a state Board of Medical Examiners. Entries in the registers give the name, place of nativity, and residence of the applicant; the medical degrees received; the dates and names of the institution that granted the degrees; and the places of continuous practice in Pennsylvania since 1871. Additional data in the second register include the date that the doctor was licensed by the Pennsylvania state Medical Council. At the bottom of each page of this register there is a dated affidavit which is signed by the physician and prothonotary. Space is also provided for indicating whether the person had moved or died. Identical returns appear in the MEDICAL REGISTER, July 18, 1881- October 11, 1894, for Bedford County; PHYSICIAN'S REGISTERS, July 19, 1881- June 10, 1939, for Bradford County; MEDICAL REGISTERS, July 16, 1881- November 10, 1920, for McKean County; and MEDICAL REGISTER, July 13, 1881- July 22, 1946, for Huntingdon County. The records are in chronological order.

MIDWIFE REGISTER, 1921-1924 (RG-47). Indexed. A record of women from Dauphin County who in compliance with the Act of June 5, 1913, registered their certificates to practice as midwives with the prothonotary of the court of common pleas. The affidavits in the register are signed by the midwives and show their names and residences; the dates that their certificates were issued by the Bureau of Medical Education and Licensure; and the place in Harrisburg where recorded. The dated and subscribed forms are signed by the prothonotary. Entries are arranged in chronological order.

MINE OFFICIAL'S CERTIFICATE RECORDS, BITUMINOUS REGION, 1903-1963 (RG-45). Indexed. Contains record books for the following mine officials:

Assistant Mine Foreman, 1911-1923. A record created to comply with registration, training, and examination standards specified in the Act of June 9, 1911. Data shown includes the name, place of birth, and age of the applicant; a description of the length and nature of his service (experience); the date and number of the certificate; and the name of the chief, Department of Mines. Entries are in numerical order by certificate number. The first volume dated 1911 and captioned "certificate of service" is in chronological order.

Assistant Mine Foreman, First Grade, 1938-1963. Information provided includes the mine district number; the name, residence, place of birth, and age of the applicant; the length and nature of the person's service; the date and number of the certificate; and the report number and date. The books are in numerical order by certificate number.

Assistant Mine Foreman, Second Grade, 1923-1963. Contains the same data found for mine foreman, first grade.

Fire Boss Mine Examiner, 1912-1961. The first nine books which cover the time period 1912 to 1923 have the same information listed for assistant mine foreman. The last two volumes, 1923-1963, contain data identical to that recorded under assistant mine foreman, first grade.

Mine Electrician, 1939-1961. Information is the same as for assistant mine foreman, first grade.

Mine Foreman, First Grade and Second Grade, 1903-1963. For the books created from 1903 to 1923, data is identical to that for assistant mine foreman. Afterwards, the information is the same reported for assistant mine foreman, first grade.

MINUTES OF THE PENSION BOARD OF THE DELAWARE, LACKAWANNA, AND WESTERN RAILWAY COMPANY, 1941-1961 (MG-300). A record of pensions funded from November 1,1941 to March 1,1961. Information shown includes the dates that the pension payments were approved and became effective; the gross monthly pension and the amounts payable by the retirement board and the company (until August, 1956, and thereafter funded and unfunded amounts); and the name, job title, date of birth, and total period of service (years and months) of each pensioner. The minutes are arranged chronologically by dates of meetings.

MUSTER AND PAYROLLS OF THE PENNSYLVANIA STATE POLICE, 1906-1939 (RG-30). The rolls are in chronological order and provide the date of the muster and roll; the name of the troop, station, and its captain; the name, rank, and enlistment date of each state police officer; and the total pay due after fines and deductions. The rolls are signed by each member of the troop and the reverse side contains casualty data, that is, the names of any individuals who left service, the dates of discharge, and the reason for separation (expiration of enlistment, transferred, injured, failure to pass required grades, etc.).

NEW CUMBERLAND FIRE DEPARTMENT RECORDS, 1898-1944 (in MG-262). Contains microfilmed copies of the foreman's roll book, 1909-1920, and roll book, 1927-1944, for Citizen's Hose Company No.1. Although the rolls as a norm just list the names of the firemen and the dates that they were in attendance, both volumes also record the deaths of members, at times, including the exact dates. The books are in chronological order.

NOMINATIONS BOOKS, 1892-1971 (RG-26). A listing of persons who filed petitions of nomination for state office. Entries are arranged by the date that the nomination was filed, and after 1919 also according to the office sought. Pertinent information found includes the candidate's name, residence, occupation, and party affiliation; the office for which nominated; and the date of filing for nomination. After 1908 the number of votes received by the candidate is recorded.

OPTOMETRY REGISTER, May 22, 1918- May 17, 1979 (RG-47). Indexed. A record of optometrists from Blair County, who in compliance with the Act of March 30, 1917, appeared before the prothonotary to exhibit their certificates and register for practice. Entries have the name, signature, and residence of the registrant; the date that the person was certified by the Board of Optometrical Education; and the volume and page number of the Optometry Register in Harrisburg where the certificate was recorded. The dated and subscribed documents are in chronological order. Other identical registers available include REGISTER OF OPTOMETRISTS [RECORD OF REGISTRATION OF LICENSE TO PRACTICE OPTOMETRY], July 29, 1918- September 21, 1967, for Dauphin County; and OPTOMETRY REGISTER, May 25, 1918- September 5, 1967, for Bradford County; June 19, 1918- March 23, 1978, for Franklin County; June 21, 1918- April 22, 1975, for Lehigh County; July 24, 1918- January 13, 1954, for McKean County; and July 5, 1918- September 14, 1961 for Schuylkill County.

OSTEOPATHIC REGISTER, 1909-1926 (RG-47). Indexed. A record of individuals from Dauphin County who in accordance with the Act of March 19, 1909, entitled "An Act to regulate the practice of Osteopathy in the State of Pennsylvania" registered with the pro-thonotary of the court of common pleas as osteopaths. The forms in the the register show the name, place of nativity, and residence of the applicant; the date that the osteopathic degree was received; the institution that granted it; and the date licensed by the Board of Osteopathic Examiners. An affidavit, dated and signed by the prothonotary and applicant, is at the bottom of each form. Entries are in chronological order.

OSTEOPATHIC REGISTER, 1909-1910, 1923 (RG-47). Indexed. A record of osteopaths who registered with the prothonotary of Franklin County and who practiced osteopathy within the Common-wealth for two consecutive years prior to the 1909. The entries in the register are signed by the osteopaths and show their names and residences; the dates that their diplomas were received; and the names of the institutions that granted them. The dated and subscribed forms are signed by the prothonotary. The register was created to comply with the Act of March 19, 1909, requiring all practitioners to be licensed by the Board of Osteopathic Examiners. Identical information appears in the OSTEOPATHIC REGISTER, 1918-1967, for Bradford County; and 1909-1926, 1960, for McKean County. Entries are in chronological order.

PENNSYLVANIA RAILROAD COMPANY RECORDS, 1847-1968 (MG-286). The Pennsylvania Railroad Company was incorporated on April 13, 1846, and by the turn of the century was both the "standard railroad of the world" and the largest single employer of men and women in the United States. Its surviving corporate archives, part of the PENN CENTRAL RAILROAD COLLECTION, 1816-1981 (MG-286), therefore, have numerous records relating to business, transportation, and labor history. While most of the more than 5,000 cubic feet of records comprising the collection do not focus on individual employees the following files are still noteworthy for their content:

Board Files, 1847-1960. Consists of documents presented at meetings of the company's board of directors. A prime source of relatively in depth coverage of major issues and challenges handled by the railroad from its inception, the files are one of the few surviving caches where nineteenth century correspondence of the company can be found. Most of the reports, letters, maps, contracts, and financial statements placed on file relate to improvements of property, construction of rail lines, abandonments, land acquisition, public relations, customer issues, labor policies, freight rates, stock investments, and corporate mergers and takeovers. Numerous files, particularly those located in the "BFA Series," however, also deal with personnel matters. Examples of such materials include, resignations, appointments, and departmental reorganizations. Documents such as these with accompanying recommendations, reports, and enclosures often describe in detail the person's background, work history, and physical and intellectual capabilities. Departmental rosters with pay rates, job titles, and data regarding promotions or transfers also are present. The board files are arranged in numerical order by file number. The files are referenced by using the INDEX TO THE MINUTE BOOKS OF THE BOARD OF DIRECTORS, 1847-1956. Besides recording minute book page numbers these index books list relevant board file numbers.

Board Memoranda, 1951-1961. Fact sheets prepared for the board of directors summarizing issues to be discussed at the meetings. Of particular note, are remarks concerning the death and retirement of employees and salary questions. The documents are in chronological order by month and thereunder in reverse order from last to first day in each month.

Board of Director's Roll Books, 1918-1967. The books consist of monthly tables which show whether each director was present or absent from board and committee meetings. Where relevant, notes appear indicating the death or replacement of a member. Committees whose meetings are documented include the committee on incidental business, the finance committee, the real estate committee, and the road committee. Loose sheets containing information about the tenure of select directors are found in the 1947-1967 roll book. The volumes are in chronological order by date of meeting.

Death and Retirement Memorials for Deceased and Retired Board Members, 1901-1958. Printed memorial statements commemorating the death or retirement of board members of the Pennsylvania Railroad Company and its diverse subsidiaries. Each memorial is certified to be an exact copy of the official announcement or eulogy appearing in the company minutes. Besides giving the name of the person, the memorial normally mentions how long the board member worked for the company and in what capacity; the date when he died or retired and how the company benefited from his service; and the date of the meeting at which the tribute was read and adopted. A brief biographical sketch then follows in which the person's date and place of birth, educational training, and work history are emphasized. The booklets are arranged in alphabetical order. There are no memorials for surnames starting with the letters A through I.

General Correspondence Files, 1860-1968. A historical records file maintained by the secretary's office. Subjects covered include everything from a photograph of the Lincoln funeral train, 1865, to files documenting what directors were offered, and accepted, chairs from the Broad Street Station's old board room, 1930. Of particular interest to family historians are files containing detailed biographical information on directors of the Pennsylvania Railroad Company, 1918-1948; historical data regarding the board of directors, 1924-1947; a list of company officers, 1847-1938; and a census of subsidiary company stockholders, 1951-1961.

Index Card File of Officers, 1920-1968. The cards (4 X 6 inch) are in alphabetical order by employees and show the company or companies that they worked for; their official position titles; and if appropriate, the date that they retired or died. Space is available to indicate if the officers were board members of any companies and in some instances the dates of appointments are noted.

Library Reference Materials, ca. 1834-1963. A collection of published monographs, limited editions, and unique studies that cover a variety of topics concerning general railroading topics and specific activities and accomplishments of the Pennsylvania Railroad Company. The library was established with the purpose of being a readily available resource to assist staff in the decision making process. While most of the materials are of a technical or historical nature the following three sets of directories can be used to find employees of the company from the level of the president down to that of chief clerks:

Lists of Officers, Chief Clerks and Heads of Sub-Departments of the Pennsylvania Railroad Company and Affiliated Lines, 1883-1912. Six published volumes that give the names of the employees, their positions and titles with the railroad; and their headquarters.

List of Officers, Chief Clerks, etc., of the Pennsylvania Lines West of Pittsburgh, 1896-1911. Two published volumes that provide the employees' names and positions for this segment of the P.R.R. system.

Directors and Officers, 1846-1896. Printed charts of varying sizes that were placed into a fiftieth anniversary book. The charts show the names of all officers of an executive office or department with their terms of service.

The library materials arc marked and organized in a Dewey decimal filing scheme.

Lists of Company Officials, ca.1896-1899. Historical compilations first prepared for the company's fiftieth anniversary that list the names of officers of the Pennsylvania Railroad Company and some of the rail lines it absorbed. Included in these tables are all offices from the president down to the superintendent level. Entries for each position show the names of all individuals holding that office from 1847 to approximately 1897; the specific dates that the office was held; and as needed, general dates for cases when different offices were created and abolished. Specific offices documented include the following: president, vice president, secretary, and treasurer for the Pennsylvania Railroad Company; superintendents for the P.R.R. and its New Jersey Division; and for the P.R.R. only, comptroller, auditors, engineers, directors, general and assistant passenger and freight agents, division freight agents, general traffic managers, and officers of the motive power department and the maintenance of way.

Minute Book of the Salary Committee, July 6, 1874- April 13, 1881. Indexed. The salary committee, which evolved from the committee on organization in charge of salaries, was responsible for the review of and implementation of any changes in the salaries of company officers. In addition to routine organizational data the minutes provide information regarding individuals whose salaries underwent review, including their salaries and position titles.

Minute Books of the Board of Directors, March 30, 1847- January 25, 1956. Indexed. Although the minutes primarily focus on corporate decisions and reports regarding earnings, expenditures, government regulations, and administrative matters, the volumes covering the period 1857 to 1887 contain narrative accounts of railroad workers, passengers, and neighboring bystanders who were killed or injured on company property. Typical information appearing includes the date and location of the accident or wreck; the name, occupation and or relationship of the victim to the railroad (passenger, widow of employee, etc.); and the extent of injuries sustained. Occasionally, the age and or date of death of the injured person is noted along with the gratuities granted. With the establishment of the voluntary relief department in 1886, a sick and death benefit plan to cover employees, entries in the minutes regarding injuries and compensation declined. From 1888 to 1891, however, several citations relating to special sick benefit requests still appear. Eulogies or memorials for significant company officers who passed away or retired are present as well. The volumes are in chronological order by dates of board meetings. There is no discrete index for identifying accident victims or retirees.

Minute Books of the Road Committee, April 22, 1847- September 15, 1948. Indexed. As might be expected, topics considered for discussion include road and equipment expenditures, abandoned property, agreements regarding crossings, property sales and leasing, and matters relating to maintenance of tracks. Because the board of directors referred cases involving injuries and deaths on the road to this committee from approximately 1867 to 1887, and special sick benefit requests from 1888-1891, this type of information appears as well. Agenda items dealing with the death or maiming of workers may range from a simple mention of the victims' names and the compensations granted either to them or their next of kin to detailed remarks about how, when, and where the accident occurred; and what the jobs of the workers were. The minutes are arranged in chronological order by date of meeting. Entries in the index that relate to gratuities generally list the names of the individuals followed by the phrase "- as to the case of."

Motive Power Personnel Records, ca. 1870-1920. Indexed. A record that includes individuals hired by the motive power department from 1864 to 1903. Entries give the name, date of birth, and place of birth for each worker; the place educated at; the date of graduation; the date of entering company service; titles of positions held and the dates of service; and the name of the person by whom recommended. A remarks section is used for recording more detailed information about projects or special assignments carried out by the employee; transfers; and even circumstances surrounding the person's death. See also: *Record of Certain Motive Power Employees*, undated, and *Record of Employees, 1899-1912.*

Pamphlet File, 1835-1946. A historical reference file that was part of the holdings of the Pennsylvania Railroad's general office library. While published pamphlets do appear in the file, press releases, awards, speeches, time schedules, passenger car menus, employee leaflets, news clippings, organizational charts, and diverse circulars are also present. Genealogical research notes relating to the twelve presidents of the company (1847-1949) and photographs of their board room portrait paintings are found as well. The file is organized in alphabetical order by titles, subjects, and names.

Payroll Sheets, 1947-1955. Bimonthly payroll sheets for employees of the treasury department of the company. The sheets have the name, position, and social security number of the worker; date of payment; gross wages; deductions; and net disbursement. The records are in chronological order. For earlier and more encompassing information regarding this department see also: *Record of Employees, ca. 1855-1940.*

Presidential Correspondence, 1899-1954, of Alexander J. Cassatt, James McCrea, Samuel Rea, William W. Atterbury, Martin W. Clement, Walter S. Franklin. Indexed. Chiefly correspondence, reports, photographs, testimony, transcripts, accounts, and news clippings relating to administrative, financial, technological, and social issues facing the company as it expanded both in size and power. The same files that record the development of major projects or topics such as the building of the New York tunnels, electrification of the northeastern corridor, and rail-air service, however, contain detailed press releases and eulogies relating to significant company officials who retired or died; letters and resumes from diverse persons seeking to make a living as prospective railroaders; farewell photographs and notes from retiring ticket agents, engineers, and executives; press releases honoring "Fifty Years of Service Button" holders; requests for assistance from disabled or sickly workers; and reports from general managers on passengers, employees, and bystanders injured or killed in train wrecks. The documents are arranged in numerical order by file numbers or a Dewey decimal code. There are name indices (5 X 8 inch cards) to the 1899-1949 correspondence. Unfortunately, the A.J. Cassatt papers, 1899-1906, an excellent source for genealogical data, have an index filled with gaps. If used creatively, Cassatt's indexed *Letter Press Books* for 1899-1906, can be utilized to determine if a relative corresponded with the company and whether a labor intensive search would be worthwhile. The index cards for the M.W. Clement papers, 1935-1949, are also not very reliable for accessing family history information.

Records of Certain Motive Power Employees (J.T. Wallis - personal), undated, indexed. The record book covers individuals who entered into service with the motive power department from as early as

1862 to at least 1913. Entries list the name, date of birth, and occupation of each worker; where educated; the date of entering service; titles of positions held; dates of appointments; months in the position; salary rates; and if relevant, dates of retirement, furlough, or death. As needed, space is available for recording the date that the employee was appointed as a special or regular apprentice; the title of the course taken; and the date that it was completed. Similar information appears for employees hired between 1862 and 1920 in *Personnel Information Book*, undated. This later volume consists of forms (M.P. 149) arranged in alphabetical order by surnames.

Record of Disablements: New York to Washington Electric Project, 1934-1936. Notices (form RD5) filed with the supevisor of motive power to notify that official and the Pennsylvania Railroad voluntary relief department of work time lost because of sickness or accidents to employees. Entries on the form generally show the name, occupation, and residence of the worker; the division and department attached to; the date that the employee reported off from work and the date of return, if back; whether the time lost was because of accident or sickness (injury also appears); the place where the notice was sent from (city and state); and the date that the notice was sent. The notice also indicates the name and title of the person reporting the disablement and the surname of the medical examiner who is to receive notification.

Record of Employees, Ca. 1855-1940. A running record of individuals employed by the treasury department of the company. Entries in the two volumes and loose papers include many of the same workers in that they are successive accounts, names being added or deleted only as new applicants were hired and old employees died or retired. The records show the names, addresses, and birth dates of the employees; the dates and departments where they first entered service with the railroad; the dates of and positions held; a history of compensations; bonding data; and the investments made to the voluntary relief department. The bound volumes are arranged randomly by employees surnames. The loose papers are in alphabetical order by surnames. For related records see also: *Payroll Sheets, 1947 1955.*

Record of Employees, October 9, 1899- September 24, 1912.
Indexed. A record of individuals hired by the motive power department from as early as 1880. Entries in the volume provide the
name, date of birth, and place of birth for each employee; the
name of the school where educated; the date of graduation; the
date of entering company service; titles of positions held and the
dates of service; and the name of the person by whom recommended. A remarks section is used for recording data regarding transfers, employment with other companies, and information about
the person's father, for example, his name and occupation. The
index has notes next to some of the workers' names indicating the
dates that they resigned. For other data see: *Personnel Records
Book, ca. 1870-1920,* and *Record of Certain Motive Power
Employees,* undated.

Record of Inscriptions on Board Room Chair Plates, ca. 1846-1963.
Indexed. Each chair in the board room of the Pennsylvania
Railroad Company had a brass plate affixed to it which listed the
name of all previous occupants. A booklet was prepared for each
chair that contains the biographies of all the occupants prior to
1964. Each booklet bears the name of the occupant as of 1964
. and provides the name, date of birth, date of death, tenure, and
position held by each past Board member.

Time Reports, 1938-1946. Payroll time sheets of employees of the
test department and chemical laboratory located at Altoona, Pa.
Each bi-monthly report is signed by the supervisor and normally
includes the name, occupation, and department of the worker; the
dates and locations of work performed; hours or days employed;
the description of the job; and the distribution code. The records
are arranged in chronological order by month and year.

Voluntary Relief Department Enrollment Cards, 1881-1968. The
Pennsylvania Railroad Company's voluntary relief department was
established on February 1, 1886. An insurance plan providing sick
and death benefits to the worker or his family, the VRD was funded by the company and voluntary contributions from the employees. The cards are arranged in five file units and thereunder in
alphabetical order by surname of person. These titles were written

on the original card cabinet drawers: 1) deceased and left service
file prior to 1938, 2) deceased and left service file prior to 1950, 3)
left service file, 4) left service since 1959 file, and 5) relief members
to The Norfolk and Western Railroad Company — 10/16/1964.
Their subdivison by the company was apparently based upon
employees' dates and circumstances of service, dates of death, and
federal government pension and retirement regulations. Because of
the number of cards involved and the size of the file (300 cu. ft.), it
is impossible to determine the exact time periods covered by the
files. Service with the company by employees however, dates back
to at least 1865. Likewise, because membership was voluntary, not
all employees of the railroad will be found on these cards, even
though coverage was system wide. None of the cards can be made
available to the public unless the employee has been dead for at
least twenty-five years. Information appearing on each set of
cards includes the following:

Deceased and Left Service File (subseries 1). Contains index
cards (5 X 8 inch) that were printed prior to 1938 and which
cover service by workers back to at least 1865. Data shown
includes the names, places of birth, dates of birth, and occupations of the employees; the names of their father, mother, and if
relevant spouse; the certificate numbers and the dates entitled
to retirement; and their employment service records, that is,
titles of positions held, divisions employed by, dates of entering
service or changing jobs; and rates of pay. An occasional social
security number is present as well. Supplemental cards contain
"disablement records" that detail when and for how long workers were sick or injured; what the cause of disablement was
(name of illness, condition suffering from, or part of body
injured); and if needed, the dates of death. Other information
that might appear includes, the dates that the employees were
last compensated for service, dates of retirement, and particulars regarding whether they were granted an annuity under the
Railroad Retirement Act of 1937. Internal accounting data, for
example, department codes (initials such as M.P. for motive
department, etc.), deduction classes, A.D.B. (annuitant death
benefit) options, and details about disbursements paid are pre-

sent as well. An extensive sampling of these cards would appear to indicate that all of the workers in this subseries have been dead for longer than twenty-five years.

Deceased and Left Service File (subseries 2). Consists of index cards (5 X 8 inch) that were printed prior to 1950 and which cover employment back to the early 1900s. The cards contain the same type of information found for subseries 1. Some personnel cards originating from the New York Central Railroad Company also are present. Such cards do not have the VRD data but they do note dates when the individuals were off duty or had left service as well as the causes. Most of the employees found on the subseries 2 cards appear to have been dead for at least twenty-five years. The dates of the employees deaths, however, are not always on the cards to verify this, and several employee cards were in fact found that listed dates of death as recently as 1970. These cards, therefore, cannot be made available without staff intervention.

Left Service File (subseries 3), 1905-1953. Index cards (3 X 5 inches) that cover service by workers dating back to at least the 1880s and which in some cases include the same employees found in subseries 1. Data can vary with the card utilized but normally entries give the employees' names, divisions, occupations, dates of birth, length of service (years and months), and dates of death; the certificate numbers; and the dates that the benefits became effective. Older cards from the early 1900s also provide the workers' present ages and rates of pay (as of 1905-1910 usually); the dates of employment (exact date of entry and leaving service); average rates of monthly pay; and period of time on the relief fund rolls. Cards dating from the 1950s list the addresses of the persons; have space for recording the dates of death; and contain references to supplemental pension plans, hollerith cards, and railroad benefit numbers. As with subseries 1 all of the workers documented on these cards died more than twenty-five years ago.

Left Service Since 1959 File (subseries 4). Has index cards (5 X 8 inches) that were for the most part printed prior to 1960 and

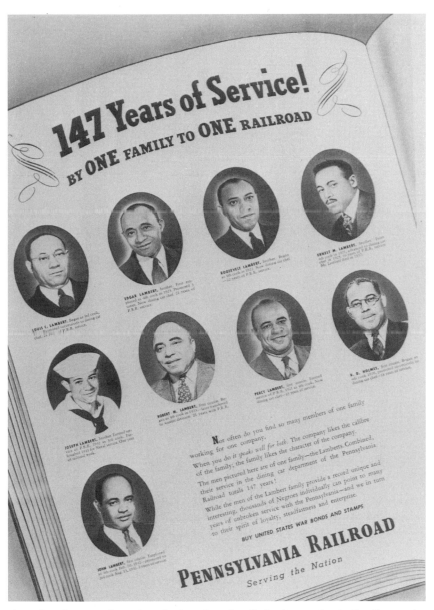

An advertisement honoring the Lambert family for its service to the Pennsylvania Railroad Company. Contained in volume 3, 1944-1945, of the *WARTIME ADVERTISING SCRAPBOOKS (MG-286), PSA.*

include individuals who left serve as late as 1963. While some cards can be found for employees who started working for the railroad in the early 1900s most of persons documented in this series were hired during the 1940 to 1950 time period. Entries on these cards usually show the names, occupations, social security numbers; divisions, departments, and pay rates of the workers; the dates of entering service changing jobs, and leaving service; and the certificate numbers. The accompanying "disablement record" cards provide the employees' birth dates; the names of the parents and spouses; and relief accounting data (dates and classes of membership, annuitant death benefit options, monthly and total contributions collected, types of disablements, time periods disabled, and amounts of disbursements paid). Cards identical to those in subseries 1 are also present. All of the cards in this series are restricted for at least twenty years.

Relief Members to Norfolk and Western Railroad Company, October 16, 1964 (subseries 5). Contains index cards (5 X 8 inches) that are the same as those described under subseries 4 and which are subject to the same access restrictions.

PERSONNEL FILES OF THE PENNSYLVANIA STATE POLICE, 1913-1943 (RG-30). Contains diverse documents ranging from incident reports to workmen's compensation claims. These forms are of particular interest:

Application for Membership in the State Employes' Retirement Association. Shows the name, sex, address, date of birth, place of birth, and signature of the applicant; the department where employed; the position held and the date of appointment; the monthly salary received; and the date that payments begin. The reverse side of the form contains a signed, witnessed, and dated authorization which records the name and address of a designated beneficiary.

Employer's Report of Accident to Employe. A form submitted to the Department of Labor and Industry, Bureau of Workmen's Compensation in Harrisburg and to an insurance carrier. Data requested include the name and address of the employer; the nature of business; the location of the place or of the plant where accident occurred (street and number, city or town, county); the number of employes involved in the accident; date, day, and hour of the accident; hour injured person began work that day; date disability began; working hours per day; average working days per week; the name, address, sex, age, nationality, race, marital status, of the injured individual; ability to speak English; the number of dependents (children under sixteen years of age) and if they are aliens; monthly earnings; work engaged in when injured; kind of machine, tool or appliance used; length of experience at machine or operation; description of how the accident occurred; the names and addresses of witnesses; nature of the injury sustained; part of the person injured; name and address of the attending physician or hospital; date that employee returned to work; if injury was fatal, date of death and name of undertaker; name of company carrying insurance; and date of report and name of person submitting it.

Enlistment Papers. Must are dated from 1925 to 1930 and record the following information: name, age, place of birth, date of birth, address, previous occupation, and physical description (height; color of hair, eyes and complexion) of the applicant; the date and place of enlistment; the period of enlistment; and the name of the troop and the station in which enlisted. Each document has an oath of allegiance, a declaration of physical and moral fitness, and a certification of inspection that is signed and dated by the trooper, the superintendent of state police, and a medical officer. The name, address, and relationship of a person to call in case of emergency appears in the lower left corner.

An alphabetical list of individuals appearing in the file is available for perusal.

PERSONNEL LISTS, PENNSYLVANIA STATE POLICE, 1912-1929 (RG-30). Typed lists of former members of the force which show the names of the state troopers; the troops that they were attached to; their file numbers; lengths of service; and reasons for discharge (general order, desertion, resignation, etc.). Also found is a list of casualties for 1929 that contains this information and has desertion, undesirable, death, and so forth, as the reasons for separation. There is no index to the lists.

PERSONNEL RECORDS, 1927-1988 (MG-393). Records relating to employees of the Pullman-Standard Car Manufacturing Company, Butler, Pa, who were either laid off or terminated from 1927 to 1988. The documents are arranged in numerical order by file check numbers within the two categories noted above. A name index is not available. Examples of the types of papers and forms present in the file appear below:

Applications for Employment. Index cards (5 X 8 inch) that provide the name, age, date of birth, height, sex, marital status, address, telephone and social security number of the applicant; the primary and secondary occupations desired; the amount (years) of experience in these fields; and a brief educational (names and locations of grammar, high school, and any colleges attended; number of years and dates there; and course work) and employment (previous employer's names and addresses; dates of employment; positions held; pay rates; and reasons for leaving) history of the person. The application card is signed and dated by the worker and lists the name, address, and telephone number of a person to contact in case of emergency. If relevant, information regarding the candidate's physical defects, dependents (number and relationship), military service (branch, dates of enlistment, rank upon discharge, and duties performed), citizenship status, and criminal background also appears.

Change in Occupation or Rate of Employee (Wage Rate Occupation) Forms. Typically lists the worker's name, file check number, department, present occupation, and pay rate; the proposed occupation and pay rate; and the reason for the change. A special data section is used to indicate the foreman recommending the change, the approval date, the effective date, and the names of the company officials concurring in and approving of the move. There is also space available on the form for recording the employee's social security number and the number of times that job classification changes had been granted.

Employee Drop Slips. Used when the worker was laid off or terminated the forms give the file check number (later clock number), name, department, and occupation of the person; the last day worked (date); and the reason for separation (laid off, leave of absence, quit, discharge or other). The slips are dated and signed by the employee, the foreman, and tool room supervisor (to indicate that locker was cleaned out and all tools turned in). Prior to the 1980s, there also is space available for both the employee and foreman to make a statement. The more modern slips have the foreman's statement and permit the worker to check a block either requesting employment in another department or passing on such a transfer.

Insurance Cards. Index cards (5 X 8 inch) that are signed and dated by the employee and record his or her name, birth date, sex, marital status (sometimes date of marriage), social security number, job class, and employment date; the names, dates of birth and relationships of eligible dependents to the worker; the name, and address of a person to whom the death benefit is to be paid, and the relationship of that individual to the insured; the insurance certificate number; the date of eligibility; and the name of the plant and insurance unit providing the coverage.

Insurance Claim Records. Index cards (5 X 8 inch) that were used to record any medical claims filed by employees or their dependents with the company's insurance carrier. Normally the cards just give the worker's name and file check number; the name of the claimant and his or her relationship to the insured (if not self); the dates that service was rendered; and the type of medical service or treatment given. A date paid section is hardly ever filled out.

Service Record. Provides details regarding the employee's work history with the company, for example, the dates first hired, rehired, laid off, and terminated; the company official requested by; the departments and occupations employed in; demerits received; and the years of accumulated service rendered. Other information recorded, however, includes the worker's name, social security number, file check number, address, phone number, nationality, citizenship status, birthplace, occupation, date of birth, race, marital standing (including number of dependents), education (highest level), physical description (height, weight, hair and eye colors) and rating (codes); previous employers (including jobs held and number of years); and if relevant, military service serial number, branch, and status.

Additional materials found include applications for military leave of absence, employee demerit reports, physical exam slips, and transfer requested by employee forms.

PERSONNEL RECORDS: PSYCHOLOGICAL TESTING, 1957 (MG-311). Psychological reports about employees of the Lehigh and New England Railroad Company. The testing was conducted by the personnel psychology center located in New York City and attempted to evaluate and project how effective employees being considered for new positions would be. Test factors measured for supervisory and management positions included mental ability, arithmetic reasoning, mechanical comprehension, social intelligence, sales comprehension, English expression, vocabulary, and executive growth factors, that is, the person's percentile rating in general information, judgment in estimating, symbolic relationships, and reading comprehension. Criteria evaluated for clerical jobs included mental ability, arithmetic reasoning, social judgment, understanding of people, clerical aptitude, clerical interests, general typing proficiency, stability, self-sufficiency, extroversion, dominance, self-confidence, and sociability. Each report has a statistical cover sheet or chart attached to it that uses these factors to grade and rank the candidate, followed by a narrative analysis which candidly describes the person's strengths and weaknesses. The files are arranged in alphabetical order by surname.

PETITIONS FOR PEDDLERS' LICENSES, 1796-1881, AND COUNTY TREASURER'S RECEIPTS FOR CLOCK PEDDLERS' LICENSES (DAUPHIN COUNTY), 1830-1845 (RG-47). The documents are arranged in chronological order by date license was granted. Information varies with each petition, but normally the person's name, residence, and reason for seeking a license (deformity, disability) to peddle or hawk appears along with the date of license. Other data often found include the amount of bond that the peddler was beholden to the Commonwealth for, his past occupation, as well as the method of hawking (on foot, by horse, or wagon). The petitions are signed, or if the person is illiterate, marked by the applicant. Clock peddler receipts dated and signed by the county treasurer also are present, but these usually only list the name of the peddler, the fee paid for the license, and the time period that the license was for.

PHILADELPHIA AND READING RELIEF ASSOCIATION RECEIPTS, 1898-1908, 1912-1914, 1916-1920 (MG-110). Three letter press type volumes that primarily consist of receipts for money paid to association members or which document the income received by the Schuylkill Navigation Company for lockage and strip tickets. Also found in the books, however, are the following forms relating to personnel actions and disability claims:

Accident Reports (Form 314). The form could be used for an employee, a customer, or unlucky bystander. Information listed includes the date and time that the incident was reported; the nature, place, and cause of the accident; the name of the person sustaining the personal injury; and remarks, that is, comments regarding witnesses that were present and or care that was administered to the individual.

Death Notices (Form 97). Entries have the date and place where the notice was being sent from; the name of the employee and the date that he was disabled; the type of disablement (natural or accident); the date and place of the member's death; the relief association certificate number and the membership class; the last date that a contribution was made to the relief fund; and the name and title of the person submitting the notice.

Notices of Disablement (Form 14). Data appearing includes the name, occupation, residence, and company division (department) of the worker; the type of disability (accident or sickness); the dates that the disability began and the member reported it; the relief class (1st, 2nd, etc.); the date and place where the notice was sent from; and the signature and title of the person issuing the notice.

Notice of Permanent Transfer, Change of Occupation, Leaving Service, Furlough, or Suspension of Member of the Relief Association (Form 9). The notice is directed to the superintendent of the relief association and records the date and place where the form was sent from; the type of personnel action; the member's name, occupation, and company division (department); the relief association certificate number; the effective date for the action; and the last month that a contribution was made to the relief fund. In some cases the employee's age also appears.

The books are in chronological order. Most of the personnel data are contained in the 1898 to 1908 volume. None of the volumes is indexed.

PHYSICIANS' ALMS HOUSE RECORD, 1868-1912 (RG-47). Indexed. A record of individuals in Bedford County who were admitted into the alms house. The book is arranged in chronological order by date of examination. Entries have the name, age, and sex of the applicant; the date examined by the physician; the name of the justice of the peace who issued the order; and the action taken, that is, whether the person was rejected or approved along with the date and the reason (cripple, poverty, old age, vagrancy, insane, deaf and dumb). There is space for recording the name of the officer executing the order, but this data is seldom provided.

PHYSICIANS' STATEMENTS AND AFFIDAVITS, 1881-1905 (RG-47). A record of individuals who registered as practitioners of medicine and surgery in Lehigh County. The statements and affidavits are usually signed and subscribed by both the applicant and the county prothonotary and show the name, place of nativity, and residence of the physician; and as relevant, the name of the institution which conferred the medical degree; the date that the degree was received; and the place or locations of continuous medical practice in Pennsylvania since 1871. Space also is available for recording information about other degrees held by the doctor and the page of the medical register where this data was recorded. Also included in many cases are transcripts of the applicant's medical diploma or a certified written statement. The statement may provide a variety of information, for example, a description of the doctor's experience in the medical field, training received, or even his age and date of birth. The documents were prepared in accordance with the Act of June 8, 1881, and the Act of May 18, 1893. The file is bundled and in rough chronological order.

PILOT APPRENTICE INDENTURE BOOKS, 1806-1931, 1942 (RG-41). Indexed. A record of apprentices to harbor pilots at the Port of Philadelphia. Normally the indenture agreements are signed by the apprentice's guardian and a master pilot and mention the novice's name and address. At times information such as the age of the indentured boy and the name and residence of his father is also listed.

PILOT LICENSE BOOKS, 1908-1982 (RG-41). Consists of pilot licenses issued for the Port of Philadelphia. The licenses are arranged according to issuance date and list the pilot's name and the dates of the bond and license. The document is ascribed by the pilot.

PROMOTION LIST FOR LIEUTENANTS, 1955-1986 (RG-30). The HISTORICAL FILE OF THE PENNSYLVANIA STATE POLICE contains a list of 339 state troopers who were promoted to the rank of lieutenant from July 16, 1955 to June 26, 1986. Entries give the name, date of birth, and place of birth of the state trooper; the date of rank as lieutenant; the date of enlistment into the service ("H.P." or "S.P." to indicate Highway Patrol and State Police, respectively); and location of duty (a code). Notations are sometimes present that record the person's date of retirement or death. The list is arranged in chronological order by date of promotion. A HIGHWAY PATROL ROSTER, 1923-1932, also is found in this file but it only has the name of the patrolman; the appointment date; and if appropriate, the date of becoming corporal, sergeant, and so forth.

PUBLIC SCHOOL EMPLOYEES RETIREMENT SYSTEM REGISTERS, 1918-73 (RG-50). A whole series of records that document active contributing members, annuitants, and individuals who withdrew from the Pennsylvania School Employees' Retirement System program. Each type of register contains the following information:

Registers of Active System Members (Account Number Registers), ca. 1918-1973. Entries in the forty-two volumes are arranged in numerical order by account numbers (1-900075) and from 1918 to 1931 give the member's name, the date that the account was dis posed of, and the method of disposal or withdrawal (retired, refund, superannuation). The maiden name of a married woman usually appears as well. After 1932-1933, in addition to this, data entries record the sex, date of birth, appointment date, and withdrawal number of the person. Similar information can be found in a sixteen volume register of new entrant withdrawals, 1933-1974 (withdrawal nos. 66110-399539) and in a three volume register of present employee withdrawals, July, 1919- July, 1970 (withdrawal nos. 1-30493).

New Entrant Registers of Superannuation Allowances Granted, July, 1933- June, 1972. The five volumes are arranged in numerical order by retirement numbers (43-37590) and give the name, sex, age, and years of service of the retiring member; the dates of birth and retirement; the active and retirement account numbers; the annual allowance granted (employee annuity and state annuity); and where appropriate, the termination number along with the date and cause of termination (usually death). In some cases a retirement option number also is listed. The same type of data appears in three volumes of present employee registers of superannuation allowances granted, July, 1933- July, 1969 (retirement nos. 3185-19737); in a present employee register of disability allowances granted, 1933-1959 (retirement nos. 997-1852); in a book of present employee disability terminations, 1919-1975 (termination nos. 1-1763); in a present employee register of withdrawal allowances granted, 1950-1960 (retirement nos. 1-111); in a book of present employee withdrawal allowance terminations, July, 1952- July, 1974 (termination nos. 1-56); in a register withdrawal of present employee superannuation terminations, 1919-59 (retirement nos. 1-7916); in a termination register of new entrant and present employee superannuations, 1931-1975 (retirement nos. 1-15498); in a new entrant register of refund annuity allowances granted, 1937-1974 (retirement nos. 1-4821); in a book of new entrant disability terminations, 1930-1975 (termination nos. 1-1483); in book of new entrant withdrawal allowance terminations, 1951-1975 (termination nos. 1-2393); and in a folder of refund annuity terminations, July, 1952- July, 1962.

Registers of Superannuation Annuitants, 1919-1970. The eight volumes are grouped by school years and thereunder arranged in alphabetical order by name of annuitant. Data found includes the annuity, retirement and or termination number; the person's name, age at retirement, years of service, and position held (teacher, principal, custodian, secretary, tax collector, etc.); the school district and county of employment/residence; the final salary earned; the amount of annuity and the date that it began; whether the retiree received social security benefits (yes or no from 1958 onward); and remarks concerning the date that the annuitant died, or may have returned to service. The more modern registers (post 1930) also mention familial relationships (mother, husband, daughter, brother, etc.) with regards to the annuity and include yearly alphabetical lists of deceased annuitants (from 1957-1958 onward). Instead of the final salary, the date that the annuity began, and the annuity's amount, however, these lists show the total value of the retirement package, the amount of accumulated deductions, and the person's date of death.

Register of Disability Annuitants, 1919-1970. The book is organized in the same manner as the registers of superannuation annuitants and contains similar information. Data identifying family members as beneficiaries, however, does not start until 1952.

RECORD BOOK OF STATE CERTIFICATES, COLLEGE GRADU-ATES, 1893-1911 (RG-22). Indexed. A registry of college graduates who were granted certificates to teach by the state Board of Education. Data entered include the name and postal address of the teacher, the college attended, the degree received, and the certificate number (with date of issue).

RECORD BOOKS OF OPTOMETRICAL LICENSES, 1918-1970 (RG-22). Consists of copies of licenses issued to optometrists by the state Board of Optometrical Education, Examination, and Licensure. Pertinent information found includes the name and address (city, state, and county) of the optometrist, the date of licensing, and in some instances comments about whether the licensee died or had his or her certificate revoked. The licenses are arranged according to the date that each was issued.

RECORD BOOKS OF OSTEOPATHS, 1909-1957 (RG-22). Indexed. A record of osteopaths licensed by the state Board of Osteopathic Examiners. Usually, entries show the application date and number; the name, address, and age of the practitioner; the school that was attended; the graduation date; the license number and date; and the fee paid. Information such as the date that the person died, the grade attained on the licensing examination, and whether the applicant was licensed on the basis of a reciprocity agreement with another state sometimes is recorded as well.

RECORD BOOKS OF PERMANENT TEACHING CERTIFICATES, 1868-1908 (RG-22). Indexed. A record of persons granted permanent teaching certificates by the state Board of Education. Entries give the name, postal address, and county of residence of the teachers; and the date and file number of the certificate granted. Notations concerning what courses the person studied or majored in frequently appear as well.

RECORD BOOKS OF THE BROTHERHOOD OF RAILROAD TRAIN-MEN, KEYSTONE LODGE 42, HARRISBURG, PA., 1910-1956 (in MG-262). While the bulk of the entries relates to routine affairs such as the election of officers, the recording of minutes, the submittal of expenditures, and the filing of reports by various committees and officers, the books include a section for reporting any brothers sick or out of work. Particulars relating to the death of members (dates, places of burial, etc.) and occasionally their wives and children appear in this space. All of the trainmen worked for the Pennsylvania Railroad Company lines east of Pittsburgh, Philadelphia Division. The volumes are arranged in chronological order by dates of meetings.

RECORD OF APPLICATIONS AND LICENSES ISSUED TO CHI-ROPODISTS, 1956-1982 (RG-22 and 26). Indexed. A record of individuals licensed as chiropodists from October 26, 1956 to October 4, 1982. Information provided by the volumes includes the name and address of the chiropodist; the date of graduation; the name and location of the institution which granted the degree; the date of application and the application number; the date that the license was issued and the license number; and the date that the license fee was paid and the amount. There is space available for recording the person's age and date of examination but it is left blank. As needed, a remarks section was used to indicate the date that the chiropodist died. The entries are arranged in numerical order by application numbers.

RECORD OF ATTORNEYS ADMITTED TO PRACTICE IN THE SUPREME COURT OF PENNSYLVANIA, 1876-1969 (RG-33). A record of attorneys admitted before the Supreme Court of Pennsylvania sitting in the Middle, 1876-1969, Eastern, and Western Districts (Philadelphia and Pittsburgh), 1924-1969. Entries list the name and residence of the lawyer, the date of admission, and the name of the person who made the motion for admittance. The names of the attorneys appearing in the registers are grouped alphabetically. Similar information is found for the state superior court in these record series: RECORD OF ATTOR-NEYS ADMITTED TO PRACTICE IN THE SUPERIOR COURT, MIDDLE DISTRICT, 1896-1969 (RG-38); and ADMISSIONS OF ATTOR-NEY DOCKET FOR PHILADELPHIA, HARRISBURG, AND SCRAN-TON, 1947-1971 (RG-38).

RECORD OF CERTIFICATES ACCEPTED IN LIEU OF PRELIMI-NARY EXAMINATION, 1904-1911 (RG-22). A registry kept by the Medical Council of Pennsylvania to provide proof that candidates for medical study had been conditioned in the preliminary branches of education. Entries generally give the name of the applicant, the high school attended, the date of graduation, the date that the certificate was issued, and the name of the examiner approving the certificate. Affidavits from school officials are oftentimes included.

RECORD OF CERTIFICATES ACCEPTED IN LIEU OF PRELIMI-NARY EXAMINATION, 1900-1911 (RG-22). A record kept by the Pennsylvania Dental Council to demonstrate that candidates possessed the educational qualifications required by law to obtain a license to practice dentistry and to matriculate in an approved dental institution. Entries are arranged chronologically and normally list the name, address, and educational credentials of each applicant. Vouchers from state examiners are pasted into the register and the number of credits earned by the registrant is frequently noted.

RECORD OF MARRIED WOMEN TO SECURE THEIR SEPARATE EARNINGS, BRADFORD COUNTY, March 19, 1873- June 13, 1891 (RG-47). Indexed. A record created as a result of the Act of April 3, 1872, that permitted married woman to enjoy the benefits and profits earned from wages for labor, salary, property or business separate from their husbands. The dated petitions were submitted to the president of the court of common pleas and normally record the name, residence (township, borough, etc., and county), and occupation of the woman; the name of her husband; the date that the sworn statement was signed and certified by the prothonotary to be true; and the date the petition was filed with the recorder of deeds. The petitions are in chronological order by filing date and often contain an acceptance clause signed by the husband.

RECORD OF PEDDLERS' LICENSES ISSUED, April 16, 1830- August 20, 1855 (RG-47) A record of individuals who were granted peddler licenses by the Dauphin County Court of Quarter Sessions. During the 1830s entries show the name and residence of the peddler, the date of the license, the mode of traveling (on foot, wagon, horse), the fee paid, and the date that the transaction was returned to the auditor general. The fact that the person was a clock peddler is also noted. Later returns seldom indicate where the applicant was from. The returns are arranged in chronological order by date license was issued.

RECORD OF THE FIRE DEPARTMENT, CITY OF SCRANTON, 1867-1893 (RG-48). A microfilmed record that is arranged according to fire companies and thereunder by the badge number of the fireman. A typical listing shows the fireman's name, age, nationality, residence (street or ward), and date of certification. Occasionally remarks appear that indicate if the firefighter died, resigned, or was discharged.

RECORDS RELATING TO THE ADMISSION AND DISCIPLINING OF ATTORNEYS AND THE REGISTRATION OF LAW STUDENTS, 1871-1985 (RG-33). The file contains motions for admittance, certificates of the state Board of Law Examiners, applications for admission, and lists of individuals admitted to practice law before the bar of the Supreme Court of Pennsylvania, Middle District. The following type of information is found on each document:

Admission Lists, 1871-1923, 1983-1985. From 1871 to 1923 the lists are arranged in alphabetical order and record the lawyer's name, the date of admittance, and the name of the person who made the motion for admittance. After 1983 these name listings are arranged in chronological order by admittance date and have the county of residence, and person making the motion typed on them.

Motions for Admittance and Certificates of the State Board of Law Examiners, 1891-1985. Motions typically provide the name of the attorney, county of residence, date of filing, and signature of the sponsor. The judicial district that the lawyer was from is periodically recorded from 1903-1960, and after 1912 his or her postal address is also noted. Prior to 1904 the documents are signed by a voucher and indicate where and for how long the applicant had experience as a law office clerk and as a lawyer before the courts of common pleas. After 1904 the motions are normally accompanied by certificates of the state Board of Examiners affirming that the applicant had successful passed the bar examination; attesting to the candidate's high moral character; and recommending his or her admission to practice law before the court. Additional information shown on the certificate include the date of certification, certificate number, the seal of the state Board of Law Examiners, and the signatures of the secretary and chairman. The documents are not arranged alphabetically but simply grouped within years by filing dates. Starting in May, 1975 typed name indexes were prepared on a monthly basis and filed with the certificates.

Applications for Admission, 1972-85. Beginning in 1972, instead of separate motions document, an application for admission was filed with the certificate. The form utilized from 1972-1976 consists of a certified personal statement submitted by the applicant, a statement of two sponsors supporting the application and giving their home and business addresses, a motion for admittance made by one of the sponsors, and a subscribed oath of admission by the applicant. The personal statement section records the applicant's name, social security number, place of birth, date of birth, and address (residential and business); lists the names of both parents, including the mother's maiden name; and describes the legal education and work experience of the person. After 1976, the application form does not include a personal statement or sponsors statement. It does give the lawyer's address and telephone number (residential in 1980 and business in 1982), however.

REGISTER BOOKS, 1909-1925 (RG-22). A record of nurses registered by the state Board of Examiners for Nurses from August 10, 1909, to April 21, 1925. The books are arranged by registration number and usually specify the name and postal address of the registrant, the school trained at, the graduation date, and the registry date. Information such as whether an applicant was registered on the basis of a reciprocity agreement with another state is also sometimes noted.

REGISTER OF ALDERMEN AND JUSTICES OF THE PEACE, ALLEGHENY COUNTY, February, 1877- May, 1891 (RG-47). The register is arranged by date of acceptance or commission. Entries record the name and district of each person and whether the commission resulted from being re-elected, succeeding himself, succeeding another named individual, or the fact that a named past official was deceased.

REGISTER OF ANIMAL CASTRATORS, January 12, 1916- April 5, 1931 (RG-22). Indexed. Data provided includes the name, date of birth, address, and county residence of the animal castrator; the date affidavit was filed; and the dates that registration fees were paid.

REGISTER OF PRELIMINARY EXAMINATIONS, 1896-1911 (RG-22). A record of examinations administered by the state medical examiners as proof that a candidate for medical studies has been conditioned in the preliminary branches of education. Entries are grouped chronologically by the date of examination and show the name of the examinee, the medical or normal school that was attended, and information regarding the subjects on which he or she was tested. Forms listing the name, residence, college, class, and educational credentials of the candidate along with the date on which the application was processed are frequently pasted into the registers.

REGISTER OF PRELIMINARY EXAMINATIONS, 1899-1911 (RG-22). A record of examinations administered by the state dental examiners to certify that candidates were conditioned in the preliminary branches of education. Normally, lists are found that give the date and location where the applicant was examined, the name of the examinee, and state whether a passing or failing grade was received. Some entries note the subjects upon which the individual was tested, the numerical grade attained, and the name of the college or normal school that was attended. Forms recording the date on which the application was processed and the name, residence, college, class, and educational credentials of the candidate are also pasted into the register. The volume is arranged by examination date.

REGISTERS OF CERTIFIED PUBLIC ACCOUNTANTS, 1899-1975 (RG-22 and 26). Indexed. A listing of persons registered as certified public accountants by the state Board of Examiners of Public Accountants. Entries list the name and address of the registrant, the certificate number and date, the application number, and the date of examination or approval. Notes concerning whether the individual has died are frequently found as well.

REGISTERS OF LAW STUDENTS, 1936-1969 (RG-33). Indexed. A record of students who registered to study law with the Supreme Court of Pennsylvania, Middle District, between June 8, 1936, and September 2, 1969. Information shown includes the name, address, and age of the student; the registration and application numbers; the date of registration; the date of the prothonotary's certificate; and the date that the registration certificate was filed.

REGISTERS OF MEDICAL LICENSES, June 23, 1881- May 18, 1959 (RG-47). Indexed. A record of physicians who applied for licenses in Franklin County. The registers are arranged in chronological order by date when medical degree was granted or by date that the person appeared before the prothonotary with his license. Entries from 1894 are signed and subscribed by both the applicant and the prothonotary and show the name, place of nativity, and residence of the physician; the name of the institution which conferred the medical degree; the date that the degree was received; time and places where continuous practice in the Commonwealth was pursued; and after 1893, the date that the Pennsylvania State Medical Council licensed the person. Space is available for recording information about other degrees held by the doctor, and volume one of this two volume series, has a column for indicating if the person died or had his license removed. The registers were created to comply with the Act of June 8, 1881, passed to provide for the registration of all practitioners of medicine and surgery and the Act of May 18, 1893, that established a Medical Council and a state Board of Medical Examiners.

REGISTERS OF MINE ACCIDENTS, 1899-1989 (RG-45). A registry of persons who were involved in coal mining accidents in the bituminous and anthracite coal fields. From 1899 to 1972 entries are arranged by coal mining districts and thereinafter according to the date of the accident. In addition to giving the name of the mine where the accident occurred information listed about the victim includes his name, age, nationality, marital status, number of children, his job in the mine, and whether he was a citizen or an alien. After 1972 the books are further divided into fatal and non-fatal (1973-1989) coal and fatal (1973-1986) and non-fatal (1973-1981) non-coal mining accidents. With the exception of the person's nationality, all of the data found in the earlier registers also appear in the accident books categorized as fatal coal mining accidents. Other information shown includes the name of the operator; the victim's experience (both in and about the mines and in the occupation engaged in when killed) and exact date of death; the number of children left that were under thirteen years old; and particulars about the accident/death (inside or outside the mine, natural causes or accidental, chargeable, and the county and time that the fatality took place). In those instances where the accident was non-fatal or non-coal related, most of the personal information columns are left blank. The person's age and occupation at the time of the accident are provided, however.

REGISTERS OF PHYSICIANS, 1912-1917 (RG-22). A record of physicians who were registered in Pennsylvania from 1870 to 1917. Normally, the doctor's name, license number (from 1895 onward), postal address, county where registered, and date of registration are given. Oftentimes information concerning the death or change of address of the practitioner is included. Prior to 1913 entries are arranged in strict alphabetical order, but after 1913 they are only grouped alphabetically by surnames.

REGISTERS OF PILOTS' NAMES AND SECURITIES, 1783-1791, 1794-1876 (RG-41). A register kept for pilots at the Port of Philadelphia. Entries are in chronological order by bond dates and there is an index which covers the period October, 1870, to March, 1876. From 1783 to 1791 the registers simply give the pilot's name, date of bond, and rate. After 1794 they also indicate where the pilot was from and the name of his surety. During the period 1795 to 1870 the registers record the surety's occupation and place of residence, and from 1804 to 1817 list also the name of any person to whom a third-rate pilot was apprenticed. After 1870 the only particulars that appear are the name of the pilot and his surety, the dates of the bond and license, and the amount of the bond.

REGISTRATION BOOKS FOR ASSISTANT PHARMACISTS, 1887-1945, 1963-1978 (RG-22 and 26). Indexed. A record of qualified assistant pharmacists registered with the Pennsylvania Board of Pharmacy. A typical listing contains the registration number, name, address, county of residence, and age of the applicant; the amount of experience in the profession; and the date of registration. Prior to 1899 the registers have renewal dates and state whether the assistant was examined or in practice before May 24, 1887. From 1963 to 1978, a record of the registrant's examination scores and the college that he or she attended appears in lieu of professional experience.

REGISTRATION BOOKS FOR PHARMACISTS, 1887-1963 (RG-22). Indexed. A record of persons registered as pharmacists by the Commonwealth. Entries ordinarily show the registration number and date, the name and address of the pharmacist, and the county of residence. Prior to 1911 the registers list renewal dates and whether a registrant was examined or in practice prior to May 24, 1887. After June 29, 1911, the registers record the age of the individual, the college attended and the grades attained. Information such as whether a pharmacist was registered because of a reciprocal agreement with another state or whether the registrant has died or moved is periodically indicated as well.

REGISTRATION BOOKS OF PHARMACY APPRENTICES, Ca.1925-1965 (RG-22). A record of pharmacy apprentices registered with the Pennsylvania Board of Pharmacy. An index is available for the names of persons registered from 1925 to 1929, but after 1929, entries are arranged numerically by certificate numbers. Data found in the registers usually include the name and address of the applicant, his or her certificate number, the application or commencement of experience date, and the certification date.

REGISTRATION CERTIFICATES OF LAW STUDENTS, 1903-1952 (RG-33). The certificates are arranged according to year and thereafter by assigned file number. A record of persons who were registered by the state Board of Law Examiners as law students with the Supreme Court of Pennsylvania, Eastern District. Data recorded include the name, age, birth date, and address of the registrant; the name of the law school attended; the name and address of the student's preceptor; and the names of the agency and officials issuing the certificate. The date that the document was issued and filed is noted, and from 1934 onward the birthplace of the applicant is regularly listed.

REGISTRATION CERTIFICATES OF LAW STUDENTS, 1905-1971 (RG-33). A record of persons who registered as law students with the Supreme Court of Pennsylvania, Western District. The certificates, which are endorsed by the state Board of Law Examiners, generally show the date that the document was issued and filed, the name of the student, and the judicial district and county where he or she resided. From 1923 to 1925 the certificates give the age and address of the applicant, the name of the student's preceptor, and the name of the law school attended. Additional information recorded after 1925 includes the birth date and birthplace of the individual and the address of the preceptor. The certificates are organized by the date that the certificate was filed and after 1932 are assigned file numbers. LAW STUDENT REGISTRATION DOCKETS (RG-33) can be used as indexes for identifying those persons who registered from 1905 to 1971.

REGISTRATION RECORD OF PRACTITIONERS OF MEDICINE AND SURGERY, 1881-1889 (RG-14). A record of registered Pennsylvania physicians. Entries are arranged by county and thereunder grouped alphabetically by doctor's surname. Usually the registers record the name, sex, race, place of birth, and residence of the practitioner. Data concerning the physician's years of continuous medical practice, particulars relating to the medical education of the registrant, and remarks about the removal or death of the practitioner regularly appear as well.

RETAIL-WHOLESALE BREWERS' AND BOTTLERS LICENSE DOCKETS, 1889-1891, 1914-1924 (RG-47). Indexed. Documentation regarding persons living in Schuylkill County who applied for licenses to sell liquor. Entries in the dockets provide the court term and date; the name and residence of the applicant; the type of business and its location; the date of filing and the district; the disposition, that is, the date that the application for license was granted or refused; the names of the petitioner's lawyer, sureties, and witnesses; and the date of the acknowledgment. In cases where the application was conveyed to someone else, the date of transfer, and the new applicant's name and residence also appear. The docket entries are numbered and arranged in order by filing date.

ROAD PAYROLLS, July, 1885- December, 1910 (MG-311). Payroll records of the Lehigh and New England Railroad Company that have the name, occupation, and signature (up to February 18, 1902) of the employee; and the time (hours, days worked), pay rate, total amount of deductions (for fines, lanterns, rent, etc.), and net amount of pay earned. From January, 1909, onward the place of employment also is recorded. Each payroll is signed by the general superintendent. The entries are in chronological order.

STATE EMPLOYEE LISTS, 1923-1926 (RG-26). The lists are grouped according to state departments, boards, or commissions. Ordinarily, an entry lists the employee's name, sex, voting residence, position or title, salary, agency, and date of birth. Information concerning the date of entry into government service and any previous state employment is also noted.

STRIKE REPORTS, 1922, 1932-1964 (RG-30). Reports submitted by the Pennsylvania State Police about labor disturbances that they were asked to investigate or quell. Typically the reports give the State Police troop and headquarters that was involved in the incident; the duties performed by the troopers and the name of each police officer who provided them; the exact dates, times, and places when events occurred; and the nature, cause, and participants in the dispute. As part of the investigation names, addresses, and occupations of pickets and strike breakers are routinely reported. In many cases the age, marital status, race, and nationality of individual workers appear as well. The file is in chronological order with the names of the labor disputes found on each folder. A container listing can be browsed to identify the dates, places, and subjects (specific companies or industries) of labor disturbances.

STUDENT OF LAW PAPERS, LEHIGH COUNTY, 1826-1883 (RG-47). The file contains statements submitted to the court of common pleas by lawyers attesting to the fact that persons named within had successfully completed a study of the law under their guidance. Other information sometimes appearing includes the ages of the law students and the exact dates their studies. The papers are in chronological order.

TAVERN KEEPERS RECOMMENDATIONS, 1797 (MG-90). The recommendations are for Cumberland County and list the name and residence of each tavern keeper. The documents are arranged by the date of the recommendation.

TAVERN LICENSES APPLIED FOR AND GRANTED, 1750-1855 (MG-90). Consists of handwritten lists for Cumberland County. The lists are arranged chronologically and give the name and residence of the licensee.

TAVERN LICENSE RECOMMENDATIONS, 1790-1809 (RG-24). Lists of persons recommended to act as tavern keepers. The amount of information given varies with each document. While some entries merely give the individual's name and county of residence along with the date of recommendation and licensing, others record the township or town where the proprietor resided. In some

140.

Tavern Licences Granted

1 William Snyder
2 Ebenezer Shaw
3 John Wathins
4 Wm F. Dininger
5 R. & A. Fowler
6 Jacob Bowman
7 Moses Coburn
8 Ezra Long
9 Humphrey Brown

10 Samuel Besley
11 John Taylor
12 John Hill
13 Wm W. Rice
14 Joseph Armstrong
15 Seth S. Barstow
16 S. M. Piollet
17 Anthony Lefever
18 John Griffin
19 Ebenezer Kendall

Sessions Expired

Venires Issued for Sept. Sess

Fines Certified

May 12th 1819 James Bullock Esq. admitted as an attorney and Counseller at Law to practice in the Courts in Bradford County and Sworn accordingly

Information regarding tavern licenses issued during the early 1800s often appears in court records such as this SESSIONS DOCKET, BRADFORD COUNTY, 1813-1821 (RG-47), PSA.

instances copies of the tavern keeper's license are also present. The items are grouped by county and thereunder arranged by recommendation date.

TAVERN VALUATION RATES, 1831 (MG-90). A record compiled for Cumberland County. The documents are grouped according to township and list the name of the tavern keeper, the valuations, and the date of the assessment.

THE CENTRAL PENNSYLVANIA QUARRY, STRIPPING, AND CONSTRUCTION COMPANY RECORDS, 1903-1961 (MG-313). The company was located in the Hazleton area of Luzerne County. Significant records covering workers include:

Workmen's Compensation Case (Accidents) and Accounts Receivable Books, 1913-1917. Besides accounts regarding routine financial expenditures, the first volume (1913-1916), contains a record of employee accidents that occurred during 1916 at the Benjamin iron and steel shops and the Buck Mountain, Beaver Meadows, Cranberry, Ebervale, Harleigh, Oakdale, Oneida, and Park Place mining facilities. Generally the narrative statements list the name, address (usually town but at times street and house number), nationality, occupation, and marital status of the employee; the date, time, and brief description of the accident and injury sustained; the compensation number; and where appropriate, a notation stating when or whether the case was closed. In some instances, additional information such as the names of witnesses, the rate of pay of the employee, the number of children in the family, and the person's race are noted. A second volume covering 1917 has less descriptive data and for the most part merely records the dates that the person was injured and returned to work; the injured man's name and compensation case number; the name of the doctor or facility that provided treatment; and remarks about when or whether the state was notified of the accident. Similar summary data for the year 1916 appears in the back of the first volume. Both volumes are grouped by the names of the sites where the accidents took place and thereafter by dates of accident. There is an alphabetical name index to the 1916 compensation cases.

Workmen's Compensation Fund Journal, 1916-1952. While account entries for the first seven years are columnar in nature and devoid of personal information, starting in May, 1924 short narratives appear that describe company awards in detail. Generally such statements mention the employee's name; describe the extent of the injury and how and when the accident occurred; the dollar amount awarded; the job/case number; and the basis for making the settlement. The volume is arranged in chronological order by dates of payment and or awards.

Workmen's Compensation Fund Ledgers, 1916-1952. The 1916-1941 ledgers normally only record the name of the person receiving compensation, the date and amount of payment, check number, and journal page number. In cases where a widow remarried, however, the date of marriage, name of husband, and names of any children to be compensated are listed as well. From 1941 to 1951 besides the information noted above the date of accident also is written. The ledgers are grouped by compensation cases and thereafter by dates of payment. The ledgers are indexed.

TIME AND CHECK ROLL BOOKS OF THE SCHUYLKILL NAVIGA-TION COMPANY, March 11, 1850- November 30, 1947 (MG-110). The payrolls are in chronological order by pay periods (usually monthly or weekly). Entries consist of a pay chart that shows the hours and days worked, the pay rate (per day or hourly), the amount earned, the name of the employee, and the nature of employment (occupation).

TIME BOOKS OF THE CIVILIAN CONSERVATION CORPS, 1931-1935 (RG-6). An example of the type of work performed by employees and the hours worked per day and month on government sponsored projects during the Great Depression. Besides listing the names of workers, many of the books record their occupations and the hourly pay rates and wages received per day. Examples of occupations include painters, watchmen, truck drivers, cooks, electricians, and clerks. The books are arranged in chronological order by dates of employment.

VETERINARY MEDICAL REGISTER, June 28, 1889- June 10, 1940 (RG-47). Indexed. A record of individuals who in compliance with the Act of April 11, 1889 registered with the prothonotary of Franklin County as practitioners of veterinary medicine. The register lists the name, place of nativity, and residence of the applicant; the medical degree held; the name of the institution that granted the degree and the date that it was received; time and places where continuous practice in the Commonwealth was pursued; and if needed, date of death or removal. Space also is available for recording information about other degrees received by the person and the back side of each register page contains a dated affidavit that is signed by the veterinarian and the county prothonotary. From 1895 onward the date that the person was licensed by the Pennsylvania Board of Veterinary Medical Examiners is included as well. The records are in chronological order.

VETERINARY MEDICAL REGISTERS, July 19, 1889- December 8, 1896, December 19, 1905- July 26, 1911 (RG-47). Indexed. A record of individuals who in compliance with the Act of April 11, 1889 and the Act of May 16, 1895 registered as veterinarians with the prothonotary of Bradford County. Each page of the registers has a form with space for recording the name, place of birth (after 1905), and residence of the registrant; the date and name of the institution that granted the degree; and the times and places of continuous practice in the Commonwealth. The bottom of the page consists of a dated affidavit that is signed by the prothonotary and the veterinarian. The entries in the register are in chronological order. Similar information is found in the VETERINARY MEDICAL REGISTER, August 26, 1889- October 4, 1904, for Dauphin County; May 13, 1890- September 7, 1897, for Huntingdon County; and August 27, 1889- February 13, 1906, for McKean County.

VETERINARY REGISTER, August 20, 1898- July 26, 1912 (RG-47). Indexed. A record of individuals who in compliance with the Act of May 16, 1895 registered as veterinarians with the prothonotary of Lehigh County. Each page in the book has the name, place of birth, and residence of the registrant; the date and name of the institution that granted the degree; and the date that the person was licensed by the Pennsylvania Board of Veterinary Medical

BALDWIN LOCOMOTIVE WORKS
SEVENTEENTH STREET DEPARTMENT
1885

J. FOREST	J. ROBERTS	GEO. ADAMS	WM. HENRY	R. CLARK	C. ELLIOT
H. FOSTER	WM. DETRICK	J. KNAPP	D. BAKER	H. GORMAN
'M. THOMAS	E. BROOKS	WM. VOLLMER	S. M. VAUCLAIN	J. GRADY	G. ALLISON	W. BOLTOI

A photograph contained in the S.M. VAUCLAIN DONATION, COLLECTIONS OF THE RAILROAD MUSEUM OF PENNSYLVANIA (MG-199), PSA.

Examiners. The bottom of the page consists of a dated affidavit that is signed by the prothonotary and the veterinarian. The entries in the register are in chronological order.

VETERINARY REGISTER, August 20, 1899- July 22, 1905 (RG-47). Indexed. A record of individuals, who in compliance with the Act of May 16, 1895, passed to provide for the registration of all practitioners of veterinary medicine and surgery, applied for the right to practice in Bedford County. Entries normally give the name, place of nativity and residence of the applicant; the degree held; the date that the degree was received and the name of the institution granting it; and as needed, the dates and places of continuous practice in Pennsylvania. Space also is provided for recording information about other degrees held by the veterinarian. The forms are signed and dated by the prothonotary and the applicant. Entries are in chronological order.

VETERINARY REGISTRATION BOOKS, September 20, 1905-
March 15, 1961 (RG-22). Indexed. Information recorded varies
with the time period. The early books give the registrant's name,
address (including county), and date of birth; the college of graduation and the date attended; the certificate number (during the
1930s); the date and county of first registration; and the dates that
registration fees were paid. The more modern books do not record
the birth date (after 1951), data regarding first registration (from
the 1940s on), or the dates fees were paid. As needed, however,
the date that the person died is written somewhere on the registration page.

In addition to these records there is also a RECORD OF DENTAL
LICENSES, 1897-1973 (RG-22 and 26); RECORD OF MEDICAL
LICENSES, 1894-1971 (RG-22 and 26); a RECORD OF CERTIFIED
PUBLIC ACCOUNTANT CERTIFICATES, 1899-1923 (RG-22); a
BOOK OF MIDWIVES, Undated (RG-22); a RECORD OF OSTHE-
OPATHS AND OSTHEOPATHIC LICENSES, 1909-1983 (RG-22 and
26); a REGISTERED NURSE CERTIFICATE BOOKS, 1917-1984
(RG-22 and 26); LICENSED ATTENDANTS [LICENSED PRACTICAL
NURSES], 1923-1984 (RG-22 and 26); APPOINTMENT BOOKS
FOR CIVIL OFFICERS, 1777-1947 (RG-26 and 27); and time and
payroll records for over thirty business enterprises in its custody.
Generally, however, these latter materials are arranged chronologically and usually just record an individual's name and occupation
along with the date. Some of the more modern personnel records
are subject to either donor or privacy restrictions. In most circumstances records of this latter type be used by the employees that
are mentioned in the documents or their immediate families.

PRISON RECORDS
(116 Cubic Feet)

The Commonwealth was one of the first political entities to abolish the use of corporal punishment for crime and to replace it with a system of rehabilitation through incarceration. In 1818 the legislature provided funds for the construction of the state's first penitentiary, the Western State Penitentiary in Pittsburgh. Subsequently, approval for the erection of the Eastern State Penitentiary at Philadelphia in 1821 and for the Industrial Reformatory at Huntingdon in 1878 was granted. The Division of Archives and Manuscripts has population records for these three penal institutions plus those of the Allegheny County Work House. Because many of these records do not appear to have readily available indices, researchers have not fully capitalized upon them. The materials, however, can offer a great deal of genealogical potential for those willing to search them.

ALLEGHENY COUNTY WORK HOUSE

Located at Claremont (Blawnox) the workhouse was established in 1866 and maintained a prison population from 1869 to 1971, when it was officially closed.

DISCHARGE DESCRIPTION DOCKETS, 1873-1971 (MG-197). The dockets are arranged and numbered in chronological order. Many of the listings from 1873 to 1899 are faded and illegible. An entry usually gives the name, register number, age (when discharged), color, sex, weight (when discharged), occupation (while imprisoned), crime, and sentence of the inmate; the date of discharge; the period of incarceration; the method of release; and the education that the prisoner received while in custody. Some of the early records also indicate the amount of money earned for overwork.

PRISON REGISTER BOOKS, 1869-1951 (MG-197). The registers are arranged alphabetically by inmate's surname and can be used to index the population records of the Allegheny County Work House. The registers list the prisoner's name, register number, and date of discharge.

REGISTERS TO INCLUDE ALL PRISONERS WHO HAVE BEEN TRIED AND SENTENCED TO HARD LABOR OR OTHERWISE, August 6, 1869-March 3, 1971 (MG-197). The registers are arranged and numbered in chronological order according to the date that the inmate was received. As a rule the registers show the name, register number, physical description (height, complexion, scars, eye and hair colors), age, occupation (before and during imprisonment), nativity, religion, literacy, habits (temperate or not), marital status, social security number (from January 29, 1960, onward), crime, and sentence of the prisoner; the dates that he or she was sentenced, received, and discharged; the person's physical and mental health upon admittance and release; the method of discharge and the period of time served in jail; the number of convictions and the places of previous incarceration; and the name of the court and county that tried and sentenced the individual (committing magistrates from 1869 to 1873). Data about whether the inmate had been in the army or navy, or had served an apprenticeship are also included. In addition, the registers provide such information as whether the person's parents were still living when he or she was age sixteen and the age at which schooling was terminated.

EASTERN STATE PENITENTIARY

Although construction of the prison at Philadelphia was authorized by the state legislature in 1821, the first inmates were not received until 1829. The Act of April 10, 1826, stipulated that prisoners sentenced from Adams, Berks, Bradford, Bucks, Centre (as of 1833), Chester, Columbia, Cumberland, Dauphin, Delaware, Franklin, Lancaster, Lebanon, Lehigh, Luzerne, Lycoming, Montgomery, Northumberland, Perry, Philadelphia, Pike, Schuylkill, Susquehanna, Tioga, Union, Wayne, and York Counties were to be incarcerated at this penal facility.

ADMISSION AND DISCHARGE BOOKS, 1844-1888 (RG-15). Normally the books list the name (after July, 1866), prisoner number, race, age, sex, marital status, nativity, occupation, date of admission, length of sentence, and date of discharge of the prisoner; the amount of time that was spent in jail; and the number of

No. A. 7499

Health Officer receipt to be found with commitment

October 20 1894 gave birth to a female child. January 14 1895 child died.

Olematina Scott

alias Olematina Scalpi

Age,	25 years,	
Native of,	Italy	
Bound,	Not	
Trade,	Housekeeper	
Complexion,	Dark	Eyes, Brown Hair, Brown
Stature,	5 ft., 1 in.	Size of foot, 9½ in. Weight, 141
Marks,	None	
No. of Convictions,	1	
Parental at 16,	Both living	
Educational,	Illiterate	Public School, Never years,
Habits,	Moderate	Private School, Never "
Conjugal relations,	Married Child ?	Age on leaving, "
Property,	None	
Crime,	Felonious wounding	
Sentence,	1 years, ——months,	
County and Court,	Lackawanna O.T.Q.S.	April T
Sentenced,	April 19ᵗ 1894	
Received,	May 23ᵗ 1894	
Relatives in Prison,	Whom:	
Fine,	$5⁰⁰	Time expires, by Commutation, 3.19.95
Discharged other than by Com. Law.		

Public Ledger p 103 # V

Judge Ly...

A listing entered in the CONVICT RECEPTION REGISTERS, 1842-1929 (not inclusive), for the Eastern State Penitentiary (RG-15), PSA. Note the data regarding the birth and death of an infant.

previous convictions. Information concerning the inmate's moral habits, hereditary diseases, vaccinations, and physical and mental health (at the time of commitment and discharge) is also included. Entries in the books are arranged by prisoner number.

BERTILLON HAND BOOKS, 1895-1937 (RG-15). The books are arranged and numbered in chronological order according to admittance date. Data usually found include the name, prisoner number, age, color, sex, and county of residence of the convict; the crime, sentence (minimum and maximum) and number of convictions; the dates of sentencing, admission, parole, and discharge; the reason for discharge; and the amount in fines paid.

CONVICT RECEPTION REGISTERS, 1842-1850, 1857-1861, 1866-1873, 1882-1883, 1885-1886, 1888-1929 (RG-15). Contains three series of registers that cover the following periods:

November 25, 1842- April 17, 1916 (not inclusive). The 1842 volume is indexed while all others are arranged and numbered in chronological order by admittance date. As can be seen from the illustration on the next page, entries generally list the name, prisoner number, age, nativity, complexion, occupation, marital status (conjugal relations), education, stature, and habits of the convict; the crime, sentence and number of convictions; the dates of sentencing and reception; the name of the judge (after 1893), county and court where he or she was convicted; the date and reason for discharge; and the amount in fines paid. Additional information such as whether the incarcerated person had any distinguishing marks or scars, owned any property, or had any relatives in prison is also included.

July 6, 1909- May 16, 1918. Besides the data found in the 1842 to 1916 registers, entries in these books show the inmate's religion, color of eyes and hair, foot size and date of birth; the nativity of his or her parents; the maiden name (after 1910) of the convict's mother; the age at which the prisoner left home; and whether the incarcerated person had any children or was living with a spouse. Specific information about the criminal's habits, for example, if he or she was profane or intemperate, smoked or was indolent when arrested is recorded, and data about whether the prisoner was an alien or had been naturalized are supplied. In addition, the names and addresses of the individual's parents, family, or correspondents are regularly noted and up until 1910 details about any crimes or previous criminal records are included. The registers are arranged and numbered in chronological order by admittance date.

March 8, 1910- January 1, 1929. Contains the information found in the 1909-1918 registers plus a record of the dates parole reports were received (until 1921) and statements of the court officers (until 1913) filed. The court officer's declaration ordinarily gives the name of the court and judge where the prisoner was tried and details of the person's crime and criminal record. The registers are arranged and numbered in chronological order by admittance date.

DESCRIPTIVE REGISTERS, October 22, 1829- September 15, 1903 (RG-15). The registers are arranged and numbered according to date of sentencing. Indices are available for prisoners received from October 22, 1829 to June 13, 1895. Normally, entries show the name, prisoner number, age, nativity, occupation, complexion, stature, length of foot, eye and hair color, and marks (scars) of the convict; the dates that he or she was sentenced, received, and discharged; the crime and sentence; the place where the person was sentenced or convicted; the number of times that he or she was convicted or incarcerated; and the date that the sentence was to expire. Written remarks about whether the inmate could read or write, or noting the number of days added to the sentence and why, are sometimes entered as well.

DISCHARGE BOOKS, 1830-1858 (RG-15). Consists of two volumes that cover the following periods:

November 7, 1830- August 29, 1858. The record is arranged by discharge date. From 1830 to 1852 entries as a rule give the name, prisoner number, age, occupation, color, and marital status (from 1835 onward) of the convict; indicate the nationality (after 1849) of the individual; state whether he or she was literate or had a drinking problem; list the person's intended residence (beginning in 1849); and record optional data such as how many times the criminal had been convicted or whether the prisoner was a slave, a runaway, or had living offspring. At various intervals between 1855 and 1858 the record includes data on the person's social relations (that is, parents living or dead), moral habits, temptation to crime, sex, religious training, industrial relations, mental state, appearance (eye and hair colors), physical condition and whereabouts; the name of the court where tried; the dates on which the prisoner was sentenced and received; the actual amount of time served in jail; and the date and method of discharge.

January 7, 1843- December 24, 1857. Entries are arranged chronologically by discharge date and normally indicate the prisoner's name, number, color, county of origin, and date of discharge. In those cases where the individual died or was paroled the date of the event is recorded. The volume would seem to have been kept in order to tabulate discharges using the variable of race.

DISCHARGE DESCRIPTIVE DOCKETS, January 7,1873- March 2,1934 (RG-15). The dockets usually list the name, prisoner number, weight, age (at discharge), sex, crime, and sentence of the prisoner; the dates of sentencing and discharge; the method of discharge; the period of incarceration; the occupation practiced (until 1917) and the education (until 1906) received during imprisonment; the intended residence after release; and the amount of money that was earned in overwork (until 1907) and received upon discharge (from 1908 onward). From 1882 and beyond, the county responsible for sending the criminal to the penitentiary is noted, and occasionally the date on which the person might have been returned to custody is recorded. The amount of property owned by the individual is also sometimes mentioned in the dockets. The dockets are arranged by prisoner discharge date.

MEDICAL STATISTICS BOOK, 1883-1886 (RG-15). A record of prisoners kept by W. D. Robinson, resident physician at the Eastern State Penitentiary. Normally a listing shows the convict's name (until January 30, 1886), prisoner number, age, color, sex, occupation, nativity, marital status, social habits (temperate or not), date of reception, sentence, and number of convictions; indicates the state of the inmate's physical and mental health, and states whether the person had any hereditary diseases in his family or had been protected against smallpox. Occasionally the person's crime and physical location within the prison are also mentioned. The book is organized by prisoner number.

MEDICAL STATISTICS BOOKS, January 1, 1886- March 24, 1900 (RG-15). Entries are arranged by prisoner number and usually record the name (until February 18, 1897), prisoner number, color, age (up to February 15, 1897), sex, nativity, conjugality (marital status), occupation, schooling, health (physical and mental condition, hereditary diseases, vaccinations), habits (that is, abstainer, intemperate, mistress), parental relations (living or dead, cause of death, and age at death), and sentence of the criminal; the number of convictions; and the names of any relatives in prison (also where and for what). Data such as the physical measurements (height and size of head) of the prisoner, the dates of admittance and release, the method of discharge, and the nativity of the parents are found from 1895 onward.

MISCELLANEOUS DESCRIPTIVE BOOKS, 1829-1842 (RG-15). Consists of three volumes that cover the following periods:

October 25, 1829- September 8, 1840. Indexed. An entry generally lists the name and description (place of birth, age, occupation, complexion, foot size, height, scars, and color of eyes and hair) of a prisoner; the crime and sentence; the name of the court where he or she was tried; the dates of sentencing, admittance, and discharge; the method by which the convict was discharged; and the name of the prosecutor in the case.

September 29, 1834- December 8, 1842. Contains short descriptive paragraphs that mention the name, prisoner number, age, place of birth, marital status, physical description (height, foot size, scars, complexion, color of eyes and hair), and occupation of the felon; the status of his or her parents (living or dead); and the number of times that he or she had been convicted. The descriptions are arranged by prisoner number.

October 12, 1839- May 30, 1840. Records the name, prisoner number, color, age, occupation, nativity, state of health, habits (temperate or not), literacy, mental condition, conjugal status, and parental relationships of the incarcerated person; his or her condition as to smallpox; the crime that was committed and the truth of the charge; the length of the individual's imprisonment prior to conviction; the number of times that he or she was convicted; and the date that the prisoner was received. Entries are arranged by prisoner number.

POPULATION RECORDS INDICES, 1900s (RG-15). Is composed of two volumes that were apparently compiled in 1914 and during the 1940s. The indices give the convict's name and prisoner number (present and previous if appropriate). Some of the prisoners whose names are entered in the books were admitted during the 1890s.

RECEPTION DESCRIPTION LIST, January 2, 1879- November 27, 1884 (RG-15). The list is arranged and numbered in order by admittance date. An index is included. Besides showing the name, prisoner number, age, marital status, color, occupation (before and after arrest), place of birth (county), and physical description (complexion, color of eyes and hair from November 19, 1884, onward) of the convict, the list calls for the following entries to be filled in: crime; date and period of sentence; date of reception; number of convictions; county where reared, arrested, tried, and convicted; cause of crime (that is, heredity, education, association); habits (abstainer, moderate, occasionally intemperate, intemperate); parental relations at age sixteen (living, mother living, father living, dead); conjugal relations (single, married, widowed, number of children living); industrial relations (that is, unapprenticed, apprenticed and left, apprenticed and served, trade); education (i.e., private, public, never went, time at, age at leaving, read and write, illiterate, read and write imperfectly); place of previous imprisonment; former prison number; and name of any relative in prison. From time to time the trade that the individual pursued at the age of twenty-one, and from twenty-one to twenty-five, is also noted.

SCRAPBOOKS, 1884-1893, 1908-1917 (RG-15). Consists of newspaper clippings that contain data about inmates, including particulars about their crimes and trials. At times photographs or newspaper sketches are also affixed. The clippings are grouped by the date of the story and thereafter labeled with a prisoner number.

PENNSYLVANIA INDUSTRIAL REFORMATORY AT HUNTINGDON

In reaction to public pressure for the creation of a middle penitentiary district the State legislature in 1878 authorized the construction of such a facility at Huntingdon. In 1881, however, because of

Governor Henry Martyn Hoyt's reforming influence, the legislature converted the institution from a prison to a reformatory for first-offender males between the ages of fifteen and twenty-five.

BERTILLON MEASUREMENT BOOK, October 24, 1907- February 12, 1925 (RG-15). The book is found in the "history file" of the Public Information Office of the Bureau of Corrections. Entries in the volume cover prisoners number 5801 to 14000 and show the name and register number of the prisoner along with his body measurements. Measurements are in centimeters and millimeters and include length and width of head, length of middle and little fingers, length of left foot, length of forearm, length of trunk, length of outstretched arms, length of right ear, and height of inmate. Entries are arranged in numerical order by prisoner register numbers.

BIOGRAPHICAL AND DESCRIPTIVE REGISTERS, 1889-1932 (RG-15). The record is arranged and numbered in chronological order and contains descriptive materials that cover the following time periods:

Biographical Registers, February 16, 1889- September 18, 1891. Entries are dated and usually give the name, prisoner number, age, and place of birth of the offender; the crime and maximum sentence to be imposed; the inmate's condition upon admittance (that is, physical and mental capability, moral susceptibility, and sensitivity); and the location of his parents. Data are also provided regarding the prisoner's antecedents (insanity, epilepsy, dissipation, education, pecuniary condition, occupation, pauperism or criminality) and rearing (family, schools, labor, religion and associations).

Reception Descriptive List, February 16, 1889- December 31, 1903. A typical entry records the name, prisoner number, age, color, physical description (complexion, stature, weight, scars, size of boot worn, color of eyes and hair), occupation (before and at arrest), nativity, habits (abstainer or not), marital status (and number of of children where appropriate), industrial relations (apprenticed or not), education (that is, type, age on leaving, and degree of literacy), crime, and maximum sentence of the prisoner;

the dates of sentencing and reception; the cause of the crime; and the name of the county where he was convicted. Additional data about the inmate, such as whether his parents were alive or dead at age fifteen, whether he had any relatives incarcerated, and what pursuits he had from age fifteen to twenty-five, are also included.

Biographical and Descriptive Registers, February 16, 1889- June 5, 1932. Besides listing the information found in the reception descriptive list, the registers record the date of birth, sex, religion, moral condition, physical status, and mental state of the prisoner; the name of the court where he was tried; and the date of his conviction. In addition, facts regarding the convict's discharge (the date of release, the place of residence, and the physical and mental condition of the subject) and familial relations (parental, sibling and avuncular habits; the occupation of the father; the places of birth of the parents; the criminal records of family members; and data about whether parents and siblings were alive or dead) are frequently included.

PHYSICIAN'S RECORD OF PRISONERS, 1889-1910 (RG-15). The materials are organized by examination date. Two types of records comprise the series:

Physician's Record of Prisoners Examined, 1889-1896, 1903-1907. A typical listing indicates the name, prisoner number, age, color, nativity, trade (that is, with or without), occupation before conviction, schooling (yes or no), habits (temperate or not), conjugal status (number of children where suitable), and sentence of the prisoner; the names of any relatives that he had in prison; his parental relations (living or dead, cause of death and age at death); and his state of physical and mental health. Diverse data about hereditary diseases and parental traits also appear.

Additional Physician's Record, July 25, 1898- February 7, 1910. Besides listing the name, prisoner number, age, color, date of birth and date of examination of the inmate, the record gives a brief medical history of the person and mentions the birthplaces (state or country) of his parents, the occupation of his father, and the parent that he most resembled.

PRISONER'S RECORD, February 16, 1889- September 30, 1921 (RG-15). Entries are arranged and numbered by reception date. Usually a listing shows the name, alias, prison number, age, color, nativity, crime, and maximum sentence of the offender; the dates that he was convicted, sentenced, and received; the name of the court and county where he was tried; and the dates that he was discharged, paroled, or reparoled (or escaped, when pertinent) from prison.

RECORD OF PAROLED MEN, 1890-1894, 1909-1913 (RG-15). The record is arranged by prisoner number and ordinarily lists the name, residence, and prisoner number of the parolee; the dates of his parole and monthly reports; the absolute release date; and the name and address of his employer. Particulars about whether the individual was returned to prison, left employment, or was arrested are also supplied.

REGISTER OF PRISONERS, February 16, 1889- July 14, 1925 (RG-15). The registers are arranged and numbered in chronological order by reception date. Normally, entries give the name and prisoner number of the confined person; the crime and sentence; the dates of sentencing and reception; and the name of the county and court where he was tried and convicted. Occasionally the age, color, and nationality of the individual is provided along with the date on which he was discharged or paroled.

WESTERN STATE PENITENTIARY

Although the state legislature authorized the erection of the prison on the outskirts of Allegheny City (now part of Pittsburgh) in 1818, the first inmates were not received until 1826. The Act of April 10, 1826, stipulated that prisoners sentenced from Allegheny, Armstrong, Beaver, Bedford, Butler, Cambria, Clearfield, Crawford, Erie, Fayette, Greene, Huntingdon, Indiana, Jefferson, Juniata, McKean, Mercer, Mifflin, Potter, Somerset, Venango, Warren, Washington, and Westmoreland counties were to be incarcerated at this penal facility.

ADMISSION AND DISCHARGE BOOKS, 1872-1900 (RG-15). The books are organized by prisoner number. From 1872 to 1891, entries show the name, prisoner number, color, marital status, age, nativity (state or country), sex, occupation, and habits (temperate or not) of the convict; the admission and discharge dates; the amount of time that was spent in county jails; the length of the sentence; the time that was actually served in prison; the number of convictions; and the individual's physical and mental health before, during, and after imprisonment. In addition the books indicate whether the prisoner was vaccinated or paroled. After 1891 the discharge sections of the books are not filled in. Entries in these latter volumes simply record the jailed person's name, prisoner number, color, age, sex, marital status, and condition of health (mental and physical).

COMPLETE REGISTER, DEPUTY'S OFFICE, January 29, 1942-January 7, 1964 (RG-15). The register is in chronological order by dates that prisoners were received and thereunder by prisoner numbers. Typically an entry records the convict's name, color, occupation, and prisoner number; the dates that the person was sentenced, received, and discharged; the length of the sentence; the crime; and the county were sentenced. Notations routinely appear that note when the prisoner was paroled, the date and prison where transferred from, the maximum sentence date, and, if relevant, the old convict number of the inmate.

CONVICT DESCRIPTION AND RECEIVING DOCKETS, January 8, 1872- April 12, 1957 (RG-15). The dockets are arranged and numbered by reception date. From 1872 to 1926, entries normally give the name, prisoner number, age (when received), color, sex, nativity (up to October 30, 1926), physical description (complexion, stature, scars, foot size, height, weight, color of eyes and hair), occupation (before conviction), mental condition (until October 27, 1927), schooling, physical health, habits, parental relations (that is, intemperate or not, whether living or dead at age sixteen), civil condition (marital status and number of living progeny where appropriate), industrial relations (data on apprenticeship and trade skills), crime and sentence of the inmate; the dates of sentencing, reception and discharge; the number of previous convictions; and the name of the county and courts where he or she was convicted. Information regarding the fashion by which the prisoner was released appears and sometimes the amount of property that he or she possessed is included. From 1873 to 1926, data about whether the person served in the army or navy are also recorded.

CONVICT DOCKET, July 31, 1826- March 19, 1859 (RG-15). Indexed. The docket records the name, prisoner number, and sentence of the convict; the dates of sentencing, admittance, and discharge; the method of discharge; and the name of the courts where he or she was tried. Physical descriptions sometimes appear that may indicate the person's age and race, while in other instances the record may state that the offender was a young man or woman. Between April 10, 1837 and February 22, 1839, the docket contains a brief account of the prisoner's trial and sentence instead of descriptive data.

COUNTY AND FEDERAL PRISONERS REGISTER, 1857-1870 (RG-15). Generally the register gives the name, prisoner number, and crime of the convict; the dates of sentencing, reception, and discharge; the length of the sentence; the amount of time that was spent incarcerated; and the name of the county (federal prisoners excepted) where he or she was sentenced. The register is grouped under county and federal headings and thereunder arranged by prisoner number.

DESCRIPTIVE BOOKS, July 31, 1826- February 25, 1873 (RG-15). The books are organized by reception date. Entries usually list the name, prisoner number, age, nativity, physical description (complexion, stature, scars, height, color of eyes and hair), occupation, conjugal status (that is, married, single, widowed; number of living offspring from 1837 onward), literacy (beginning in 1837), crime, and habits (from 1837 onward) of the inmate; the name of the county where he or she was sentenced; the dates of sentencing, reception, and discharge; the length of the sentence; the number of previous convictions; and the number of living offspring that he or she had (from 1837 onward). From 1864 to 1873 the sex, color, residence and means by which the convict was released appear along with the date that the sentence was to expire. Occasionally, remarks are entered in the books that indicate when the individual escaped or died. Of the four books contained in this series, only the volume covering the years 1864 to 1873 is not indexed.

DESCRIPTIVE LISTS, April 24, 1876- February 8, 1956 (RG-15). In most instances the lists record the name, prisoner number, age, sex, color, nativity, mental condition, occupation, marital status (number of living children if apropos), religious belief, physical health, residence, habits (abstainer or not), physical description (build, scars, height, foot size, complexion, and eye and hair colors), fingerprint classification (from March 31, 1922 onward), and sentence of the prisoner; the dates of sentencing and reception; the number of convictions, former prisoner numbers, and locations; the places of previous imprisonment; the nativity of the person's parents (from January 17, 1881 onward); the age at which school was left; the number of years residence in the United States and Pennsylvania (as of September 24, 1897); and the name of the county and court where he or she was convicted. In addition the lists mention whether the inmate served in the army or navy, worked as an apprentice, was naturalized or an alien (as of September 24, 1897), could read and write, or attended a public or private school. From 1876 to 1939, detailed physical measurements (length of arms, trunk, left middle finger, forehead, etc.) of the convict are given, and after August 16, 1922, the prisoner's place and date of birth are recorded. The record is arranged and numbered in chronological order by reception date.

DESCRIPTIVE REGISTER, May 9, 1826- May 13, 1876 (RG-15). The register is arranged and numbered according to the date that the person was sentenced. Entries usually mention the name, prisoner number, age, occupation, nativity, stature, complexion, foot size, marks (scars), and eye and hair colors of the inmate; the dates of sentencing and reception; the crime and sentence; the method of discharge; the number of previous convictions; and the date that the sentence was due to expire. Remarks recording the date on which the imprisoned person died or escaped are sometimes found as well.

DISCHARGE DESCRIPTIVE DOCKETS, January 2, 1873- April 29, 1957 (RG-15). The dockets are organized by prisoner discharge date. Besides recording the criminal's name, prisoner number, age, color, physical condition, mental state, sex, crime, sentence, and occupation (only up to February 27, 1923) while in custody, the dockets list the dates of sentencing and discharge, the time served in prison, and the person's intended residence (until July 31, 1922). The weight of the prisoner when admitted and discharged is at times indicated, and from 1930 onward parole statistics are included. In addition the dockets provide data about the inmate's method of release and county of origin.

HOSPITAL RECORD BOOK, February of 1895 to January of 1902 (RG-15). Entries are grouped by hospitalization date, and usually show a prisoner number, an ailment suffered, the length of treatment, and the dates of death, transfer, or release. Population Indexes must be utilized to determine the actual names of the prisoners.

POPULATION INDEXES, ca. 1826-1960 (RG-15). Contains five volumes of prisoner names and numbers that may be used to extract information from any of the records for the Western State Penitentiary. The following time periods and prisoner numbers are covered by the indices:

July 31, 1826- September 17, 1892, containing prisoner numbers 1-10000; November 7, 1859- April 24, 1902, containing prisoner numbers 2250-A3500; September 17, 1892- June 6, 1918, containing prisoner numbers A1-A9999. May 5, 1902- June 7, 1915, containing prisoner numbers A3501-A8723; June 6, 1918, ca. 1960s, containing prisoner numbers A10000-C3265 inclusive and prisoner numbers up to G2174 not inclusively; March 16, 1934, ca. 1970s, containing prisoner numbers B4000-C33000.

PRISONER IDENTIFICATION CARDS, 1907-1963 (RG-15). A record filed with or created by the Bureau of Identification of the Western Correctional Diagnostic and Classification Center located at Pittsburgh, Pa. The cards are arranged in numerical order by register number (A4683-C7339, not inclusive) and cover individuals sentenced between 1907 and 1963. There are many identification cards missing for the 1907-1920 time period, however. In addition to having a black and white photograph of the inmate from a front and side view, the cards record the name, color, height, weight, age, build (for example, tall or medium stature), complexion (fair, dark brown, black, etc.), eye and hair color, nativity, occupation, address, and register number of the prisoner; the date and county where sentenced; the crime; the term (length) of sentence; the dates of minimum and maximum sentence; and the date and place where the photograph was taken. Space is available for indicating the presence of any identifying marks and scars on the inmate. Likewise, a remarks section is used to report the convict's old register number or, if applicable, date of death. The back of the card has a complete set of fingerprints on it. Some cards bear captions which indicate that they were once part of the files of Eastern State Penitentiary and there is one carton that contains facsimiles of identification records relating to escaped criminals from other prisons (1920-1930s).

VARIOUS

HISTORY FILE OF THE PRESS OFFICE, BUREAU OF CORRECTIONS, 1829-1981 (RG-15). A historical file preserved by the Public Information Office consisting of newspaper clippings and albums, photographs, prisoner identification records, commitment papers, correspondence, receipts, pardons, commutations, histories, publications, reports, annual statements, a Bertillon measurement book, and annual reports which relate to prison institutions at Camp Hill, Dallas, Graterford, Greensburg, Huntingdon, Muncy, Philadelphia (Eastern State Penitentiary), Pittsburgh (Western State Penitentiary), and Rockview. The documents are filed in alphabetical order under prison institution. A container listing is available for reference

LAND RECORDS

(1,115 Cubic Feet)

With the exception of the Revolutionary War years, the Land Office of the Commonwealth has operated continuously since William Penn arrived in Pennsylvania in 1682 and began to administer and sell land. In 1981 the land records and the functions of the office were transferred to the Pennsylvania Historical and Museum Commission. As a result, staff from the Pennsylvania State Archives are responsible for carrying out many of the traditional operations of the Land Office, that is, selling and giving titles to unpatented tracts of land; compiling warrantee township tract maps; constructing connected drafts; processing applications for patents; recording, indexing, and filing deeds applying to land owned or to be acquired by the Commonwealth; and dealing with matters relevant to establishing and marking Pennsylvania's boundaries. Private deeds transferring titles to land are maintained at the office of the recorder of deeds for the appropriate county. While microfilmed copies of many of these deeds are available in the search room of the Archives, they are not searched by staff nor are they filed with the records of the Land Office (Record Group 17). Likewise, researchers who wish to search federal land grants (including military grants made by the United States government) should find them deposited with the National Archives and Records Administration (Washington, D.C. 20408). It should be noted, however, that no such grants were issued in Pennsylvania.

In order to successfully conduct research with the state land records the researcher must first identify the full name of the land purchaser, that is, the applicant, the warrantee, or patentee; the county in which the land was owned; and the approximate date of the transaction. As a general rule, the state land records are not going to provide extensive genealogical information about the purchasers of land, for example, personal data such as the person's nativity, age, marital status, or occupation. They can be used, however, to document the presence of a particular settler in a specific place at a given time, a good starting point to begin or continue a family history. The three basic documents created in the land title process include the warrant, a written certificate authorizing the surveying of land; the survey, a sketch of the warranted land's boundaries (meets and bounds) and total acreage; and the patent, the official deed by which the land passes from the Commonwealth to the private owner. For a thorough understanding of both the history of the Land Office and potential research use and contents of the state land records, researchers should consult Donna Bingham Munger's *Pennsylvania Land Records: A History and Guide for Reseach* (1991). Nonetheless, the following select list of record holdings can be used as a quick reference tool:

ABSTRACTS OF WARRANTS, 1706-1741, 1 volume
ACCOUNTS OF WILLIAM ALLEN'S LAND HOLDINGS, 1733-1753, undated, 1 folder
ACCOUNTS OF WILLIAM PETERS' (ESTATE PAPERS), 1739-1754, 1 box
ALLEGHENY TOWN AND OUT LOTS, 1788-1797, 1806, 1 volume
APPLICATION BOOK - WEST SIDE (OF SUSQUEHANNA RIVER), 1767-1769, 1 volume
APPLICATION BOOKS - EAST SIDE (Nos. 1 and 2), 1765-1769, 2 volumes
   Applications, 1742-1865, 2 cartons
   Applications for and Release of Liens, 1850 (1870-1873)
   1898, 1929, 1 carton
APPLICATIONS FOR ISLANDS, 1757 (1757)-1793, 1912, 3 cartons
APPLICATIONS FOR ISLANDS, 1791-1811, 1 volume
APPLICATIONS FOR PATENTS, 1870-1953, 6 cartons
APPLICATIONS FOR SURVEY LAST PURCHASE, 1769-1774, 1 volume
APPLICATIONS FOR WARRANTS, 1732-1767, 8 volumes
APPLICATIONS FOR WARRANTS, 1734-1952, 70 cartons
APPLICATIONS FOR WARRANTS [PREEMPTION], 1785, 1 box
APPLICATIONS FOR WARRANTS [LARGE LOTS], 1792, 1 box
APPLICATIONS FOR WARRANTS TO RIVER BEDS, 1803, 1848-1865, 20 folders
APPLICATIONS FOR WARRANTS WITHDRAWN, 1874-1912, 1 carton
APPLICATIONS FOR VACANT LAND UNDER THE ACT OF ASSEMBLY APPROVED MARCH 28, 1905, 1905-1927, 1 volume

APPLICATIONS NEW PURCHASE, 1769, 1 volume

BAYNTON (JOHN) AND WHARTON (SAMUEL) WARRANTS, 1762-1766, 5 folders

BEAVER TOWN LOTS, 1793-1848, 1 volume

BOARD OF PROPERTY DOCKETS, 1808-1952, 2 volumes

BOARD OF PROPERTY MINUTE BOOKS, 1765-1980, 14 volumes

BOARD OF PROPERTY PAPERS, 1682-1947, 18 cartons

   Board of Property Petitions, 1682-1903, 4 cartons

CAVEAT BOOKS, 1748-1940, 17 volumes

   Caveats, 1700 1910, 7 cartons

CERTIFICATES OF EXONERATION, 1765-1856, 1 carton

CERTIFICATES OF INDEBTEDNESS (vouchers for providing supplies in the revolution), 1780, 1 box

CERTIFICATES OF PAYMENT OF PURCHASE MONEY, 1786-1809, 5 cartons

CERTIFIED TOWNSHIPS OF LUZERNE COUNTY (SURVEYS AND PATENTS), undated, 1 volume

   Classification Seventeen Townships of Luzerne County, undated, 1 volume

COATES ESTATE, ABRAHAM, 1782, 1 volume

   Commission Books, 1733-1809, 6 volumes

COMMISSIONERS OF PROPERTY MINUTES (Books C-I,K), 1685-1692, 1701 1709,1712-1741 (includes a deed book and other records for Philadelphia County), 8 volumes

COMMONWEALTH DEED BOOKS (relates to instruments pertaining to the capitol park, Department Of Forestry, and state institutions between 1822-1921) undated, 7 volumes

CONNECTICUT CLAIMANTS [MINUTES OF EVIDENCE RESPECTING TITLES], undated, 3 volumes

COPIED SURVEYS, ca. 1682-1900s, 477 volumes

COPIED SURVEYS (Henry Houck, Secretary of Internal Affairs), 1910-1912, 4 volumes

DEED BOOK OF (JOHN) NICHOLSON LANDS [SOLD UNDER ACT OF 1840], 1 volume

DEED REGISTER OF THE STATE FORESTRY RESERVE PROPERTY IN THE DEPARTMENT OF INTERNAL AFFAIRS UNDER ACT OF 1919 (contains instruments dated 1763-1908), ca. 1919, 1 volume

Warrant No.65 dated February 14, 1782, to survey 319 1/4 acres of land in Westmoreland County. The land was purchased by George Washington from John Bishop. WARRANTS, 1682-Present (RG-17), PSA.

DEED REGISTERS - GAME PRESERVES UNDER 1919 ACT, 1919-1964, 31 volumes

> *Depositions, 1717-1867* (relating to property, 1683-1867), 5 cartons

DEPRECIATION LAND MAPS, 1785-1789, 15 folders

> *Deputy Surveyors' Certificates,* 1792-1795, 1 carton

DEPUTY SURVEYORS' LISTS OF RETURNS, 1762-1887, 10 volumes

DONATION LAND CLAIMANT PAPERS AND MISCELLANEOUS PATENTS, ca. 1785-1810, 4 cartons

DONATION LAND MAPS, 1785-1786, 27 folders

EAST SIDE APPLICATIONS REGISTERS, 1765-1769, 2 volumes

EAST SIDE APPLICATIONS BOOK (compiled in 1949), undated, 1 volume

EAST SIDE OF SUSQUEHANNA APPLICATION BOOK, 1765-1769, 1 volume

ERIE LOTS, 1801-1810, 1 volume

ERIE LOTS - RESERVE TRACTS - WATER LOTS, 1796-1815, 1 volume

ERIE, FRANKLIN, WARREN, AND WATERFORD TOWN OUT LOTS, 1797-1809, 1 volume

ESCHEATS, 1846-1946, 1 carton

GENERAL CORRESPONDENCE OF THE SECRETARY, 1713-1882, 60 boxes

GENERAL CORRESPONDENCE OF THE SURVEYOR GENERAL, 1682-1873, 2 boxes

HOLLAND LAND COMPANY PREVENTION CERTIFICATES, 1798, 1 carton; 1 box

INDEX TO CAVEAT BOOKS, 1748-1798, 2 volumes

INDEX TO EAST SIDE APPLICATIONS (Nos. 1-4160), 1765-1767, 1 volume

INDEX TO NEW PURCHASE APPLICATIONS (Nos. 1-3854), 1769, 1 volume

ISLANDS IN THE RIVERS (WARRANT REGISTERS), 1797-1903, 2 volumes

ISLANDS IN THE RIVERS DELAWARE, OHIO, ALLEGHENY, SCHUYLKILL, ETC. (WARRANT REGISTER), 1798, 1806-1903, 1 volume

ISLANDS IN THE SUSQUEHANNA RIVER (REGISTER OF APPLICATIONS), 1793-1812, 1 volume

ISLANDS - ORDERS RELATING TO, 1793-1901, 4 cartons

ISLANDS IN THE SUSQUEHANNA RIVER (WARRANT REGISTER), 1797-1857, 1 volume

JOURNAL FOR DEPRECIATION LANDS, BEAVER AND PHILADELPHIA LOTS, 1785-1896, 1 volume

JOURNALS FOR ERIE, FRANKLIN, WARREN, AND WATERFORD LOTS, 1801-1920, 5 volumes

LAND LIEN DOCKETS, 1864-Present, 4 volumes

LAND WARRANT AND PATENT RECEIPTS, 1781-1809, 8 cartons

LAST PURCHASE (WARRANT REGISTERS), ca. 1785-1820s, undated, 4 volumes

LAST PURCHASE MAPS, 1791-1799, 30 folders

LEASES AND RELEASES, 1684-1706, 3 volumes

LEDGER OF DEPRECIATION LANDS, PHILADELPHIA AND BEAVER TOWN LOTS, 1785 (1785-1809)-1897, 1 volume

LEDGERS FOR ERIE, FRANKLIN, WARREN, AND WATERFORD LOTS, 1801-1923, 4 volumes

LETTER BOOKS OF THE SECRETARY, 1800-1811, 1838-1839, 2 volumes

LETTER BOOKS OF THE SURVEYOR GENERAL, 1762-1764, 1810-1821, 2 volumes

LETTER PRESS BOOKS OF THE SURVEYOR GENERAL, 1870-1875, 6 volumes

LETTERS OF ATTORNEY AND INDEXES, 1684-1812, 22 volumes

LETTERS - PENNSYLVANIA CLAIMANTS, 1800-1804, 1 volume

LISTS OF DEPUTY SURVEYORS, 1713-1850, 1 volume

LISTS OF COUNTY SURVEYORS, 1850-1957, 2 volumes

LISTS OF SALES, PHILADELPHIA LOTS, 1781-1782, 1 volume

LUZERNE RELEASE BOOKS, 1800-1822, 2 volumes

Logan Correspondence, James, 1712-1722, 1 folder

LONDON LAND COMPANY PAPERS, 1689, 1783, 1 folder

MAPS OF CERTIFIED LUZERNE TOWNSHIPS (includes Bedford, Braintrim, Exeter, Hanover, Huntingdon, Kingston, Newport, Northmoreland, Pittston, Plymouth, Providence, Putnam, Salem, Springfield, Ulster, and Wilkes-Barre), ca.1804-1810, undated, 18 items

MAPS AND RELATED RECORDS OF THE COMMONWEALTH'S BOUNDARIES (includes copies of maps dating back to 1786), 1837-1982, undated, 13 boxes; 1 map drawer

MAPS OF LAST PURCHASE DISTRICTS, 1791-1799, 30 items

MAPS OF PROPRIETARY MANORS, 1717-1776, 34 items

MAPS OF PROPRIETARY TOWNS (includes Bedford, Carlisle, Easton, Reading, Sunbury, and York), ca. 1762-1767, 16 items

MARKHAMS [WILLIAM] BOOK (844 Warrants), 1682-1685, 1 volume

Melish Maps - Papers Relating to, 1815-1826., 2 boxes

MINUTES OF THE NICHOLSON COURT OF PLEAS, 1841-1843, 1 volume

Muster Rolls, 1782-1834, 1 folder

NEW CASTLE COUNTY SURVEY NOTES [WALTER WHARTON'S LAND SURVEY REGISTER], 1675-1679, 1 volume

NEW CASTLE, KENT, AND SUSSEX SURVEYS, 1683-1722, 1 volume

NEW PURCHASE BLOTTERS [DAY BOOKS OF LAST AND NEW PURCHASES, nos. 1-2], 1785-1794, 1799-1801, 2 volumes

NEW PURCHASE DAY BOOKS OF THE RECEIVER GENERAL (nos. 1-5), 1785-1809, 5 volumes

NEW PURCHASE JOURNALS, 1785-1900, 6 volumes

NEW PURCHASE LEDGERS AND INDEXES, 1785-1900, 9 volumes

NEW PURCHASE REGISTERS, 1769, 2 volumes

NICHOLSON (JOHN) LANDS - COMMISSIONERS RETURN OF SALES, ca. 1806, 1 volume

OLD PURCHASE BLOTTERS (Nos. 1-8), 1784-1802, 8 volumes

OLD PURCHASE DAY BOOKS OF THE RECEIVER GENERAL (Nos. 1-46), 1720-1779, 1781-1809, 46 volumes

   Old Purchase Journals, 1701-1710, 1712-1779, 1781-1836, 1839-1955, 41 volumes

OLD PURCHASE LEDGERS AND INDEXES, 1701-1955, 71 volumes

OLD RIGHTS, 1682-1729, 4 volumes

OLD RIGHTS [BUCKS AND CHESTER COUNTIES], 1682-1740, 1 volume

OLD RIGHTS, BUCKS COUNTY, 1682 (1683-1752)-1758, 2 volumes

OLD RIGHTS, CHESTER COUNTY, 1682 (1684-1717)-1763, 1 volume

OLD RIGHTS, PHILADELPHIA, 1682-1725, 1 volume

OLD RIGHTS, PHILADELPHIA, CHESTER, BUCKS, NEW CASTLE, KENT, AND SUSSEX COUNTIES, 1685-1691, 1712-1720, 1 volume

ORDERS TO SURVEY FOR USE OF PROPRIETARIES, 1746-1747, 1 volume

ORIGINAL PURCHASES (covering warrants, surveys, and returns of survey for first purchasers and their under purchasers, 1682-1764), undated, 1 volume

PATENT BOOKS, SERIES A, AA, P AND H, 1683-Present, 189 volumes

PATENT BOOKS (Nos. 1-2011), 1733-1759, 3 volumes

PATENT INDEXES, 1730-present, 12 volumes

PATENT REGISTERS, 1700-1728, 2 volumes

PATENT REGISTERS, 1781-1786, 1873-1933, 3 volumes

PATENTS BY THE ROYAL GOVERNORS OF NEW YORK, 1667-

1679, 1681-1682, 1 volume
PATENTS, 1677-1682, PROPRIETARY WARRANTS [RECORD OF
LANDS, WITHIN UPLAND COURT JURISDICTION IN DELAWARE
RIVER - RECORDED IN THIS BOOK JULY OF 21ST 1759],
1670-1685, 1 volume
PHILADELPHIA CITY LOTS - PAPERS RELATING TO, 1682-1797,
4 folders
PHILADELPHIA OLD RIGHTS, 1682-1745, 1 volume
POPULATION LAND COMPANY PREVENTIVE CERTIFICATES,
ca.1792-1798, 1 carton
PROOF OF SETTLEMENT CERTIFICATES, ca. 1792-1865, 4
cartons
PROPRIETARY RIGHTS INDEX (AND TRANSCRIPT), 1683-1772,
Undated, 2 volumes
PROPRIETARY TOWNS - PAPERS RELATING TO, 1754-1811, 9
folders
   Purchase Vouchers (New and Old Purchase), 1784-1949, 59
   cartons
QUIT RENT BOOKS,1741-1742, 1757-1776, 2 volumes
QUIT RENT ROLLS, 1703-1744, 22 volumes
RECEIVER GENERAL'S DAY BOOK OF SALES BY AUCTION,
1785-1809, 1 volume
RECORD OF DEEDS FOR PENAL AND CHARITABLE INSTITU-
TIONS (relates to instruments recorded between 1765-1897),
undated, 1 volume
RECORD OF LAND APPLICANTS, 1784-1786, 1794, 6 volumes
RECORDS RELATING TO TOWN AND OUT LOTS, ca. 1787-
1795, 2 cartons
RENT ROLLS, 1683-1776, Indexed, 22 volumes
RETURN OF SURVEYS, 1678-1870, 103 cartons
RETURNS OF SURVEY, 1674-1870, 21 volumes
SEVENTEEN CERTIFIED TOWNSHIPS (CONNECTICUT
CLAIMS), ca. 1799-1810, 11 cartons; 9 flat boxes
SEVENTEEN CERTIFIED TOWNSHIPS, SURVEYS AND CER-
TIFICATES, 1895-1912, 12 volumes
SPECIAL APPLICATIONS,, 1760-1765, 1 volume
STEEL'S RENT ROLL FOR PHILADELPHIA, 1731, 1 volume

SUNBURY, FRANKLIN, WARREN, AND BEAVER TOWN LOTS -
FRANKLIN, WARREN, WATERFORD RESERVE TRACTS (REGIS-
TER), undated, 1 volume
SURVEYS, 1682-Present, 152 cartons; 1 box
TITLE PAPERS, 1695-1836, 6 cartons
   Town Lots - Papers Relating to, ca. 1787-1795, 1 carton
TRACT PATENT NAME INDEX, undated, 4 volumes
TRANSMITTAL OF WARRANTS, 1781, 1789-1809, 3 cartons
UNPATENTED LAND LISTS, 1820-1837, 5 boxes
UNPATENTED LAND TICKETS, 1822-1827, 3 boxes
VIRGINIA CLAIMS, 1779-1780, 2 volumes
WARRANT BOOKS, 1682-1797, 4 volumes
WARRANT BOOKS, 1733-1753, 8 volumes
WARRANT BOOKS (COPIES OF WARRANTS, ETC.), 1682-1741,
4 volumes
WARRANT BOOKS (Nos. 8-25), 1775-1776, 1781-1814, 1827-
1848, 1863-1888, 16 volumes
WARRANT REGISTER INDEX OF THE SURVEYOR GENERAL,
1684-1864, 6 boxes
WARRANT REGISTERS (GREEN AND WHITE BOOKS), 1733-
present, 31 volumes
WARRANT TRACT MAPS, 1907-1993, 15 cubic feet
WARRANTS, 1682-1715, 4 volumes
WARRANTS, 1682-present, 208 cartons; 3 boxes
WARRANTS (COPIES OF NEW WARRANTS IN SURVEYOR GEN-
ERAL'S OFFICE), 1682-1759, 12 volumes
WARRANTS - PETER GROVENDIKE [A LIST OF WARRANTS
RENEWED OF PETER GROVENDIKE BY THE GOVERNOR'S
WARRANT BEARING DATE THE 31ST DAY OF THE 5TH
MONTH 1684], 1675-1684, 1 volume
WEST SIDE (OF SUSQUEHANNA RIVER) APPLICATIONS REG-
ISTER, 1766-1769, 1 volume
   West Side Applications, 1766-1769, 2 volumes
WHITESIDE MAPS, 1817-1818, approximately 50 items

In order to locate untitled tracts of land, the Land Office started
preparing warrant tract maps in 1907. Besides listing the names
of the warrantees and patentees, the maps show the size (acres

and perches) and boundaries (courses and distances) of the tracts; the location of each piece of land in relation to other adjoining property holders and occasionally physical landmarks (rivers, streams, lakes); the dates that the land was warranted, surveyed, and patented; and where relevant, the name of the tract or an indicator that the person might be deceased. Warrantee tract maps are currently complete for twenty-four counties (Allegheny, Beaver, Cameron, Dauphin, Elk, Erie, Fayette, Greene, Lackawanna, Lancaster, Lawrence, Luzerne, McKean, Mercer, Perry, Pike, Potter, Sullivan, Susquehanna, Tioga, Venango, Warren, Washington, and Wayne). Select townships have been mapped for ten other counties. A complete list of township maps available by counties is found in the appendices to this book.

Other pertinent official land records in the custody of the of the State Archives include these series: GOVERNOR'S ACCOUNTS (contains fees paid for patents issued, November 1, 1759- October 29, 1760), 1742-1752, 1759-1763 (RG-21); MORTGAGES AND RELATED VALUATIONS, 1773-1793 (RG-8); MORTGAGE BOOKS, 1774-1788 (RG-8); SHERIFF'S DEED BOOKS, 1796-1876 (RG-33); and INDIAN DEED BOOK, ca. 1815 (RG-26). Unfortunately, with the exceptions of the mortgage books, the mortgages and valuations, and the sheriff's deed books, none of these records is indexed. On the other hand, the mortgage materials were created by the General Loan Office and are indexed by mortgagor's surname. Usually the documents give the name, residence and occupation of the mortgagor; a description of the land being mortgaged; and the amount of the mortgage. The sheriff's deed books are dockets filed with the Eastern District of the Supreme Court of Pennsylvania and relate to property sold at public auction. Except in rare cases they seldom give more than a description of the property and the names of the new and old owners.

CHURCH AND CEMETERY RECORDS
(6 Cubic Feet)

The State Archives has acquired a modest number of church and cemetery records relating primarily to the central Pennsylvania region, by virtue of its location in Harrisburg. Most of these materials, however, have traditionally either been retained by the churches that generated them or deposited at local historical societies. Some of the genealogically significant records which the Division of Archives and Manuscripts has obtained include these:

ALLEGHENY COUNTY HOME FOR THE INSANE AND TUBERCULOSIS SANITARIUM, CEMETERY DIAGRAM, 1920 (RG-23). The diagram, from the Woodville State Hospital records, is dated 1920 and drawn to a one inch equals twenty feet scale. There are 196 burial plots depicted, with each grave site listing the plot number and name of the person interred. Researchers must obtain written permission from the Department of Public Welfare before examining this item.

CHAPEL CEMETERY (BEAVER COUNTY) DOCUMENTATION, 1982 (MG-8). A mimeographed report prepared by Michael E. Lutz that shows the following information extracted from gravestones for each individual buried in this Monaca, Pa. cemetery: name, date or year of birth, date or year of death, location of burial plot, and often familial relationship (father, wife, son, daughter, etc.). In cases where the deceased was a member of the military, his rank, unit, and the war he served in are recorded. A plan showing the location of each numbered gravestone in the cemetery is included in the report as an index. Entries on the list appear in numerical order by gravestone number.

CHISUK EMUNA CONGREGATION OF HARRISBURG (DAUPHIN COUNTY) RECORDS, 1883-1983 (MG-3). For the most part microfilmed copies of minutes, membership accounts, news clippings, and business records. Also include, however, are cemetery lot records, 1937-1968, and cemetery records, 1879, 1884, 1904, 1931, 1949-1974, that contain data about burials and deaths.

CHRIST LUTHERAN CHURCH (LUZERNE COUNTY) PAMPHLET, 1910 (MG-8). Found among the J. Augustus Schmidt Papers, 1894-1911, is a pamphlet called "In Memory of Those Who Died During the Twenty Years from October 1, 1890- October 1, 1910, and Were Buried by Rev. J.O. Schlenker, Pastor of Christ Lutheran Church, Hazelton, Pa." Entries are in chronological order and give the person's name, date of death, and age (years, months, and days).

CONCORD CONGREGATION OF PLEASANTVILLE (VENANGO COUNTY) SESSION BOOK, 1843-1882 (MG-3). Entries in the book are grouped by events and thereunder arranged chronologically. The following information is found:

Record of Marriages. Entries show the names of the couple being married and the date of their union.

Record of Baptisms. Information varies with each entry, but normally researchers may expect to find the name of the baptized person, the date of the christening, and the names of the parents.

Record of Deaths. A typical listing usually gives the name of the deceased person and the date of his or her death. At times the age of the individual at death is noted and familial relationships designated.

CORNWALL METHODIST EPISCOPAL CHURCH (LEBANON COUNTY) RECORDS, 1849-1974 (MG-262). Contains microfilmed membership lists, Sunday school class records, and the following baptism, marriage and death records:

Record of Baptisms, April 4, 1859- April 15, 1973. The books are arranged by dates of baptism and include church members who were born from 1842 to 1972. Information recorded includes the baptized person's name, address (after August 5, 1956), date of birth, and date of baptism; the place of birth (after July 10, 1864); and the names of the parents, officiating minister, and witnesses. Remarks sometimes appear that note the date of death of the person (1864-1878) or the church status of the parents (1956-1973).

Record of Marriages, September 22, 1859- December 24, 1930, March 23, 1935-April 6, 1973. Normally the registers give the names and residences of the couples; the date of marriage; the marriage or license number (from 1895 onward); and the names of the officiating minister and witnesses. At various intervals, however, the ages of the husband (1865-1878, 1895-1956) and wife (1895-1956); the occupation of the male (1865-1878, 1895-1930); and the skin color of the man (1895-1930) are recorded. Likewise from 1895 to 1930, there is space for recording the maiden name of the wife, if a widow; the names of the couple's parents and their nationality; and the maiden name of the couple's mothers. Unfortunately, in most instances this data is not filled in. The books are arranged in chronological order by date of marriage.

Record of Funerals-Deaths, March 22, 1935- April 26, 1973. From 1935 to 1970 entries usually show the name and age of the deceased person; the date and place of the funeral; the names of the officiating minister and the funeral director; and the date of death (from October 22, 1952). Occasionally familial relationships also are recorded. After January 6, 1970, the date of burial is no longer listed. The records are arranged in chronological order by either date of burial or date of death.

CURTIN IRON WORKS, LEDGER, October 25, 1899- April 19, 1937 (MG-155). The ledger has accounts of burials by the Eagle Cemetery Association. Besides recording the fee collected, the record mentions the name of the person buried, the date of burial, and the lot number. Entries are in chronological order by burial date.

DIXMONT STATE HOSPITAL, LISTING OF PERSONS BURIED IN GRAVES ON HOSPITAL GROUNDS, May 26, 1863- June 5, 1937 (RG-23). A typed list in alphabetical order that gives the deceased patient's name, age, sex, and nativity; the date of death; and the grave number. The information was extracted from the hospital's MORTUARY RECORD, 1857-1951 (RG-23) and contains 1,354 grave sites. The original index cards used to create this list and a listing arranged in numerical order by grave number also are available. Researchers must obtain written permission from the Department of Public Welfare before being able to use these records.

FIRST PRESBYTERIAN CHURCH OF CARLISLE RECORDS (CUM-
BERLAND COUNTY), 1785-1920 (MG-262). The collection is on
microfilm and comprises these records:

Minute Book, 1816-1834. May contain data about the church
member's familial relationships, race, and dates of admittance or
dismissal. In those cases where a church elder died the date of
death is normally indicated.

Miscellaneous Lists, 1785-1914. Consists of lists of subscribers,
and the following:

An Alphabetical List of the Members in Communion of the
Presbyterian Church, ca. 1785-1914. Entries show the person's name and where appropriate the dates of his or her
admittance, dismissal, suspension, or death.

A Register of Children Baptized, 1835-1838. A typical listing
gives the name of the child baptized, the names of the parents, the dates of birth and baptism, and the name of the
minister who performed the ceremony.

Baptisms, October 30, 1806- July 3, 1815. Usually, entries
simply record the person's name and date of baptism, but at
times familial relationships are mentioned along with the
name of the baptizer.

Persons Married by Robert Davidson at Carlisle, 1785-1789.
In actuality the list has the names of married couples and the
dates of their unions from March 1, 1785, to November 6, 1817.

Pew Records, 1828-1841. A typical entry simply mentions the
name of the church member, the date, and the amount of
money paid for pew usage.

Register, 1785 -1812. Has the following sections:

Admissions by Certificates and Professions of Faith, 1785-1813,
1816-1854. Ordinarily a listing shows only an individual's name
and the date of admission.

Adult Baptisms, November 11, 1820- January 14, 1892, March

24, 1895- December 11, 1899. Each entry usually gives the name of the person baptized, the date of the baptism, and the name of the person performing the ceremony. Occasionally family relationships are also depicted.

Child Baptisms, October 30, 1806- September 14, 1918. Data found include the name of the baptized child, the date of the baptism, the names of the parents, and the name of the officiating minister.

Marriages, ca. 1789-1800, 1819-1835, 1848-1925. Usually, entries record the name of the couple, the date of their union, and the name of the individual marrying them. From 1824 to 1835 the residence of the married couple is regularly listed. Many of the listings from 1789 to 1800 are illegible.

All of the materials are arranged chronologically. A printed copy of church marriages, ca. 1785-1812, which is arranged alphabetically by couple's surname, also appears on the microfilm.

GERMAN LUTHERAN PARISH REGISTERS, 1745-1972 (MG-262). Microfilmed transcripts of Adams County church records that were compiled and collected by Pastor Frederick S. Weiser and a staff of volunteers. The following records are included among the holdings:

Benders Church, near Biglerville (Butler Township). Parish Registers, 1860-1898. Indexed. Consists of baptisms, marriages, and burials. The baptisms are from June 9, 1860 to November 9, 1898, and show the name, date of birth, and date of baptism of the child; the parent's names; and the sponsors. Burial entries, September 11, 1880- March 27, 1899, record the name, age, and date of death of the deceased. Only two marriage records for 1895 and 1896 are present. These entries give the names of the couples and the dates of their unions.

Bethlehem Lutheran Church, Bendersville (Menallen Township). Parish Registers, 1879-1965. Indexed baptism, marriage, and burial data. The entries for baptisms record the child's name, date of birth, and date of baptism along with the parents' names. Adult baptisms normally do not include the names of parents but do sometimes note that the baptized was the spouse of a named church member. Marriage entries have the names and residences (up to March 24, 1948) of the couples as well as the date of union. Burial information consists of the deceased person's name, age, date of death, and place of burial (cemetery).

Chestnut Grove Evangelical Lutheran Church (Latimore Township). The indexed membership records, 1867-1967, have the following categories of data:

Births and Baptisms, 1867-1899, 1905-1906, 1908-1967. Contains birth data for members from 1848-1903, not inclusive. Entries identify the parents and sponsors and give the child's name, date of birth, and date of baptism.

Deaths, September 12, 1867- October 14, 1967. Data normally appearing includes the name, age, and date of death of the church member. From 1867-1907 and 1904-1967, however, the cause of death and the place of burial are shown, respectively.

Marriages, June 16, 1868- May 27, 1967. Information recorded can be as little as the names, residences, and dates of union of the couple to inclusion of the parent's, witness's, and minister's names.

Christ Evangelical Church, also known as Lower Bermudian Church (Latimore Township). Registers, 1865-1909. Indexed. Includes baptism records, December 2, 1865- October 24, 1909, that list the child's name, date of birth, date of baptism, and parent's names; marriage records, January 1, 1866- January 16, 1910, that give the date of the marriage along with the names of the couple and the bride's father; and death records, March 29, 1866- July 14, 1909, that show the church member's name, age, date of death, and often, cause of death.

Christ Lutheran Church, Gettysburg (Cumberland Township). Record Books, 1837-1930. The volumes are indexed and have the following entries:

Admissions, 1838-1854. Lists the member's name and date of admission, the mode of admission, and in the form of remarks whether he or she was removed from the rolls or died.

Baptisms, 1837-1911, 1914-1928. Shows the baptized person's name, age, or birthday; if a child, the parent's names; by whom baptized (1837-1839); and the sponsors (from 1840 to 1899).

Deaths, 1841-1911, 1914-1930. Gives the dead person's name, age, date of death, and place of interment (1914-1930). A remarks section sometimes is utilized to record familial relationships that existed, the cause of death, or the names of clergy conducting the burial services.

Marriages, 1847-1910, 1914-1930. Provides the names and residences of the husband and wife; the name of the officiating pastor; and the date of marriage.

Christ Reformed Church, Littlestown (Germany Township). Registry, 1747-1871. Consists of a record of baptisms that covers member's births from 1734 to 1870. Entries list the name, date of birth, and date of baptism of the child; the parent's names; and the names of the sponsors. Often, the sponsor's relationship to the child is noted.

Conewago Chapel, Roman Catholic (Conewago Township). Register, 1790-1835. Indexed. Contains information about marriages (names of parties and date of) from February 23, 1796 to April 21, 1835; baptisms (name, dates of birth and baptism of child; names of parents and sponsors), November 18, 1790 to April 30, 1815; and deaths and burials (dates of; and name, age, and familial status of the deceased), November 4, 1791 to October 9, 1833.

Evangelical Lutheran and Reformed Congregation (Menallen Township). Contains a communicant's list, ca. 1805-1857, and the following:

Joint Baptismal Protocol, December 27, 1780- April 24, 1852. Shows the name, date of birth, and date of baptism of the child; the names of the parents; and the sponsors' names.

First Evangelical Lutheran Church, New Oxford (Oxford Township). Parish Registers, 1881-1966. Indexed and including baptisms of infants, November 12, 1881- July 10, 1966, that identify the parents and sponsors and show the baby's name,

date of birth, and date of baptism; burials, August 23, 1884-
June 30, 1966, that record the church member's name, age,
date of death, date of burial (1949-1966), and place of burial;
and marriages, July 24, 1892- August 20, 1966, that list the
date of wedlock and the names and residences of the husband
and wife. There are several marriage entries that date from
1852-1885, and a couple of death records for 1879 and 1881.

*Flohr's Evangelical Lutheran Church, McKnightstown (Franklin
Township)*. Indexed records of baptisms, burials, and marriages for
the following periods:

Baptisms, June 8, 1866- June 9, 1935. Includes birth data from
1861 to 1935 and shows the child's name, date of birth, date of
baptism, and parents.

Burials, August 14, 1887- June 14, 1935. Lists the name, age,
date of death, and place of burial of the deceased. Remarks,
that give the dead person's family status, that is, mother, wife,
child of, etc. are also present.

*German Reformed and Evangelical Lutheran Congregations at
Mark's or White Church (Mount Joy Township). Register, 1836-1926*.
Indexed. Has these sections:

Baptisms, February 6, 1836- April 19, 1924. Entries record the
name, date of birth, and date of baptism of the child; the names
of the parents; and if not the parents, the names of the sponsors.

Funerals, September 13, 1884- June 7, 1926. Typically provides
the name and age of the deceased; the date of the funeral; and
the officiating pastor's name.

*Grace Evangelical Lutheran Church, Two Taverns (Mount Joy
Township). Church Records, 1888-1959*. Indexed and including
baptisms of infants, July 8, 1888- December 20, 1959, that identify the parents and show the baby's name, date of birth, date of
baptism, and sometimes, date of death; baptisms of adults, April
14, 1946- March 27, 1958, that have the name, date of birth, and
at times, family status (wife, son, etc.) of the proselyte; burials,
April 26, 1888- February 25, 1928, that list the church member's

name, age, and date of death along with the name of the officiating pastor; and marriages, August 6, 1889- August 14, 1929, that record the date of the wedding, the names and residences of husband and wife, and usually, the name of the pastor who conducted the service.

Holy Trinity Lutheran Church, York Springs (Huntingdon Township). Church Records, 1831-1857 include the following:

Records of the Huntingdon Church, 1831-1855. Besides lists of communicants, 1839-1847, records of the church council's minutes, 1831-1855, the record has an index to baptisms and baptismal entries, April 9, 1840- April 28, 1842, that give the name, birth date, and christening date of the child; and the names of the parents and sponsors.

Records, 1831-1957. Indexed. Consists of baptisms, February 15, 1854- August 16, 1866, that provide the child's name, date of birth (1854-1859, 1866), date of baptism, and parent's and sponsor's names; marriages, November 28, 1842- January 17, 1867, that record the date of wedlock, names and residences of the couples, and pastor's name; and deaths, November 21, 1842- January 1, 1867, that give the name, age, and date of death of the deceased along with the minister conducting the burial service. At times, the cause of death and place of burial also are noted.

Record Book of the Petersburg Charge, 1842-1870. The book is in alphabetical order by surnames and contains baptismal entries, December 10, 1842- December 10, 1854, that record the child's name, date of birth, and date of baptism along with the identities of the parents and sponsors.

Church Register of the Petersburg Charge, 1848-1855. A list that shows the names of church members and in some cases the spouse to whom they were married. Notations appear too that indicate the passing away of members, usually with the exact dates of death.

Records, 1866-1890. Indexed. Consists of births and baptisms, April 20, 1867- April 2, 1886; marriages, April 18, 1867-

December 28, 1886; and deaths, May 29, 1867- November 5, 1888. For the most part, the information recorded is similar to that found in the 1831-1957 record. Under marriages, however, the names of the parents or witnesses appear. Likewise, the death records normally include the cause of death and the place of interment.

Parochial Register, 1890-1957. Indexed. Contains baptisms of infants, April 4, 1890-December 9, 1956, that were born between 1889-1956; marriages, August 29, 1889- February 14, 1957; and burials, April 29, 1889- December 8, 1956. The data is the same as that provided in the 1831-1957, and 1866-1890 records.

Lutheran and Reformed Congregations, Arendtsville (Franklin Township). Became the Trinity Lutheran Church and the Zion United Church of Christ, both of Arendtsville.

Joint Church Register and Baptismal Book, 1785-1874. Indexed. Contain entries regarding church baptisms that list the names of the parents and sponsors along with the child's name, date of birth, and date of baptism.

Register of Marriages, 1804. Six records that give the names of the parties, the date of union, and whose daughter the wife was.

Lutheran and Reformed Union Congregation, Lower Bermudian. Has a church book with the following data:

Baptisms, March 19, 1745- October 6, 1864. Identifies the parents and witnesses and gives the infant's name and date of christening. The date of birth of the child starts to appear in the 1760s but not on a consistent basis until 1775.

Marriages, October 10, 1758- November 30, 1772. Data varies but in addition to the names and date of marriage of the couple, entries usually mention their parent's names.

Names of the Dead, 1763-1767, 1830, 1834, 1860-1864. Information found can be inclusive and record the person's date of birth, date of arrival in America, parent's names, spouse's name, and date of death or it can be a short comment which simply reports the dates when the member was born and passed away.

Mount Joy Evangelical Lutheran Church (Mount Joy Township). Church Books, 1824-1943. Indexed and including baptisms, November 10, 1824- May 31, 1829, November 2, 1851-November 14, 1941, that identify the parents and sponsors and give the child's name, date of birth, and date of baptism; marriages, October 28, 1851- September 24, 1937, that provide the date of the wedding, the names of the husband and wife, and the pastor officiating at the service; and burials, November 6, 1851- January 23, 1943, that have the church member's name, age, date of burial, and place of burial (from August 10, 1881). Remarks are present that also note what the cause of death was or that depict familial relationships.

St. James Evangelical Lutheran Church, Gettysburg (Cumberland Township). Parish Registers, 1818-1904. Indexed and containing the following sections:

Baptisms, April 25, 1819- July 17, 1904. Gives the child's name, dates of birth and baptism; parents names; and if not the parents, the name of the sponsors.

Burials, May 13, 1832- October 20, 1851, March 15, 1855- April 17, 1904. Provides the name, age, and date of death of the dead person; and from 1836 to 1851, the place of burial. A remarks column occasionally mentions the cause of death or the place of interment from 1861 to 1904.

Marriages, July, 1830- April 4, 1904. From 1830-1861 entries only record the married couple's names with the date of marriage. After 1861, the couple's residences and the name of the officiating pastor appear too.

St. James Evangelical Lutheran Church, Wenksville (Menallen Township). Church Records, 1902-1965. Indexed and including baptisms of infants, August 5, 1903- March 29, 1964, that identify the parents and show the baby's name, date of birth, and date of baptism; marriages, December 31, 1903- May 26, 1917, that list the date of the wedding and the names and residences of the husband and wife; and burials, March 14, 1903- January 6, 1918, that provide the church member's name, age, date of death, place of burial, and cause of death.

St. John's Evangelical and Reformed Church, Fairfield (Hamiltonban Township). Parish Registers, 1854-1967. Indexed. Consists of these entries:

Baptisms, 1854-1886, 1892-1904, 1913-1967. Entries record the child's name and date of baptism along with the parent's - names. Other data found includes the date of birth (1854-1886, 1939-1967) and the names of the child's sponsors (1913-1939). There are two baptismal returns for 1839 at the end of the first register.

Burials, 1854-1886, 1892-1967. Normally entries show the name, age, and date of death of the person. At times, a remarks column is used to record the cause and place of death of the church member.

Marriages, 1892-1967. Entries have the names and residences of the couples and the date of the marriage.

St. John's Evangelical Lutheran Church, Abbottstown (Berwick Township). Parish Registers, 1884-1920. The birth, marriage, and burial records are in chronological order. Information provided about births includes the name of the parents and the name and dates of birth and baptism of the child. Marriage entries have the names and residences of the husband and wife followed by the date of marriage. Burial data includes the name and age of the deceased, the date of death, and the place of burial. Remarks appear from December 29, 1897 to January 4, 1906 that may mention anything from the cause of the person's death to comments regarding what parish he or she belonged to. From December 6, 1911 to February 14, 1911 the date of the funeral also is recorded.

St. John's Evangelical Lutheran Church, Littlestown (Germany Township). Parish Registers, 1763-1868. Indexed. Include baptisms, November 9, 1763- April 9, 1868, that record the child's name, date of birth, date of baptism, and parent's names; burials, January 8- September 2, 1858, that show the name, age, and date of death of the deceased; and marriages, 1858, that give the dates of union and the names of the husband and wife.

St. John's Lutheran Church, Abbottstown (Berwick Township). *Registers, 1837-1877,* containing data regarding births, marriages, and deaths. The birth returns give the person' name, dates of baptism and birth, the names of the parents, and sometimes the witnesses. Marriage returns show the names and residences of the couples, the date of the union, and the place where married. Death returns record the name of the deceased and the date and place of death. The transcripts are in alphabetical order by surname.

St. Luke's Evangelical Lutheran Church, near Bonneauville (Mount Pleasant Township). Church Records, 1888-1959. Indexed and including baptism of infants, November 20, 1888- November 15, 1959, that identify the parents and show the baby's name, date of birth, and date of baptism; adult baptisms, 1939, 1942, 1951, 1954, that record the name, date of birth, date of baptism, and address of the proselyte; marriages, 1888-1921, 1931-1949, 1953-1956, that provide the date of the wedding, the names and residences of the husband and wife, the name of the officiating pastor, and the license number (after 1949); and burials, 1888-1922, 1930-1957, that list the church member's name, age, date of burial, and place of burial.

St. Paul's Evangelical Lutheran Church, Biglerville (Butler Township). Contains these indexed records:

Baptisms of Infants, August 5, 1881- November 30, 1934. Entries record the child's name, date of birth, and date of baptism along with the parent's names.

Marriages, March 12, 1915 - November 17, 1934. Lists the names and residences of the husband and wife and the date of marriage.

Burials, April 7, 1915- February 22, 1935. Provides the name, age, date of death, and place of interment of the deceased.

St. Paul's Evangelical Lutheran Church, Littlestown (Germany Township). Parish Registers, 1867-1938. Indexed and consisting of baptisms, September 22, 1867- April 17, 1938, that record the identity of the parents and the child's name, date of birth, and date of baptism; marriages, August 21, 1867- June 3, 1939, that provide the names and residences of the husband and wife, and the date of the wedding; and burials, December 26, 1867-May 16, 1939, that show the church member's date of death, age, place of burial, and at times, cause of death.

St. Paul's Evangelical Lutheran Church, near New Chester (Straban Township). Also known as "The Pines." Parish Registers, 1862-1960. Indexed. The registers have a record of church baptisms, April 19, 1862- October 2, 1960, that give the child's name, date of birth, and date of baptism along with the names of the parents and sponsors; marriages, November 14, 1861- May 22, 1960, that provide the date of marriage, the couple's names and residences, and from 1936 onward, often the parent's names; and deaths, December 17, 1861- March 5, 1960, that show the name, date of death, and age of the deceased, the place of burial and cause of death (after 1866), and the date of burial (after 1950). Occasionally, the maiden name of a deceased woman is included as well.

St. Paul's Evangelical Lutheran Congregation, Gettysburg (Cumberland Township). The indexed church book, 1859-1864, has these entries:

Baptisms, January 16, 1859- September 18, 1864. Contains births from 1856 to 1864. Entries list the name, date of birth, and date of baptism of the youngster; the names of the parents; and the names of the sponsors.

Marriages, May 31, 1860- June 1, 1864. Provides the date of marriage; the names, residences, places of birth, and occupations of the couples; and the names of their parents.

St. Paul's Lutheran Church, McSherrystown (Conewago Township). Record Book, 1893-1943. Indexed and consisting of baptisms, July 1, 1894- July 18, 1943, that cover individuals born between 1863 and 1943 and which show the person's date of baptism, names of parents, and the officiating pastor (until 1914); marriages, May 3, 1896-June 26, 1943, that record the date of wedlock and identify the couples and their residences; and burials, July 8, 1894-April 17, 1943, that provide the name, age, date of death, and place of burial of the deceased church member.

United Methodist Church Of Gettysburg (Cumberland Township). Indexed parochial registers are found that contain this information:

Baptisms, March 21, 1854- April 17, 1925. Entries give the name, date of birth, and date of baptism of the church member; if a child, the names and residence of the parents; and the identities of the sponsors.

Initial Membership Roll, October 24, 1891- May 24, 1903. The listing provides the name, age, and marital status of the church member; the date when received; and if married, the date of marriage and the name of the individual's spouse.

Marriages, April 11, 1854- April 7, 1925. Data shown includes the names and residences of the husband and wife, and the date of the union.

Upper Bermudian "Ground Oak" Church (Huntingdon Township).

Baptismal Records of Ground Oak Church, October, 21, 1791- May 12, 1872, January 14, 1874. Indexed. Entries identify the parents and sponsors and list member's name, date of birth, and date of baptism.

Parish Registers, 1868-1905. Indexed. Includes baptismal records, March 27, 1867- December 28, 1905, that show the child's name, date of birth, date of baptism, and parent's names; marriage records, March 10, 1867- December 24, 1901, that identify the couple's parents and give their names, residences, and date of marriage; and death records, December 31, 1866- October 6, 1901, that list the deceased person's name, age, date of death, cause of death, and burial location.

Zion Evangelical Lutheran Church, Fairfield (Hamiltonban Township). Parish Registers, 1853-1967. Indexed. Includes entries regarding the following:

Baptisms, 1853-1902, 1910-1967. Provides the name, date of birth, and date of baptism of the child along with the names of the parents.

Marriages, 1853-1889, 1908-1929, 1945-1967. Records the names and residences of the husband and wife and the date of union. The residences of the couple are not always present from 1945 onward.

Burials, 1853-1892, 1910-1967. Gives the name, age, and date of death of the deceased. A remarks column sometimes notes the cause of death or the place of interment. From 1946 to 1954 the date of birth of the person appears.

GERMAN REFORMED SALEM CHURCH (UNITED CHURCH OF CHRIST) OF HARRISBURG (DAUPHIN COUNTY) DEPOSIT, 1787-1916 (MG-292). Contains the following materials:

Registry, 1809-1879. Usually, entries are in chronological order by the date of the event. Information on the following topics appears in various sections of the book:

Baptisms, September 10, 1841- August 30, 1879. Ordinarily a listing shows the name, date of birth, and date of baptism of the child; the names of the parents; and the name of the minister.

Funerals, January 18, 1841- October 8, 1879. Has information about members who died from January 16, 1841, to October 6, 1879. Entries give the name and age (years, months and days) of the deceased person, and the dates of death and burial. Sometimes the place of interment is also mentioned.

Marriages, April 22, 1841- October 21, 1879. Data found include the name and residence of the married couple, the date of marriage, the name of the minister performing the ceremony, and the names of the witnesses.

Members' Names, April 22, 1809- May 25, 1879. Encompassing

members who were living and receiving the sacraments as of 1855 and 1879, the registry records the member's name, date of reception, mode of reception (confession, confirmation, certificate, etc.), and where appropriate, date of death, dismissal, suspension, excommunication, or restoration.

Receipt Book, August 3, 1827- June 23, 1859. The record of Sexton George Snyder of fees received for digging graves. Entries are in chronological order by burial date and list the name of the person paying the fee and his or her relationship to the deceased.

List of Sunday School Scholars, 1820-1826. Contains an "Alphabetical List of the Names of Children that Attended the Salem Sunday School of Harrisburg" together with their place of residence, time of admission, and situation in learning.

Roll Books, 1836-1841, 1859. Entries normally show the name of the pupil attending Sunday school class, the dates of attendance, and the name of the teacher. The books are organized numerically by assigned class numbers, and differentiate between students who were males, females, or seniors.

Sunday School Receiving Books, 1839-1842, 1850-1851. A typical listing gives the name and class of the pupil; the name, occupation, and residence of the parent or guardian; and the relationship of the guardian to the student (aunt, uncle, etc.). From 1850 to 1851 information regarding a child's withdrawal from school (date and reason) appears regularly, and occasionally the age of the would-be scholar is entered. The books are organized by the date that the pupil was received into school.

HILL LUTHERAN CHURCH RECORDS (LEBANON COUNTY), 1731-1850 (MG-262). The collection consists of microfilmed records in German which furnish information about church births and baptisms, 1736-1836; burials, 1794-1839; communicants, 1794-1850; and marriages, 1731-1784. Entries are arranged chronologically.

MORAVIAN CHURCH, DIARIUM OF BETHLEHEM (LEHIGH COUNTY), 1742-1871 (MG-262). Entries are arranged in chronological order. While most of the text relates to commentaries about scripture; the moral lessons learned from life experiences; and insights gained from interaction with the community of others, marginal notations and remarks appear regarding the deaths, funerals, and baptisms of Moravian Church members and even Native American converts. Prior to June 12, 1865, the record is written in German, afterwards it is in English.

MORAVIAN CHURCH, RECORDS OF THE MORAVIAN MISSION AMONG THE INDIANS OF NORTH AMERICA, 1737-1917 (MG-262). A micropublication prepared by Research Publications, Incorporated, of New Haven, of original records in the custody of the archives of the Moravian Church in Bethlehem, Pa. The materials consist of diaries, correspondence, accounts, maps, registers and catalogues that describe both the religious activities of the missionaries and the day-to-day lives of the Indians. Most of the records are written in German script. Of particular interest to researchers are the microfilm rolls dealing with Pennsylvania (boxes 116-137, 1371) that contain either catalogues or registers. Normally, such records provide the names of Indian converts and the dates when they were born, baptized, confirmed, married, died, or buried. The relationship of family members to each other often appears as well. An *Index to the Records of the Moravian Mission Among the Indians of North America* compiled by Rev. Carl John Fliegel was published in 1970 and can be used for finding the names of Indians, white persons, geographic places, Indian Nations, non-Indian nations, and land topics. Card entries give the index term, the box and folder number where the item can be found; the date of the document; and a brief description of the records content. The collection is arranged by names of states where mission contact occurred (New York, Connecticut, Pennsylvania, Ohio (some Michigan), Indiana, Kansas, Georgia, and Oklahoma) or by topic (Personalia, Generalia, Indian Languages, and Other) and thereunder by box, folder, and item numbers. Most of the documents are in rough chronological sequence and there is a microfilmed list of contents at the beginning of each box.

PATH VALLEY AND FALLING SPRINGS CHURCH (FRANKLIN COUNTY) RECORD BOOK, 1794-1844 (MG-3). The record book has the following listings:

Baptisms, October 17, 1803- February 12, 1839. Entries are in chronological order by baptismal date and indicate the person's name and whether he or she was an adult or infant.

Marriages, June 5, 1794- March 21, 1844. Data entered include the date of the marriage, the names of the individuals being married, and the name of the minister conducting the service. The listings are arranged by marriage date.

REFORMED CHURCH OF LANCASTER RECORDS, 1736-1947 (MG-262). Consists of records of the First Reformed Church of Lancaster, Pa., 1736-1947, and Reformed Church and Family records of eastern Pennsylvania from the collections of Franklin and Marshall College Library, 1752-1850. The former are written or transcribed in English while the latter are for the most part in German script. Information such as this is found:

Baptisms, 1736-1947. Data varies but generally the child's name, date of baptism, and date of birth (from as early as 1729) appear along with those of the parents and sponsor. Registries prepared by Johann Heinrich Hoffmeier, such as that begun on October 19, 1806, are in German script. Others such as those of Martin Bruner (1832-1849) and the Rev. M. Harbaugh (starting in 1850) are in English, however. Bruner also transcribed and translated the baptismal entries found for the period 1736 to 1848.

Deaths, 1752-1947. Typically show the name, age (years, months, and days), and date of death of the deceased. In cases where the dead person was a child or wife, the name of the parents or husband is recorded. From 1847-1851, 1932-1947, the date of burial or place of interment is also provided.

Marriages, 1742-1931. Entries list the names of the couples, the dates of unions, and oftentimes their residences.

Entries on each of the lists are in chronological order.

ST. JOHN'S CHURCH OF CARLISLE (CUMBERLAND COUNTY) PARISH REGISTER, 1793-1882 (MG-262). Entries are arranged by type of ceremony and thereunder chronologically. The register, which is on microfilm, contains data on these topics:

Baptisms, 1793-1805, 1819-1830, 1847-1881. Has the following categories of data: name of person baptized, date of baptism, age or date of birth, names of parents, name of sponsor, and name of officiating rector. At times the place of birth of the individual also appears.

Confirmation, 1821, 1842-1849, 1852-1866. Entries generally list the confirmed person's name, the date of confirmation, and the name of the officiating bishop.

Deaths or Burials, 1819-1830, 1842-1881. Information that may appear includes the name, age, and familial relationships of the deceased and the date of his or her demise.

Marriages, 1819-1830, 1842-1866. A typical listing might show the names of the married couple and the date of their marriage. Sometimes the residence of the newlyweds is noted.

ST. LUKE'S EPISCOPAL CHURCH (LEBANON COUNTY) DEPOSIT, 1856-1963 (MG-312). The deposit contains these volumes:

Register of the Parish of St. Luke's Church, 1857-1896. The register is arranged topically and thereunder chronologically. The following categories of information are found:

Lists of Parishioners and Families, May 1, 1865- April 6, 1896. The data appearing differ with each entry. While some listings simply indicate the parishioner's name, residence, and familial relationships, others also note particulars about the person's occupation, habits, and inclinations.

Baptisms, September 26, 1858- November 29, 1896. Entries list the name, date of birth, and date of baptism of the church member along with the names of the parents, sponsors, and officiating clergyman.

Confirmations, August 7,1859- June 2, 1895. A listing gives the date of the ceremony, the name of the confirmed, and the name of the officiating bishop.

Communicants, 1857-1896. A typical entry usually records the name and residence of the parishioner, the date, and where apropos, information about his or her removal, dismissal, or death.

Deaths, May 26, 1860- November 4, 1896. Data shown include the name and age (years, months, and days) of the deceased, the date of death, the place of interment, and the name of the officiating clergyman. Starting on July 9, 1879, the date of the funeral is also recorded.

Marriages, December 8, 1861- November 21, 1896. Entries provide the names of the couple, the date and place of their marriage, and the names of the witnesses and officiating clergyman.

Private Register of Alfred M. Abel, June 7, 1857- July 5, 1908. A record of marriages, baptisms, funerals and other public services performed by the Reverend Mr. Abel while officiating as a clergyman at Hope Church (Mount Hope, Lancaster County) and St. Luke's Church (Lebanon, Lebanon County), 1857-1878; St. John's (Olympia), St. Peter's (Tacoma), St. Luke's (New Tacoma), and Trinity (Portland) churches in the Washington and Oregon territories, 1878-1881; and St. Luke's (Lebanon, Lebanon County) and St. Mark's (Jonestown, Lebanon County) churches, 1881-1908. The same type of information described as being in the parish register appears in this private register. Although the register has lists of persons baptized, married, and buried, most of it was recorded using a diary format.

ST. PATRICK'S ROMAN CATHOLIC BURIAL ASSOCIATION (LEBANON COUNTY) DUES BOOK, 1906-1907 (MG-182). Besides providing the names of members and the amounts of dues and funeral assessments that they paid, the book records the dates of death for members who passed away during the fiscal period. The members' surnames are in alphabetical order.

ST. STEPHEN'S EPISCOPAL CHURCH, THOMPSONTOWN (MIF-FLIN COUNTY), BAPTISMAL, BURIAL, AND MATRIMONIAL REGIS-TER, 1825-1838, 1890-1970 (MG-262). Indexed. The register is on microfilm and divided into these sections:

Baptisms, July 31, 1825- November 14, 1970. Entries usually give the name, date of birth, and date of baptism of the church member; the names of his or her parents and sponsors; and the name of the officiating minister. Familial relationships are frequently depicted and in a few cases the adult's birthplace is also mentioned.

Confirmations, May 1, 1838- April 13, 1967. Contains little information other than the name of the confirmed, the date of the confirmation, and the name of the person performing the ceremony. Names of sponsors sometimes appear.

Deaths, 1827-1852, 1894-1934, 1962-1965. A typical listing might show the name of the deceased, the date of death, the place and date of burial, and the name of the person conducting the burial ceremony. Some of the earliest listings indicate the deceased individual's residence, age, and familial relationships. From 1962 to 1965 his or her date of birth is entered.

Marriages, September 6, 1900- February 7, 1968. Although there are only a few entries, those that appear list the names of couples, the date and place of their marriage, and the names of the minister and witnesses officiating at the ceremony.

SHOOP'S CHURCH, LUTHERAN AND REFORMED CONGREGA-TIONS (DAUPHIN COUNTY) RECORD BOOK, 1830-1872 (MG-3). The book is arranged chronologically and is composed of the following parts:

Baptisms, November 19, 1831- May 28, 1871. Among the information recorded is the name and date of birth of the baptized, the date of the baptism, and the names of the sponsors and parents.

Burials, November 28, 1850- September 4, 1867, January 22-July 31, 1871. A typical entry shows the name and age (years, months, and days) of the deceased and the date of his or her burial.

TABOR FIRST REFORMED CHURCH OF LEBANON (LEBANON COUNTY), CHURCH RECORD, ca. 1750-1900 (MG-262). Entries in the volume are arranged chronologically by the date of the ceremony. The record is on microfilm and contains the following materials:

Baptisms, November 24, 1764- August 1, 1898. Ordinarily an entry might provide the name of the baptized, the names of the parents and sponsors, the dates of birth and baptism, and the name of the individual performing the baptism.

Deaths, March 1, 1851- November 20, 1897. Data entered include the name, age (years, months, days), and date of death of the person. A list of church members drawn up by Rev. Henry Kroh, 1826-1835, also appears that indicates the dates of death of some members.

Marriages, June 7, 1803- August 28, 1898. Information supplied varies with the time period. From 1851 to 1898, the listings usually give the names of the married couple, the date of their wedding, and the name of the minister marrying them. Prior to June, 1851, the names of witnesses regularly appear.

TULPEHOCKEN CHURCH, STOUCHSBURG (BERKS COUNTY) CHRISTENING REGISTER, 1762-1848 (MG-3). The script is in German and lists the name of the person christened and the date of the ceremony.

TUSCARORA OLD SCHOOL BAPTIST CHURCH RECORDS (JUNIATA COUNTY), 1794-1947 (MG-262). The record consists of two microfilmed minute books that contain references regarding the deaths and baptisms of members. Normally an entry only shows the name of the person who died or was baptized and the date of the occurrence. In a few instances, however, the date of birth is also found. Included is a list covering the years 1793 (births) through 1818 (deaths) that records the dates members were baptized, dismissed, or died. There is a name index for the 1794-1828 book.

UNITED PRESBYTERIAN CHURCH, MERCERSBURG (FRANKLIN COUNTY) RECORD BOOK, 1866-1882 (MG-3). Entries are arranged chronologically. The volume can supply researchers with data about these events:

Baptisms, May 7, 1866- October 23, 1874. A listing gives the name of the child, the date of baptism, and the names of the parents.

Communicants, 1866-1882. Usually entries list the name of the member and the date that he or she joined the congregation. Written remarks are also found that depict familial relationships and the dates on which a member died, moved, or was dismissed from the sect.

Deaths, May 25, 1866- November 2, 1882. Data entered include the name and age of the late church member, the date of death, and the relationship of the person to the church. The cause of death is sometimes noted as well.

Marriages, February 1, 1866- December 7, 1870. An entry records the names of the couple, their residence, and the date of the ceremony.

UNITED STATES NAVAL CEMETERY, GUANTANAMO BAY, CUBA, INFORMATION FROM GRAVESTONES, 1980 (MG-8). A mimeographed nine page booklet compiled by A.C. Trapp and dated April 14, 1980, that contains the names, dates of births, dates of deaths, and oftentimes the origins (nation and or state) of individuals buried in the cemetery at Guantanamo Bay, Cuba. At times, the branch of military service or the fact that the person was a civilian employee is noted as well. The names are in alphabetical order.

COUNTY RECORDS
(3,817 Cubic Feet)

Although the State Archives has increased its holdings of original county records, most county records, including will books, letters of administration, deeds, tax lists and the like, are still kept at the county courthouses, in custody of the respective county officers. As a rule these officials do not make extended searches for genealogical data. The Division of Archives and Manuscripts has microfilm copies (RC 47) of the following materials:

ADAMS COUNTY RECORDS. INDEX TO WILLS, 1800-1864; WILLS, 1800-1851; INDEX TO ORPHANS' COURT DOCKETS, 1800-1936; ORPHANS' COURT DOCKETS, 1800-1853; INDEX TO DEATH RECORDS, 1852-1899; DEATH RECORDS, 1852-1855, 1893-1905; INDEX TO BIRTH RECORDS, 1852-1855; BIRTH RECORDS, 1852-1855, 1893-1899; DELAYED BIRTH RECORDS, 1941-1950 (for 1870-1906); INDEX TO MARRIAGE RECORDS, 1852-1855; MARRIAGE RECORDS, 1852-1855; MARRIAGE LICENSE DOCKETS, 1885-1950; DEEDS, 1800-1851; INDEX TO DEEDS, GRANTEES AND GRANTORS, 1800-1937; TAX LISTS, 1800-1842; TAX ASSESSMENT BOOKS, 1842-1959; and REGISTER OF NEGROES AND MULATTOES, 1800-1820 (See reproduction on page 227).

ALLEGHENY COUNTY RECORDS. ESTATE INDEX, 1788-1971; INDEX TO BIRTHS, 1893-1905; INDEX TO MARRIAGE LICENSE DOCKETS, 1885-1925; MARRIAGE LICENSE DOCKETS, 1885-1906; PROCEEDINGS INDEX, 1788-1971; WILLS, 1789-1906; ORPHANS' COURT DOCKETS, 1789-1905; DEATH RECORDS, 1874-1903; NATURALIZATION DOCKETS, 1816-1903; LISTS OF ATTORNEYS AND LAW STUDENTS, 1788-1981; MINUTES OF THE BOARD OF HEALTH, 1957-1986; and TAX RECORDS, 1877-1899.

ARMSTRONG COUNTY RECORDS. REGISTER'S (OF WILLS) DOCKET, 1805-1881, and INDEX, 1805-1935; ADMINISTRATOR BONDS, 1832-1868; PROBATE ACCOUNTS, 1850-1867; DEATH RECORDS, 1852-1855; WILLS, 1805-1873; INDEX TO WILLS,

1797-1961; INDEX TO ORPHANS' COURT DOCKETS, 1805-1931; ORPHANS' COURT DOCKETS, 1817-1868; INDEX TO DEEDS, GRANTEES AND GRANTORS, 1805-1941; DEEDS, 1805-1866; LAND SURVEYS, 1801-1906; INDEX TO MORTGAGES, MORT-GAGEES AND MORTGAGORS, 1805-1943; NATURALIZATION DOCKETS, 1807-1906; APPLICATIONS FOR BURIAL OF VETER-ANS AND VETERANS' WIDOWS, 1885-1937; ROAD AND BRIDGE VIEWS, 1889-1919; ROAD PETITIONS, 1904-1924; and BRIDGE DOCKET, 1917-1974.

BEAVER COUNTY RECORDS. INDEX TO DEEDS, GRANTEES AND GRANTORS, 1800-1918; DEEDS, 1803-1866; INDEX TO MORT-GAGES, MORTGAGEES AND MORTGAGORS, 1800-1918; REGIS-TER OF BIRTHS, 1893-1906; DELAYED BIRTH RECORDS, 1942-1971 (for 1872-1905); REGISTER OF DEATHS, 1852-1854, 1893-1907; REGISTER OF MARRIAGES, 1852-1854; MARRIAGE LICENSE INDEX, 1885-1916; MARRIAGE LICENSE DOCKETS, 1885-1916; INDEX TO REGISTER'S (OF WILLS) OFFICE, 1812-1965; REGISTER'S (OF WILLS) DOCKETS, 1834-1916; WILLS, 1803-1917; INDEX TO ORPHANS' COURT DOCKETS, 1804-1952; ORPHANS' COURT DOCKETS, 1804-1881; ARGUMENT DOCKET, 1864-1895; and PARTITION DOCKET and INDEX, 1895-1920.

BEDFORD COUNTY RECORDS. INDEX TO WILLS, 1771-1963; WILLS, 1771-1906; WIDOWS' APPRAISEMENTS, 1876-1953; ADMINISTRATORS', EXECUTORS', AND GUARDIANS' ACCOUNTS, 1849-1901; GUARDIANS' BONDS, 1832-1906; ORPHANS' COURT DOCKETS, 1772-1900; INDEX TO DEEDS, GRANTEES AND GRANTORS, 1771-1950; DEEDS, 1771-1905; INDEX TO MORT-GAGES, MORTGAGEES AND MORTGAGORS, 1771-1963; MORT-GAGES, 1830-1900; BIRTH RECORDS, 1894-1906; DELAYED BIRTH RECORDS, 1941-1963 (for 1867-1905); MARRIAGE LICENSE DOCKETS, 1885-1963; DEATH RECORDS, 1894-1906; OATHS OF DEATHS, 1890-1901; NATURALIZATION PAPERS, Ca. 1802-1934; RECORD OF NEGRO AND MULATTO SLAVES, 1780, 1798; RECORD OF NEGRO AND MULATTO CHILDREN, 1821-1825, 1828; RETURNS OF NEGRO AND MULATTO CHILDREN AND MISCELLANEOUS SLAVE RECORDS, Ca. 1780-1834; DEN-TAL REGISTERS, 1883-1898, 1931; MEDICAL REGISTER, 1881-1894; VETERINARY REGISTER, 1889-1905; RECORD OF COUNTY

APPLICATION FOR MARRIAGE LICENSE.

Mr. _Alexander Russell_
—TO—

Miss _Margaret McCance_

MARRIAGE LICENSE

No.

On this _9th_ day of _March_ A. D. 188_8_ appeared Mr. _Alexander Russell_ and applied for a License for the marriage of Mr. _Alexander Russell_ white _a resident of the_ _township_ of _North Beaver_ County of _Lawrence_ State of _Pennsylvania_ aged _53_ years _8_ months and _five_ days, to _Miss Margaret McCance_ white _a resident of the township_ of _North Beaver_ County of _Lawrence_ State of _Pennsylvania_ aged _45_ years _five_ months and _seven_ days.

Same day _J W McClelland_ J. P. having inquired upon oath of the said applicant relative to the legality of the said contemplated marriage, and it appearing that there is no legal impediment thereto, the Clerk of the Orphans' Court can issue a certificate authorizing any Minister of the Gospel, Justice of the Peace, or other person authorized by law to solemnize marriages, to join said _Alexander Russell_ and _Margaret McCance_ together in the Holy State of Matrimony.

And the said _____ being _____ minor the consent of _____ of the said minor to the contemplated marriage was first given before said _____ personally (by proper legal certificate filed and duly signed, attested and acknowledged.)

Occupation of Man _Farmer_

Occupation of Woman _none_

Relationship of parties, if any, before marriage _None_

Former State of Man, Married or Single _Married_

Former State of Woman, Married or Single _Single_

If Married; Date of Death or Divorce of Man's Wife _1st wife died June 3rd 1886_

If Married; Date of Death or Divorce of Woman's Husband _X_

LAWRENCE COUNTY, ss.

Personally appeared before me _J W McClelland a Justice of the Peace_ of said County, _Alexander Russell_ and _Margaret McCance_ who, being duly qualified according to law, did depose and say that the statements above set forth are correct and true, to the best of their knowledge and belief.

Sworn and subscribed before me, this _9th_ day of _March_ A. D. 188_8_

J W McClelland
Justice of the Peace

Alexander Russell
Maggie E McCance

The 1888 Application For Marriage License submitted by Alexander Russell, a widowed farmer from North Beaver township. From the Lawrence County MARRIAGE RETURNS, 1885-1910 (RG-47), PSA.

PRISONERS, 1899-1931; ASSESSMENT BOOKS, 1776-1867 (incomplete); and TAX RECORDS, 1772-1850.

BERKS COUNTY RECORDS. INDEX TO WILLS, 1752-1915; WILLS, 1752-1860; WILLS (unrecorded German wills), 1753-1779; INDEX TO LETTERS OF ADMINISTRATION, 1752-1915; LETTERS OF ADMINISTRATION, 1752-1852; ADMINISTRATION BONDS, 1815-1851; INDEX TO ORPHANS' COURT DOCKETS, 1752-1860; ORPHANS' COURT DOCKETS, 1752-1857; INDEX TO MISCELLANEOUS ORPHANS' COURT RECORDS, 1757-1947; INDEX TO ORPHANS' COURT REAL ESTATE RECORDS, 1752-1937; INDEX TO APPOINTMENTS AND DISCHARGES, 1752-1938; INDEX TO DEEDS, GRANTEES AND GRANTORS, 1752-1926; DEEDS, 1752-1866; DEEDS, PENN BOOK NO.1, 1826-1853; INDEX TO BIRTHS, 1894-1906; BIRTH RECORDS, 1894-1906; INDEX TO DELAYED BIRTH RECORDS, 1941-1949; DELAYED BIRTH RECORDS, 1941-1949 (for 1870-1905); INDEX TO MARRIAGE LICENSE DOCKETS, 1885-1909; MARRIAGE LICENSE DOCKETS, 1885-1906; MORTGAGES, 1752-1822; INDEX TO MORTGAGES, MORTGAGORS, 1752-1926; INDEX TO MISCELLANEOUS DOCKETS, GRANTEES, 1752-1936; INDEX TO MISCELLANEOUS DOCKETS, GRANTORS, 1752-1936; MISCELLANEOUS RECORDER OF DEEDS DOCKETS, 1821-1869; DEEDS (unrecorded), 1769-1886; DEATH RECORDS, 1852-1855,1894-1906; INDEX TO DEATH RECORDS, 1894-1906; COMMISSION BOOK P, 1778, 1781, 1783-1854 and DEEDS, 1783-1786; INDEX TO NATURALIZATION PAPERS, 1798-1914; NATURALIZATION PAPERS, 1798-1852; MINUTES, 1793, 1809-1819, 1822-1825, TRIAL LISTS and ARGUMENTS, 1805-1832, OF THE COURT OF COMMON PLEAS; INDEX TO APPEARANCE DOCKETS, 1776-1778; APPEARANCE and CONTINUANCE DOCKETS, 1753-1788; TRIAL LISTS OF THE CIRCUIT COURT, 1800-1804, 1834; OYER AND TERMINER DOCKET, CIRCUIT COURT, 1804; MINUTES OF THE COURT OF GENERAL QUARTER SESSIONS, 1767-1776, 1778-1804, 1822-1826; PETITIONS TO GRAND JURIES AND ORDERS, 1800-1808; EXECUTION DOCKETS (Judicial Process), 1765-1778; JUDGMENTS, 1752-1775; JURY RECORD, 1807; JUSTICE OF THE PEACE DOCKETS, 1829-1834; ALMSHOUSE MINUTE BOOKS, 1858-1869, 1877-1883; ALMSHOUSE AND PRISON ACCOUNT BOOKS,

1911-1921; ANIMAL BOUNTIES, 1760-1762; BOND SALES, 1822-1846; BRIDGE BOOKS, 1837-1859, 1864-1874; FINANCIAL RECORDS (includes account books of the Wyomissing Manufacturing Company, 1853-1858), 1758-1901; MILITIA RECORDS, 1780-1892; POOR CHILDREN'S RECORD OF BERKS COUNTY, 1839-1842; DOG LICENSE TAX PAID, 1913-1916; TAX RECORDS, 1779-1871; TAX ASSESSMENT AND RETURNS OF NORWEGIAN TOWNSHIP, 1806-1811; TAX ASSESSMENT RECORDS, 1829-1866; and TAX LISTS (for thirty-two townships; not complete for each), 1753-1832.

BRADFORD COUNTY RECORDS. LAND TITLES, 1799-1830; DENTAL REGISTERS, 1883-1896, 1898-1956; OPTOMETRY REGISTER, 1918-1967; OSTEOPATHIC REGISTER, 1909-1924; PHYSICIANS REGISTERS, 1881-1916, 1897-1939; RECORD OF MARRIED WOMEN TO SECURE THEIR SEPARATE EARNINGS, 1873-1895; STALLION REGISTERS, 1893-1950; and VETERINARY REGISTERS, 1889-1896, 1905-1911.

BUCKS COUNTY RECORDS. INDEX TO WILLS, 1684-1939; WILLS, 1682-1906; INDEX TO ORPHANS' COURT DOCKETS, 1683-1958; ORPHANS' COURT DOCKETS, 1683-1866; INDEX TO DEEDS, GRANTEES AND GRANTORS, 1684-1919; MORTGAGES, 1782-1821; INDEX TO MORTGAGES, MORTGAGEES AND MORT-GAGORS, 1684-1919; DEEDS, 1684-1866; MARRIAGE RECORDS, 1835-1845; RECORD OF MARRIAGES BY MAHLON VAN BOOSKIRK AND TRANSCRIBED BY WILLIAM SUMMERS, 1812-1839; MUSTER ROLLS, 1784, 1799; REGISTER'S (OF WILLS) DOCKET, 1839-1913; REGISTER OF INHABITANTS, 1682-1689; REGISTRY OF WILLS AND LETTERS OF ADMINISTRATION, 1684-1693; RECORD OF INVENTORIES, 1684-1688; MINUTES OF THE BOARD OF DIRECTORS OF THE POOR AND HOUSE OF EMPLOYMENT, 1865-1892; LIST OF PAUPERS IN THE ALMSHOUSE, 1810-1833; ALMSHOUSE REGISTER OF ADMISSIONS AND DISCHARGES, 1843-1849, 1889-1895, 1906; ALMSHOUSE AND HOSPITAL REGISTER, 1872-1889; POOR HOUSE REGISTER, 1810-1838; DEATH REGISTER, 1810-1924; MINUTES AND RECORDS OF THE BOARD OF RELIEF, 1863-1865; RECORD OF INDENTURED SERVANTS AND APPRENTICES, AND ACCOUNTS OF THE DIREC-

TORS OF THE POOR AND THE HOUSE OF EMPLOYMENT, 1809-1893; MISCELLANEOUS (RECORDER OF DEEDS) RECORDS, 1776-1868; TREASURER'S ACCOUNTS, 1747-1796; and REGISTER OF SLAVES (includes manumission records), Ca. 1783-1830, not inclusive.

BUTLER COUNTY RECORDS. INDEX TO WILLS, 1800-1971; WILLS (incomplete), 1804-1910; INDEX TO ORPHANS' COURT RECORDS, 1800-1971; ORPHANS' COURT DOCKETS, 1804-1866; MORTGAGES, 1804-1848; DECLARATIONS OF INTENTION, 1874-1919; NATURALIZATION DOCKETS, 1804-1903; PETITIONS FOR CITIZENSHIP, 1804-1931; and INDEX TO PETITIONS FOR CITIZENSHIP, 1804-1982.

CAMBRIA COUNTY RECORDS. MINUTES OF THE BOARD OF INSPECTORS OF THE COUNTY JAIL, 1911-1972; and MINUTES OF THE SALARY BOARD, 1911-1945.

CAMERON COUNTY RECORDS. INDEX TO WILLS, 1863-1972; WILLS, 1862-1907; INDEX TO DEEDS, 1860-1902; DEEDS, 1860-1867; and NATURALIZATION DOCKET, 1862-1906.

CARBON COUNTY RECORDS. MINUTES, 1876-1878, TRIAL SUMMARIES, 1872, 1876-1878, and TRIAL TRANSCRIPTS, 1876-1878, OF THE COURT OF OYER AND TERMINER.

CENTRE COUNTY RECORDS. INDEX TO REGISTER'S (OF WILLS) AND ORPHANS' COURT DOCKETS, 1800-1949; BIRTH RECORDS, 1893-1906; DEATH RECORDS, 1893-1906; DELAYED BIRTH RECORDS, 1941-1942 (for 1879-1906); DENTAL REGISTERS, 1883-1962; MEDICAL REGISTERS, 1881-1931; OPTOMETRY REGISTER, 1918-1968; BIRTH RETURNS FOR NEGROES AND MULATTOES, 1803-1820; and REVOLUTIONARY WAR PENSION DECLARATIONS, 1819-1826, 1832-1833, 1835.

CHESTER COUNTY RECORDS. INDEX TO WILLS AND ADMINISTRATIONS, 1712-1923; WILLS, 1712-1924; INDEX TO ORPHANS' COURT DOCKETS, 1716-1968; ORPHANS' COURT DOCKETS, 1716-1916; INDICES TO BIRTH, MARRIAGE, AND DEATH RECORDS, 1852-1855; BIRTH, MARRIAGE, AND DEATH RECORDS, 1852-1855; BIRTH, MARRIAGE, AND DEATH RECORDS (UNOFFI-

CIAL), 1799-1866, undated; INDEX TO DEEDS, GRANTEES AND GRANTORS, 1688-1922; DEEDS, 1688-1903; MISCELLANEOUS DEEDS, 1821-1844, 1848-1856; INDEX TO MISCELLANEOUS DEEDS, GRANTEES, 1688-1860, and GRANTORS, 1688-1853; INDEX TO SHERIFF'S DEEDS, 1773-1905; SHERIFF'S DEEDS, 1773-1905; SHERIFF'S ORIGINAL DOCKETS, 1804-1916; PARTITION DOCKETS, 1891-1937; RECOGNIZANCE DOCKETS, 1820-1847; ADMINISTRATORS' ACCOUNTS AND AUDITOR'S REPORTS, 1850-1901; INDEX TO MORTGAGES, MORTGAGEES, 1688-1913; INDEX TO MORTGAGES, MORTGAGORS, 1688-1920; MORTGAGES, 1774-1852; INDEX TO LETTERS OF ATTORNEY, 1774-1909; LETTERS OF ATTORNEY, 1774-1903, WARRANTS AND SURVEYS, 1701-1727; ALIENS' DECLARATIONS OF INTENTIONS, 1834-1906; RECORDS OF NATURALIZATION, 1798-1860, 1887-1906; BURIAL FILE (A-Z by last name) and CEMETERY FILE (A-Z by cemetery), ca. 1775-1985, OF THE OFFICE OF VETERANS' AFFAIRS; SOLDIERS' WIDOWS BURIAL DOCKETS, 1917-1961; SOLDIERS' BURIAL DOCKETS, 1885-1927; SOLDIERS' BURIAL DOCKETS FOR THE SPANISH-AMERICAN WAR, WORLD WAR I, WORLD WAR II, KOREA, and VIET NAM, 1927-1979; COURT OF QUARTER SESSIONS DOCKETS, 1714-1906, and INDEX, 1777-1826; COURT OF OYER AND TERMINER DOCKETS, 1802-1911, and INDEX, 1802-1935; REVOLUTIONARY WAR SERVICE CLAIMS (typescripts, most dealing with Berks County veterans), Ca. 1911-1936; BOARD OF COUNTY COMMISSIONERS' INDEX TO PAY ORDERS, 1807-1813; MINUTES OF THE PROVINCIAL COURT, 1756-1778; PROVINCIAL TAXES, 1715, 1757-1776; STATE TAXES, 1777-1791; COUNTY TAX ASSESSMENTS, 1810, 1820; COUNTY TAXES, 1718-1800; and TAX LISTS (by years, not complete), 1715-1850.

CLARION COUNTY RECORDS. NATURALIZATION DOCKET, 1841-1906; DECLARATIONS OF INTENTION, 1849-1906; and POOR BOARD AND ROAD TAX RECORDS OF ELK TOWNSHIP, 1880-1891.

CLEARFIELD COUNTY RECORDS. ORPHANS' COURT DOCKET BOOKS and INDEXES, 1824-1916; ORPHANS' COURT PROCEEDINGS INDEX, ca. 1842-1955; WILLS, 1863-1919; REGISTER OF WILLS AND ORPHANS' COURT ESTATE INDEX, ca. 1855-1985;

BIRTH RECORDS, 1852-1854, 1893-1905 (includes delayed birth entries); DELAYED BIRTH CERTIFICATES, 1941-1963 (for 1867-1905); DEATH RECORDS, 1892-1905; REGISTRATION OF MAR-RIAGES, 1852-1854, 1868, 1877-1878; MARRIAGE LICENSE DOCKETS, 1885-1916; INDEX TO DEEDS, 1804-1935; DEEDS, 1805-1901; MISCELLANEOUS DOCKETS OF THE REGISTER OF WILLS, 1863-1948; NATURALIZATION PETITIONS, 1820-1903, ALIEN DOCKETS, 1805-1906; and MILITARY DISCHARGES (includes Civil War soldiers, 1862-65), 1868-1902.

CLINTON COUNTY RECORDS. WILLS, 1839-1907; INDEX TO ORPHANS' COURT AND REGISTER'S (OF WILLS) DOCKETS, 1839-1974; and ORPHANS' COURT DOCKETS, 1839-1869.

COLUMBIA COUNTY RECORDS. INDEX TO WILLS AND ADMINIS-TRATIONS, 1813-1974; WILLS AND ADMINISTRATIONS, 1813-1921; DEATH RECORDS, 1852-1855, 1893-1905; INDEX TO DEATH RECORDS, 1852-1855; BIRTH RECORDS, 1852-1854, 1856, 1893-1905; DELAYED BIRTH RECORDS, 1941-1943 (for 1879-1905); MARRIAGE LICENSE DOCKETS, 1885-1907; and ANNUAL AND TRIENNIAL ASSESSMENT RECORDS, 1814-1817, 1820-1832, 1834-1840.

CRAWFORD COUNTY RECORDS. WILLS, 1820-1907; REGISTER'S (OF WILLS) DOCKETS, 1800-1889, and INDEX, 1800-1970; DEATH AND MARRIAGE RECORDS, 1852-1854; DELAYED BIRTH RECORD, 1941-1968,1970-1971 (for 1865-1907); BIRTH RECORDS, 1893-1906; MARRIAGE LICENSE DOCKETS, 1885-1907, and INDEX, 1885-1951; DEATH RECORDS, 1893-1905; ORPHANS' COURT DOCKETS, 1825-1868, and INDEX, 1800-1921; and TAX RECORDS, 1829-1871.

CUMBERLAND COUNTY RECORDS. INDEX TO WILLS AND AD-MINISTRATIONS, 1750-1937; WILLS, 1750-1877; ADMINISTRA-TION RECORDS, 1750-1880; ORPHANS' COURT DOCKETS, 1751-1863; INDEX TO DEEDS, GRANTEES AND GRANTORS, 1750-1950; DEEDS, 1750-1860; BIRTH, DEATH, AND MARRIAGE RECORDS, 1852-1855; BIRTH RECORDS, 1894-1905, DELAYED BIRTH RECORDS 1941-1949 (for 1875-1905); MARRIAGE LICENSE DOCKETS, 1886-1930 and INDEX, 1885-1930; DEATH RECORDS,

1894-1905; SLAVE RETURNS, 1780,1789,1814; RETURNS FOR NEGRO AND MULATTO SLAVES, 1780-1833, not inclusive; NATURALIZATION RECORDS, 1798-1905; PAUPER CHILDREN RECORDS, LISTS, 1807-1836, undated; APPEARANCE DOCKETS, 1765-1767, 1784-1793, 1797-1807; CONTINUANCE DOCKETS, Ca. 1750-1845; JURORS LISTS, GRAND AND TRAVERSE, 1806-1856, undated; TAVERN RECORDS AND LICENSES, 1750-1855; INDEX TO CORPORATIONS, GRANTEES AND GRANTORS, 1750-1950; ASSESSOR'S DUPLICATE TAX LISTS, 1783-1817; TAX RETURNS (SETTLEMENTS), 1779-1843, undated; TAX RETURNS (COLLATERAL INHERITANCE), 1836-1839, 1842-1843; and TAX LISTS (by years, not complete and including taxes paid by townships, 1736-1749), 1750-1850.

DAUPHIN COUNTY RECORDS. WILLS, 1785-1875; INDEX TO ORPHANS' COURT DOCKETS, 1785-1946; ORPHANS' COURT DOCKETS, 1785-1852; INDEX TO DEEDS, GRANTEES AND GRANTORS, 1785-1917; DEEDS, 1785-1850; BIRTH RECORDS, 1852-1854, 1893-1906; DELAYED BIRTH RECORDS, 1941-1947 (for 1870-1905); MARRIAGE RECORDS, 1852-1855; INDEX TO MARRIAGE DOCKETS, 1885-1950; MARRIAGE LICENSE DOCKETS, 1885-1950; DEATH RECORDS, 1852-1855, 1893-1904; APPEARANCE DOCKETS, 1785-1876; JUSTICE OF THE PEACE DOCKETS, 1797-1801; MEDICAL REGISTERS, 1881-1928; TAVERN LICENSE PETITIONS, 1785-1790, 1796-1797, 1802-1803; ALMSHOUSE PATIENT'S REGISTER, 1914-1930; POORHOUSE REGISTER OF DEATHS, 1866-1919, 1921-1924; REGISTER OF ADMISSIONS AND DISCHARGES FOR THE DAUPHIN COUNTY ALMSHOUSE, 1889-1931; REGISTER OF ADMISSIONS AND DISCHARGES FOR THE DAUPHIN COUNTY POORHOUSE, 1865-1873, 1889, 1894, 1904-1923; TAX ASSESSMENT rolls, 1830-1899; and TAX LISTS, 1785-1850.

DELAWARE COUNTY RECORDS. WILLS, 1789-1908; INDEX TO MORTGAGES, MORTGAGORS, 1789-1912; MORTGAGES, 1789-1825; ORPHANS' COURT DOCKETS, 1789-1865; ORPHANS' COURT DOCKETS, 1790-1882; INDEX TO WILLS AND ADMINISTRATIONS, 1789-1973; LETTERS OF ADMINISTRATION, 1790-1917; RECOGNIZANCE RECORDS, 1835-1888; INDEX TO

DEEDS, GRANTEES AND GRANTORS, 1789-1914; DEEDS, 1789-1866; and NATURALIZATION PAPERS, 1795-1906.

ELK COUNTY RECORDS. ADMINISTRATORS' AND EXECUTORS' ACCOUNTS, 1851-1896; INDEX TO ESTATE RECORDS, 1844-1971; WILLS, 1845-1915; MISCELLANEOUS DOCKETS, 1844-1868; INDEX TO MISCELLANEOUS DOCKETS, 1844-1971; ORPHANS' COURT DOCKETS, 1857-1886; BIRTH RECORDS, 1852-1853, 1893-1906; DELAYED BIRTH RECORDS, 1941-1977 (for Ca. 1875-1905); DEATH RECORDS, 1852-1853, Ca. 1893-1907; MARRIAGE LICENSES, 1853-1854; MARRIAGE LICENSE DOCKET BOOKS, 1885-1916; DEEDS, 1844-1887; INDEX TO DEEDS, 1844-1910; NATURALIZATION DOCKET, 1844-1906; NATURALIZATION PAPERS, 1844-1906; and MILITIA ENROLL-MENTS, 1864, 1870-1876, 1888-1889.

ERIE COUNTY RECORDS. WILLS, 1823-1916; ESTATE INDEX, 1823-1971; REGISTER'S (OF WILLS) DOCKET, 1839-1864; ORPHANS' COURT DOCKETS, 1822-1868; ORPHANS' COURT PROCEEDINGS INDEX, 1823-1958; INDEX TO DEEDS, GRANTEES AND GRANTORS, 1823-1919; DEEDS, 1823-1866; INDEX TO MISCELLANEOUS AND CONTRACT DOCKETS, GRANTEES, 1823-1946; BIRTH RECORDS, 1893-1906; DELAYED BIRTH RECORDS, 1941-1955 (for 1867-1905); DEATH RECORDS, 1892-1906; MAR-RIAGE LICENSE DOCKETS, 1885-1907; INDEX TO MARRIAGE LICENSE DOCKETS, 1885-1919; MORTGAGES, 1815-1836, and INDEX, 1823-1919; TAX RECORDS, 1816-1870; TAX RECORDS (Fairview Borough to Venango Township), 1851-1906; and TAX RECORDS (Borough and City of Erie) 1850-1857, 1867, 1869-1870, 1871-1920.

FAYETTE COUNTY RECORDS. ADMINISTRATORS' AND EXECU-TORS' ACCOUNTS, 1850-1871; ORPHANS' COURT DOCKETS, 1784-1869, and INDEX, 1784-1950; MINUTES OF THE ORPHANS' COURT, 1851-1860; ORPHANS' COURT DOCKET, 1783-1802, AND MINUTES OF THE COURT OF GENERAL QUARTER SES-SIONS OF THE PEACE, 1783-1808; EXECUTION DOCKETS, 1784-1818; CONTINUANCE DOCKETS, 1784-1786, 1791-1812; DEATH RECORDS, 1852-1855; INDEX TO WILLS, 1784-1949;

WILLS, 1784-1875, and BONDS, 1784-1866; SHERIFF'S DEED BOOK, 1785-1875, and COURT DOCKET, 1784-1804; SHERIFF'S and TREASURER'S DEEDS, 1827-1836; MARRIAGE RECORDS, 1852-1854; BIRTH RETURNS FOR NEGROES AND MULATTOES, 1788-1826 (includes CERTIFICATES OF REGISTRY RECEIVED FROM OTHER COUNTIES, 1785, 1803, 1805, 1807-1808, and MISCELLANEOUS PAPERS, 1823,1830, undated); TAX RECORDS, 1785-1882; and TAX RECORDS OF LUZERNE TOWNSHIP, 1816-1840.

FOREST COUNTY RECORDS. DEEDS, 1857-1871; INDEX TO DEEDS, GRANTEES AND GRANTORS, 1858-1933; and SHERIFF'S DEEDS, 1852-1903.

FRANKLIN COUNTY RECORDS. ESTATE PAPERS, 1784-1822; INDEX TO MINORS' ESTATES, 1786-1958; INDEX TO WILLS, 1784-1963; WILLS, 1784-1905; WIDOWS' APPRAISEMENTS, 1855-1961; INDEX OF ADMINISTRATIONS, 1784-1962; APPOINT-MENT OF GUARDIANS RECORD, 1864-1908; ADMINISTRATORS', EXECUTORS', AND GUARDIANS' ACCOUNTS, 1847-1900; INDEX TO ORPHANS' COURT DOCKETS, 1819-1963; ORPHANS' COURT DOCKETS, 1785-1903; INDEX TO DEEDS, GRANTEES AND GRANTORS, 1785-1963; DEEDS, 1785-1883; INDEX TO PLOTS IN DEEDS, undated; MORTGAGES, 1811-1868; BIRTH RECORDS, 1894-1906; DELAYED BIRTH RECORDS, 1941-1963 (for 1873-1906); MARRIAGE LICENSE DOCKETS, 1885-1963; DEATH RECORDS, 1893-1906; FUNERAL DIRECTORS REGISTERS, 1916-1963; SOLDIERS' DISCHARGE BOOK, 1919-1933; MEDICAL REGISTERS, 1881-1959; DENTAL REGISTER, 1899-1953; OPTOMETRY REGISTER, 1918-1978; OSTEOPATHIC REGISTER, 1909-1923; STALLION REGISTERS, 1894-1927; VETERINARY MEDICAL REGISTER, 1889-1940; and TAX RECORDS, 1794-1848.

FULTON COUNTY RECORDS. WILLS, 1842-1908; WIDOWS' APPRAISEMENTS, 1863-1962; ADMINISTRATORS', EXECUTORS', AND GUARDIANS' ACCOUNTS, 1851-1909; INDEX TO ORPHANS' COURT DOCKETS, 1851-1936; ORPHANS' COURT DOCKETS, 1851-1901; ESTATE INVENTORY AND APPRAISEMENT LISTS, ca. 1850-1937; INDEX TO DEEDS, GRANTEES AND GRANTORS,

1850-1937; DEEDS, 1850-1900; MORTGAGES, 1851-1899; BIRTH RECORDS, 1894-1905; DELAYED BIRTH RECORD, 1941-1958, 1960-1963 (for 1872-1905); MARRIAGE RECORDS, 1852-1854; MARRIAGE LICENSE DOCKETS, 1885-1963; DEATH RECORDS, 1852-1854, 1874-1881, 1895-1905; SOLDIERS' DISCHARGE BOOK, 1919-1924; RECORD OF HONORABLE DISCHARGED SOLDIER BURIALS, 1896-1927; ROAD BOOK, 1851-1910; DENTAL REGISTER, 1883-1943; MEDICAL REGISTERS, 1881-1953; OPTOMETRY REGISTER, 1919-1956; STALLION REGISTERS, 1894-1967; and VETERINARY SURGEONS REGISTER, 1889-1897.

GREENE COUNTY RECORDS. INDEX TO DEEDS, GRANTEES AND GRANTORS, 1796-1941; DEEDS, 1796-1866; INDEX TO ORPHANS' COURT DOCKETS, 1799-1949; ORPHANS' COURT DOCKETS, 1797-1867; and ADMINISTRATORS' ACCOUNTS, 1850-1868.

HUNTINGDON COUNTY RECORDS. INDEX TO WILLS AND LETTERS OF ADMINISTRATION, 1787-1918; WILLS, 1787-1908; INDEX TO ORPHANS' COURT DOCKETS, 1788-1972; ORPHANS' COURT DOCKETS, 1788-1866; BIRTH REGISTERS, 1852-1853, 1893-1905 (includes delayed birth entries, 1941); DEATH REGISTER, 1852-1854; MARRIAGE REGISTER, 1852-1854; MARRIAGE LICENSE DOCKETS, 1885-1907; INDEX TO DEEDS, GRANTEES AND GRANTORS, 1786-1972; DEEDS, 1786-1866; MISCELLANEOUS DEED INDEX, GRANTEES AND GRANTORS, 1790-1877; MISCELLANEOUS DEED BOOK, 1856-1866; and INDEX TO MORTGAGES, MORTGAGEES AND MORTGAGORS, 1786-1891.

INDIANA COUNTY RECORDS. INDEX TO DEEDS, GRANTEES AND GRANTORS, 1803-1928; DEEDS, 1806-1866; ORPHANS' COURT DOCKETS, 1807-1867; INDEX TO ORPHANS' /COURT DOCKETS, 1803-1970; DECLARATIONS OF INTENTION, 1885-1906; NATURALIZATION DOCKETS, 1903-1906; and NATURALIZATION INDEX, 1806-1902.

JEFFERSON COUNTY RECORDS. WILLS, 1852-1906; DEATH RECORDS, 1853-1854; MARRIAGE RECORDS, 1852-1855; INDEX

TO DEEDS, GRANTEES AND GRANTORS, 1818-1910; DEEDS, 1828-1866; REGISTER'S (OF WILLS) DOCKETS, 1832-1906; ORPHANS' COURT DOCKETS, 1833-1868; INDEX TO ORPHANS' COURT DOCKETS, 1832-1944; NATURALIZATION RECORDS, 1831-1906.

JUNIATA COUNTY RECORDS. INDEX TO DEEDS, GRANTEES AND GRANTORS, 1831-1973; DEEDS, 1831-1866; MISCELLANEOUS RECORDER OF DEEDS DOCKETS, 1851-1867 and INDEX, 1831-1067; INDEX TO WILLS, 1831 1973; WILLS, 1831-1910, INDEX TO DECEDENTS' ESTATES, 1852-1973; INDEX TO ORPHANS' COURT DOCKETS, 1831-1881; ORPHANS' COURT DOCKETS, 1831-1869; and MINUTE BOOK OF THE BOARD OF RELIEF, 1861-1865.

LANCASTER COUNTY RECORDS. INDEX TO WILLS, 1729-1947; WILLS, 1729-1908; INDEX TO ORPHANS' COURT DOCKETS, 1742-1890; ORPHANS' COURT DOCKETS, 1742-1850; MISCELLA-NEOUS REGISTER'S (OF WILLS) AND ORPHANS' COURT BOOKS, 1742-1867; INDEX TO BIRTH RECORDS, 1852-1854; BIRTH RECORDS, 1852-1855, 1894-1907; INDEX TO DELAYED BIRTH RECORDS, 1941-1959; DELAYED BIRTH RECORDS, 1942-1959 (for 1869-1906); BIRTH REGISTERS FOR COLUMBIA BOROUGH, 1901-1911; BIRTH REGISTERS FOR LANCASTER CITY, 1905-1913; DEATH AFFIDAVITS, 1874-1907; INDEX TO DEATH AFFI-DAVITS, 1874-1950; MARRIAGE LICENSE DOCKETS, 1885-1906; INDEX TO MARRIAGE LICENSE DOCKETS, 1885-1936; INDEX TO DEEDS, GRANTEES AND GRANTORS 1729-1894; DEEDS, 1729-1867; MISCELLANEOUS RECORDER OF DEEDS BOOKS, 1847-1871; INDEX TO MORTGAGES, MORTGAGORS, 1729-1940; MORTGAGES, 1812-1821; MINUTES OF THE DIREC-TORS OF THE POOR AND HOUSE OF EMPLOYMENT, 1798-1866; ALMSHOUSE ADMISSIONS AND DISCHARGES, 1866-1912; LAN-CASTER CITY MAYOR'S REGISTRY OF COLORED PERSONS, 1820-1849; LANCASTER COUNTY HOSPITAL BIRTH REGISTER, 1864-1923, 1925-1927, 1931; LIST OF PAUPERS IN THE HOUSE OF EMPLOYMENT AND HOSPITAL, 1809-1825; RECORD OF OUT-DOOR RELIEF, 1885-1893, 1898-1937; RETURNS OF NEGRO AND MULATTO CHILDREN BORN AFTER THE YEAR 1780, 1788-

1793; INDEX TO SLAVES, 1780-1834; JUSTICE OF THE PEACE DOCKETS, 1784-1791; ROAD DOCKET BOOKS, 1729-1856, 1869-1885; ROAD INDEX (alphabetical by township), 1730-1988; ROAD INDEX, 1830-1855; ROAD PETITION INDEX, 1837-1879; TAX ASSESSMENTS, 1802, 1811, 1815-1847; and TAX RECORDS (incomplete), 1750-1855.

LAWRENCE COUNTY RECORDS. CORONER'S INQUISITIONS, 1852-1910.

LEBANON COUNTY RECORDS. INDEX TO WILLS, 1813-1935; WILLS, 1813-1881; ORPHANS' COURT DOCKETS, 1813-1855; INDEX TO DEEDS, GRANTEES AND GRANTORS, 1813-1932; DEEDS, 1813-1850; BIRTH RECORDS, 1853-1855, 1893-1906; DELAYED BIRTH RECORDS, 1941-1950 (for 1869-1905); INDEX TO BIRTH RECORDS, 1853-1854, MARRIAGE RECORDS and INDEX, 1852-1855, MARRIAGE LICENSE DOCKETS, 1885-1949; DEATH RECORDS, 1852-1855, 1893-1906; INDEX TO DEATH RECORDS, 1852-1854; SOLDIERS' DISCHARGE BOOK, 1869-1950 (discharges, 1862-1898); VETERANS' GRAVE REGISTER, 1800-1932; MILITARY ENROLLMENT LISTS, 1865-1879; ASSESSORS MILITARY ROLLS, 1878-1882; DESCRIPTIVE COMPANY ROLL, 1861; JUSTICE OF THE PEACE DOCKETS, 1811-1827, 1830-1905, 1860-1882; MEDICAL REGISTERS, 1881, 1953; OPTOMETRY AND OSTEOPATHIC CERTIFICATES (RECEIPT STUBS), 1909-1921; OSTEOPATHIC REGISTER, 1909-1917, AND OPTOMETRY REGISTER, 1918-1958; REGISTER OF DENTISTS, 1899-1958; VETERINARY MEDICAL REGISTER, 1889-1902; REGISTRY OF AUTOMOBILES OR MOTOR VEHICLES, 1903-1905; TAX LISTS (for ten townships, incomplete), 1841-1846, 1849.

LEHIGH COUNTY RECORDS. TAX LISTS, 1813-1817.

LUZERNE COUNTY RECORDS. REGISTER'S (OF WILLS) INDEX, 1788-1875; INDEX TO WILLS, 1786-1918; WILLS, 1786-1905; INDEX TO ORPHANS' COURT DOCKETS, 1787-1874; ORPHANS' COURT DOCKETS, 1787-1905; BIRTH RECORDS, 1893-1905; BIRTH REGISTRATION RETURNS, 1895-1904; DELAYED BIRTH RECORDS, 1941-1968 (for 1877-1903); DEATH RECORDS, 1893-1905; MARRIAGE LICENSE DOCKETS, 1885-1906; INDEX TO

Typical entries made in the REGISTERS OF NEGROES AND MULATTOES, 1800-1820, for Adams County (RG-47), PSA.

DEEDS, GRANTEES AND GRANTORS, 1787-1907; DEEDS
(includes Civil War discharges in volume 112), 1787-1901; and
TAX ASSESSMENT RECORDS, 1803-1842 (See: Wyoming County.)

LYCOMING COUNTY RECORDS. DELAYED BIRTH RECORDS,
1956-1970 (ca.1867-1905); and MORTGAGES, 1825-1873.

MCKEAN COUNTY RECORDS. BIRTH RECORDS, 1893-1906;
DELAYED BIRTH RECORDS, 1941-1971 (for 1880-1905); DEATH
RECORDS, 1893-1905; MARRIAGE LICENSE DOCKETS, 1885-
1908; INDEX TO DEEDS, GRANTEES, 1806-1971; INDEX TO
DEEDS, GRANTORS, 1806-1900; DEEDS, 1806-1868; ALIEN
DOCKETS, 1842-1906; DENTAL REGISTERS, 1883-1941, not
inclusive; MEDICAL REGISTERS, 1881-1920, not inclusive;
OSTEOPATHIC REGISTER, 1909-1960, not inclusive; and REGIS-
TER OF CERTIFICATES OF MEDICAL PRACTITIONERS, 1880.

MERCER COUNTY RECORDS. WILLS, 1804-1907; INDEX TO
ESTATES, 1800-1971; INDEX TO PROCEEDINGS, 1804-1971;
REGISTER'S (OF WILLS) DOCKETS, 1805-1907; ORPHANS'
COURT DOCKETS, 1804-1867; BIRTH RECORDS, 1898-1905;
DELAYED BIRTH RECORDS, 1941-1970 (for 1868-1905); DEATH
RECORDS, 1893-1906; MARRIAGE LICENSE DOCKETS, 1885-
1908; INDEX TO DEEDS, GRANTEES AND GRANTORS, 1803-
1919; DEEDS, 1803-1866; and TAX ASSESSMENT DUPLICATES,
1804-1814.

MIFFLIN COUNTY RECORDS. REGISTER'S (OF WILLS) DOCKET,
1789-1899; ORPHANS' COURT CHANCERY DOCKETS, 1865-
1875; DEATH RECORDS, 1852-1855; 1893-1906; CORONER'S
INQUESTS, 1875-1919; BIRTH RECORDS, 1853-1854, 1893-
1906, DELAYED BIRTH RECORDS, 1941-1969 (ca. 1867-1905);
AFFIDAVITS CORRECTING BIRTH RECORDS, 1941-1964; MAR-
RIAGE RECORDS, 1852-1853; DEEDS, 1790-1953; DECLARA-
TIONS OF INTENTION AND INDICES, 1851-1907; NATURALIZA-
TION DOCKETS, 1802-1913; NATURALIZATION PAPERS, 1810-
1912; APPLICATIONS FOR BURIAL OF DEAD SOLDIERS, 1885-
1920; RELIEF BOARD, DOCKETS OF PAYMENT TO FAMILIES OF
CIVIL WAR SOLDIERS, 1861-1865; MEDICAL REGISTER, 1895-
1919; DENTIST REGISTER, 1898-1950; VETERINARY SURGEON

REGISTER, 1889-1915; JUSTICE OF THE PEACE DOCKET, 1850-1852; MINUTE BOOK, 1850-1876, and TREASURER'S BOOK, 1854-1866, OF THE DIRECTORS OF THE POOR; CIRCUIT COURT DOCKETS, 1792-1809, 1826-1834; APPEARANCE PAPERS OF THE COURT OF COMMON PLEAS, 1851-1905; and TAX DOCKETS, 1823-1827.

MONTGOMERY COUNTY RECORDS. INDEX TO WILLS, 1784-1942; WILLS, 1784-1863; INDEX TO ADMINISTRATIONS, 1794-1941; ORPHANS' COURT DOCKETS, 1784-1850; INDEX TO DEEDS, GRANTEES AND GRANTORS, 1784-1877; DEEDS, 1784-1820; MISCELLANEOUS BAPTISM, MARRIAGE, AND DEATH RECORDS (official and unofficial records, incomplete), 1730-1929; MISCELLANEOUS MILITARY SERVICE RECORDS (incomplete), 1775-1809; LIST OF RETAILERS, INNS, AND TAVERNS, LICENSES, AND ELECTED OFFICIALS, 1830-1861; LIST OF POOR CHILDREN, 1820-1823, 1833-1839, 1841; MINUTES OF THE BOARD OF DIRECTORS OF THE POOR, 1889-1900; RECORDS OF ADMISSIONS AND DISCHARGES AT THE ALMSHOUSE, 1904-1913; REGISTERS OF BIRTHS AND DEATHS AT THE COUNTY ALMSHOUSE, 1884-1907; RECORDS OF WEARING APPAREL AT THE ALMSHOUSE, 1886-1912; APPRENTICE BOOK OF THE DIRECTORS OF THE POOR AND OF THE HOUSE OF EMPLOYMENT (RECORD OF INDENTURES), 1872-1906; APPOINTMENT BOOK, 1826-1890, AND POOR HOUSE DAY BOOK, 1808-1821; and TAX LISTS (thirty townships and two boroughs, incomplete), 1785-1847.

MONTOUR COUNTY RECORDS. WILLS, 1850-1912; BIRTH RECORDS, 1892-1905; DELAYED BIRTH RECORDS, 1941-1968 (for 1870-1905); DEATH RECORDS, 1893-1905; MARRIAGE LICENSE DOCKETS and INDEX, 1885-1909; INDEX TO DEEDS, GRANTEES AND GRANTORS, 1850-1958; DEEDS, 1850-1866; and MISCELLANEOUS (DEED) INDEX, 1850-1958.

NORTHAMPTON COUNTY RECORDS. INDEX TO REGISTER'S (OF WILLS) DOCKETS, 1752-1966; WILLS, 1752-1907; INDEX TO ORPHANS' COURT DOCKETS, 1752-1882; ORPHANS' COURT DOCKETS, 1752-1866; MISCELLANEOUS COURT RECORDS (includes township histories and lists of county officers, 1752-1834), 1749-1838; BIRTH RECORDS, 1893-1908; DELAYED BIRTH RECORDS, 1941-1952 (for 1868-1934); DEATH RECORDS, 1893-1903; MARRIAGE RECORDS, 1852-1854; MARRIAGE LICENSE DOCKETS, 1885-1907; INDEX TO DEEDS, GRANTEES AND GRANTORS, 1752-1926; DEEDS, 1752-1866; MISCELLANEOUS RECORDER OF DEEDS DOCKET, 1815-1866; INDEX TO MORT-GAGES, MORTGAGEES AND MORTGAGORS, 1752-1922; MORT-GAGES, 1799-1822; TRACTS OF LAND (property of Messrs. Penn taken by Lucius Carter), 1754-1776; WARRANTS AND SURVEYS, 1734-1879; and TAX ASSESSMENTS AND LISTS (by years, incomplete), 1761-1815.

NORTHUMBERLAND COUNTY RECORDS. WILLS, 1772-1908; INDEX TO REGISTER'S (OF WILLS) DOCKETS, 1792-1930; ORPHANS' COURT DOCKETS, 1772-1868, and INDEX, 1772-1974; BIRTH RECORDS, 1852-1853, 1893-1905; DELAYED BIRTH RECORDS, 1941-1968 (for 1869-1906); INDEX TO DE-LAYED BIRTH RECORDS, 1950-1968; DEATH RECORDS, 1852-1855, 1893-1905; MARRIAGE RECORDS, 1852-1855; MARRIAGE LICENSE DOCKETS, 1885-1907; INDEX TO MARRIAGE LICENSE DOCKETS, 1885-1974; INDEX TO DEEDS, GRANTEES AND GRANTORS, 1772-1913; DEEDS, 1772-1866; MORTGAGES, 1793-1838; INDEX TO MORTGAGES, MORTGAGEES AND MORT-GAGORS, 1772-1974; TAX RECORDS, 1774-1843; and TRIENNIAL ASSESSMENTS, 1802-1811.

PERRY COUNTY RECORDS. WILLS, 1820-1880; INDEX TO ORPHANS' COURT DOCKETS, 1820-1950; ORPHANS' COURT DOCKETS, 1820-1869; INDEX TO DEEDS, GRANTEES AND GRANTORS, 1820-1950; DEEDS, 1820-1851; INDEX TO BIRTHS, 1852-1854; BIRTH RECORDS, 1852-1854, 1893-1919; MARRIAGE RECORDS and INDEX, 1852-1855; MARRIAGE LICENSE DOCK-ETS, 1885-1950; INDEX TO DEATH RECORDS, 1852-1855; DEATH RECORDS, 1852-1855, 1893-1919; and TAX LISTS (by townships, incomplete), 1820-1849.

PHILADELPHIA COUNTY RECORDS. INDEX TO WILLS, 1682-1900; WILLS, 1682-1901; INDEX TO ADMINISTRATIONS, 1682-1900;

ORPHANS' COURT DOCKETS, 1719-1852; INDEX TO ORPHANS' COURT DOCKETS, 1719-1852; INDEX TO DEEDS, GRANTEES AND GRANTORS, 1683-1851; DEEDS, 1684-1847; INDEX TO EXEMPLIFICATIONS, 1684-1800; EXEMPLIFICATIONS, 1683-1785; PATENTS (CITY LOTS), 1781-1785; and MISCELLANEOUS RECORDS such as ACCOUNTS OF REDEMPTIONERS CUSTOM HOUSE, LONDON, FEB. 7, 1774-JULY 29, 1775; SHIP REGISTERS, 1763-1776; REGISTER OF ARRIVALS IN PHILADELPHIA (part), 1682-1686; REGISTRY OF THE REDEMPTIONS, GERMANS, indexed, 1785 1831; INDEX TO DEEDS RECORDED IN PHILADELPHIA FOR LANDS NOW IN MONTGOMERY COUNTY, 1682-1743; LIST OF NAMES OF THE INHABITANTS OF THE COUNTY OF PHILADELPHIA WITH THE QUANTITY OF LAND THEY HOLD IN 1734; REPORT OF COMMISSION ON CITY LOTS, 1700; MUSTER ROLLS, 1777-1789; GENERAL RETURN OF THE 1ST BATTALION OF MILITIA OF PHILADELPHIA COUNTY FOR FINES FOR NON-ATTENDANCE ON THE DIFFERENT MUSTER DAYS IN 1779; ROLL OF THE 7TH COMPANY, 5TH BATTALION, PHILADELPHIA MILITIA, 1782; ROLL OF STATE GUARDS, PHILADELPHIA, 1814; RETURN OF ABSENTEES OF THE 4TH COMPANY, 2ND BATTALION, 98TH REGIMENT, PHILADELPHIA, 1828-1830; ROLL OF THE 7TH COMPANY, 84TH REGIMENT, PHILADELPHIA, 1828-1830; REGISTER OF BIRTHS,1817-1873; RECORD OF DEATHS IN PHILADELPHIA (part), 1791-1851; RECORD OF DEATHS (in German, no place given), 1793-1844; REGISTER OF DEATHS IN GREENWICH TOWNSHIP, 1817-1886; CERTIFICATES OF MARRIAGE BEFORE JOHN DENNIS, ALDERMAN OF PHILADELPHIA, 1846-1852; MARRIAGE REGISTER, PHILADELPHIA MAYOR'S OFFICE, 1857-1865; and MARRIAGE LICENSES, 1763-1776.

POTTER COUNTY RECORDS. REGISTER'S (OF WILLS) DOCKETS, 1836-1908 and INDEX, 1836-1972; BIRTH AND DEATH RECORDS, 1893-1906; MARRIAGE LICENSE DOCKETS, 1885-1906; INDEX TO DEEDS, GRANTEES AND GRANTORS, 1806-1972; DEEDS, 1806-1866; and INDEX TO MORTGAGES, 1804-1931.

SCHUYLKILL COUNTY RECORDS. BIRTH RECORDS and INDEX, 1893-1905; DEATH RECORDS and INDEX, 1893-1905; INDEX TO

DEEDS, GRANTEES AND GRANTORS, 1811-1915; DEEDS, 1811-1902; and TAX ASSESSMENTS AND RETURNS, 1811-1850.

SNYDER COUNTY RECORDS. ORPHANS' COURT DOCKETS, 1855-1883; WILLS, 1855-1882; DEATHS OF TESTATORS AND INTESTATES, 1816-1980; BIRTH RECORDS, 1893-1905; DELAYED BIRTH RECORDS, 1941-1962 (for ca. 1867-1905); DEATH RECORDS, 1893-1905; and MARRIAGE RECORDS, 1885-1920.

SOMERSET COUNTY RECORDS. WILLS, 1795-1902; INDEX TO WILL BOOKS, 1795-1922; ESTATE DOCKETS, 1796-1904; ESTATE DOCUMENTS, 1795-1882; INDEX TO ESTATES, 1795-1921; EXECUTORS AND ADMINISTRATION RECORDS, 1850-1912; INDEX TO BIRTH RECORDS, 1852-1854, 1893-1908; BIRTH RECORDS, 1853-1854, 1893-1908; DELAYED BIRTH RECORDS, 1941-1965 (for 1876-1905); CORONER'S INQUISITIONS, 1853-1922; MARRIAGE RECORDS, 1797-1824; MARRIAGE REGISTER, 1852-1854 (includes 1855-1923); MARRIAGE LICENSE DOCKETS, 1885-1968; INDEX TO DEEDS, GRANTEES AND GRANTORS, 1795-1949; DEEDS, 1795-1901; SHERIFF'S AND TREASURER'S DEEDS, 1829-1905; INDEX TO SHERIFF'S DEEDS, 1803-1905; EQUITY DOCKETS, 1856-1870; PARTITION DOCKETS, 1889-1937; INDEX TO MORTGAGES, MORTGAGEES AND MORTGAGORS, 1795-1964; MORTGAGE RECORDS, 1846-1871; LUNATICS, DRUNKARDS, INJUNCTIONS, AND DIVORCE INDEXES, 1879-1954; GRAVE REGISTRATION RECORDS OF THE OFFICE OF VETERANS AFFAIRS; SOLDIERS DISCHARGE RECORDS (discharges, 1862-1865), 1862-1943; GENERAL INDEX TO DISCHARGED SERVICE PERSONS, 1864-1968; VETERANS' DISCHARGE BOOKS AND INDEXES, 1862-1986; SURVEY WARRANTS, ca. 1767-1899; INDEX TO PLOTS, undated; NATURALIZATION BOOKS AND PAPERS, ca. 1829, 1855-1860; CONTINUANCE DOCKET BOOKS, 1796-1877; MEDICAL REGISTER, 1881-1934; VETERINARY REGISTER, 1889-1931; COURT OF OYER AND TERMINER DOCKET, 1855-1899; COURT OF QUARTER SESSIONS DOCKETS, 1800-1902, and INDEX, 1795-1920; ROAD AND BRIDGE RECORDS, ca.1795-1980, and INDEX, undated; and TAX ASSESSMENTS, 1795-1878.

SULLIVAN COUNTY RECORDS. INDEX TO ORPHANS' COURT
DOCKETS, 1848-1937; ORPHANS' COURT DOCKETS, 1848-1870;
REGISTER'S (OF WILLS) DOCKETS AND WILL BOOKS with
INDEX, 1847-1913; INDEX TO DEEDS, GRANTEES AND GRAN-
TORS, 1847-1876; DEEDS, 1848-1866; DEATH RECORDS, 1893-
1905; MARRIAGE RECORDS, 1852-1855; NATURALIZATION
RECORDS, 1848-1906; MARRIAGE LICENSE DOCKETS, 1885-
1913; BIRTH RECORDS (includes delayed birth records, 1904,
entered in 1941), 1894-1906; and DELAYED BIRTH RECORD,
1941-1967 (for 1879-1906)

SUSQUEHANNA COUNTY RECORDS. INDEX TO WILLS AND
ADMINISTRATIONS, 1810-1882; INDEX TO REGISTER'S (OF
WILLS) DOCKETS, 1810-1949; BIRTH RECORDS, 1893-1906;
DELAYED BIRTH RECORDS and INDEX, 1941-1942, 1948-1967
(for 1867-1905); DEATH RECORDS, 1893-1906; and MARRIAGE
LICENSE DOCKETS, 1885 1917.

TIOGA COUNTY RECORDS. LAND TITLES, 1799-1830.

UNION COUNTY RECORDS. PROBATE RECORDS, 1777-1788;
WILLS AND INDEX TO ADMINISTRATIONS, 1813-1838; WILLS,
1815-1819; APPLICATIONS FOR BURIAL OF DECEASED SOL-
DIERS, 1886-1915; TREASURER'S LICENSE BOOKS, 1836-1856;
DEPUTY SURVEYOR, WARRANTS RECEIVED, 1813-1818; TAV-
ERN LICENSE PETITIONS, 1814-1887; and TAX RECORDS, 1814-
1882.

VENANGO COUNTY RECORDS. INDEX TO WILLS AND REGIS-
TER'S (OF WILLS) DOCKET, 1800-1969; WILLS, 1819-1906; WILL
DOCKETS, 1906-1916; ORPHANS' COURT DOCKETS, 1806-1870;
BIRTH RECORDS, 1893-1905; DELAYED BIRTH RECORDS, 1941-
1969 (for 1863-1906); DEATH RECORDS, 1893-1906; MARRIAGE
RECORDS, 1852; MARRIAGE LICENSE DOCKETS, 1885-1916;
INDEX TO DEEDS, GRANTEES AND GRANTORS, 1800-1925;
DEEDS, 1805-1889; INDEX TO MORTGAGES, MORTGAGORS,
1800-1926; and NATURALIZATION DOCKETS, 1806-1906.

WARREN COUNTY RECORDS. INDEX TO ORPHANS' COURT
DOCKETS, 1844-1947; ORPHANS' COURT DOCKETS, 1844-1866;

REGISTER'S (OF WILLS) DOCKETS, 1820-1908, and INDEX, 1823-1971; BIRTH RECORDS, 1893-1905; DELAYED BIRTH RECORDS, 1941-1970 (for 1869-1905); DEATH RECORDS, 1893-1905; MARRIAGE RECORDS, 1852-1853; MARRIAGE LICENSE DOCKETS, 1885-1909; INDEX TO DEEDS, GRANTEES AND GRANTORS, 1819-1897; and DEEDS, 1819-1866.

WASHINGTON COUNTY RECORDS. INDEX TO WILLS, 1808-1939; WILLS, 1781-1915; INDEX TO ORPHANS' COURT DOCKETS, 1781-1952; ORPHANS' COURT DOCKETS, 1781-1868; INDEX TO BIRTHS, 1852-1853; BIRTH RECORDS, 1893-1906; DELAYED BIRTH RECORDS and INDEX, 1941-1970 (for 1869-1906); DEATH RECORDS, 1893-1906; MARRIAGE LICENSE DOCKETS, 1885-1932, and INDEX, 1885-1940; MARRIAGE LICENSES, 1885-1924; INDEX TO DEEDS, GRANTEES AND GRANTORS, 1781-1924; DEEDS, 1781-1866; INDEX TO MORTGAGES, 1781-1925; MORT-GAGES, 1841-1854; DECLARATIONS OF INTENTION INDEX, 1800-1944; NATURALIZATION INDEX, 1802-1962; NATURALIZA-TION FILES, 1802-1906; MISCELLANEOUS CLERK OF COURTS PAPERS, Ca. 1784-1829; VETERANS GRAVE REGISTRATION RECORD, 1932-1982; CEMETERY MAPS OF SOLDIERS' GRAVES REGISTRATIONS, undated; MILITIA ROLLS, 1846, 1852-1855, Undated; NEGRO REGISTER, 1782 (1782-1820)-1851; INVENTO-RIES OF ESTATES (Yohogania County, Virginia), 1776-1781; and TAX RECORDS, 1785-1859.

WAYNE COUNTY RECORDS. INDEX TO WILLS, 1798-1925; WILLS, 1798-1907; ORPHANS' COURT DOCKETS, 1802-1869; BIRTH RECORDS, 1893-1904; DELAYED BIRTH RECORDS, 1941-1968 (for 1864-1906); DEATH RECORDS, 1893-1904; MARRIAGE LICENSE DOCKETS, 1885-1906; INDEX TO DEEDS, GRANTEES AND GRANTORS, 1798-1941; DEEDS, 1798-1866; INDEX TO MORTGAGES, MORTGAGEES AND MORTGAGORS, 1798-1941; MORTGAGES, 1798-1834; MISCELLANEOUS RECORDER OF DEED RECORDS, 1824-1825, 1879-1912; and MISCELLANEOUS COURT OF COMMON PLEAS RECORDS, 1824-1825, 1879-1912.

WESTMORELAND COUNTY RECORDS. INDEX TO WILLS, 1773-1918; WILLS, 1773-1970; ABSTRACTS OF WILLS, 1815-1819; PROBATE RECORDS, 1777-1778; REGISTER'S (OF WILLS) GENERAL INDEX, 1773-1970; BIRTH RECORDS, 1893-1905; DELAYED BIRTH RECORDS and INDEX, 1941-1981 (for 1870-1906); DEATH RECORDS, 1893-1906; MARRIAGE LICENSE DOCKETS, 1885-1916, and INDEX, 1885-1920; INDEX TO DEEDS, GRANTEES AND GRANTORS; and DEEDS, 1773-1897.

WYOMING COUNTY RECORDS. WILLS, 1843-1908; INDEX TO REGISTER'S (OF WILLS) DOCKETS, 1842-1938; ORPHANS' COURT DOCKETS, 1843-1866; BIRTH RECORDS and INDEX, 1893-1905; DELAYED BIRTH RECORDS, 1941-1966 (for 1872-1906); DEATH RECORDS and INDEX, 1853-1854, 1893-1906; MARRIAGE LICENSE DOCKETS, 1885-1906; INDEX TO DEEDS, GRANTEES AND GRANTORS, 1842-1916; DEEDS, 1842-1866 NATURALIZATION DOCKETS, 1843-1916; and TAX ASSESSMENT RECORDS, 1803-1889, not inclusive.

YORK COUNTY RECORDS. INDEX TO WILLS, 1749-1940; WILLS, 1749-1882; INDEX TO ORPHANS' COURT DOCKETS, 1749-1887; ORPHANS' COURT DOCKETS, 1749-1881; INDEX TO DEEDS, GRANTEES AND GRANTORS, 1749-1912; DEEDS, 1749-1859; BIRTH RECORDS, 1893-1907; DELAYED BIRTH RECORDS, 1941-1958 (for ca. 1867-1905); MARRIAGE LICENSE DOCKETS, 1885-1916; AFFIDAVITS OF DEATHS, 1877-1916; DEATH RECORDS, 1877-1890, 1893-1907; NATURALIZATION PAPERS, 1799-1822, 1824-1906; DECLARATION OF INTENTION DOCKET, ca. 1799-1906; NATURALIZATION ADMISSION DOCKET (INDEX), ca. 1795-1906; DISTRICT COURT DAY BOOK, 1826-1835; DISTRICT COURT DOCKETS, 1826-1835; COMMON PLEAS COURT DOCKETS, 1757-1791, not inclusive; NOTARIAL DOCKET OF JOHN MORRIS, 1792-1805; NOTARIAL DOCKET OF GEORGE CARUTHERS, 1810-1812; COURT OF GENERAL QUARTER SESSIONS DOCKETS, 1749-1794; ROAD DOCKETS, 1791-1844; ROAD PAPERS, 1749-1831, undated; INDEX TO ROADS AND BRIDGES, 1750-1933; INDEX TO STREETS, ALLEYS AND BRIDGES, 1882-1932; DENTAL HYGIENISTS REGISTER, 1923-1937; REGISTRATION OF DENTIST DIPLOMAS, 1883-1897; REGISTER

OF DENTISTS, 1899-1957; DOG REGISTERS, 1884-1915; OSTEO-
PATHIC REGISTER, 1909-1955; REGISTER OF MOTOR VEHI-
CLES, 1903-1905; REGISTER OF PHYSICIANS AND SURGEONS,
1881-1955; REGISTERS OF STALLIONS, 1894-1907, 1910-1925;
VETERINARY REGISTERS, 1899-1905, 1912-1917; MILITARY
ENROLLMENT LIST, 1865; RECORD OF INDIGENT DECEASED
SOLDIERS AND SAILORS, 1891-1932; MINUTES OF THE BOARD
OF DIRECTORS OF THE POOR, 1845-1918; LIST OF TAXABLE
INHABITANTS, DEAF, DUMB AND BLIND PERSONS IN YORK
COUNTY FOR 1871; ALMSHOUSE TRAMP RECORD, 1886-1895;
RECORDS OF APPRENTICES, 1860-1911; SURVEYOR'S RECORDS,
1875-1943; and TAX RECORDS, 1758-1849, not inclusive.

The Division of Archives and Manuscripts also owns microfilm copies
(MG-262) of some miscellaneous federal, municipal, township, and
county records that researchers should be aware of. Among these are:

PITHOLE CITY ASSESSMENT BOOK (Venango County), 1866-1877.

POTTER COUNTY RECORDS, HARRISON TOWNSHIP, 1823-1880,
containing tax lists for seated and unseated lands, 1836-1846.

RECORD OF DEEDS FOR THE DISTRICTS OF AUGUSTA AND
WEST AUGUSTA (southwestern Pennsylvania), at a Virginia Court
held at Fort Dunmore (Pittsburgh), 1775-1776.

UNITED STATES DIRECT TAX OF 1798, for all existent Pennsylvania counties.

Film readers are available for public use in our search room.
Because searching microfilm requires a great deal of time and
effort, staff can neither answer requests for information contained
on these films nor furnish certificates based on data found in
them. Certifying the authenticity of such information falls within
the jurisdiction of the county officers in whose custody the original
records remain, and consequently we cannot make copies of these
items.

Besides having these microfilmed materials, the State Archives
continues to acquire permanently valuable county records that
have been retired, microfilmed, or digitized by county officers. The
records listed below represent those series that might be of particular interest to family historians.

ALLEGHENY COUNTY

BOARD OF COUNTY COMMISSIONERS TAX RECORDS, 1877-1935, not inclusive (RG-47) for the boroughs of Aspinwall, 1893-1935; Avalon, 1893-1935; Beechview, 1909; Bellevue, 1882-1935; Beltzhoover, 1881-1898; Ben Avon, 1893-1935; Ben Avon Heights, 1915-1935; Blawnox, 1930-1935; Brackenridge, 1905-1935; Braddock, 1883-1935; Bradford Woods, 1920-1935; Brentwood, 1920-1935; Bridgville, 1904-1935; Brushton, 1891-1892; Carnegie, 1895-1935; Carrick, 1905-1925; Castle Shannon, 1920-1935; Chalfont, 1920-1935; Chartier, 1880-1894; Cheswick, 1905-1935; Christy Park, 1894-1899; Churchill, 1935; Coraopolis, 1888-1935; Crafton, 1893-1935; Dormont, 1910-1935; Dravosburg, 1905-1935; East McKeesport, 1897-1935; East Pittsburgh, 1896-1935; Edgewood, 1891-1935; Edgeworth, 1910-1935; Elizabeth, 1886-1935; Elliott, 1893-1900; Emsworth, 1896-1935; Esplen, 1892-1905; Etna, 1883-1935; Forest Hills, 1920-1935; Fox Chapel, 1935; Glassport, 1905-1935; Glenfield, 1879-1935; Greentree, 1887-1935; Hays, 1905-1925; Haysville, 1905-1935; Heidelberg, 1905-1935; Homestead, 1883-1935; Ingram, 1905-1935; Knoxville, 1882-1925; Leetsdale, 1910-1935; Liberty, 1915-1935; McDonald, 1935; McKess Rocks, 1893-1935; Mansfield, 1880-1893; Millvale, 1880-1935; Montooth, 1898-1905; Mount Oliver, 1893-1935; Manhall, 1905-1935; North Braddock, 1898-1935; North Clairton, 1920; Oakdale, 1894-1935; Oakmont, 1890-1900; Osborne, 1886-1935; Overbrook, 1920-1925; Pitcairn, 1895-1935; Plum, 1884-1935; Port Vue, 1893-1935; Rankin, 1893-1935; Reynoldton, 1887-1898; Rosslyn Farms, 1915-1935; Sewickley, 1883-1935; Sharpsburg, 1883-1935; Sheraden, 1895-1905; Springdale, 1910-1935; Spring Garden, 1884-1915; St. Clair, 1915-1920; Swissvale, 1900-1935; Tarentum, 1883-1935; Thornburg, 1910-1935; Trafford, 1935; Turtle Creek, 1893-1935; Verona, 1881-1935; Versailles, 1893-1935; Wall, 1905-1935; West Bellevue, 1884-1899; West Elizabeth, 1879-1935; West Homestead, 1903-1935; West Liberty, 1887-1905; West View, 1910-1935; Westwood, 1915-1925; Whitaker, 1905-1935; Wilkinsburg, 1889-1935; Wilmerding, 1890-1935; and Wilson, 1910-1920; the cities of Allegheny, 1879-1905; Clairton, 1905-1935; Duquesne, 1892-

1935; McKeesport, 1882-1935; and Pittsburgh, 1877-1935; and the townships of Aleppo, 1880-1935; Baldwin, 1880-1920; Bethel, 1887-1935; Braddock, 1886-1935; Chartier, 1881-1920; Collier, 1883-1935; Crescent, 1881-1935; East Deer, 1879-1935; Elizabeth, 1883-1935; Fawn, 1880-1935; Findlay, 1879-1935; Forward, 1880-1935; Franklin, 1883-1935; Frazier, 1915-1935; Hampton, 1883-1935; Harmar, 1879-1935; Harrison, 1883-1935; Indiana, 1883-1935; Jefferson, 1879-1935; Kennedy, 1905-1935; Kilbuck, 1882-1935; Leet, 1880-1935; Lincoln, 1884-1935; Lower St. Clair, 1883-1920; McCandless, 1879-1935; Marshall, 1879-1935; Mifflin, 1884-1935; Moon, 1882-1935; Mount Lebanon, 1915-1935; Neville, 1887-1935; North Fayette, 1879-1935; North Versailles, 1883-1935; O'Hara, 1879-1935; Ohio, 1880-1935; Patton, 1881-1935; Penn, 1880-1935; Pine, 1883-1935; Reserve, 1880-1935; Richland, 1881-1935; Robinson, 1880-1935; Ross, 1880-1935; Scott, 1879-1935; Sewickley, 1883-1935; Sewickley Heights, 1905-1935; Shaler, 1883-1935; Snowden, 1880-1935; South Fayette, 1880-1935; South Versailles, 1883-1935; Springdale, 1880-1935; Sterrett, 1883-1905; Stowe, 1883-1935; Union, 1880-1925; Upper St. Clair, 1883-1935; Versailles, 1886-1935; West Deer, 1887-1935; and Wilkins, 1880-1935.

Several pertinent original records transferred to the State Archives from the county and not described elsewhere include a RECORD OF INQUESTS HELD BY THE CORONER, 1899-1927; an INDEX TO INQUESTS HELD, A-Z, 1905-1925; and PITTSBURGH RIOT CLAIMS, 1877-1882, relating to damages caused by the Great Railroad Strike of 1877.

BEAVER COUNTY

BOARD OF COUNTY COMMISSIONERS TAX RECORDS, 1842-1926, not inclusive (RG-47) for the boroughs of Aliquippa, 1895-1925; Ambridge, 1906-1925; Baden, 1871-1926; Beaver, 1860-1925; Beaver Falls, 1871-1925; Bridgewater, 1861-1926; College Hill, 1893-1925; Conway, 1903-1925; Darlington, 1871-1925; Eastvale, 1923; Fallston, 1871-1925; Frankfort, 1871-1898; Frankfort Springs, 1895-1925; Freedom, 1893-1912; Georgetown, 1871-1925; Glasgow, 1871-1909; Hookestown, 1871-1925; Midland, 1916-1925; Monaca, 1898-1925; New Brighton, 1842-

1925; Patterson Heights, 1900-1925; Phillipsburg, 1871-1885; Rochester, 1913; St. Clair, 1871-1898; Shippingport, 1911-1923; South Heights, 1912-1925; and the townships of Big Beaver, 1853-1925; Borough, 1853-1925; Brighton, 1842-1925; Center, 1915-1925; Chippewa, 1871-1913; Darlington, 1853-1925; Daugherty, 1894-1925; Economy, 1853-1925; Franklin, 1876; Greene, 1853- 1925; Hanover, 1853-1925; Harmony, 1897-1924; Hopewell, 1882-1884; Independence, 1853-1922; Industry, 1865-1925; New Sewickley, 1871-1925; North Sewickley, 1871-1925; Ohio, 1871-1925; Patterson, 1871-1925; Potter, 1913-1925; South Beaver, 1871; and White, 1902, 1916.

BEDFORD COUNTY

ESTATE PAPERS, 1770-1790, 1912-1960 (RG-47). The file is arranged in chronological order by date of will with each document thereinafter numbered. Normally besides containing the person's will which specifies who will be the executor and how the estate is be divided, the file includes an inventory of the deceased individual's goods and chattel. Administration bonds, accounts of expenditures, and oaths of death routinely appear in the papers as well. These latter oaths are dated and subscribed before the register of probate wills by the executor or administrator of the estate. Besides affirming that the estate will be faithfully administered, the document records the late residence (township, borough, or city) of the deceased, and the date, approximate time, and place of death (home, etc.).

Other original records for the county which are located at the State Archives include APPOINTMENTS, ca. 1839-1848; BONDS, ca. 1874-1913; DEPUTATIONS, ca. 1875-1900; and OATHS, ca. 1874-1910 from the prothonotary's office; and DEED BOOKS 1771-1948, 1954-1957, 1962-1963; MISCELLANEOUS DOCKETS (agreements, bonds, letters patents, powers of attorney, oaths, etc.), 1864-1977; MORTGAGE BOOKS, 1829-1966; SHERIFF'S DEED BOOKS, 1905-1964; and WILL BOOKS, 1892-1966, from the recorder of deeds and register of wills respectively.

BRADFORD COUNTY

DIVORCE INDEXES, 1876-1977 (RG-47). Entries are grouped alphabetically and give the name of the person against whom a decree in divorce was granted; the date of the decree; the name of the petitioner; the court term, year, and case number; the docket number; and the nature of the decree. Decrees involving drunkards, lunatics, and persons restrained from selling or encumbering real estate are recorded as well.

LOCALITY INDEXES, 1903 (1903-1939)-1983 (RG-47). The volumes are arranged by townships and boroughs and thereinafter by date that tax claims were filed against property holders or their estates. Data shown include a description of the property, that is, the name of the owner or reputed owner, street or road location, street number, and property boundaries (really other real estate owners surrounding it); the type (county, poor, school, build-ing, sewer, bond, penalty, etc.) and amount of the tax claim; the year that the tax was levied; the date of filing the tax claim and the pertinent court case number, term, and year; and where applicable, the date that a *scire facias* was filed and or satisfaction received by the county or municipality (as late as 1981). Although most of the data entered is between 1903-1946 municipal claims appear for as late as 1983.

In addition to these records, the prothonotary's office has placed the following original materials at the State Archives: APPEAR-ANCE DOCKET INDEXES, 1813-1870, 1873-1890; ADSECTUM INDEXES, 1813-1870, 1873-1890; AUDITORS' REPORTS DOCK-ETS and INDEX, 1846-1957; CHATTEL MORTGAGES INDEX, 1850-1858; DEFENDANTS INDEX, 1871-1873; EJECTMENT INDEX, 1856-1891; EXECUTION DOCKETS, 1822-1861; EXECU-TION INDICES, 1858-1934; INDEX TO ASSIGNED JUDGMENTS, 1878-1915; JUDGMENT DOCKETS, 1827-1886, and INDICES, 1871-1873; JUDGMENT INDICES, 1881-1923; MECHANICS LIEN DOCKETS and INDEX, 1840-1938; PARTITION DOCKETS, 1878-1912; OYER AND TERMINER DOCKETS, 1851-1956, and INDEX, 1851-1904; PLANTIFFS INDEX, 1871-1873; SESSIONS DOCKETS, 1813-1842, 1850-1884, 1887-1968, and INDEXES, 1814-1968, 1980-1985; STALLION REGISTERS, 1893-1950; SURPLUS BOND

RECORD, 1898-1975, and INDEX, 1898-1976. Fairly recent TAX DUPLICATES, 1926, 1930, 1935, 1940, 1945, 1950, 1955, from the county's tax assessment office are also available.

BUCKS COUNTY

DECEASED AND CANCELLED FOREIGN BORN VOTER REGIS-TRATION FORMS, 1937-1974 (RG-47). A record found among the records of the Bucks County Board of Elections and voters registration. Entries on the forms provide the name, occupation, sex, color, date of birth, place of birth, address, and physical description (height; color of hair and eyes) of the person; the date on which the individual was naturalized; the court and place where naturalized; the naturalization certificate number; the election ward and district; the borough, town, or township; the party affiliation and year of registration; and the date and reason (failure to vote) for registration being cancelled. The dated registration form bears the signatures of both the foreign born voter and the registrar. The forms are in alphabetical order.

Additional original records received by the State Archives from the county include

APPLICATIONS FOR BURIAL OF DECEASED SOLDIERS AND DECEASED SOLDIERS' WIDOWS, 1909-1923; BOUNTY CLAIMS FOR KILLING NOXIOUS ANIMALS, 1905-1907, 1909, 1911; and LISTS OF DEATHS RETURNED BY THE ASSESSORS, 1893-1907.

CARBON COUNTY

CORONER'S RECORDS (NATURAL/UNNATURAL DEATHS), 1857, 1867-1887 (RG-47). The file is arranged in chronological order by date of inquest and contains narrative reports (inquisitions) that describe in the form of testimony the circumstances which caused the victim's death; the approximate date of death; and when possible, the deceased person's name, age, occupation, residence, and relationship to other members of the community. Normally, the documents are dated and signed by the witnesses and coroner. Expenses incurred for conducting the inquest may also be noted.

Other original Carbon County records located at the State Archives include APPLICATIONS FOR PEDDLERS LICENSES, ca.

1882; JURORS LISTS, 1847-1893; LISTS OF VOTERS, 1907; MIS-
CELLANEOUS CIVIL COURT PAPERS, 1879-1920; MISCELLA-
NEOUS ELECTION PAPERS, 1875-1937; OATHS OF ELECTION
OFFICER, 1902-1907; and VOTER AFFIDAVITS, 1905.

COLUMBIA COUNTY

ANNUAL AND TRIENNIAL TAX ASSESSMENTS, 1841-1910, not
inclusive (RG-47). Returns for all existing municipalities for 1841,
1843, and 1845, and for the boroughs of Benton, 1895-1910;
Berwick, 1859-1910; Catawissa, 1883-1910; Centralia, 1867-1910;
Millville, 1893-1910; Orangeville, 1900-1910; and Stillwater,
1900-1910; and the townships of Beaver, 1853-1910; Benton,
1853-1910; Bloom, 1853-1910; Briar Creek, 1853-1910;
Catawissa, 1853-1910; Centre, 1853-1910; Cleveland, 1893-1910;
Conyngham, 1856-1910; Fishing Creek, 1853-1910; Franklin,
1853-1910; Greenwood, 1853-1910; Hemlock, 1853-1910; Jackson,
1853-1910; Locust, 1854-1910; Madison, 1853-1910; Maine,
1852-1910; Mifflin, 1853-1910; Montour, 1853-1910; Mount Pleasant, 1853-1901; Orange, 1853-1910; Pine, 1853-1910; Roaring
Creek, 1853-1910; Scott, 1854-1910; and Sugarloaf, 1853-1910.

MARRIAGE LICENSE RETURNS AND CONSENTS, 1885-1957 (RG-
47). Applications for marriage licenses filed with the clerk of the
orphans' court of Columbia County. The following forms are present:

Applications for Marriage Licenses. From 1913 to1957 the application contains statements of the male and female applicant's which
give their names, colors, occupations, birthplaces, residences,
ages, and previous marital status (not married, or if yes, date of
spouse's death or of the divorce); and the names, residences, color,
occupations, birthplaces of their parents. Other questions asked
include whether either party was related by blood; afflicted with a
transmissible disease; an imbecile, epileptic, of unsound mind; or
under the influence of any intoxicating liquor or narcotic drug. The
applications are dated and signed by both the couples and a court
official. From 1887 to 1913 the dated and signed marriage license
affidavits simply list the names, ages, residences, occupations, and
previous marital status of the parties. Prior to 1887 the affidavits

only record the names and ages of the man and woman, and the fact that no legal impediment to marriage existed. The applications are in numerical order by application numbers. Numbers (nos. 1-26869) were assigned according to the dates that the applications or affidavits were filed with the court.

Consents to the Marriage of a Child or Ward. Entries on the form record the name, residence, and relationship of the parent or guardian to the minor; the name and age of the minor; and the relationship of the minor to the adult filing the form. The consent certificates are dated and signed by the parent or guardian, two witnesses, and a notary public.

Duplicate Marriage Certificates. Filed with the application and sometimes in lieu of it, the certificate (really a stub) provides the names of the couples; the name of the minister, justice of the peace, or alderman conducting the ceremony; and the date and place of the marriage. The front side of the form has the application and certificate number, the surnames of the couple, and the date that the form was filed with the court written upon it.

The State Archives also has original COMMON PLEAS CIVIL PAPERS, 1836-1865, and LITTLE COMMON PLEAS RECORDS, 1814-1968, relating to the board of county commissioners and the prothonotary's office.

CUMBERLAND COUNTY

DUPLICATE TAX LISTS (assessor's valuation lists) (MG-4 and MG-90) for the townships of Allen, 1797-1798, 1825; Buffalo, 1808-1809; Dickinson, 1793, 1802-1803, 1825; East Pennsboro, 1798, 1809, 1810, 1825; Fannet, 1783; Frankfort, 1804; Greenwood, 1798, 1801, 1810; Hopewell, 1798, 1825; Middleton, 1798-1809; Mifflin, 1798, 1804, 1809, 1812, 1814, 1825; Newton, 1798, 1817, 1825; Rye, 1798, 1817; Shippensburg, 1817, 1825; South Middleton, 1813; Southampton, 1803, 1809, 1812, 1825; Toboyne, 1798; Tyrone, 1798, 1809; and West Pennsboro, 1798, 1804, 1811, 1817. The lists are grouped alphabetically according to resident's surname and show the individual's name, township of residence, valuation, and the amount of tax paid.

NEGRO SLAVE NAME AND AGE RETURNS, 1780, 1789, 1791 (MG-90). The returns are arranged by the date of the document and usually give the slave's name, sex, age, and owner's name. Occasionally, the slave's job is mentioned and quite often the owner's residence and occupation are listed.

TAX RETURNS, 1779-1843 (MG-90). The returns are organized in the same manner as the duplicate tax lists and contain the same type of information.

DAUPHIN COUNTY

BOARD OF COUNTY COMMISSIONERS TAX RECORDS, 1785-1960, not inclusive (RG-47) for the boroughs of Berrysburg, 1870-1960; Dauphin, 1857-1960; Elizabethville, 1893-1960; Gratz, 1852-1960; Halifax, 1876-1960; Highspire, 1905-1960; Hummelstown, 1875-1960; Lykens, 1872-1960; Middletown, 1831-1960; Mifflin, 1868-1899; Millersburg, 1857-1960; Paxtang, 1915-1960; Penbrook, 1895-1960; Royalton, 1892-1960; Steelton, 1880-1960; Uniontown, 1864-1960; and Williamstown, 1888-1960; the city of Harrisburg, 1792-1960; and the townships of Annville, 1789-1813; Bethel, 1785-1813; Conewago, 1851-1960; Derry, 1785-1960; East Hanover, 1785-1960; Halifax, 1805-1960; Hanover, 1825-1831; Heidelberg, 1785-1813; Jackson, 1830-1960; Jefferson, 1843-1960; Lebanon, 1785-1813; Londonderry, 1785-1960; Lower Paxton, 1785-1960; Lower Swatara, 1817-1960; Lykens, 1811-1960; Middle Paxton, 1785-1960; Mifflin, 1820-1868, 1900-1960; Paxton, 1785-1798; Reed, 1849-1960; Rush, 1827-1960; South Hanover, 1843-1960; Susquehanna, 1816-1960; Swatara, 1802-1960; Upper Paxton, 1785-1960; Upper Swatara, 1820-1824; Washington, 1847-1960; Wayne, 1879-1960; West Hanover, 1785-1960; West Londonderry, 1900-1960; Williams, 1869-1960; and Wisconisco, 1840-1960.

INDEXES TO DIVORCES, LUNATICS, AND DRUNKARDS, 1880-1930 (RG-47). Found among the records of the prothonotary of Dauphin County, entries are grouped in alphabetical order by first letter of surname and give the person's name; the court term and year; the docket number; and information about whether the case is a lunatic, drunkard, or divorce proceeding. If the latter, the first name of the spouse is also listed.

LIST OF FREEHOLDERS, TENANTS, AND SINGLE MEN, undated (RG-47). A record of male residents of Dauphin County. The volume is grouped by townships and boroughs with names thereunder in alphabetical order. Entries list the name of the resident followed in many cases by notations that indicate whether the person removed, was dead, or might live in another county since the last enumeration was taken. The following county subdivisions are contained in the record: Conewago, Derry, East Hanover, East Wisconisco, Elizabethville, Halifax, Harrisburg (north and south wards), Highspire, Hummelstown, Jackson, Jefferson, Londonderry, Lower Paxton, Lower Swatara, Lykens, Middle Paxton, Middletown, Mifflin, Millersburg, Perrysburg, Port Royal, Portsmouth, Reed, Rush, South Hanover, Swatara, Uniontown, Upper Paxton, Washington, West Hanover, Wisconisco.

MANUSCRIPT CENSUS REPORT, 1860 (RG-47). Handwritten returns for Dauphin Borough, Rush Township, and Middle Paxton Township that were preserved by the prothonotary of Dauphin County. These enumerations contain the same data described as being on the federal census returns.

RAILROAD AND CANAL DAMAGES BOOK, 1826-1833 (RG-47). Inquisitions held in Dauphin County to examine and determine whether property damage claims made by residents against the Pennsylvania Canal Company and later the Pennsylvania Railroad Company were justified. Entries in the docket give the name of the claimant and the defendant; the date and court term; the names of the jury members; an explanation of the complaint or dispute; a description of the property (size, that is perches, and location in relationship to neighboring properties); the findings of the jury; and if relevant, the compensation granted. Entries are in chronological order by date of inquisition.

RETURNS OF POOR CHILDREN TO THE COUNTY COMMISSIONERS OFFICE, 1832-1841 (MG-4). The listings are arranged by township and generally record the name and age of the child, and the names of the parents. Data about whether the child was an orphan, black (colored), or even a twin are frequently provided.

SOLDIERS' BURIAL RECORD BOOKS, October 16, 1902-March 24, 1933 (RG-47). Indexed. Consists of printed forms entitled "application for burial of deceased soldier" that show the name, rank, regiment, date of discharge, and occupation (immediately preceding death) of the deceased veteran; the date of death and place of burial; and the cost of the funeral (laying out of the body, coffin, grave, and hearse). Post World War I forms also provide additional data about the deceased soldier, for example, the place of death, the cemetery where he was buried, and the war that he served in. Each application has an affidavit at the bottom that is dated and signed by county residents, a representative of the county commissioners, or an undertaker. The volumes are arranged in chronological order by dates of affidavits.

Other original records available for Dauphin County include these from the prothonotary and clerk of courts: ACCOUNTS OF THE OLIVE ENCAMPMENT, NO. 56, INTERNATIONAL ORGANIZATION OF ODD FELLOWS; ADSECTUM INDEXES, 1792-1935; APPEAR-ANCE DOCKETS, 1879-1887; ARBITRATION DOCKETS, 1832-1843; EJECTMENT INDEX, 1856-1924; EXECUTION DOCKETS, 1791-1868, 1872-1906; EXECUTION DOCKET INDEXES: DEFEN-DANT (ADSECTUM), 1787-1792, 1886-1908, 1910-1912, 1919-1933, 1935-1967, and PLAINTIFF, 1886-1891, 1893-1899, 1904, 1907-1908, 1919-1933; EXECUTION DOCKET OF THE CIRCUIT COURT, 1800-1834; EXECUTION DOCKET OF THE DISTRICT COURT, 1823-1828; DELINQUENT NOTES, 1857-1858, 1865-1866; GENERAL INDEX OF BONDS, 1785-1837; INDEX TO STREETS, Undated; JURY LISTS, 1895-1933; JUSTICE OF THE PEACE AND ALDERMEN'S DOCKETS, 1836-1843, 1900-1931; LOCALITY INDEXES, 1901-1929, undated; MIDDLETOWN CAR AND MANUFACTURING COMPANY ACCOUNT RECORD ASSIGN-MENT, 1874; MINUTES OF THE COURT OF COMMON PLEAS, 1822-1848, 1853-1860, 1871-1904, 1910-1948; PAPERS OF THE COURT OF QUARTER SESSIONS AND OYER AND TERMINER, 1785-1903 (including five folders dated 1861 containing Dauphin County prison discharges, 1789-1860; a calendar of prisoners committed in the jail; records of the Overseers of the Poor; appointments and report of road viewers; and duplicate schedules

of property taken on discharge from the Dauphin County prison);
PLEA DOCKETS OF THE COURT OF COMMON PLEAS, 1841-
1863, 1874-1912; PROCESS RETURNABLE OF THE COURT OF
COMMON PLEAS, 1797-1800; RECORD OF INSOLVENTS, 1807-
1847; REGISTERS OF DOGS, 1879-1921; SENTENCE DOCKETS,
1886-1929; SESSIONS DOCKETS, 1898-1899, 1916-1922;
SESSION MINUTES OF THE COURT OF COMMON PLEAS, 1809-
1815; SESSION MINUTES OF THE COURT OF OYER AND TER-
MINER AND THE COURT OF QUARTER SESSIONS, 1809-1812,
1834 1020; STALLION REGISTER, 1804-1919; and TRIAL LISTS
OF THE COURT OF COMMON PLEAS, 1841-1846, 1854-1861,
1887-1892.

ERIE COUNTY

INDEX TO WILLS FOR ERIE COUNTY, 1822-1908 (RG-47). Entries
are grouped in alphabetical order by first letter of surname.
Information recorded includes the names of the testator and
executors; the date that the will was registered; the date of the
will; the date of letters testamentary; and the letter of the will book
and page number on which recorded.

PROOF OF DEATH DOCKETS, 1925-1953 (RG-47). Indexed.
Found among the records of the register of wills for Erie County,
the volumes provide a sworn and subscribed estimate of the value
of estates (personal and real estate) of deceased residents. Other
data appearing include the name, date of death, and township of
residence of the decedent; the names, residences, and relationship
to the deceased of any surviving family, heirs or kin; and the
amount (acres) and location of any real estate owned by the
deceased person in the county. Entries are in chronological order
by date affidavit was filed.

TAX RECORDS OF THE COUNTY COUNCIL, 1816-1965, not inclusive (RG-47) for the boroughs of Albion, 1930-1965; Corry, 1928-
1965; Crainesville, 1921-1965; East Springfield, 1921-1965;
Edinboro, 1922-1965; Elgin, 1921-1965; Fairview, 1869-1965;
Girard, 1848-1965; Lake City, 1956-1965; Lockport, 1871-1903;
Middleboro, 1862-1965; Mill Village, 1871 1965; North East, 1838-
1965; North Girard, 1926-1955; Plateau, 1904-1965; South Erie,

1867-1870; Union City, 1864-1958; Waterford, 1835-1965; Wattsburg, 1835-1965; and Wesleyville, 1913-1965; the city of Erie, 1823-1965; and the townships of Amity, 1926-1965; Beaverdam, 1823-1841; Concord, 1924-1965; Conneaut, 1926-1965; Elk Creek, 1925-1965; Fairview, 1824-1965; Franklin, 1895-1965; Girard, 1833-1965; Greene, 1842-1965; Greenfield, 1817-1965; Harborcreek, 1823-1965; Lawrence Park, 1926-1965; Leboeuf, 1823-1965; McKean, 1824-1965; Millcreek, 1819-1965; North East, 1823-1965; Springfield, 1823-1965; Summit, 1855-1965; Union, 1823-1965; Venango, 1823-1965; Washington, 1837-1965; Waterford, 1816-1965; and Wayne, 1827-1965.

Other significant records transferred to the Archives include ADSECTUM INDEXES, 1821-1940; APPEARANCE DOCKETS, 1823-1851; DIRECT INDEXES, 1830-1940; EXECUTION DOCK-ETS, 1823-1970, and INDICES, 1825-1973; INDEX TO CITY OF ERIE LIENS EXCEPT GENERAL LIENS, 1879-1899; JUDGMENT DOCKETS, 1827-1830, 1839-1950; and MECHANICS LIEN DOCK-ETS, 1837-1954, 1956-1969, and INDICES, 1856-1981, from the county prothonotary; GRANTEE and GRANTOR INDEXES, 1920-1958; GRANTEE and GRANTOR MISCELLANEOUS AND CON-TRACT INDEXES, 1824-1958; an INDEX OF POWER OF ATTOR-NEY, 1824-1935; and MORTGAGOR INDEXES, 1920-1958, from the county recorder of deeds; and ADMINISTRATIVE BONDS, 1873-1953, 1956-1959; ARGUMENT LISTS FOR ORPHANS' COURT AND QUARTER SESSIONS COURT, 1883-1927; BOND BOOKS, 1950-1953, 1956-1959; ESTATE FILES, 1823-1959; INVENTORY BOOKS, 1929-1954; LETTERS OF ADMINISTRATION DOCKETS, 1926-1953; and LETTERS TESTAMENTARY PETI-TIONS, 1926-1953, from the county register of wills.

FRANKLIN COUNTY

COUNTY LEVIES, ASSESSOR'S DUPLICATIONS AND RETURNS (TAX AND EXONERATION LISTS), 1794-1847, not inclusive (MG-4), for Antrim, Fannett, Franklin, Greene, Guilford, Hamilton, Letterkenny, Lurgan, Metal, Montgomery, Peters, Quincy, St. Thomas, Southampton, Warren and Washington Townships. During the 1800's (excluding 1845 and 1847) entries normally list the name, township of residence and property owned (slaves, acres, livestock, etc.) of the taxpayer; the valuation; and the amount of tax that was paid. The status of residents as single free-man, tenant or trader (peddler, etc.) is sometimes indicated as well. There is an "occupation list," 1835, for Guilford Township that records the name, occupation, and sex of the individual. The returns for each township are grouped alphabetically according to taxpayer's surname.

HUNTINGDON COUNTY

ARBITRATION DOCKETS, 1850-1885 (RG-47). The books are in chronological order by court date and show the names of the defendant and plaintiff; the court term, year, and case number; the date that a "rule to reference" was entered by the plaintiff; the names of the arbitrators selected to hear the case; the ruling or decision; and when appropriate, the date and amount of the award. Notations appear in some instances which indicate that the subject of the litigation was an estate, the defendant in fact being deceased. The cause of the suit or particulars about the dispute are rarely stated, however.

Additional records transferred to the State Archives from the pro-thonotary's office include APPEARANCE DOCKETS, 1792-1919; CHATTEL MORTGAGE DOCKETS, 1943-1973; CONDITIONAL SALES DOCKETS, 1925-1954; CONTINUANCE DOCKETS, 1789-1850; EQUITY DOCKETS, 1849-1897; EXECUTION DOCKETS, 1788-1859; JUDGMENT DOCKET INDEX, 1827-1958; MECHAN-ICS LIEN DOCKETS, 1836-1962; MINUTE BOOKS OF THE COURT OF COMMON PLEAS 1821-1872, 1890-1905; RECORD OF REGISTRATION OF MOTOR VEHICLES, 1903; SECURED TRANSACTION DOCKETS, 1954-1961; STALLION REGISTERS, 1894-1934; AND TAX LIEN DOCKETS, 1901-1953.

JEFFERSON COUNTY

INSOLVENCY PETITIONS, 1831-1921 (RG-47). The petitions were filed with the prothonotary of Jefferson County by debtors seeking financial relief. The dated petitions are signed by the debtor and county prothonotary and provide the names of creditors; a schedule of property owned; and an explanation for the financial distress (unemployment, poor health, death of spouse). Depending on the circumstances, information regarding arrests, convictions, fines, and plaintiffs may also appear. The documents are in chronological order.

Other original records of Jefferson County preserved by the State Archives include CIVIL CASE FILES, 1823-1912; EQUITY PAPERS, 1856-1910; EXECUTIVE DOCKET PAPERS, 1831-1910; FICTITIOUS NAME PAPERS, 1917-1973; MECHANICS LIEN DOCKET PAPERS, 1843-1932; PARTITIONS, 1857-1917; ROAD PAPERS, 1830-1885; and COURT OF QUARTER SESSIONS PAPERS, 1831-1915.

LAWRENCE COUNTY

CORONER'S INQUISITIONS, 1852-1910 (RG-47). Normally the documents are signed by the coroner and witnesses, and give, when possible, the name of the deceased, and how, when, where, and by what manner he or she died. The record is arranged by filing date.

DELAYED BIRTH RECORDS, 1941-1975 (RG-47). Petitions filed with the Orphan's Court of Lawrence County concerning delayed registrations of births. Each petition has three parts, a section for recording personal information; dated and subscribed affidavits from a priest or minister, a relative, or non-relatives regarding the validity of the data recorded; and the order of the court. Personal information reported includes the name, place of birth (state, county, township, and hospital or institution), date of birth, sex, and occupation of the applicant; the name, race, birthplace, occupation, and age (at time of applicant's birth) of the person's father; the maiden name, race, birthplace, age (at time of applicant's birth), and occupation of the individual's mother; the number of children born to the mother and still living; the parent's residence; and whether the applicant was a twin and the birth was legitimate. The documents are filed in numerical order by petition numbers. The record covers individuals born from 1875 to 1906 and was authorized by the Act of July 16, 1941. For similar data about other counties see the microfilm holdings section.

MARRIAGE RETURNS, October 5, 1885-December 28, 1910 (RG-47). Marriage affidavits, applications, and duplicate certificates filed by residents of Lawrence County with the clerk of the orphans' court. The following types of documents are filed in numerical sequence:

Marriage License Affidavits. Apparently used up to July, 1890, the forms have the same information listed for marriage license affidavits, 1885-1912, of Columbia County.

Applications for Marriage License. Forms that are filed on an occasional basis from 1888 to 1905. Information shown includes the names, residences , ages, occupations, race, and prior marital status (single, or if married, date of spouse's death or of the divorce) of the couples; the date of filing; and the signatures of the applicants and court official accepting the application. The couples also indicate whether any relationship exists between them before the marriage.

Duplicate Marriage Certificates. Forms filed on a routine basis from approximately July, 1890 onward. As needed, consent of parent or guardian forms are included with the certificates. Both forms have the same type of information described previously for Columbia County.

Besides these records the Archives also has custody of the county's ORPHANS' COURT PAPERS, 1850-1908; EQUITY PAPERS, 1855-1907; and FICTITIOUS NAMES FILE (for recording business names and their owners), 1917-1977.

LEHIGH COUNTY

ADSECTUM INDEX TO SHERIFF'S RETURN FOR SALE OF REAL ESTATE, 1812-1906 (RG-47). Entries are grouped alphabetically by surname of purchaser and list the name of the defendant; the volume and page number of the docket; the court case number, term, and year when the real estate was litigated; the month, day, and year that the property was sold; and the location of the real estate.

INQUEST DOCKETS, January 1, 1928-September 16, 1941 (RG-47). Indexed. A record of inquests held in Lehigh County. Entries in the books show the name, age, color, sex, and date of death of the person; the place and date of the inquest (from 1932 onward); and the verdict, that is, the cause of death. The inquests are numbered.

Other records received from the clerk of courts include APPLICATIONS FOR REGISTRATION OF AN AUTOMOBILE, 1903-1905; ASSIGNMENT DOCKETS, 1839-1928; ASSIGNMENT FOR BENEFIT OF CREDITORS CASE FILE, 1839-1949; CIRCUIT COURT PAPERS, ca. 1826-1843; DIRECT INDEX TO SHERIFF'S RETURN FOR SALE OF REAL ESTATE, 1812-1949; INDEX TO CONDEMNATIONS, 1812-1949; INDEX TO JUDGMENTS AGAINST LUNACIES, 1812-1929; PARTITION DOCKETS, 1863-1954; SHERIFF'S DEED DOCKETS, 1877-1905; SHERIFF'S EXECUTIVE DOCKETS, 1815-1959; SOLDIERS' PEDDLERS LICENSES, 1875-1970; and a TREASURER'S DEED DOCKET, 1933-1934.

LUZERNE COUNTY

BOARD OF COUNTY COMMISSIONERS TAX RECORDS, 1809-1965, not inclusive (RG-47) for the boroughs of Ashley, 1872-1965; Avoca, 1892-1960; Conyngham, 1905-1950; Courtdale, 1900-1960; Dallas, 1880-1960; Dorranceton, 1890-1920; Dupont, 1920-1965; Duryea, 1905-1965; Edwardsville, 1885-1960; Exeter, 1885-1938; Forty-Fort, 1887-1933; Freeland, 1877-1950; Hughestown, 1880-1965; Jeddo, 1865; Kingston, 1858-1925; Lafflin, 1965, Larksville, 1955; Luzerne, 1935-1965; Nescopeck, 1945-1950; New Columbus, 1935-1950; Nuangola, 1945; Parsons, 1888-1899; Pleasant Valley, 1872-1875; Plymouth, 1878-1891; Schickshinny, 1872-1960; Sugar notch, 1935-1945; Swoyerville, 1935-1950; Warrior Run, 1930-1940; West Hazelton, 1930-1935; West Wyoming, 1935-1945; White Haven, 1945; Wyoming, 1930-1945; and Yatesville; the cities of Hazelton, 1859-1955; Nanticoke, 1879-1965; Pittston, 1853-1955; and Wilkes-Barre, 1860-1965; and the townships of Bear Creek, 1859-1965; Black Creek, 1850-1965; Buck, 1834-1965; Butler, 1840-1940; Conyngham, 1880-1965; Dallas, 1818-1965; Dennison, 1840-1965; Dorrance, 1842-1965; Exeter, 1820-1899; Fairmount, 1835-1898; Fairview, 1888-

1900; Foster, 1859-1899; Franklin, 1844-1960; Hanover, 1821-1955; Hazel, 1845-1953; Hollenback, 1859-1965; Hunlock, 1880-1965; Huntington, 1815-1899; Jackson, 1859-1950; Jenkins, 1853-1965; Kingston, 1895-1905; Lake, 1965; Marcy, 1894; Nescopeck, 1833-1935; Newport, 1809-1955; Plains, 1933-1955; Plymouth, 1955; Rice, 1935-1960; Ross, 1935-1965; Salem, 1811-1950; Slocum, 1935-1950; Sugar Loaf, 1880-1945; Union, 1814-1945; White Haven, 1855-1858; Wilkes-Barre, 1898-1937; and Wright, 1935-1945.

The following original records of the clerk of courts are also among the holdings of the State Archives: OYER AND TERMINER DOCKET, 1892-1899; QUARTER SESSIONS DOCKETS, 1827-1840, 1849-1965; QUARTER SESSIONS INDEXES, 1918-1965; and QUARTER SESSIONS AND OYER AND TERMINER PAPERS, 1788-1883, not inclusive.

NORTHUMBERLAND COUNTY

TAX RECORDS, 1770-1921, undated, not inclusive (RG-47) for the boroughs of McEwensville, 1858-1900; Milton, 1848-1900; Mount Carmel, 1855-1899; Riverside, 1872-1900; Shamokin, 1866-1900; Snydertown, 1898, 1921; Sunbury, 1848-1900; Turbutville, 1859-1900; and Watsontown, 1800-1899; and the townships of Augusta, 1770-1846, undated; Bald Eagle, 1774-1782; Beaver, 1785-1799; Bloom, 1808; Buffaloe, 1773-1801; Cameron, 1852-1898; Catawissa, 1785-1797; Chillisquaque, 1787-1894, undated; Coal, 1840-1900; Delaware, 1848-1900; Derry, 1785-1796; East Buffaloe, 1796-1797; East Cameron, 1898-1900; East Chillisquaque, 1895-1900; Fishing Creek, 1793-1808, undated; Gearhart, 1891-1900; Hemlock, undated; Jackson, 1837-1921; Jordan, 1852-1900; Lewis, 1848-1900; Little Mahanoy, 1814-1920; Lower Augusta, 1848-1900; Lower Bald Eagle, 1787-1795; Lower Mahanoy, 1811-1908; Loyalsock, 1787-1794; Lycoming, 1783-1793; Mahantango, 1796-1797, undated; Mahoning, 1782-1808, undated; Mahanoy, 1778-1808; Mifflin, 1805, undated; Milton, 1818-1846; Northumberland, 1787, 1830-1900; Nippenose, 1787-1795; Pine Creek, 1786-1795; Point, 1786-1900; Ralpho, 1883-1900; Rockerfeller, 1881-1900; Rush, 1820-1900; Shamokin,

1773-1900; Sunbury, 1770-1848, undated; Turbut, 1773-1900; Upper Augusta, 1850-1900; Upper Bald Eagle, 1787-1789; Upper Mahanoy, 1787-1898; Washington, 1785-1900; West Buffalo, 1781-1797; West Cameron, 1898-1900; West Chillasquaque, 1895-1900; White Deer, 1778-1801; Wyoming, 1774-1793; and Zerbe, 1853-1900; and the townships/cities of Haines, 1792-1800, undated; Miles, 1789-1799; Muncy, 1774-1795; Penns, 1773-1811; and Potter, 1787-1813.

SCHUYLKILL COUNTY

SESSIONS BLOTTERS, 1844-1964, not inclusive (RG-47). Normally the volumes show the court case number, term, and year; the defendant's name and the charge; the name of the person providing the information under oath; the dates of court appearances; the amount of bail and the names of the sureties; the name of the justice of the peace making the return; and the dates that the return was made and delivered to the district attorney. Entries are in numerical order by case number.

Additional records transferred to the Archives from the county include COURT APPOINTMENT DOCKETS, 1933-1976; COURT OF OYER AND TERMINER DOCKETS, 1824-1967; COURT OF QUARTER SESSIONS DOCKETS, 1811-1969 and MISCELLANEOUS DOCKETS, 1917-1971; a DOG REGISTER, 1854-1912; LICENSE DOCKETS, 1889-1933; MINUTE BOOK DOCKETS, 1857-1976; and SETTLED CASE DOCKETS, 1884-1939, from the clerk of courts; and COAL TAX APPEALS, 1926-1942, from the board of county commissioners.

SOMERSET COUNTY

REPORTS OF THE DIRECTORS OF THE POOR AND OF THE HOUSE OF EMPLOYMENT AND MANAGERS OF SOMERSET COUNTY, December 31, 1902- December 31, 1926 (RG-47). The reports contain lists of persons admitted to the poor house, county home, county hospital or the county hospital for the insane that record the name, age, and sex of the resident and the dates of admittance, discharge, parole, death, or escape. From 1902 to 1908 the reports have listings of indentured children. Besides providing the name and age of the child, these lists also mention the name of the master and the date when the indenture was to expire. The record is arranged by filing date. From 1914 onward the names appearing on the lists are usually in alphabetical order.

APPOINTMENT PETITIONS, 1854-55, 1857-1880, 1882-1933, 1937-1938, and CORONER'S INQUISITIONS, 1853-1922, from the Somerset Clerk of Courts are also among the county record holdings of the State Archives.

TIOGA COUNTY

JURY LISTS, 1878-1977 (RG-47). The lists are dated and subscribed by the jury president and commissioners and give the names, occupations, and municipal residence of potential jurors. The file is in chronological order.

CONSTABLE BONDS, 1835-1979, and MISCELLANEOUS CIVIL PAPERS, 1898-1900, from the prothonotary's office of Tioga County are also among the holdings of the State Archives.

OTHER ORIGINAL COUNTY RECORDS

RECORDS OF THE COURT OF QUARTER SESSIONS, 1800-1903, of Crawford County; CIVIL RECORDS, 1807-1830, 1837-1838, for Indiana County; MINUTES OF THE COURT OF QUARTER SESSIONS, 1878-1969, for Lackawanna County; COUNTY ASSESSMENT ROLLS, 1945, 1950, 1955, 1960, for Lebanon County; JUDGMENT INDICES, 1828-1891, for Montgomery County; BONDS, 1837-1955, for Union County; COMMISSION BOOKS, 1890-1976, for Wayne County; and COMMISSION BOOKS, 1792-1973, and INDEXES, 1792-1964, for Westmoreland County.

CENSUS RECORDS

(107 Cubic Feet)

There have been no state censuses in Pennsylvania. The so-called SEPTENNIAL CENSUS RETURNS, 1779-1863 (RG-7), were merely enumerations of taxpayers every seven years for the purpose of determining representation in the General Assembly. Only a few (11 per cent) of these records have survived, and usually they just list the name and at times the occupation of the taxable white inhabitant. Data concerning slaves residing in the counties are often more extensive in content. Beginning with the year 1800, the name, age, sex, and residence of each slave is frequently noted, and occasionally even the owner's name is provided. A few returns (for Franklin County, 1828, 1835, 1842; Columbia County, 1821; Mifflin County, 1821; and Philadelphia City, 1863) also contain data (such as names, ages, and sex) about deaf, dumb, and blind persons.

The State Archives has original returns for thirty counties and the city of Philadelphia. Inhabitants are listed according to township or other political subdivision, with subdivisions arranged in alphabetical groupings in some, but not all, instances. The chart which appears on the next page illustrates what types of information are found on the returns from each county. Because of geographic proximity and as part of its local records preservation functions the Archives possesses a rough draft of the SEPTENNIAL CENSUS ENUMERATION FOR DAUPHIN COUNTY, 1856 (RG-47). Entries on these returns are grouped by boroughs and townships and have columns for recording the name, occupation, and sex of each taxable; and as needed, the number of male and female slaves owned and their ages; and the names, ages, color, and sex of any blind, deaf, and dumb household members. No data regarding slave holdings is provided on the returns. Apparently by mistake, however, the age of each taxable is entered in this space for Jackson, Jefferson, Londonderry, Mifflin, Rush, Upper Paxton, and Washington Townships and the borough of Millersburg. Other communities found on the enumeration include Conewago, Derry, Halifax, Hanover (East, West, North, and South), Harrisburg (East, West, North, and South), Londonderry, Lykens, Middletown,

Paxton (Lower and Middle), Reed, Susquehanna, Swatara (also Lower), and Wisconisco Townships and the boroughs of Dauphin and Gratz. The volume has an index but it is used to locate the pages on which county subdivisions appear rather than taxables.

The Division of Archives and Manuscripts also has custody of FARM CENSUS RETURNS (RG-1), generated by the Commonwealth during the years 1924 and 1927. The returns are arranged by county, and thereinafter by subdivision. Entries normally list the name and post office address of the occupant or person operating the farm; whether that person owned, rented, or simply managed the farm; the number of members in the household; the number of males and females comprising the family unit; and during 1927, the number of males and females in the family who were under ten years of age. Diverse data concerning livestock and the number of acres in the farm and its usage are included as well.

The decennial census is a national and not a state record. The federal census for 1790 was published in 1907 under the title *Heads of Families at the First Census of the United States Taken in the Year 1790: Pennsylvania* (Washington, 1908). This volume is completely indexed and may be consulted at the State Archives or at most large public or private libraries and historical societies. Entries show the name of a head of family, the number of free white males under sixteen years of age, the number of free white females, the number of all other free persons, and the number of slaves.

Enumerations for later census years have not been printed, but microfilm copies of Pennsylvania's schedules from 1800 to 1920 are available for use in the Archives search room. Entries are generally arranged by county, and thereunder by subdivision. Researchers may expect to find the following genealogical data:

CENSUS OF 1800. Covers all nineteen counties, with a typical entry listing the name and address of a head of family; the number of free whites under ten years of age, ten and under sixteen, sixteen and under twenty-six, twenty-six and under forty-five, and forty-five years and upward in the household; the number of all other free persons except Indians not taxed; and the number of slaves.

CENSUS OF 1810. Contains information for all twenty-four counties with entries usually showing the name and address of a head of family; the number of free white males and females under ten years of age, ten and under sixteen, sixteen and under forty-five, and forty-five years and upward in the household; the number of all other free persons except Indians not taxed; and the number of slaves.

CENSUS OF 1820. Includes data on all fifty-one counties with a listing normally showing the name and address of a family head; the number of free white males and females under ten years of age, ten and under sixteen, between sixteen and eighteen, sixteen and under twenty-six, twenty-six and under forty-five, and forty-five years and upward in the household; the number of foreigners not naturalized; the number of persons engaged in agriculture, commerce, or manufacturing; the number of free blacks and slaves by various age and sex categories; and the number of all other persons except Indians not taxed.

CENSUS OF 1830. Gives information for all fifty-two counties with an entry ordinarily enumerating the name and address of a head of family; the number of free white males and females in five-year groups to twenty, ten-year age intervals from twenty to one hundred, and one hundred years old and upward in the household; the number of free male and female black persons by age and sex; the number of slaves by age and sex; and the number of aliens.

CENSUS OF 1840. Has enumerations for all sixty-three counties with a representative listing normally recording the name and address of a head of family; the number of free white males and females in five-year age groups to twenty, ten-year age groups from twenty to one hundred years old and over in the household; the number of free male and female black persons and slaves according to various age groups; the number of persons classified as deaf, dumb, blind, insane, or idiotic in public and private charge; the number of persons in each family employed in various classes of occupations; the number of white persons over age twenty who were illiterate; and the names and ages of any military pensioners.

CENSUSES OF 1850 AND 1860. Data for all sixty-three and sixty-four counties respectively are found with a typical entry giving the name, postal address, age, sex, race, and occupation for each free person; the occupation and value of real estate owned for all free males over the age of fifteen years; the state, territory, or country where the individual was born; and data about whether the person was married, over twenty years of age and illiterate, attended school within the year, or was a pauper or convict. Entries regarding slavery generally show the name, age, sex, and color of the slave; information about whether the individual was at that time a fugitive from the state; and the slaveowner's name. A microfilmed copy of the HEADS OF FAMILIES INDEX FOR THE 1850 FEDERAL CENSUS, COUNTY OF PHILADELPHIA (MG-262) is also included among the census holdings. Prepared by the Genealogical Society of Pennsylvania, the index lists by county subdivisions and thereunder in alphabetical order all heads of households as well residents with differing surnames. The city of Philadelphia is not included but the other twenty-six boroughs and townships of the county are.

CENSUS OF 1870. Records information for all sixty-six counties with a listing normally showing the name, postal address, age (if under one year, the number of months), sex, race, and birthplace for each person in a household; the occupation and estate (personal and property) value of all males over the age of twenty-one years; whether the person attended school or was married within the year; whether the individual's parents were of foreign birth; and for a person ten years of age or older, whether he or she was deaf, dumb, blind, insane, idiotic, or able to read and write.

CENSUS, U.S. SCHEDULES FOR PITTSBURGH AND ALLEGHENY CITIES, 1850, 1860, 1870. Consists of a computerized listing of the 1850 through 1870 federal censuses that was prepared by the Pittsburgh Regional Historical Data Archives. The listings are in alphabetical order by resident's surname and show the name, age, sex, color, ward, and occupation of the individual along with the page and line number of the census manuscript from which the information was extracted. Occasionally data also appear concerning property owned.

CENSUS OF 1880. Contains data for all sixty-seven counties with entries usually recording the name, address, sex, race, birthplace, age (if less than one year, number of months), marital status (whether married during the census year), relationship to the head of the family, profession, occupation, or trade of the person; the number of months unemployed during the census year; and whether the individual was sick, temporarily disabled (if so what sickness or disability), literate, blind, deaf, dumb, idiotic, insane, maimed, crippled, or bedridden. Information about school attendance and parental birthplaces is also noted. A SOUNDEX INDEX to the census, which is based on the phonetic sounds of surnames, has been acquired from the National Archives. The index provides users with the soundex code; the state covered by the index; and the volume, enumeration district, sheet number, and line of the return where the data appears on the census. Additional information shown on the index includes the name, color, sex, age, birthplace, address, and citizenship status of the head of the family; and the name, age (also month and year of birth), place of birth, citizenship status, and relationship of each member of the family to that person. The index cards are grouped in alphabetical order by the first letter of the family or person's surname and thereunder arranged in numerical order by soundex number and alphabetically by the first name of the head of household.

SPECIAL CENSUS OF 1890 (SCHEDULE ENUMERATING UNION VETERANS AND WIDOWS OF UNION VETERANS OF THE CIVIL WAR). Covers all sixty-seven counties with an entry commonly giving the surveyed person's name and postal address plus the veteran's rank, company, regiment (or vessel attached to), length of service, dates of enlistment and discharge, and, where apropos, any disability incurred.

CENSUS OF 1900. Has data for all sixty-seven counties with the following recorded: the name, address, race, sex, date of birth, age at last birthday, and marital status (and number of years if married) of each person in the household; the relationship of that individual to the head of the family; the number of children that each mother gave birth to and the number of offspring that were still alive at the time of the census; the place of birth of the person and his or her parents; the occupation, trade, or profession of everyone ten years and over; the number of months that every able-bodied person was unemployed during the year; and how many months of school each household member attended. In those cases where the surveyed person was an immigrant, he or she was asked to provide information regarding the year of migration to the U.S., the number of years residency in the country, and whether naturalization had occurred. In addition data concerning literacy and home or farm ownership are also found. A SOUNDEX INDEX is available for for this census.

CENSUS OF 1910. Covers all sixty-seven counties and provides information such as this: the name, address, race, sex, age at last birthday, and marital status (and number of years in present marriage if married) of each person in the abode; the relationship of that individual to the head of the family; the number of children born to each woman and the number alive at the time of the census; the birthplace of both the person being polled and his or her parents; the occupation, trade, profession, or work done by the resident; the nature of the industry, business or establishment in which the person worked and whether as an employer, employee, or working on own account; if an employee, whether working on April 15, 1910, and the number of weeks without a job in 1909; and the literacy (able to read, write), school status (any attendance since Sept. 1, 1909) of each person counted. In addition, a foreign-born resident was asked whether he or she could speak English, was a naturalized citizen or an alien, and the year of arrival in the United States. Data regarding home or farm ownership; mortgages; and whether the individual was a Civil War veteran, blind, deaf and dumb also appears. A SOUNDEX INDEX is available for accessing the microfilm. The typed index cards show the soundex code; the state covered by the index; and the volume, enumeration district, sheet number, and line of the census return where the data can be found. Besides this retrieval data, the following information appears about the families and individuals enumerated: the name, color, sex, age, birthplace, and address of the head of the household; and the names, ages, birthplaces, and relationship of each member of the family to that person.

CENSUS OF 1920. Is complete for all sixty-seven counties and records the following data: name, address, race, sex, age at last birthday, and marital status of each person in the household; the relationship of that individual to the head of the family; the place of birth of both the person being enumerated and his or her parents; the occupation, trade, profession, or work done by the resident; the nature of the industry, business or establishment in which the person worked and whether as an employer, a wage or salary worker, or working on own account; the literacy (able to read, write) and school status (any attendance since Sept. 1, 1919) of each household member. Other questions asked of the foreign born include the year of immigration to the United States; whether the person was a naturalized citizen or an alien; if naturalized, the year of naturalization; whether the individual could speak English and the mother tongue of that person and his or her parents. Data about home ownership, that is, whether the dwelling was owned or rented, free or mortgaged, is recorded as well. A SOUNDEX INDEX can be used for accessing the microfilm. Entries on the index will provide the user with the soundex code; the state covered by the index; and the volume, enumeration district, sheet number, and line of the census return where the data can be located. Additional information shown on the index includes the name, color, sex, age, birthplace, address, and citizenship status of the head of the household and each member of the family related to that person.

For the convenience of researchers, published indexes to Pennsylvania's 1800-1860 censuses are available for use in the search room. In addition to the census materials relating to Pennsylvania the Division of Archives and Manuscripts has a CENSUS BOOK (MG-48) for the New York communities of Addison, Bath, Canisteo, Cohocton, Dansville, Jasper, Painted Post, Prattsburg, Pulteney, Troupsburg, and Wayne. Kept by the census marshall of Steuben County, John Magee, the book was compiled for the federal census of 1820 and contains information appropriate for that enumeration. The volume is not indexed.

Because the septennial censuses and the farm censuses are not indexed, the Archives staff cannot respond to inquiries for specific information contained in them. Likewise, we do not service search requests relating to the federal censuses, nor do we make copies for them. Questions regarding these federal returns should be addressed to the National Archives and Records Administration (Washington 20408).

DATA RECORDED IN THE SEPTENNIAL CENSUSES, 1779-1863

County	Year	Taxables				Slaves or Blacks			
		Name	Occupation	Age	Sex	Owner's Name	Name	Age	Sex
Adams	1800	X	–	–	–	O	X	X	X
Allegheny	1800	X	X	–	–	X	–	X	X
Bedford	1779	X	–	–	–	–	–	–	–
"	1786	X	–	–	–	–	–	–	–
"	1800	X	–	–	–	O	–	X	X
Berks	1779	X	–	▪	▪	▪			
"	1786	X	–	–	–	–	–	–	–
"	1793	X	–	–	–	–	–	–	–
"	1800	X	X	–	–	X	X	X	X
Bucks	1786	X	–	–	–	–	–	–	–
"	1800	X	–	–	–	–	–	–	–
Centre	1800	X	–	–	–	X	–	X	X
Chester	1779*	X	–	–	–	–	–	–	–
"	1786*	X	–	–	–	–	–	–	–
"	1800	X	–	–	–	–	X	X	X
Columbia	1821	X	X	–	–	X	–	X	X
Cumberland	1793	X	X	–	–	–	–	–	–
"	1800	X	X	–	–	–	X	X	X
Dauphin	1786	X	–	–	–	–	–	–	–
"	1800	X	–	–	–	–	X	X	X
" (Derry Twp.)	1807	X	X	–	–	X	X	X	–
Delaware	1793*	X	X	–	–	–	–	–	–
"	1800	X	–	–	–	X	–	X	X
Fayette	1786	X	–	–	–	–	–	–	–
"	1800	X	–	–	–	–	–	–	–
Franklin	1786	X	–	–	–	–	–	–	–
"	1800	X	X	–	–	X	–	X	X
"	1807	X	X	–	–	X	X	X	X
"	1814	X	X	–	X	–	X	O	X
"	1821	X	X	O	X	X	X	X	X
"	1828	X	X	O	X	–	X	X	–
"	1835	X	X	O	X	X	X	X	X
"	1842	X	X	–	X	X	X	X	X
Greene	1800	X	–	–	–	X	X	X	X
Huntingdon	1800	X	X	–	–	–	–	–	–
"	1821	X	X	–	–	–	–	–	–
Lancaster	1779	X	–	–	–	–	–	–	–
"	1786	X	–	–	–	–	–	–	–
"	1793	X	–	–	–	–	–	–	–
"	1800	X	O	–	–	X	O	X	X

		Taxables				Slaves or Blacks			
County	Year	Name	Occupation	Age	Sex	Owner's Name	Name	Age	Sex
Luzerne	1800	X	–	–	–	–	X	X	O
Lycoming	1800	X	X	O	O	–	X	X	X
Mifflin	1800	X	–	–	–	–	O	O	O
"	1821	X	X	–	–	O	O	O	O
Montgomery	1786	X	O	–	–	–	–	–	–
"	1793	X	–	–	–	–	–	–	–
"	1800	X	X	–	–	–	X	X	–
"	1807	X	X	–	–	–	–	–	–
"									
(Pottsgrove Twp.)	1842	X	–	–	–	–	–	–	–
Northampton	1786	X	–	–	–	–	–	–	–
"	1800	X	–	–	–	–	X	X	X
Northumberland									
	1800	X	O	–	–	–	X	X	–
Philadelphia City									
	1793*	X	X	–	–	–	–	–	–
" "	1800	X	X	–	–	O	O	O	O
" "	1863	X	X	X	X	also race	X	X	X
Philadelphia County									
	1793*	X	X	–	–	–	–	–	–
Somerset	1800	X	X	–	–	–	–	–	–
Washington	1786	X	–	–	–	–	–	–	–
"	1800	X	X	–	–	X	X	X	X
Wayne	1800	X	X	–	–	–	X	X	–
Westmoreland									
	1786	X	–	–	–	–	–	–	–
" & Armstrong									
	1800	X	O	–	–	–	X	X	X
Wyoming	1849	X	X	–	–	–	–	–	–
York	1786	X	–	–	X	–	–	–	–
"	1793	X	O	–	–	–	–	–	–
"	1800	X	O	–	–	X	–	X	X
"	1807	X	X	–	–	O	O	X	X

KEY: X = Information is usually found
= Information is not found
O = Information is occasionally found
* = Not grouped alphabetically

FAMILY PAPERS
(576 Cubic Feet)

The State Archives possesses numerous manuscript groups that contain the personal papers of Pennsylvania families. For a more comprehensive listing of such materials researchers should consult Harry E. Whipkey's *Guide to the Manuscript Groups in the Pennsylvania State Archives* (Harrisburg, 1976). The list appearing here consists only of those collections that contain any of the following items: wills, deeds, indentures, genealogies, land papers, and documents relating to the marriages and deaths of members of select families. Collections that are available only on microfilm (MG-262, General Microfilm Collection) and have not been cataloged in other guides are also included.

Achey Family Collection, 1834 (1894-1919)-1919 (MG-140), of Bucks County.

J. Simpson Africa Papers, 1734 (1772-1891)-1891 (MG-14), from Huntingdon County.

Albert family, ca. 1915 (in MG-445), from Shellsville, Dauphin County.

John Anderson Papers, 1684-1904 (MG-147), of Bedford County. Materials of the marriage-related Espy, Woods and Watson families are included.

Anshutz-Berry families, 1791-1936 (in MG-262), from the Huntingdon County region.

Barton Collection, Robert R., 1823-1976 (MG-460) containing papers relating to the Barton family of Lexington, Virginia and the marriage related Hume family of Memphis, Tennessee.

Bear Papers, John, 1783-1836 (MG-21), of Cumberland County.

Beaver Records, James A., 1790-1915 (MG-389), of Centre County. Contains deeds, patents, a biography of the governor, and genealogy of his ancestors.

Bell Insurance Company Records, E.A., 1893-1949 (MG-266), of Monroe County includes a Bell family history.

Bellamy Family Papers, 1846-1934 (in MG-8), of Wisconsin; contains data on the Sherwood and Thomas families and Beyer family, 1732-1923 (in MG-8), from Tyrone, Blair County. Includes birth records of the marriage related Crum family.

Bierer Papers, Jacob J., 1795-1907 (MG-253), from Latrobe, Westmoreland County.

Bloss Family Collections, 1863-1904 (MG-25), from Luzerne County.

Bodey-Cooper Collection, ca. 1806-1882 (MG-26), of Montgomery County and the city of Philadelphia, respectively.

Bowerman Papers, Solomon, 1823-1922 (MG-337), having land papers pertaining to the Diddy family, 1823-1922, of Dauphin County.

Brady Family Papers, 1814-1964 (MG-249), from Shippensburg, Cumberland County.

Brooke family, 1779-1824 (in MG-262), from the Birdsboro area, Berks County.

Bryant Family Papers, 1807-1808, 1833-1857, 1903 (MG-27), from western Pennsylvania.

Buchanan family, 1780-1900 (in MG-8), from Greene County.

Bucher-Hummel families, 1764-1963 (MG-382), from Dauphin County.

Bucher family, 1768-1837 (in MG-262), from the Birdsboro area, Berks County.

Burd-Shippen Family Collection, 1715-1834 (MG-30), of Lancaster County.

Campbell Family Papers, 1796-1877 (MG-34), of Juniata County.

Carter and Henry families, 1756-1877 (in MG-262), of Lancaster County.

Casey Family Collection, 1946-1986 (MG-406), of Lackawanna County. Microfilmed copies of photographs, scrapbooks, and notations about the family's history.

Chandler family, 1830-1842 (in MG-262), from the Philadelphia vicinity.

Claypoole family, 1657-1811 (in MG-8), of Philadelphia.

Coleman Family Collection, 1757-1940 (in MG-182), the Lebanon County Historical Society manuscript collections of Lebanon County.

Conrad Family Papers, 1762-1796 (MG-37), from Middletown, Dauphin County.

Cope Family Papers, 1793-1937 (MG-38), of Philadelphia, Chester, Bucks, and Susquehanna Counties.

Corbett family, 1870-1897 (in MG-262), from Clarion County.

Denny-O'Hara families, 1778-1912 (in MG-262), from the Pittsburgh area.

Ditmer-Lehmer Family Papers, 1863-1914 (MG-151), of York County.

Dobbins family, 1793-1908 (in MG-262), of Erie County.

Dock Family Papers, 1865-1951 (MG-43), originally from Lancaster and Cumberland counties. Genealogical data on the Knight family of the Philadelphia area are also found.

Earle Papers, George H., 1935-1939 (MG-342), of Chester County. Contains biographical and military service, and genealogical data among his official papers.

Elder Family Collection, 1752-1918 (MG-45), from Dauphin County.

Endsley Family Papers, 1847-1941 (in MG-8), from Somerset County.

Engle Family Papers, 1854-1858 (in MG-8), from Dauphin and Lancaster Counties.

Evans family, 1752-1907 (in MG-262), of Chester County.

Evans Collection, Samuel, 1752-1918 (MG-47), of Lancaster County. Contains genealogical data on the Evans, Fall, Hughes, Lowery, Lukens, Slaymaker, and Watson families.

Eyre family genealogy, Col. John, 1738-1905 (in MG-193), of Philadelphia. The data is recorded in a handwritten and annotated copy of a 1760 day book. Information regarding the family's Kensington property, 1919, also appears in the back of the volume.

Farley family, 1846-1870 (in MG-8), of Philadelphia.

Fenn Collection, George Washington, 1829, 1861-1927 (MG-333), from Harrisburg. Includes a family bible and genealogical data on the Fenn-Dietrich-Roberts families of Dauphin County.

Ferree Papers, Ozias, 1865-1909, 1971 (MG-251), of Adams County. Includes genealogical materials on the Ferree and Leaman families.

Fisher Papers, Benjamin Franklin, 1862-1915 (MG-375), from Montgomery County.

Flickinger Family Papers, 1834-1891 (in MG-8), of Perry County.

Foster family, 1837-1869 (in MG-262), from Luzerne County.

Frazer Papers, Reah, 1739 (1821-1856)-1879 (MG-53), from Lancaster County.

Fulton Papers, J. Alexander, 1846 (1846-1861)-1900 (MG-54), from Kittanning, Armstrong County.

Garner Collection, Ignatius, ca. 1834-1888 (MG-417), containing historical notes and a genealogy for the Garner family of Schuylkill County.

Gilson Family Papers, 1887-1889, 1958 (in MG-8), from Ohio and Pennsylvania.

Greason Collection, Samuel M. (MG-62), relating to the Greason and Gracey families of Cumberland County.

Gregg Collection, Theodore, 1851-1874 (MG-233), of Centre County.

Gross Family Papers, 1805-1918 (MG-63), of Union County.

Hall Papers, Wilmer C., 1860-1879 (MG-65), from Cumberland County.

Harper Collection, John W., 1767-1982 (MG-420), of Centre County. Contains *taufschein*, land surveys, deeds, wills, and genealogical materials.

Harris Family Papers, 1768-1849 (MG-67), of Dauphin County.

Harris-Fisher Family Collection, 1749-1881 (MG-68), from Harrisburg and Middletown, Dauphin County.

Harris-Silverthorn Family Papers, 1827-1924 (MG-69), from the Erie County area.

Hastings-Hickok Estate Papers, 1766-1901 (MG-336), primarily land titles relating to family activities in Bedford County. Contains materials relating to the Woods, Watson and Espy families.

Haudenshield Papers, John R., 1901-1962 (MG-142), of Allegheny County.

Hershey Family Papers, 1826-1863 (in MG-262), of Lancaster County. Contains Scott Funk Hershey's printed family history.

Hickok Papers, Ross A., 1768-1943 (MG- 146), from Harrisburg, Dauphin County.

Hiester Family Papers, 1750-1865 (MG-72), of Berks and Dauphin counties.

Hillegass family, Conrad, 1822-1825 (in MG-8), of Montgomery County. Includes a naturalization certificate, 1760, of John Kunnius of Berks County.

Hines Family Papers, 1773-1872 (in MG-8), from Philadelphia.

Hocker Family Collection, 1851-1954 (in MG-8), originally from Carlisle; includes a genealogy of the Watson family of West Virginia.

Hoover Family Papers, 1845-1933 (in MG-8), from Lancaster County.

Keith Family Papers, 1861-1906 (in MG-8), of New England and Bucks County.

Kelly Family Papers, 1815 (1836-1865)-1937 (MG-189), from the borough of Indiana.

Kerr Papers, Lewis B., 1794-1889 (MG-77), of Perry County.

King Collection, Alfred, 1801-1929 (MG-177), of Erie County.

Kinkead-Armstrong-Hollenbach Collection, 1765-1850 (MG-158), of Toboyne Township, Perry County (formerly a part of Cumberland County).

Knight family; see Dock Family Papers.

Knoedler Family Collection, 1900-1940 (MG-330), of Economy, Beaver County.

Kramer Collection, Thomas, 1780, 1786, 1800-1819, 1835-1882, 1889 (MG-296), from Palmyra in Lebanon County; contains materials pertaining to the Kramer and Segner families.

Kuhnert family photographs, ca. 1920-1976 (MG-281), from Harrisburg, Dauphin County.

Kunkel Family Collection, 1801-1885 (MG-256), from Harrisburg, Dauphin County.

Kunkle Collection, John Crain, 1798, 1830-1873, 1938-1966 (MG-301), of Harrisburg, Dauphin County. Materials relating to the Rutherford family, ca. 1870's are also present.

Leitzell Family Collection, 1742-1955 (in MG-8), originally of Dauphin County; includes materials on the Rupley, Shrenck (Shrenk) and Leige families.

Lightfoot-Meredith families of Berks County, ca. 1700-1900s (in MG-8).

Logan Papers, Algernon Sydney and Robert Restalrig, ca. 1680-1945 (MG-247), from Philadelphia; containing photographs and genealogical materials relating to the Logan and Wister families.

Maclay Family Papers, 1788-1933 (MG-352), of Franklin County.

McAllister Family Papers, 1775-1850, (MG-81), of York, Lancaster and Dauphin counties.

McCalmont Family Papers, 1925-1947 (MG-371), from Franklin, Venango County. Includes personal letters and "family bulletins."

McCoy Family Papers, ca. 1930-1950 (in MG-8), from Harrisburg, Dauphin County.

McFarland Papers, J. Horace, 1859-1866, 1898-1951 (MG-85), of Harrisburg, Dauphin County. Contains a biographical sketch, a genealogy, and family Bible with birth, marriage, and death notations, 1804-1903.

Meginness Collection, John F., 1828-1899 (MG-255), from Williamsport, Lycoming County; contains genealogical materials concerning central Pennsylvanians.

Merkel Family Papers, 1818-1912 (MG-88), of Cumberland County.

Meseroll Collection, Sarah R., 1733-1939 (MG-143), having papers of the Preston family of Buckingham and Plumstead Townships in Bucks County, and at Stockport in Wayne County.

Metcalf Collection, Daniel, 1783-1825 (MG-183), of Potter County.

Mifflin Collection, Lloyd, 1835-1961, 1965 (MG-165), of Columbia, Lancaster County.

Mish Papers, John W., 1811-1916 (MG-91), from Lebanon County.

Mohn Family Papers, Henry, 1844-1958 (MG-332), containing photographs and an 1871 Bible relating to the Mohn and marriage-related Feucht family of Leetsdale (Allegheny County) and Economy (Beaver County).

Moore Family Papers, 1749 (1749-1887)-1934 (MG-93), of Carlisle, Cumberland County; includes items relating to the Parker family as well.

Nauman Papers, Gertrude Howard, 1780-1972 (MG-201), from Harrisburg, Dauphin County.

Nicholson Papers, John, Sequestered 1765 (1778-1800)-1852 (MG-96), of Philadelphia.

Orbison Family Papers, 1750-1902 (MG-98), of Huntingdon County; contains items relating to the Cox, Barton and Binney families of Philadelphia, and the Cromwell, Smith and Thompson families of Huntingdon.

Ott Family Papers, 1838-1971 (in MG-354), from Beaver County.

Pennypacker Papers, Samuel W., 1703 (1851-1916)-1916 (MG-171), from Philadelphia.

Potts Family Papers, 1704-1853, 1904 (MG-104), of central Pennsylvania.

Priestley Papers, Joseph, 1794-1874 (MG-414), from Northumberland County. Chiefly deeds and the 1802 will of the discoverer of oxygen.

Ream Family Papers, 1750-1862 (in MG-8), from Reamstown, Cocalico Township, Lancaster County.

Rex Collection, Millicent Barton, 1762 (1814-1880)-1949 (MG-180), containing materials relating to James White of Hartstown in Crawford County.

Richardson Collection, George A., 1869-1974 (MG-263), from Bethlehem, Lehigh County. Includes research notes on the family's history.

Robbins Collection, Lucy, 1684-1906 (MG-423), containing legal and family papers of the Baldwin-Williams-Swain families of Bucks County and Philadelphia.

Schaffner Family Collection, 1859-1866 (MG-232), of Dauphin County.

Schmidt Papers, J. Augustus, 1894-1911 (in MG-8), from Hazleton, Luzerne County.

Selden Family Collection, 1820-1891, 1906 (MG-102), of Masthope in Pike County.

Sloan-Gordon Family Papers, 1813-1934 (in MG-8), from Monongahela in Washington County.

Snyder Family Collection, 1787-1843 (MG-116), of Snyder County (formerly Union County).

Staake Papers, William H., 1773 (1871-1895)-1895 (MG-118), containing papers of the Davidson and Ewing families of Philadelphia and the wills and settlements of Lewis Bremer, William S. Clark, Caroline Cook, Maria Elisabeth Feichtenberger, Isaac Flickinger, Peter Gelzer, James Golcher, Anton Gruber, Christian Hahn, Delphine T. Hopper, Charles W. McNeely, John Reyle, Samuel Schrack, Joseph A. Speel, Daniel Springer, J. George Wagner and Joseph Wayne.

Stackhouse Family Papers, 1797-1819, 1861-1922 (MG-119), of Bucks County.

Stevens-Outman Family Papers, 1856-1972 (MG-149), of Potter County; includes items relating to the Swetland and Watrous lines of the family.

Stover Papers, Edward, 1857-1935 (MG-320), of Middletown and Hummelstown, Dauphin County.

Swope family, ca. 1880-1960 (in MG-218) of Mapleton Depot. Includes photographs of the Boring, Hess, Smithson, and Brooks families.

*A photograph found in the PENNSYLVANIA COLLECTION, 1626- present
(MG-8), PSA. Unfortunately for researchers, such photographs are not
usually so clearly identified as this one is.*

Tate family genealogy, Major Magnus, 1732-1808 (in MG-8), of Philadelphia and Berkeley County, Virginia. Includes a copy of the royal descent of the "Shooter's Hill" Smiths of Virginia.

Thompson Collection, Edward Shippen, 1684 (1746-1904)-1941 (MG-125), having materials of the Shippen, Burd and Patterson families of Perry, Dauphin and Lancaster Counties.

Thompson-Ullery Collection, Kathleen, 1783-1972 (MG-305), of Juniata County.

Treziyulny Family Papers, 1758-1921 (MG-128), of Centre County.

Vensell family, 1863-1894 (in MG-262), from Clarion County.

Weaver-Lebo families, 1885-1886 (in MG-8), from Dauphin County.

Weidner Family Papers, 1828-1880 (in MG-8), from Berks County.

Weiser Family Collection, 1742-1927 (MG-132), from Lancaster County.

Welles Family Papers, 1805-1898 (MG-133), of Wyalusing in Bradford County; includes materials relating to Mathias Hollenback of Wilkes-Barre.

Williams Family Collection, Edward C., 1848-1923 (MG-318), from Dauphin County. Contains records about the marriage related Hetzel family.

Woods Family Collection, 1794 (1861-1866)-1952 (MG-188), of Centre County.

Zehner-Zaner families, 1971 (in MG-8), consisting of a one-volume lineage.

Zundel Family Papers, 1918-1945 (in MG-354), from Phillipsburgh (now Monaca), Beaver County. Contains genealogical data, 1816-1866, on the Zundel and marriage-related Forstner families.

MISCELLANEOUS RECORDS

(624 Cubic Feet)

ABSTRACTS OF OBITUARIES IN THE *CARLISLE EVENING SENTINEL*, 1906-1915, by John C. Fralish, Jr. (MG-262). A microfilm copy of typed information extracted from the published obituaries of the *Sentinel* which is located in Cumberland County. Entries are in alphabetical order by surnames and normally give the name, age, date of death, and place of death of the deceased person; the date of the funeral; and particulars regarding whether data about surviving family members appeared in the newspaper. Other information which appears on occasion include the occupation of the person, his or her most recent residence if not living in the city of Carlisle at time of death, name of spouse, and place of birth.

ACCOUNTS OF LOTS SOLD, 1832-1937 (MG-311). Indexed. A record of property sold by the Lehigh Coal and Navigation Company in Allentown, Ashton, Bethlehem, Coaldale, Easton, Hecklebernie, Landsford, Mauch Chunk, Nesquehoning, Rockport, South Easton, Summit Hill, Tamaqua, Taylorsville, West Haven, and sundry places. Information appearing includes the name of the purchaser, the property's location and lot number, the date of deed or agreement, the price of the lot, the date and the amount of any bonds and mortgages, cash amount, and date of entry or settlement.

DR. KARL ARNDT HARMONY SOCIETY COLLECTION, 1749-1949 (MG-437). Contains alienated documents that were once part of the Harmony Society's archives. The Harmony Society was a German religious communal group that was established in western Pennsylvania on February 15, 1805, by George Rapp and his followers and that lasted until December 13, 1905. The legal file has a few items in each of the following categories: birth records for Johann Georg Rapp, November 1, 1757, and Johann Georg Bentel, December 31, 1758; certificate of safe passage for John Langenbacher, a laborer and native of Knittlinger, to travel from France to the United States, February 27, 1806; citizenship paper of Johan Friedrich Reichert, July 9, 1798; coroner's inquisitions held in Beaver County regarding the death of an unidentified man who drowned as a result of an explosion on the steamboat *Mayflower*, May 16, 1848, and concerning the drowning of a new-born, September, 13, 1849; death certifications, 1813-1884, for John Mayer (1813), John George Shaffer (1804), Jacob Steck (1812), a child of Carolina Teiling (1884), Elisabeth Wahl (1878), Anna Catharina Wolfangel (1848), and Gottfried (Nikander) Wolfangel (1849); divorce papers pertaining to Christop Mohl , 1807, 1824, 1831, 1849; extracts of deeds, 1854, 1873; guardian-ship papers of Barbara, Godfray, and Theophilus Lively, December 26, 1808; indenture servant papers for Gotlieb Napper (Knapper), October 22, 1804, and for Henry and Elisabeth Knapper, January 16, 1818; land patents of Peter Shriver for a lot in Jefferson County, Oh., 1805, and of John S. Duss for land in Webster County, Neb., 1887; lists of names of the Harmony Society who filed their declaration of intention to become citizens on the 25th day of September, 1810 and the 12th day of November, 1811; surveys, courses, and distances, 1804-1930; and certified copies of the wills of Susannah E. Crees of Beaver County (1897), Jacob Fruit of Beaver County (1875), William T. Henrici of Beaver County (1877), Mary Elizabeth Creese Spitzer of Marengo, Ill. (1901), and Henry Sybert of Lancaster County (1806). There also is an 1868 application of Caroline Duss, widow of deceased Civil War soldier John Rutz (alias Duss), for an additional bounty.

BANKRUPTCY FILE, 1785-1790 (RG-27). Contains bonds and peti-tions filed with the president of the supreme executive council by debtors, creditors, and the commissioners of the bankrupt. Data found on the documents differ with each case, but usually the bankrupt person's name, occupation, and amount of debt appears. Specifics concerning the claims of creditors are occasionally noted and the amount of bond submitted is recorded. The file is arranged alphabetically and a name listing has been created for reference purposes.

BRIEFS OF TITLE, 1880-1918 (MG-311). Indexed. Abstracted transactions which trace the ownership of select land holdings of the Lehigh Coal and Navigation Company from current ownership by the company back to the original warrant and patent holders. Representative properties include the Francis Yarnall tract; South

Second Street and Easton; the Francis B. Nichols tract; Ballstown (Philadelphia City); the "Biddle" (Luzerne County) and John Farnum (Pottsville) estates; real estate purchased for the Lehigh and Susquehanna Railroad Company (the Hazardville, Penobscot, and White Haven tracts); the Gerard Lock, Hauto, Kettle, Mauch Chunk, and Pine Forest tracts; Lehigh Coal Mine Company land holdings; and water power and rights of the Lehigh and Delaware Division Canals. With the exception of the Ballstown tract which was in Philadelphia City all of the property holdings are in Carbon, Lehigh, Luzerne, Northampton, and Schuylkill Counties. Each volume covers a specific geographic region and is thereunder in chronological order. Hand drawn maps of the various tracts often appear immediately after the name indexes.

BUCHER-HUMMEL FAMILY PAPERS, 1763-1963 (MG-382). Correspondence, receipts, business accounts, legal documents, engravings, photographs, and family papers pertaining to John Conrad Bucher and his descendants. Included in the collection are the following:

Diary of JOHN CONRAD BUCHER, November 5, 1818- October 26, 1827. Entries provide comments regarding social, political and cultural matters at both the national and local level. Numerous references to the marriage and death of family members, personal acquaintances, and Harrisburg residents appear as well.

Papers Relating to the FRENCH AND INDIAN WAR ERA, 1763-1764. Several versions of a monthly return for the Second Battalion, Pennsylvania Regiment, commanded by Lt. Col. Asher Clayton dated October 24, 1764, and stationed at the forks of the Muskingum, 128 miles from Fort Pitt; a roll of Capt. James Pepers' Troop of Light Horsemen, Second Battalion, Pennsylvania Regiment, September 8, 1764, while at Fort Bedford; appointment by John Penn of Conrad Bucher as Captain of the Pennsylvania Regiment of Foot, July 1, 1764; and accounts relating to military supplies and troop movements, 1763-1764.

CADAVER RECEIVING BOOKS, 1901-1908, 1916-1925, 1942-1965 (RG-11). A record of bodies donated to and received by the anatomical board of the state of Pennsylvania (now Human Gifts

Registry) and distributed to medical and dental schools in the state for teaching purposes. Entries in the books give the name, sex, color, age, nativity, social state (single, married, widow), and occupation of the deceased; the date and cause of death; the date that the body was delivered and the tag number; the attending physician's name and dates of treatment; the names of the institution that provided the cadaver and the school receiving it; and the condition of the body (good, bad, cut, uncut). The volumes are in chronological order by delivery date with some books also having monthly groupings by areas (usually Philadelphia and Pittsburgh).

CAMBRIA IRON COMPANY HOSPITAL RECORDS, 1887-1931 (MG-262). The Cambria Iron Company which operated in Johnstown, Pa. opened its own hospital on November 7, 1887, exclusively to treat employees who were injured on the job. It was the first such industrial hospital established in Pennsylvania and probably the United States. Included among the microfilmed records are patient registers, November 9, 1887-October 29, 1931. The volumes are arranged in chronological order by admittance dates and have columns for recording the injured employee's name, nativity, age, sex, marital status, occupation, and color; the diagnosis upon being admitted, and if relevant, as revised; the result of treatment; number of days spent in the hospital; the hospital ward; patient admittance and discharge numbers; and if appropriate, the date of death. The more modern registers (1923-1931) have space for indicating whether the person was a paying or poor patient.

CENTURY FARMS PROGRAM APPLICATIONS AND RELATED CORRESPONDENCE, 1988-1990 (RG-1). The Century Farm Program was established to recognize those farm families of the Commonwealth who are the backbone of the state and nation. Applications cover farms whose ownership dates from as early as 1717 to 1887 and show the name, telephone number, postal address, township, and county of the owner; the current number of acres in the farm; the main business, specialty of the farm; the date of original purchase by the family's ancestors; and a list of family owners from the first owner to the present. Supplemental and voluntary information collected for the use of future historians appears on the back of the application. Data solicited include who the farm was originally purchased from; how many acres were in the parcel; what was the cost of land per acre; where was the first owner born; where did he live prior to the farm; was this a homestead; did the first owner farm the land; did he engage in any trades or occupations other than farming; how many children did he have; children's names and where did they move; is the original home or any portion of the original buildings still standing or in use; when was the home built; and any other related information or historical facts. The form is notarized, dated, and signed by the applicant and has a legal description of the land from a deed, abstract, or tax statement attached to it. A brief family history may be included as well. The applications are grouped by counties. A computerized listing showing the county, year farm was acquired, name and address of owner (or couples), and the year that the farm was certified as a Century Farm, is available for reference purposes.

CLEMENCY FILE, 1775-1900, 1906-1907, 1948-1962, (RG-15, 26 and 27). Individual case files that may contain diverse documents (summary sheets, letters, petitions, court transcripts, newspaper notices, copies of death warrants, pardon proclamations or respites) about persons seeking pardons from the president of the Supreme Executive Council, the governor, or the Board of Pardons. The information found in the file varies with each dossier and the time period. While one case file may merely enumerate a person's name and reason for being imprisoned, another may also list the incarcerated individual's occupation and particulars about his or her life and family. In a few instances photographs of the persons are included. From 1790 to 1873 the documents are filed chronologically. All other materials are arranged alphabetically according to petitioner's surname.

COLLECTIONS OF THE LANDIS VALLEY MUSEUM, 1749-Present (MG-447). Contains microfilmed deeds, patents, confirmation and condition of sale papers, frakturs, and family bibles, 1749-1893, relating to residents in or near the site of of the Landis Valley Museum in Lancaster County. For the most part the records on the microfilm are in chronological order.

COMMISSION BOOKS, August 9, 1733- April 1, 1809 (RG-17). Indexed. Besides containing data pertaining to commissions for offices ranging from aldermen of the city of Philadelphia to treasurer of Pennsylvania, the volumes also have lists of persons who took the oath of allegiance and fidelity to the Commonwealth from 1789 to 1794; diverse charters of incorporation; and copies of select patents recorded in them.

COURT PAPERS OF THE COURTS OF OYER AND TERMINER, 1757-1787 (RG-33). The documents are filed among the records of the Supreme Court of Pennsylvania, Eastern District, and are organized according to name of county and then chronologically by date of of item. The materials are from the oyer and terminer courts of Bedford, Berks, Bucks, Chester, Cumberland, Lancaster, Northumberland, Philadelphia, and York Counties. Types of documents include case files, judicial and administrative papers, and diverse records of the mayor's court of Philadelphia; minutes from the *nisi prius* courts of Northampton and York Counties; and liquor license petitions from the city of Philadelphia. Papers in the administrative files include precepts and diverse lists of jurors, judges, justices of the peace, constables, sheriffs, marshals, and prisoners. The case files are composed of warrants, grand jury inquests and presentments, coroner's inquisitions, recognizances, depositions, examinations, trial minutes, and other papers pertinent to the prosecution of a case (that is, writs, subpoenas, jury excuses, and search and extradition papers). Cases represented pertain to crimes such as misdemeanors, arson, rape, horse stealing, burglary, murder, and high treason.

COURTS OF OYER AND TERMINER AND GENERAL GAOL DELIVERY DOCKETS, 1778-1828 (RG-33). A record of criminal cases (that is, robbery, assault, rape, treason, larceny, murder, etc.) heard and tried by the Supreme Court of Pennsylvania. Normally, entries record the name and alleged crime of the accused person, the name of each jury member, and the decision and sentence of the court. In those cases where the defendant was a slave, however, his of her value and master's name is also provided. The record is arranged chronologically by court term.

Besides testimony and petitions, the DAMAGE CLAIMS, 1828-1861 (in RG-17), PSA presented to the Board of Canal Commissioners sometimes contain maps such as this one showing the flooded land holdings of John and William Frazier in Meadville, Pa.,1835.

DAMAGE CLAIMS, 1828-1861 (in RG-17). Indexed or arranged alphabetically by name of claimant. Chiefly depositions, appraiser's reports (1830-1840), releases, and or supporting materials pertaining to damages to real estate caused by the construction and operations of the state's canal system. The dated documents usually describe the property's location; the name of the owner; the date, cause and extent of damage; and the remedy or compensation sought. Maps of the damaged property sometimes accompany the claims. Property holders claims against the Allegheny Portage (1831-1858) and Columbia and Philadelphia railroads (1832-1857) and the Beaver Division (1829-1843); the Delaware Division (1827-1856); the Eastern Division (1828-1835); the Erie Extension Canal (1837-1861); the French Creek Division (1829-1848); the Juniata Division (1832-1858); the North Branch Division (1830-1858); the Susquehanna Division (1829-1855); the West Branch Division (1829-1857); the Western Division (1829-1860); and the Wiconisco Feeder (1837-1841) of the Pennsylvania Canal are included. While not part of the state built canal system, DAMAGE CLAIMS, 1812-1867 (MG-174) against the Union Canal Company and RIGHT-OF-WAY DAMAGE RECORDS, 1889-1896 (MG-110), relating to the Schuylkill Navigation Company's canal works in Robeson and Union Townships, Berks County, can also be consulted for similar information.

DEATH WARRANTS FILE, 1775-1899, 1912-1952 (RG-15 and 26). The file is arranged according to the date of the warrant. The documents usually indicate the person's name and crime, the name of the court and the place where he or she was tried, the type of execution to be utilized, and the dates of conviction and execution. In most cases the name of the official charged with carrying out the sentence is recorded, and occasionally clemency petitions and trial transcripts are also found.

DECLARATIONS OF BRITISH REGISTRY OF VESSELS, 1727- 1729, 1731-1733, 1744-1745, 1761-1764, 1774-1776 (RG-41). A record of vessels that registered with the British authorities at the Port of Philadelphia during the colonial period. The documents are arranged by affirmation date and give the name, tonnage, and classification of the vessel; the place where it was built; the name of the master; and the name, occupation, and residence of the owner.

DEEDS AND DRAUGHTS RELATING TO SAMUEL RICE FARM IN PERRY COUNTY, 1797-1850 (MG-5). Documents pertaining to the Milligan family in what was originally Tyrone Township, Cumberland County, but is now Saville Township in Perry County. Papers found include deeds, mortgages, patents, and land draughts. There also is an 1881 justice of the peace commission for Alexander K. Dobbins Jr.

DENTAL REGISTER, August 16, 1902-January 1, 1916 (MG-324). A unique item that provides a record of dental care received by residents of central Susquehanna County. The register lists the patient's name and residence, the date of treatment, the type of dental work performed, and the fee paid. A chart that shows a drawing of each tooth in the mouth is utilized to indicate both the location and appearance of fillings inserted in the person's teeth. Remarks also appear that note whether the fillings were gold, or if plates were fashioned. Entries are in chronological order.

DIARY OF WALLACE K. KEELY, 1905-45 (RG-30). A personal scrapbook of State Police officer Wallace K. Keelly who served with the force from 1906 to 1940. The diary has newspaper clippings, postcards, and photographs of state troopers as well as "mug" shots, biographical profiles, and background information pertaining to criminals and cases involving the State Police, with emphasis on the activities of Troop C which was headquartered at Pottsville, Pa. The "mug" shots are usually accompanied by descriptive cards that provide the name, residence, occupation, race, age, height, weight, hair and eye color, and build of the person; the date and place of arrest; the nature of the crime (date, place, means, object); the date and time of the crime; and the names of any associates, places frequented, or peculiarities that might make apprehension of the person easier. The diary is in chronological order.

DOCKETS OF THE COURTS OF OYER AND TERMINER AND GENERAL GAOL DELIVERY, 1778-1828 (RG-33). The dockets are found among the records of the Supreme Court of Pennsylvania, Eastern District, and consist of criminal cases heard and adjudged in Allegheny, Bedford, Berks, Bucks, Chester, Cumberland,

A page from the DIARY OF WALLACE K. KEELEY, 1905-1945 (RG-30), PSA, describing the activities and appearance of William Z. Foster, a socialist labor agitator who was arrested at Tamaqua, Pa. in 1920.

Dauphin, Delaware, Fayette, Franklin, Huntingdon, Lancaster, Luzerne, Lycoming, Montgomery, Northampton, Northumberland, Philadelphia, Washington, Westmoreland, and York Counties. Information provided includes date of session; names of defendant, witnesses, judge, sheriff, and jurors; nature of the crime committed; the verdict; and if relevant, the sentence. Cases range from misdemeanors to high treason, and have in many cases personal details about the defendants and victims. The prosecutor may be either the Commonwealth of Pennsylvania or the Republic of the United States. Entries in the volumes are in chronological order by court terms.

ESTREAT OF FINES, SUPREME COURT OF PENNSYLVANIA, 1780-1783, 1803-1827 (RG-33). True copies of revenues collected from fines, amercements, and recognizances; marriage, tavern, and public housekeeper licenses; subpoenas; precepts; and bench warrants that were sent to the comptroller general by the courts of quarter sessions, the courts of oyer and terminer, and the city court of Philadelphia. Enumerations of fines can have the arrested individual's name, residence, marital status (for example, spinster) and occupation; the type of crime committed and the location; the amount of the fine; and the date of the returns. The fact that the person fined was a negro or a slave is often indicated as well. The lists of tavern and public housekeeper licenses usually only give the name of of the person obtaining the license, the township of residence, the fee paid, and the court session. Marriage license returns vary as to content. In most cases entries on the lists simply record the name of the male paying the license fee, the date that the fee was received, the amount paid, and the name of the county and or official that submitted the list. On occasions, however, the name of the wife and the couple's township of residence are also reported. License returns for the following counties are found:

Bedford County. Marriages and Public Housekeepers, October, 1781- January, 1783.
Bucks County. Public Housekeepers, June, 1780.
Chester County. Public Housekeepers, September, 1780.
Cumberland County. Public Housekeepers, July, 1783.
Lancaster County. Marriages, May- September, 1780, August, 1781-March, 1782; Public Housekeepers, August, 1780.
Northampton County. Marriages, September- December, 1780; Public Housekeepers, September, 1780- March, 1783.
Philadelphia City and County. Marriages and Taverns, April, 1780- September, 1780, September, 1781- November, 1782.
Westmoreland County. Public Housekeepers, April, 1782- March, 1783.
York County. Marriages, June, 1779- May, 1780.

ETHNIC STUDIES COLLECTIONS, 1789-P (MG-215). Primarily ethnic newspapers (1893-1990s) and anniversary histories celebrating church openings from 1745 to the present. Frequently the anniversary books have photographs and information about church founders. On occasion lists of parishioners, sometimes with their dates of birth and death, also appear. The newspapers which are published in foreign languages for the most part highlight the careers and accomplishments of native sons and daughters. Representative ethnic groups found in the collection include African Americans, Bulgarians, Croatians, Germans, Greeks, Hungarians, Irish Americans, Italians, Lithuanians, Polish Americans, Russians, Serbians, Slovaks, Ukrainians, and the Welsh.

FOWLER'S [THADDEUS] PANORAMIC MAPS, 1884-1905 (MG-11). These popular maps can be used by researchers to obtain a bird's-eye view of what an ancestor's community looked like at the turn of the twentieth century. Maps for the following Pennsylvania municipalities are available: Alburtis (1893), Altoona (Pennsylvania Railroad Company's Car Shops, 1895), Ambler (1894), Apollo (1896), Archbald (1892), Avoca (1892), Beaver (1900), Belle Vernon (1902), Bellwood (1895), Benjamin (1894), Berlin (1905), Bernville (1898), Birdsboro (1890), Boswell (1905), Bradford (1895), Brooklyn (1893), Brownsville (1902), Butler (1896), California (1902), Cambridgeboro (1895), Canonsburg (1897), Carbondale (1890), Carnegie (1897) Chambersburg (1894), Charleroi (1897), Clarion (1896), Clearfield (1895), Collegeville (1894), Columbia (1894), Confluence (1905), Connellsville (1897), Corry (1895), Curwensville (1895), Dawson (1902), Derry Station (1900), Donora (1901), Downington (1893), DuBois (1895), Dunbar (1900), Duquesne (1897), Edwardsville (1892), Elizabeth (1897), Elizabethtown (1894), Ellwood City (1896), Emmaus (1893), Emlenton (1897), Evans City (1900), Factoryville (1891), Fleetwood (1893), Ford City (1896), Forest City (1889), Frackville (1889), Franklin (1901), Gallitzin (1901), Gettysburg (1888), Girardsville (1889), Glassport (1902), Greensburg (1901), Greenville (1896), Grove City (1901), Hamburg (1889), Harmony (1901), Homestead (1902), Honesdale (1890), Indiana (1900), Irvona (1895), Irwin (1897), Jeannette (1897), Jermyn (1889), Johnsonburg (1895),

Kittanning (1896), Knox (1896), Kutztown (1893), Latrobe (1900), Lewisburg(h), (1884), Lewistown (1895), Ligonier (1900), Lindsey (1895), Lockridge (1893), McDonald (1897), McKees Rocks (1901), Macungie (1893), Mahanoy City (1889), Mars (1900), Marysville (1904), Mendelssohn (1902), Meyersdale (1900), Middletown (1894), Mifflintown (1895), Mill Creek (1892), Millersburg (1894), Millersville (1894), Miner's Mills (1892), Minersville (1889), Monaca (1900), Monongahela City (1902), Montrose (1890), Morrisville (1893), Moscow (11891), Mount Joy (1894), Mount Pleasant (1900), Mountville (1894), New Brighton (1901), New Castle (1896), New Kensington (1902), Newmanstown (1898), Newville (1903), Nicholson (1891), North East (1896), Oakmont (1896), Oil City (1896), Patterson (1895), Patton (1900), Peckville (1892), Pen Argyl (1894), Perkasie (1894), Pitcairn (1901), Pittsburgh (1902), Pittston (1892), Plains (1892), Pottstown (1893), Pottsville (1889), Punxsutawney (1895), Ridgway (1895), Rochester (1900), Roscoe (1902), Royersford (1893), Saint Mary's (1895), Salisbury (1905), Schwenksville (1894), Scottdale (1900), Scranton (1890), Sellersville (1894), Sharon (1901), Sharpsville (1901), Sheffield (1895), Shenandoah (1889), Sheridan (1898), Shippensburg (1894), Somerset (1900), Souderton (1894), South Fork (1900), Spring City (1893), Strasburg (1903), Tacony (1898), Tarentum (1901), Telford (1894), Tidioute (1896), Tionesta (1896), Titusville (1896), Turtle Creek (1897), Tyrone (1895), Union City (1895), Uniontown (1897), Verona (1896), Warren (1895), Washington (1897), Waynesboro (1894), Waynesburg (1897), West Bethlehem (1894), West Elizabeth (1897), West Newton (1900), West Pittston (1892), Wilkes-Barre (1899), Wilmerding (1897), Wilson (1902), Windber (1900), Wrightsville (1894), and Zelienople (1901).

IGNATIUS GARNER COLLECTION, ca. 1834-1888 (MG-417). Contains papers relating to the settlement St. Marys Borough (1842-1850s) in Elk County by the German Catholic Brotherhood with roots in Baltimore, Md., and Philadelphia, Pa. Besides correspondence, several deeds and passports, and family history information about the Garner–Bertrand families, the collection contains a biographical sketch of Ignatius Garner and military service records (most in the form of G.A.R. transfer cards) for Civil War veterans G.C. Branden, W.B. Hartman, David Kennedy, Michael Stibich, and Xavier Sachien-heimer (Socenhiemer). Generally these transfer cards list the names and numbers of the G.A.R. posts; the names, ages, places of birth, and occupations of the veterans; the dates of enlistments and discharges; their rank and military unit; the reasons for discharge; and the terms of service (years and months).

GENERAL CORRESPONDENCE OF THE COMMISSIONER OF THE PENNSYLVANIA STATE POLICE, 1905-1946 (RG-30). The file is arranged in alphabetical order by names and or subjects. Of particular interest are the following two topics:

State Police War Activity File, 1917-1920. Chiefly reports of special duty submitted by state troopers who were asked to go into Pennsylvania communities to investigate allegations of anti-American activities by labor organizers, immigrants, socialists, Bolsheviks, communists, fascists, and outspoken residents. Typically, the reports which were really background checks, contain diverse personal data about each suspect. The investigations were conducted under authority of the Espionage Act, the Selective Service Act, and other national legislation passed to protect American institutions and values from foreign influences during the World War I period. The file is arranged in chronological order. A name index is not available.

War Prisoners, 1942-1946. Papers pertaining to escaped war prisoners, 1942-1946. The bulletins that were issued give the name, age, and physical description (height, weight, color of complexion, hair, and eyes) of the soldier; his serial number and rank; whether he spoke English; and the date, time, and place of the escape. Occasionally the prisoner's past occupation and religion are also noted. Documents are arranged in chronological order.

HARMONY SOCIETY RECORDS, 1786-1951 (MG-185). The Harmony Society was a German separatist religious group that was founded by George Rapp in western Pennsylvania in 1805. A communal society that was in fact highly successful, the Harmonists invested in railroads and real estate; manufactured wool, cotton, and silk goods; owned and operated oil, lumber and brick companies; and exported domestic goods, produce, wine, whiskey, and merchandise into the Ohio-Mississippi Valley from Pittsburgh to New Orleans for well over seventy-five years. As a result, the society's administrative, legal, and business records often contain documents that provide interesting data about members, the workers who were hired by them, and the communities that they did business with. Some of the more noteworthy materials include these:

Administrative File, 1805-1951, undated. Has registers, 1822, undated, that contain birth (*gebren*), death (*gestorbun*), and membership (*angekomen*) data, 1734-1946; marriage information, January 27, 1805-September 28, 1817; population summaries, 1820-1854; names of society members buried at Economy, Pa., 1825-1951; names of non-society members buried at Economy, Pa., 1865-1922; a list of society children born at New Harmony, Ind., 1814-1824; and a list of persons born to the society, 1897-1900. Also found are a register of burial plots, 1840-1857; a register of souls, undated; a list of names and occupations, ca. 1840; lists of male members of the Harmony Society, 1866, 1869; and genealogical materials, ca. 1848-1900, pertaining to the Davis, Eppeler, Henrici, Kroll, Lenz, Linnenbrink, Rall, and Rapp families. Most of the records are arranged in chronological order. There are no name indexes.

Business File, 1788-1928, undated. Includes the following time and payroll books: miscellaneous wage books, 1840, 1881-1896; time payroll book for the Economy Oil Company, 1864-1869; George Kirschbaum's record book of men employed by the Harmony Society, 1876-1887; time books of Michele Nardi (contractor), 1882-1883; time books of Charles Lander, 1883-1891; wage and expense account of William W. Werner, 1886-1895; time book of Godfried Lauppe, 1887-1892; time book of Hermann Fischern and Hugo Miller, 1891-1901; Economy Planing Mill time books, 1892-1894; time book of the French Point Planing Mill and Lumber Company, 1894-1899; Harmony Brick Works time book, 1897-1901; time book of H. Frank Blackstone (brick works), 1897-1901; and payroll book of The

Harmony Society, 1903-1910. Although the incoming correspondence, 1788, 1804-1905, chiefly consists of materials relating to the buying and selling of goods, it also contains letters
asking for assistance from the children and relatives of past
society members, requests for employment, and personal correspondence that are rich in family history information. Likewise,
on occasions, notations regarding the deaths of acquaintances
and or comments about individuals wishing to obtain employment appear in the memorandum books, 1815-1890. With the
exception of the incoming correspondence which is arranged in
alphabetical order by name of correspondent on a yearly basis,
these records are either in chronological order or consist of random entries.

General File, ca. 1751-1951. Has hand colored and drawn maps
by Wallrath Weingartner that show the layout of the town and
the location of the homes of each family when the society was in
Harmony, Pa. (Butler County) from 1804-1815, and in New
Harmony, Ind. (Posey County) from 1815-1824.

Legal File, 1786-1943. Contains abstracts of titles, 1852-1921;
agreements, assignments, contracts, and releases, 1790, 1805-
1908; citizenship papers, 1815-1888; commitment papers,
1858-1870; deeds, 1796-1949; a judgment and mortgage docket, September term, 1869- December term, 1885; land
draughts, surveys, and miscellany, 1786-1924; land patents,
1786-1828; leases, 1816-1904; passports and visas, 1804-1872;
powers of attorney, 1805-1893; vital statistics, 1796-1890; and
wills, estates documents, guardianship certificates and trust
fund materials, 1806-1907. All of these materials have indexes
that can be used for reference purposes. In addition, this file has
a deed book, 1883-1892, and mortgages, 1808-1900, that are in
chronological order.

Public Records File, 1828-1914. The file primarily consists of
alienated public documents that society members accumulated
while serving in the capacity of tax assessors and justices of the
peace. Some of the materials also were in the custody of the
Harmonists because of the dominant role that the society

played in the community's economic and political life. Included are tax books for Economy Township, 1834-1872, Harmony Township, 1852-1907, and Ambridge Borough, 1905-1906, in Beaver County, Pa.; justice of the peace dockets and indexes, Beaver County, Pa., 1828-1853, 1883-1889, 1893-1910; and justices of the peace docket of J.P. Houser, Warren County, Pa., 1858-1893.

For a more comprehensive summary of contents of this collection consult the *Guide to the Microfilmed Harmony Society Records, 1786-1951, in the Pennsylvania State Archives* compiled by Robert M. Dructor (1983).

JOHN W. HARPER COLLECTION, 1767-1982 (MG-420). Primarily *taufschein*, surveys, deeds, patents, and other papers pertaining to John W. Harper's ancestors and to Centre County. The collection also includes copies of ships' passenger lists, wills, and materials relating to family history.

HARRISBURG *HOME STAR* COLLECTION, 1895 (1962-1971)-1971 (MG-217). The *Home Star* was a weekly newspaper published in Harrisburg from 1948 to 1971. The collection contains photographs of local, state, and national politicians, businessmen, civic leaders, entertainers, and prominent personalities. There is an alphabetical name listing to the photographs.

HERSHEY MUSEUM LOCAL HISTORY COLLECTION, 1734-1933 (MG-411). Deeds, tax records, estate papers, fiscal items, and miscellaneous family papers relating to residents of Berks, Clinton, Cumberland, Dauphin, Franklin, Lancaster, Lebanon, and Snyder Counties. Justice of the peace dockets for Dauphin County, 1836-1931, and several marriage licenses, 1842-1892, also are included. A container listing at the folder and or item level is available for retrieval purposes.

INSOLVENT DEBTOR PAPERS, 1789-1805, 1812-1814 (RG-33). Papers relating to insolvency cases brought before the Supreme Court of Pennsylvania, Eastern District. Types of papers filed include petitions, bonds, assignments, renunciations of assignments, debt schedules, and certificates of discharge, reference, and naturalization. Typically petitions provide the names of the debtor, creditors, assignees, and arbiter; the amount of debt; and references to relevant insolvency laws. In those instances where the debtor owned slaves they were listed, usually by name, with the rest of the property as assets. The file is arranged in alphabetical order by surname. There also is an alphabetical list of insolvent debtors that shows the person's creditors and the filing date of the petition for insolvency.

INSTITUTIONAL POPULATION RECORDS, 1882-1909 (RG-23) Contains a record of patient admittances to the following treatment facilities: Allegheny City Home, 1884-1886, 1888; Burn Brae, 1884-1888; Danville State Hospital, 1883-1888; Pennsylvania Hospital for Insane (Philadelphia), 1883-1888; Pennsylvania State Lunatic Hospital (Harrisburg), 1883-1888; Philadelphia Hospital, 1884-1888; Pittsburgh City Farm Insane Asylum, 1884-1886, 1888; St. Francis Hospital (Pittsburgh), 1887-1888; Schuylkill County Almshouse, 1883-1888; and the Friends Asylum (Frankford), 1883-1888. The materials are arranged and numbered in chronological order. Of particular value to researchers are the forms called "order for the reception of a patient." Categories of data normally found on these forms include: name, sex, age, residence (during past year), marital status (if apropos, number of children), occupation, trade, or employment of the patient; names of parents if living; residence of any living brother or sister; name and residence of any known relative; time at which insanity was supposed to have existed and the circumstances that induced such belief; name and address of all medical attendants treating the patient for the last two years; name, occupation, and relationship of the petitioner for commitment to the patient; certification particulars (that is, dates of certification and the name, residence, and credentials of each certifying physician, magistrate, or judicial officer); and date of admission.

JUSTICE OF THE PEACE DOCKETS, LEBANON COUNTY, 1811-1827, 1830-1925 (MG-4). Along with the routine reporting of proceedings in cases involving assault, mischief, gambling, swearing and the like are entries pertaining to child indentures, illegitimate births, inquests, and marriages. The 1830-1905 docket is particu-

larly noteworthy, since it contains some actual marriage certificates, 1897-1901, themselves. The docket are arranged in chronological order.

KEATING LAND COMPANY RECORDS, 1814-1918 (MG-265). The
records contain the papers of three land companies: John Keating
and Company (1796-1856), Keating and Company (1856-1884),
and Hamlin and Forest (1884-1900s). Included are correspondence, 1855-1868, from John and William V. Keating of Philadelphia, Pa., to their lawyer and agent, Bryon D. Hamlin of
Smethport, Pa., concerning land sales in McKean County; land
ledgers, 1816-1918, relating to properties in Clinton and Clearfield
Counties; agreements, 1855-1907; surveyor field notes, 1852-
1856; and application books, 1871-1877, pertaining to Hamlin's
activities on behalf of the firm in McKean County; and a hand
drawn and colored map book, 1876, of plats in McKean, Potter,
Cameron, Clinton, and Clearfield Counties.

KENT COUNTY COURT HOUSE RECORDS, ca. 1680-1843 (MG-
262). Microfilm of select records located in the Kent County
Courthouse in Delaware. Records appearing include chancery
dockets, 1806-1843, and deed books, ca. 1680. Some volumes are
indexed.

LAND APPRAISAL RECORDS, ca. 1918-1920 (MG-457). Valuation
records of the Buffalo and Susquehanna Railroad Corporation for
Cowanshannock Township in Armstrong County; Dubois
Township in Clearfield County; Grove Township in Cameron
County; Benezette and Jay Townships in Elk County; Plumville
Borough, and North and South Mahoning Townships in Indiana
County; Bingham, Genesee, Ulysses, West Branch, and Wharton
Townships in Potter County; and Clearfield, Clymer, Deerfield,
Gaines, and Westfield Townships in Tioga County. Also present are
papers relating to Wellsville and Willing Township in Allegany
County, New York. Most of the valuation documents consist of
annotated blueprints that are dated June 30, 1919, and which are
identified as "right-of-way and track maps." These maps show the
exact locations of properties, facilities, and municipalities located
along the rail line and have charts which list the number of each

land tract identified on the map; the names of the grantor and grantee; the date and type of instrument used to obtain the right or property (agreement, release, etc.); the number of the book and page where the instrument was recorded; the date recorded; the custodian number; and any pertinent remarks. In addition to valuation maps, however, the following appraisal forms also are found:

Sales of Adjacent Lands, undated. The document provides the name of the land's owner (the B. & S. R.R. Corp.), the division (Main Line, Sagamore to Juneau, Germania to Gaines Junction, Gaines Junction to Knoxville, Knoxville to State Line, etc.); the valuation zone, map, and section numbers; the date of the deed and the deed book and page number where it was recorded; the names of the grantor and grantee; the area (square feet or acres), description (buildings present, proximity to rail lines), location, and dimensions of the land; the recited and real dollar value of the real estate; the estimated value of improvements and the indicated land value; and an analysis of improvements, assessment information, and pertinent comments. Space was available for also indicating whether the sale was made under normal conditions; whether the sale was representative of values in the vicinity; and who was responsible for providing the actual consideration.

Local Opinions of Values of Adjacent Lands, undated. The form gives the name of the land owner (the railroad); the division; the zone, map, and valuation section numbers; the state, county, and municipality where the land was situated; the local appraiser's, name, approximate age, occupation, qualifications, and length of residence in the community; type and location of land discussed; opinion as to the lands value; and the appraised value per square foot or acre unit.

Latest Assessment of Adjacent Lands, 1918-1919. Has the land owner's name (the railroad company); the division; the zone, map, and valuation section numbers; the adjacent land's owner, area, assessed value, and per acre or square foot value; the established ratio; and the resulting value.

Zone Summary of Land Field Notes, 1920. Records the name of the owner (the railroad); the division; the zone, map, and valuation section numbers; the state, county, and municipality where the land was located; the boundaries of zone; description and use of adjacent land on both sides of right of way; statistical details (units of vacant and improved land; naked land units, that is, high, middle, or low; and appraiser's conclusion of the dollar value (per acre) of naked land adjacent to the right of way; and pertinent remarks, for example, the observation that the railroad cut through the best lands of the farm.

The forms are grouped by geographic regions or railroad divisions.

LAND RECORDS OF THE ERIE RAILROAD COMPANY, 1847-1914 (MG-300). Approximately 140 volumes of transcribed deeds, abstracts of titles, land draughts, agreements, rights-of-way, and ordinances belonging to the Real Estate Department of the Erie Railroad Company and relating to real estate holdings in New York, New Jersey, Ohio, and Pennsylvania. The records include land records for the Allegheny, Buffalo, Bradford, New York, Rochester, and Susquehanna Divisions and the Niagara Falls Branch. Representative rail lines include the Buffalo and Jamestown Railroad; Elmira State Line Railroad; Greenwood Lake Railway, Long Dock Company; Newburg and New York Railroad; New York, Pennsylvania and Ohio Railroad; Nypano Railroad; and Paterson and Ramaparo Railroad. The volumes are grouped by divisions or railroads and thereunder in chronological order by date of document.

LETTERS OF ATTORNEY, 1684-1812 (RG-17). Chiefly powers of attorney, bonds, and releases relating to land transactions and issues. Of particular interest is the book for 1746-1755 [D-2; volume 3] which contains Ann Speechley's pedigree as of 1754, including marriages, baptisms, and burials (1694-1747) pertaining to the Bedford County family of Thomas Kline and his wife, Hester (Esther) Lawton. The volumes are in chronological order. Indexes are available for approximately half of the twenty volumes.

MACLAY FAMILY COLLECTION, 1788-1933 (MG-352). The collection consists of family correspondence, 1788-1933; legal papers, 1794-1914; account books, 1812-1887; political memorabilia, ca. 1800-1930; and a genealogy of the Maclay family compiled by

David Maclay (1762-1839) in 1824. Of particular value are the MEMORANDUM BOOKS of David Maclay, 1824-1830; the DIARIES, 1831-1873, and JOURNAL OF VISITS TO PATIENTS, 1840-1865, of Charles Templeton Maclay (1812-1888) who resided in Lurgan Township in Franklin County. The journal of Charles T. Maclay includes a "record of deaths," May, 1840-December 30, 1843, and a "register of births and deaths," July 1, 1852- August 23, 1852. In addition to comments regarding crops, the weather, and family activities, the diaries and memorandum books contains frequent entries about the deaths of neighbors and acquaintances from 1824-1855, as well as occasional references to marriages which took place. Unfortunately, there are no indexes to these books. Entries are for the most part in chronological order.

MAP BOOKS OF THE BOARD OF CANAL COMMISSIONERS, 1810-1881, undated (in RG-17). Contains original and pastel colored drawings, plans, and profiles of canal routes and facilities (locks, dams, raft chutes, viaducts, and some building prototypes) which show the locations of the waterways, neighboring property holders, and geographic and man-made features. Representative canal and rail routes include those between Pittsburgh and Conneaut Lake (1827); a railroad from Belmont Plane to Broad and Vine Streets in Philadelphia (1855); map of the Philadelphia and Columbia Railway (1851); map of the Covington and Lexington Railroad (1851); profile and map of the Delaware Division canal from Carpenter's Point to Easton (1828-1829); the North Branch Extension Canal (1836, 1838); the Erie Extension Canal (1839); and a map and profile for the Middle and Conemaugh routes of a proposed Harrisburg and Pittsburgh Railroad (ca. 1839-1840). A complete and detailed list of map holdings is found in Hubertis M. Cummings *PENNSYLVANIA BOARD OF CANAL COMMISSIONERS' RECORDS WITH ALLIED RECORDS OF CANAL COMPANIES CHARTERED BY THE COMMONWEALTH: DESCRIPTIVE INDEX* (1959).

MAPS OF THE DELAWARE DIVISION CANAL SURVEYS, 1868 (RG-6). Bound hand drawn and colored maps showing properties, facilities, and municipalities along the Delaware River from Easton to Bristol, Pa. Owners of the tracts of land appear on the maps, but there is no name or place index included in the books. The books were prepared for the Delaware Division Canal Company and the Lehigh Coal and Navigation Company by Thomas S. McNair from surveys made in April and May, 1868. The original field notes with sketches are located among the RECORDS OF THE BOARD OF CANAL COMMISSIONERS (in RG-17).

MAPS OF THE SCHUYLKILL NAVIGATION COMPANY, 1827-1948 (MG-110). Seventy-two maps, most hand drawn and colored, that pertain to the operations of the company's canal works from Port Carbon in Schuylkill County to Philadelphia. Besides providing information about the actual canal facilities, the maps are a striking visual record of land ownership along the Schuylkill River from 1851-1864. Related to this series are BLUEPRINTS AND TRACINGS, 1846-1948, that depict water power resources and property holdings of the Schuylkill Water Company in the counties of Berks, Chester, Montgomery, Philadelphia, and Schuylkill.

MARITIME RECORDS FOR THE PORT OF PHILADELPHIA, 1766-1937 (RG-13). Microfilmed transcriptions of historical records that were copied by employees of the Work Projects Administration as part of the Pennsylvania Historical Survey, 1931-1937. The following materials are noteworthy:

Alphabetical List of Crews, Port of Philadelphia, 1789-1880. Gives the name of the crew member along with the year and page number of the record.

Chronological List of Crews, Port of Philadelphia, 1798-1880. Contains two varieties of listings. One type shows the name and type of vessel, the captain or master in charge, the craft's destination, and the date of voyage. A second style of listing, of more interest to family historians, includes all of the above information plus, in most cases (after 1802), each crew member's name, age, birthplace, residence, and physical description (that is, the person's height; type of complexion; color of hair and eyes; and hair style, for example short, long, and/or curly). Comments regarding the presence of scars on the individual or the fact that the crew member was a citizen of the U.S., a colored man, or might have deserted also appear. Prior to 1802 very little crew data is listed other than the person's name and an occasional job class (cook, mate, etc.)

Slave Manifests, 1800-1841. The manifests are arranged in chronological order by date manifest was signed and sworn to by the captain of the vessel and attested to by the collector of the port. The actual dates of the manifests cover the period Nov. 2, 1817, to Feb. 16, 1861. Approximately a dozen vessel names are listed with each manifest recording the name of the captain or master; the vessel's name, destination, and tonnage; the name of the shipper or slave owner and his or her residence; and generally the slave's name, sex, age, stature (height in feet and inches), and class or color (dark, black, yellow, etc.)

MISCELLANEOUS PAPERS OF THE SUPREME COURT OF NISI PRIUS OF THE STATE OF PENNSYLVANIA, ca. 1786-1800 (RG-33). Indexed. Bound scrapbooks and volumes containing court minutes, coroner's inquisitions, proceedings in cases, and lists of marriage, public housekeepers, and tavern licenses issued. The license returns are found in volume 45 and normally show the name of the official submitting the list, the county where the license was issued, the name of the individual paying the fee, the dates that the return covers, the fee paid, and the total amount collected. The following returns are present:

Marriage Licenses Issued

Lancaster County, September, 1780- April, 1781, August, 1781-
    March, 1782.
Northampton County, August- September, 1780.
Philadelphia City and County, April, 1780- November, 1782.
York County, March- September, 1782.

Licenses Issued To

	Public Housekeepers	Taverns
Bedford County	1780-1781	1780
Bucks County	1781-1782	1781 (June)
Chester County	1781-1782	1780-1781
Cumberland County	1781-1782	1780
Lancaster County	1781-1782	1780-1782

Northampton County	1780-1782	1780
Philadelphia County/City	None	1780-1781

MISCELLANEOUS RECORDS OF THE SUPREME COURT OF PENNSYLVANIA, EASTERN DISTRICT, 1704-1899 (RG-33). The documents are arranged in chronological order and consist of recognizances, narratives, deeds, wills, estate papers, coroner's inquisitions, petitions, depositions, assignments, pleas, charters for churches, and diverse types of writs.

MISCELLANEOUS RECORDS RELATING TO LUZERNE, NORTHUMBERLAND, AND SUSQUEHANNA COUNTIES, 1787, 1804-1863 (MG-4). Consists of a lot book, 1787, for Luzerne County; land tracts in Northumberland County (1774-1787) that were copied in 1804, 1815, 1850, and 1852 and estate and case papers for Susquehanna residents, 1813-1863. The estate papers pertain to Asahel Avery, Chapman Carr, Dr. Benjamin A. Denison, Dr. Mason Denison, Elder Davis Dimock, Daniel Gregory, Garner Isbell, Rosewell Morse, Joshua W. Raynsford, and Samuel Warner.

MONTHLY REPORTS OF THE PENNSYLVANIA STATE POLICE FORCE, 1905-1916 (RG-30). The reports consist of a narrative in which each call for assistance or investigation is described in one paragraph, followed by an addendum that lists the criminal charge, the name, sex, and nationality of the perpetrator; the case number; and its disposition. Unfortunately, the name of the arrested person is not included nor can it be ascertained from any files currently at the Archives. The narrative or conditions report generally includes the names of the persons being investigated or arrested; the date and place of incident; the reason for the call or complaint; the names of the police officers making the call; and as relevant, the names, ages, occupations, nationality, or race of both the accused and victim. The reports are filed in chronological order on a monthly basis.

MOTHERS' PENSION ACCOUNTS, 1913-1917 (RG-28). A record of indigent, widowed, and abandoned mothers who were beneficiaries of state money provided for by the Act of April 29, 1913. Data found in the accounts include the name and address of the mother, her claim number, and the names and dates of birth of her children. The entries are arranged by county and thereinafter by claim number.

ORAL HISTORY COLLECTION OF THE PENNSYLVANIA HISTORICAL AND MUSEUM COMMISSION, 1970-present (MG-409). The collection consists of more than 1,000 taped interviews conducted throughout the Commonwealth over the last twenty-five years. Oral history projects (approximately 775 hours) that shed light on the common folk and their backgrounds as southern born African American migrants; European immigrants; Hispanics; Jews; and workers in the coal, steel, and electrical industries include the following:

1919 Steel Strike Project, 1973 (3 tapes, 3 interviews, 1 hour); Chester Oral History Project: The Black Experience, 1976-1977 (29 tapes, 20 interviews, 21 hours); Cornwall Oral History Project, 1981-1982 (41 tapes, 25 interviews, 45 hours); Delta Oral History Project, 1976 (38 tapes, 16 interviews, 32 hours); Eckley Oral History Project, 1972, 1976 (86 tapes, 54 interviews, 56 hours); Electrical Workers of Western Pennsylvania Project, 1976-1977 (56 tapes, 36 interviews, 42 hours); Harrisburg Jews Project, 1975, 1979 (2 tapes, 2 interviews, 2 hours); Harrisburg Oral History Project, 1975-1977 (45 tapes, 21 interviews, 33 hours); Lancaster Oral History Project: The Greek Community, 1973 (9 tapes, 8 interviews, 6 hours;) Military Nurses Project, 1971-1972 (20 tapes, 25 interviews, 24 hours); Monessen Community Project, 1981 (47 tapes, 26 interviews, 50 hours); Monessen Project: The Croatians, 1977 (30 tapes, 30 interviews, 20 hours); Nanticoke Oral History Project (Anthracite Peoples), 1981 (21 tapes, 19 interviews, 22 hours); Nanticoke Women Oral History Project, 1977-1978 (57 tapes, 52 interviews, 34 hours); Pennsylvania's New Deal Project, 1990 (18 tapes, 11 interviews, 14 hours, also 8 video tapes); Pittsburgh Oral History Project, 1974-1978 (303 tapes, 191 interviews, 215 hours); Scranton Oral History Project, 1977 (73 tapes, 60 interviews, 47 hours); Steelton Oral History Project, 1971-1977 (16 tapes, 14 interviews, 8 hours); Washington County Project: Life and Customs in Mining Towns, 1975 (144 tapes, 78 interviews, 103 hours).

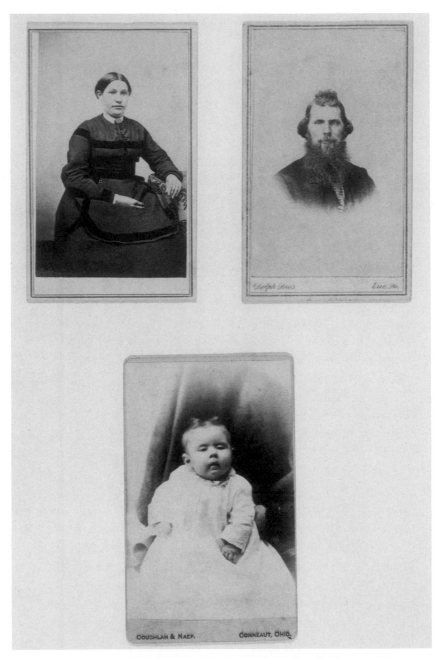

The ABBY FAMILY: Wife, Melissa Harris Abby; Husband, George Abby ; Daughter, Imogene. Family portraits contained in the PHOTOGRAPH COLLECTIONS (MG-218), PSA.

For more detailed descriptions of each project's content and background information about the individuals interviewed consult the finding aid to the collection in the State Archives and Matthew S. Magda's *Oral History in Pennsylvania: Summary Guide to the Oral History Collections of the Pennsylvania Historical and Museum Commission* (1981).

PASSENGER LISTS, 1831, 1835-1836, 1839 (RG-17). A sampling of accounts that have survived for Pennsylvania's state canal system and which often record the canal boat's name, master, and voyage dates; the name of the passengers and the distances that they traveled; and the amount in fares collected. At times, the number of members constituting a family or the fact that a wife was traveling with her husband is also noted. Lists are found for the Eastern Division (1835-1836), the Juniata Division (1835-1836), the Western Division (1831, 1836) of the Pennsylvania Canal and the Allegheny Portage (1839) and Columbia and Philadelphia (1836) Railroads. The PASSENGER LISTS are filed with the CHECK ROLLS, WORK ESTIMATES, RECEIPTS, AND MISCELLANEOUS ACCOUNTS (RG-17) of each division, etc.

PENNSYLVANIA COAL COMPANY RECORDS, 1838-1975 (MG-282). Contains a two–volume land record (1848-1894), maps, and copies of deeds, rights of way, leases, and land drafts relating to property holdings in northeastern Pennsylvania. Besides providing data regarding neighboring lot owners, estate information and details about how, when, and from whom the land was obtained is sometimes noted. Representative communities include Avoca, Carbondale, Dunmore, Exeter, Everhart, Griffins Corners, Hawley, Hughstown, Inkerman, Jermyn, Lackawanna, Laflin, Marcy, Moosic, Old Forge, Olyphant, Oregon Heights, Pittston, Plains, Port Griffith, Roaring Brook, Welsh Hill, and Yatesville. The materials are not indexed. A typed listing that is arranged by file numbers, and which lists the name of the lot and its location is available for reference purposes.

PENNZOIL COMPANY DEEDS, 1849-1890 (MG-245). Historic deeds of the Pennzoil Company for property holdings in Crawford, Elk, Forest, Jefferson, McKean, and Warren Counties. The papers are not in any discernible order.

PHOTOGRAPH COLLECTIONS, ca. 1853-1974 (MG-218). Contains photographs relating to the Abby (example, page 314), Craven, Gould, Harris, Silverthorn, Bliss, Spalding, Frack, Shunck, Wilcox, Forrest, and Cowperthwaite families of Pennsylvania. In many instances the photographs also have notes concerning familial relationships written upon them. Also included in the collections are diverse photographs featuring the Pennsylvania National Guard and some of its prominent personalities.

PILOTS' REPORTS, 1793-1974 (RG-41). A record of vessels arriving and leaving from the Port of Philadelphia as reported by their pilots. Data usually appearing include the name, classification, and draft (from 1880 and onward) of the vessel; the name of the captain or commander; the name of the pilot; the date of entry or clearance (after March, 1898); and the number of persons aboard (until August 30, 1880). The reports are in chronological order according to the date that the vessel left or reached Philadelphia.

PRINTED ABSTRACTS OF TITLE, 1869, 1875 (MG-286). The record belonged to the general real estate agent of the Pennsylvania Railroad Company and consists of two items: "brief of title to Bryn Mawr in Merion Township, Montgomery County, Pa.," 1869, and "abstract of title to the tract of land situated in the First Ward of the city of Philadelphia between Prime and Reed Streets and extending from Front Street to the Delaware River, belonging to the United States of America and known as the Philadelphia Navy Yard," 1875. Both records contain abridged accounts of all transactions related to the many properties located in these two areas. Abstracted transactions include letters patents, wills, deeds, indentures, petitions, acts, and other related instruments. Both abstracts also contain a map of their respective tracts. The volumes are in chronological order.

JOSEPH PRIESTLEY HOUSE COLLECTION, 1785-1851, undated (MG-414). Chiefly deeds, with several articles of agreements, bonds, patents, and leases relating to properties owned by Joseph Priestley Jr. in Northumberland County. The documents are in chronological order.

PROPERTY MAPS AND ATLASES, 1876-1905 (MG-286). The over-sized volumes contain maps of properties contiguous to Pennsylvania Railroad Company rights of way. Each atlas consists of a running series of maps that illustrate land ownership for specific regions within main, branch, and subsidiary lines. The maps vary in size and content, but generally include the name of the railroad company; the division, branch, or geographic region; the names of adjacent property owners; political subdivisions (townships, cities); cartographic symbols and scales; and indexes. The maps primarily are hand drawn with black ink and water colors. Some paper and blueprint copies, however, also are present. Atlases of the Pennsylvania Schuylkill Valley Railroad Company and the Trenton Cut Off Railroad Company as well as the Pennsylvania Railroad Company are included. Local historians and genealogists interested in Lancaster County residents will find the drawings of the Philadelphia Division of the Main Line of the P.R.R. from Thorndale to Mount Joy (1876) both attractive and useful.

REAL ESTATE TRUST COMPANY OF PHILADELPHIA (RETCO) RECORDS, 1861-1963 (MG-338). A Philadelphia–based company that was incorporated in 1887 and which served as trustees for railroad, transit, mining, and manufacturing enterprises. The collection consists of BENEFICIARY DOCUMENT FILES, 1861-1963, that contain correspondence, mortgages, real estate papers, and agreements of the German American Title and Trust Company. Significant estates represented include those of Ida Butler, George H. Earle Jr., Marguerite Grant, the Stanley B. Haddock heirs, Kate A. Jewell, Joseph McIllhenny, Nelson Andrew Manship, John Eyre Shaw, Mary Shields, and E.O. Thompson. Also present is an indexed LETTER BOOK, December 28, 1881- November 10, 1882, of the Fidelity Insurance, Trust, and Safe Deposit Company. While much of the data in this volume is routine investment business some of the letters have information regarding the client's marital status and the dates that wills, deeds, and other estate documents were filed. Besides listing the name of the individual and the page number, the index to the letter book frequently has "decd." written after entries. The beneficiary file is arranged in alphabetical order by company name or personal surname.

RECORD OF CONTAGIOUS AND INFECTIOUS DISEASES, 1919-1947 (RG-48). A record created by the health department of the City of Johnstown and covering the period from December 25, 1919 to March 31, 1947. Entries are dated and show the name, age, sex, address, and ward of the patient; name of the attending physician; name of disease and whether it was a new case or hospital; date of fumigation; and date that quarantine was lifted. In the case of children, the name of the school is noted. The volumes are arranged in chronological order by the date that the disease was reported.

RECORD OF INHERITANCE TAX APPRAISEMENTS AND RECEIPTS, 1898-1965 (RG-42). A record of inheritance taxes collected by the register of wills from each county for payment to the state treasury. The bound volumes are filed by county and thereafter arranged in order by date of appraiser returns. Three types of accounts exist:

Appraisements of All Estates Subject to Transfer Inheritance Tax, 1917-1965. The top of each page lists a county and the name of the register of wills for it. The following columns of data appear: the name and date of death of the person whose estate is being appraised; the rate of tax (percentage); appraised value of realty; appraised value of personalty; value of life estate or annuity; amount of tax per appraisement; date of the appraiser's return; remarks (adjustments); date and number of register's receipt; date when charged, sealed, and countersigned at Department of Revenue; total value of estate per appraisement filed; debts and expenses of administration; five percent for prompt payment; penalty for interest; amount of tax paid to register; amount of tax paid into Department of Revenue; date of payments into the state treasury by Department of Revenue; date of demand for payment by the secretary of Revenue; and answer made by the register to the demand for payment when not paid.

Appraisements of Estates Subject to Direct Inheritance Tax, 1917-1950. With the exception of not having a column for the rate of tax percentage, each volume contains the same information found in the "estates subject to transfer inheritance tax" records.

*Appraisement of All Estates Subject to Collateral Inheritance Tax,
1898-1950.* The volumes are organized like the other two sets of
accounts but do not record the date of death of the person whose
estate is being appraised or the tax percentage. Other minor differ-
ences include information about how payments are made, that is,
to the state treasury directly by the register; and regarding
demands for payment, by the auditor general rather than the
Department of Revenue. The remarks column is also used to indicate the names of annuitants or beneficiaries of life estates.

RECORD OF LANDS OWNED BY THE LEHIGH VALLEY RAILROAD
COMPANY, undated (MG-274). The volumes are grouped by names
of subsidiary companies and or facilities and thereafter arranged
in numerical order by tract numbers. Besides giving routine information regarding the location (city or town, township, county, and
state), description, and ledger value of the land tracts, entries
record brief histories of how each parcel was acquired (names of
grantor and grantee, number of acres, type and date of conveyance,
amount of consideration named in deed, and the book, page and
date recorded); the purpose for which the land was acquired; and
any rights or privileges gained by the railroad. Significant subsidiary company holdings contained in the volumes include the
Auburn and Ithaca Railway; the Bay Shore Connecting Railroad;
the Depew and Tonawanda Railroad; the Buffalo and Geneva
Railroad; the Buffalo Creek Railroad; the Cayuga and Susquehanna
Railroad; the Consolidated Real Estate Company; the Delaware,
Susquehanna and Schuylkill Railroad; the Easton and Northern
Railroad; the Geneva and Ettenville Railroad; the Geneva, Ithaca
and Sayre Railroad; the Elmira, Cortland and Northern Railroad;
the Lehigh Valley Railway; the the Lehigh and Lake Erie Railroad;
the Loyalsock Railroad; the Middlesex Valley Railroad; the Mont-
rose Railroad; the Newark and Roselle Railroad; the Pioneer Real
Estate Company; the Rochester and Southern Railroad; the Roselle
and South Plainfield Railroad; the Schuylkill and Lehigh Valley
Railroad; the Seneca County Railroad; the State Line and Sullivan
Railroad; Tift Farm (Erie County, N.Y.); and the United Real Estate
Company.

RECORDS OF THE KU KLUX KLAN, INCLUDING CORRESPON-
DENCE, BILLS AND RECEIPTS, ENLISTMENT PAPERS, AND MIS-
CELLANEOUS PUBLICATIONS, 1922-1940 (RG-30). The materials
were confiscated by the Pennsylvania State Police and contain
information about Klan membership and activities in Pennsylvania,
New Jersey, and Delaware. Of particular interest to researchers
are the following materials:

Enlistment Papers, 1924-1926. A record of persons from Adams,
Allegheny, Carbon, Clarion, Crawford, Erie, Indiana, Lawrence,
Mercer, Northumberland, Venango, Washington, and
Westmoreland Counties who applied and were accepted for membership in the Pennsylvania State Klavaliers. The applications are
grouped by county and call for the following entries: name,
address (street, city, and county), age (years and months), occupation, physical description (that is, height, weight, complexion, distinguishing marks, and eye and hair color), marital status, military
service (number of years and branch), educational advantages,
qualifications, character, and signature of the recruit; date and
term of enlistment; date and place of taking oath of enlistment;
name and rank of recruiting officer; and name and rank of commanding officer.

Election Returns, 1923-1940. Contain "reports of officers elected"
from the various Pennsylvania branches of the Ku Klux Klan.
Normally the returns list the name, number, and location of the
Klan; the date, time, and location of regular klonklaves; and the
name, office, and address of the elected officer. The materials are
not arranged in any discernible pattern.

*Quarterly Reports and Registrations of the Delaware Realm, 1929-
1940.* Includes these materials:

> Alphabetical Membership Lists, 1929-1940. Various listings of
> Delaware Klansmen who were naturalized into the organization,
> suspended for non-payment of dues, or considered members in
> good standing. The dated lists are arranged chronologically and
> record the member's name and address along with the Klan
> number, name, and realm.

Registrations, 1938. Entries on the forms usually give the klansman's name, address, and membership card number; the date that dues were paid up to; and the Klan name and number.

Quarterly Reports of the New Jersey Realm, 1938-1940. Contains a half dozen forms entitled "Applications for Citizenship in the Invisible Empire - Knights of the Ku Klux Klan," 1939-1940. The applications were submitted by residents of New Jersey and usually show the applicant's name, address (residential and business), age, weight, height, and occupation; the dates of election to membership and naturalization; the name and address of a reference; and the Klan number and realm. The forms are signed by the Kligrapp and at times also indicate the name of the applicant's employer.

RECORDS OF THE PENNSYLVANIA SOCIETY OF SONS OF THE AMERICAN REVOLUTION (PASSAR), ca. 1901-1978 (MG-370). The National Society of Sons of the American Revolution was organized in 1889. After a great deal of interest and lobbying, particularly in the Pittsburgh area, a Pennsylvania branch was set up in 1893. Of interest to family historians are the following items:

Account Book, 1901-1960. Primarily registration records that are organized according to society chapters. Information noted includes the member's name and registration numbers (national and state), the date of registration, the date that the charters was granted to the chapter, and as pertinent, and the date that the member may have been dropped from the rolls, transferred, or died. Other subdivisions in the volume deal with "members in the Second World War," "casualties reported in World War II," "World War medal awards," "deaths," "resignations," "dropped," and so forth. Most of the entries are in chronological order.

Membership Index Cards, 1929-1978. Consists of two sets of cards that list the full name and mailing address of each member. As needed, the dates that the person resigned, was dropped from the rolls (usually for not paying dues), or died is recorded. One set of cards (3 X 7 inches) is arranged in alphabetical order by the member's surname and has data regarding dues paid from 1929-1959. The other set of cards (3 X 5 inches) is for the most part undated, arranged by counties or society chapters, and thereafter by member surnames. Various notations concerning deaths, resignations, etc. occurring in 1978, however, are inscribed on these cards.

REGISTER OF DRAWBACKS ON GOODS EXPORTED, 1785-1786 (RG-4). A record of goods exported from the Port of Philadelphia and of drawbacks (duties refunded). The register is in chronological order by export date and lists the vessel's name and type; the names of the master, exporter, and importer; the dates of arrival and clearance; the port of origin and destination; the type of cargo exported; the value of the goods imported; and the amount of drawback.

REGISTER OF DUTIES PAID ON IMPORTED GOODS, 1781-1787 (RG-4). Recorded at the Port of Philadelphia, an entry usually gives the name of the vessel's master, the port of origin, the value of the goods imported, the name of the importer, and the duty paid. A brief description of the cargo also appears in most cases. The registers are arranged by import date.

REGISTER OF MEMBERS OF THE HARMONY SOCIETY, 1805-1905 (RG-13). The data that appears in this bound volume was apparently compiled on index cards (3 X 5 inches) by staff from the Federal Writer's Project, a Works Progress Administration (WPA) sponsored effort that was terminated early in 1942. From 1965 to 1971 staff from Old Economy Village used these cards to create the alphabetical list that appears in this register. Entries generally show the member's name and birth date, the date of arrival, the dates when the individual's signature appears on documents, and when pertinent, the date of withdrawal. Miscellaneous information, for example, family relationships or the person's country of origin are recorded in a column captioned "notes." Depending on the person's membership and marital status, the date of death or the woman's maiden name, may be found as well. Approximately 1,500 names are included.

REGISTERS OF VESSEL ARRIVALS AND CLEARANCES, 1784-1791, 1793-1797, 1802-1840, 1843-1956 (RG-41). A record of shipping at the Port of Philadelphia. The listings are signed by the vessel's captain and for the most part show the name, classification, nationality (from 1902 onward), and oftentimes the tonnage of the vessel; the port of arrival or clearance; the name of the owner or consignee; and the names of the pilot and captain. A brief description of the vessel's cargo is usually given as well. The registers are arranged chronologically according to the date that the vessels reached or left Philadelphia, and the following indices can be used to retrieve data from them:

INDEX OF VESSEL ARRIVALS, 1862-1879, 1881-1882, 1884-1890, 1894-1937.

INDEX OF VESSEL CLEARANCES, 1862-1863, 1879, 1882-1884, 1892-1894, 1899-1907, 1915.

INDEX OF COASTAL VESSEL ARRIVALS, 1873-1878.

It should be noted that the indices are in alphabetical order, but by vessel name and not captain's surname.

REPORTS, DAMAGE CLAIMS, AND CLAIMS ABSTRACTS AND CERTIFICATES RELATING TO BORDER RAID CLAIMS AND THE COMMISSIONERS TO ASSESS DAMAGES IN THE BORDER COUNTIES, 1869-1879 (RG-2). Contains bound volumes and papers such as these:

DAMAGE CLAIM APPLICATIONS (SUBMITTED UNDER ACTS PASSED 1863- 1871), 1871-1879. The claims cover residents of Adams, Bedford, Cumberland, Franklin, Fulton, and York Counties. Each application consists of a handwritten petition and a printed form called an "abstract of application for damage" (primarily relating to the Acts of April 9, 1868 and May 22, 1871) that are arranged by county and thereunder by surname of claimant. Information shown includes the claim number and filing date; the name and residence (county and township) of the applicant; an inventory of personal property and real estate lost or damaged; the estimated monetary loss (aggregate as well as discrete) incurred; and the amount and date of the award granted (from 1871). Particulars, for example, the names of southern commanders responsible for the damage are sometimes noted. A typed name listing of claimants is available for reference purposes. Researchers can also consult an INDEX TO DAMAGE CLAIM APPLICATIONS (SUBMITTED UNDER ACTS PASSED, 1863-1871), ca. 1871-1879, and an INDEX TO ISSUED WAR DAMAGE ADJUDICATED CLAIM CERTIFICATES, 1872-1879.

WAR DAMAGE CLAIM ABSTRACTS, 1868-1871. Entries in the volumes are grouped by county and thereunder by first letter of claimant's surname. Most books simply give the person's name, county of residence, claim number, and amount claimed. Several also provide the monetary amount claimed for losses of both personal property and real estate.

Similar data appear in CHAMBERSBURG WAR DAMAGE CLAIM APPLICATIONS SUBMITTED UNDER ACT OF FEBRUARY 15, 1866 (RG-2).

JULIUS SACHSE COLLECTION OF EPHRATA CLOISTER MATERI- ALS, 1680-1939 (MG-351). Original documents, photocopies, tran- scripts, and heliographic facsimiles of correspondence, articles, books, wills, and hymnals collected or written by Julius Friedrich Sachse (1842-1919) concerning the history and religious develop- ment of Ephrata Cloister by the Seventh Day German Baptist Brethern. Also included among the records are biographical mater- ial pertaining to leaders and members of the cloister as well as information relating to similar pietistic and religious communal groups in Lancaster and Chester Counties.

SANITARY ENGINEER EPIDEMIC REPORTS, 1904-1919 (RG-11). Etiologies prepared by staff from the Health Department's Bureau of Sanitary Engineering to explain why outbreaks of disease occurred in communities throughout Pennsylvania. The reports usually start with a brief history in which the population, econo- my, geography, environment, and socio-cultural features of the borough or township are described. This local history is followed by a narrative and statistical analysis of the problem; a discussion of possible improvements that could serve as a remedy; and rec- ommendations. As part of the report's content, details regarding the residents who became ill or died are reported, including in some cases their names, residences, ages, and activities prior to the epidemic. The reports are organized by county, then communi- ty, and thereunder by the date of investigation.

NANCY SHEDD COLLECTION, 1747-1870 (MG-458). The documents are from the estate of John W. Surgart, the donor's father, and consist of several indentures, deeds, and land patents relating to South Carolina, Virginia, and Northampton and Chester Counties of Pennsylvania. Also included are land grants and petitions to the courts of Cumberland County for roads.

SHIPPING BONDS AND CERTIFICATES, 1752-1775 (RG-41). A record created at the Port of Philadelphia to comply with British maritime regulations during the colonial period. Normally the record is arranged by pass number, and thereunder according to the date of the document. Included among the materials are the following items:

Bonds, 1752-1775. The bonds are dated with a typical listing giving the name, signature, and occupation of the vessel's bonder; the amount of the bond that was paid; the name of the vessel's master; and the name and type of vessel that was bonded. The owner of the vessel is sometimes noted.

Oaths, 1752-1775. Entries are dated and list the name, classification, gun power, and tonnage of the vessel; the region where the vessel was built (plantation or not); the place where the vessel was owned; the destination to which the vessel was bound; the name of the master; the name of the naval officer who surveyed the sailing craft; the date of the oath; and the name and residence of the person making the affirmation. The number of crew members who were foreigners or British subjects is also indicated.

WILLIAM W. STOEY COLLECTION, 1893-1925 (MG-240). Has photographs of the Berrier, Butler, Lingle, Peiffer, Read, Sullenberger, and Yingst families that were taken by William W. Stoey, Harrisburg conservationist and naturalist.

EDWARD STOVER PAPERS, 1857-1935 (MG-320). Business accounts, family materials, and legal papers of Edward Stover, Middletown lumber merchant. The legal papers, 1861-1928, consist of agreements, bonds, insurance policies, leases, mortgages, and a deed and release. Many of the agreements, 1865-1898, relate to the leasing of farms to tenants near what today is known as Hummelstown, Pa. In addition to giving the name of the person leasing the farm; the period of the lease; and a description of the property being rented; the document lists detailed information regarding what crops were to be grown; and the planting, sowing, animal husbandry, and labor services that the family was required to provide Stover as conditions for occupancy.

SUSQUEHANNA COMPANY RECORDS, 1754-1803 (MG-344). The collection consists of positive photostatic copies of original deeds and conveyances (ca.1794-1803) and a reproduction of the typed summaries of deeds and conveyances that are deposited at the Wyoming Historical and Geological Society in Wilkes-Barre, Pa. These summaries are abstracts from original record books of the Susquehanna Company (1754-1798) that are located at the Connecticut Historical Society in Hartford, Conn. Entries on the summaries give the name and residence of the grantee, the date of deed, the location of the grant, the consideration (amount paid, terms), and the page reference, that is, the page number placed on the copies of the original deeds and conveyances.

TAX AND EXONERATION LISTS, 1762-1794 (RG-4). Consists of diverse tax (supply taxes, carriage, and billiard table taxes, property returns, etc.) and exoneration returns for Allegheny, Bedford, Berks, Bucks, Chester, Cumberland, Dauphin, Fayette, Franklin, Huntingdon, Lancaster, Montgomery, Northampton, Northumberland, Philadelphia, Washington, Westmoreland, and York Counties. Depending on the time period and the type of returns compiled, the dated lists may show the name, residence (county and township), and trade of the taxable; the number of acres and type (patent, warrant, and improved) of land that he possessed; the number of livestock (cattle and horses) and negroes that he owned; the tax rate; and the tax that he paid. Frequently the lists also indicate whether the individual was a single freeman and whether he operated a distillery, sawmill, or gristmill. The returns are arranged by county, and thereunder according to political subdivision. The surnames appearing on the lists are grouped alphabetically.

TITLE INDEX TO LEHIGH COAL AND NAVIGATION COMPANY'S PROPERTY THROUGH WYOMING VALLEY PENNSYLVANIA, September 1, 1909 (MG-311). A record prepared by Sturdevant Engineering Company, Ltd. of Wilkes-Barre, Pa. The index consists of columns which show the property number, the names of the grantor and grantee, the date (1837-1900) and type of conveyance (condemnation, release, deed, etc.), the book and page where the title was recorded, the map number, and remarks, for example, whether the land had no reservations, was coal reserved, or was only partially owned. The index is followed by a series of numbered maps that usually depict property boundaries; the arrangement of buildings; road and track locations; the presence of rivers, streams, and waterways; and at times, the owners of real estate in the following Luzerne County communities: Ashley, Hanover, Jenkins, Laflin, Miners Mills, Nanticoke, Newport, Parsons, Pittston (both city and township), Plains, Sugar Notch, Warriors Run, and Wilkes-Barre (both the city and township).

TREZIYULNY FAMILY PAPERS, 1758-1900, undated (MG-128). Chiefly drafts of single tracts and connected tracts of land surveyed by Charles S. and Henry P. Treziyulny in the central counties of Pennsylvania or copies of surveys made by a number of deputy surveyors of the Commonwealth. Representative counties include Bedford, Blair, Centre, Clearfield, Clinton, Cumberland, Huntingdon, Lycoming, Mifflin, and Northumberland. Also present are survey field notes, 1769-1888; select deeds, 1794-1857; family correspondence, 1859-1893; Graff family land papers, 1773-1809; and a passport of Wilhelm Rohrigs from the Kingdom of Hanover, 1845. An alphabetical county and township list is available for referencing the surveys.

UPPER ALLEN SCHOOL DISTRICT RECORDS, 1890-1939 (MG-319). Teacher's monthly reports, enrollment books, census books, and school tax records for the Cumberland County school district of Upper Allen. Some of the records pertain to the Center Square and Pleasant Schools. The following information appears in these records:

Census of Children Between the Ages of Six and Sixteen Years, 1923-1924, 1933-1934, 1937-1938. Entries in the volumes have space for recording the name of the school and the district; the name, date of birth, age at last birthday (blank for 1934), sex, nationality, and residence of each student; and the name of the parent or guardian. From 1923-1924 there is a notarized oath of the enumerator attesting to the accuracy of the data. After 1936 with the exception of the names and residences of the students and their parents, and an occasional reference to the grade last attended, most of the data columns are blank. The volumes are not in any type of discernible order after 1924. Prior to 1925 entries are grouped together by school enrolled in.

Enrollment of Children Between the Ages of Six and Sixteen Years, 1914-1916, 1918, 1920, 1937-1938. The students names appear in the volumes under the school in which they are enrolled. Data given includes the child's name, age, date of birth, sex, nationality (prior to 1937), and residence; name of parent or guardian; school enrolled in; district and county; and if relevant, name of employer of child under sixteen. The returns are notarized, dated, and signed by the enumerator as to correctness.

School Tax Duplicates, Upper Allen Township, 1933-1936. These four volumes list the name, address, and occupation of each taxable person along with the per capita tax paid. Entries in the books are grouped in alphabetical order by first letter of surname.

Teachers' Monthly Reports, October 11, 1881-March 12, 1890. Provides the name of the school district; the name of the school and the teacher; the name and age of each student; and statistics regarding days attended, number of girls and boys attending class and specific courses (arithmetic, spelling, etc.), and visits by guests or parents. Space on some of the forms is available for reporting what books were used and the amount of money received from the treasurer of the district. Entries are in chronological order.

VALUABLE PAPERS FILE, ca. 1850-1967 (MG-286). Indexed. Records found among the holdings of Pennsylvania Railroad Company, the secretary's office. The file is arranged in numerical order by file numbers and consists of agreements, contracts, incorporation papers, charters, deeds, mortgages, leases, and abstracts of titles of the Pennsylvania Railroad and many of the companies that it gained control over.

VALUABLE PAPERS FILE, 1850-1966 (MG-286). Indexed. Records belonging to the secretary of the Lehigh Valley Railroad Company and which primarily consist of agreements, contracts, leases, mortgages, and deeds. Each item generally provides the purpose of the document and the effective date; the names of the individual, companies, or government entities that are parties to the negotiations; the financial terms; and a description of the principle right or property conveyed. Records vary as to scope and nature, including pipe and wire, track and crossing rights, real estate, physical facilities, financial obligations, joint operations with other companies, governmental authorizations, purchases, and so forth. The documents are arranged in numerical order by file numbers.

SAMUEL WALLIS COLLECTION, 1763-1873, 1921, undated (MG-167). General correspondence, 1766-1830; legal papers, 1770-1845; and land papers, 1763-1873, of Samuel Wallis, a native of Northumberland County and a surveyor who worked for the Surveyor General's Office of Pennsylvania from 1781 to 1809. Accordingly, a major portion of the papers pertain to the surveying of land in Pennsylvania, particularly in the north central region. Representative land drafts, 1767-1873, include tracts in Bedford, Berks, Lycoming, and Northumberland Counties.

LUCILLE WILSON COLLECTION, 1793-1881 (MG-298). Contains a half dozen group photographs of students and teachers attending Linden Hall Seminary For Young Ladies in Lititz, Pa., probably during the 1870s to 1880s. The photographs have the names of the class members on the reverse side, but in German script.

WOMEN IN HISTORY PROJECT FILES, Undated (MG-350). The original biographies and materials submitted by branches of the American Association of University Women for consideration and possible inclusion in the publication *Our Hidden Heritage: Pennsylvania Women in History*. In addition to a biography, each nomination has a cover form which provides the name, date of birth, date of demise, residence (city or county) of the woman researched; her area of significant contribution (education, politics, etc.); the name of the branch submitting the name; the name, address, and telephone number of the writer(s) of the biography; the names of any other contributors to be credited, and why; the name of the local archives where the research materials on the nominee will be stored; and the name, address, and telephone number of the project chairman or other responsible party submitting the materials. Other data requested about the historical figure include whether the woman was nationally known (if yes, proof thereof); was the person of statewide prominence (if yes, evidence thereof); if non-living and primarily of local significance, how would she rank in comparison to other local women submitted (1 to 14); and was a glossy photograph of the individual available and included with the application. The applications are organized in alphabetical order by surnames.

WRITS OF HABEAS CORPUS FOR NEGRO SLAVES, 1786-1787 (RG-33). The documents were filed with the Supreme Court of Pennsylvania, Eastern District, and contain diverse data that vary with each writ. Many of the writs provide the slave's name, place of residency, and name of master. In some instances familial relationships are depicted and particulars are entered about where the slave worked and when he or she was purchased. The documents are dated and arranged in chronological order.

List of children educated at the public expense in Bucks County, 1830. There are 1,025 names in this volume and 1,132 children listed in another 1829-1830 book. For similar information researchers should examin folders marked as "common school" in the GENERAL ACCOUNTS, 1809 (1809-1896) – 1929, of the Auditor General (RG– 2), PSA.

APPENDIX A

SELECT LIST OF PENNSYLVANIA VITAL RECORDS LEGISLATION

Proprietary Level

11/04/1676 Ministers or town clerks of every parish required to record all births, marriages and (Duke of York's Laws) burials.

05/05/1682 Register of the county called upon to keep a register of births, burials and 12/17/1682 (Great Law) marriages. There shall be a registry for births, marriages, burials, wills, the (Laws Agreed Upon in England) names of executors, etc.

03/10/1683. Register of the county to register certificates of marriage. Set registers fees for 05/10/1684 recording births, deaths, wills, marriages and recording a marriage certificate in (Laws of Assembly) parchment.

05/10/1690 Religious societies required to keep a registry of marriages, births and burials (Laws of Assembly)(abrogated in 1693 by William and Mary and re-enacted later in 1693 and 1700).

Municipal Level

03/08/1860 (PL 130) Effective July 1, Philadelphia City health officer to keep registration books for marriages, births and deaths. Physicians, clergy, etc. required to register and provide uniform information on vital statistics to him. Supplemental 02/27/1867 (PL 32) and 4/9/1869 (PL 821).

04/16/1870 (PL 1194) Effective May 1, Pittsburgh City Board of Health authorized to operate a registration system for vital statistics comparable to Philadelphia.

04/10/1873 (PL 724) Effective May 1, Allentown city health officer authorized to operate a registration system for vital statistics comparable to that of Philadelphia and Pittsburgh.

05/23/1874 (PL 230) Pennsylvania third class cities given power to create a board of health that could create a complete and accurate system of registration of marriages, births, deaths and interments for purposes of legal and genealogical investigations.

05/05/1876 (PL 113) Boards of health, wherever established by law in cities of the Commonwealth, authorized to keep registration books for marriages, births and deaths. Physicians, clergy, etc. required to register by July 1st with the secretary of the board and provide uniform data on vital stats to him.

06/07/1881 (PL 51) Boards of health in third class cities authorized to keep registration books for marriages, births and deaths. Physicians, clergy, etc., required to register with a health officer by July 1st and provide uniform data on vital stats to him.

05/24/1887 (PL 204) Cities of the fourth to seventh class could create a board of health with powers to keep a complete and accurate registration system for marriages, births and deaths and to compel obedience to do so on the part of physicians, clergy, etc.

04/29/1937 (PL 487) Registrar of vital statistics of every borough, town and township required to provide written reports on deaths of residents to the registration commission in their community.

05/31/1959 (PL 62) Registrar of vital statistics required to provide written reports to the registration commission of every city of the second class, third class, borough, town or township regarding the deaths of residents.

11/10/1959 (PL 1467) Exclusive jurisdiction concerning birth records, changes and appeals from the Department of Health by residents of Philadelphia given to the municipal court instead of the orphans' court.

County Level

04/02/1804 Court of common pleas as well as the supreme court and circuit courts authorized to receive and decide upon applications for divorce. Jury trials also approved with appeals to be filed before the supreme court or court of error and appeals.

03/13/1815 (PL 150) Court of common pleas authorized to receive and decide upon all applications for divorce. Appeals to be heard by the supreme sourt of the state. Elaboration of powers, procedures or circumstances: 02/26/1817 (PL 67); 04/13/1843 (PL 233); 04/15/1845 (PL 455); 04/26/1850 (PL 590); 05/08/1854 (PL 644); 03/09/1855 (PL 68); 04/22/1858 (PL 450); 04/14/1859 (PL 647); 04/11/1862 (PL 430); 05/25/1878 (PL 156); 06/11/1891 (PL 295); 06/20/1893 (PL 471); 06/25/1895 (PL 308); 03/10/1899 (PL 8); 03/09/1903 (PL 19); 04/18/1905 (PL 211); 04/22/1905 (PL 293); 04/26/1905 (PL 309); 05/01/1909 (PL 374); 04/16/1911 (PL 53); 04/13/1911 (PL 60); 04/20/1911 (PL 71); 06/08/1911 (PL 720); 05/09/1913 (PL 191); 04/21/1915 (PL 154); 06/01/1915 (PL 674); 05/08/1919 (PL 164); 05/11/1921 (PL 499); 03/19/1923 (PL 20); 06/28/1923 (PL 886); 04/04/1925 (PL 124); 03/29/1927 (PL 71); 04/27/1927 (PL 406); 05/02/1929 (PL 1237); 07/13/1953 (PL 449); 04/02/80 (PL 63).

04/10/1849 (PL 549) Under threat of penalties, all persons who because of care or profession might possess marriage records were required to provide transcripts of the materials to any applicants paying the proper fees.

01/12/1852 (PL 2) Register of wills to keep marriage, birth and death registers. Physicians, clergy, etc., to submit certificates to them. Appropriations provided 05/04/1852 (PL 542) and 4/19/1853 (PL 590).

01/31/1855 (PL 4) Registration Act of 1852 repealed.

05/15/1874 (PL 194) Register of wills required to record the day and hour of death of testators and intestates.

06/23/1885 (PL 146) Clerk of orphans' court, effective October 1st, authorized to issue and record all marriage licenses. Amendments, supplements, etc., 05/23/1887 (PL 170); 03/27/1903 (PL 80; 102); 07/24/1913 (PL 1013); 05/17/1939 (PL 148); 03/09/1945 (PL 41); 05/16/1945 (PL 576).

06/06/1893 (PL 340) Clerk of orphans' court authorized to keep birth and death registers (did not affect cities where a system of registration was already established).

05/22/1895 (PL 99) Clerk of orphans' court required to make

marriage license dockets open for inspection or examination by the public (persons could make copy or abstracts of the entries for publication in any regularly published newspaper printed in the Commonwealth).

05/22/1895 (PL 105) Prothonotaries, clerks of court or notaries public authorized to take affidavits, petitions and all papers and proceedings concerning divorces.

07/16/1941 (PL 405) Orphans' court, upon petition, required to perfect or record birth records of persons born prior to January 1, 1906. (A special docket book or register was to be kept by the Court for this purpose.)

07/24/1941 (PL 497) Prothonotaries and clerks of court required to make out certificates of divorce, annulment of marriage or adoption to be forwarded to the state Department of Health for inclusion in its record of vital statistics.

05/21/1943 (PL 322) County officers to provide free of charge certified copies of death, birth, marriage and divorce certificates to disabled war veterans and their dependents in death and compensation cases.

06/29/1953 (PL 304) "Vital Statistics Law of 1953" – clerks of orphans' court to transmit to the state Department of Health transcripts of all marriage license applications filed with them. A certificate of each divorce, annulment of marriage, adoption decreed or ordered in the Commonwealth was also to be sent to the department by the prothonotaries or clerks of orphans' courts. Persons requiring copies of such documents were to apply to the court or county officer that issued them.

08/22/1953 (PL 1344) "The marriage Law" – act that consolidated the marriage laws of the Commonwealth and repealed the Act of June 23, 1885. Clerk of orphans' court reauthorized to issue and record all marriage licenses. Supplemented 10/07/1976 (PL 1056); 10/17/1977 (PL 211).

08/04/1955 (PL 303) Orphans' court given exclusive jurisdiction over all court proceedings required for determining issues concerning recordation of birth or the alteration of birth records.

08/09/1955 (PL 322) Coroners in third–eight class counties authorized to issue certificates of cause of death in all cases referred to them by the local registrar of vital statistics. Updated 05/09/1961 (PL 197).

08/18/1961 (PL 1011) "Vital Statistics Law of 1953"– amended to include that the Department of Health would report monthly, in writing to the registration commission of each county the deaths of residents occurring in their communities.

07/24/1970 (PL 620) Established regulations for the adoption of minors and adults and designated what form and style the decrees, papers, etc., were to be recorded in (Effective January 1, 1971).

State Level

09/16/1785 State supreme court authorized to receive petitions or libels for divorce after an affadavit was first entered with one of the justices, a justice of the court of common pleas or a justice of the peace. Trial by juries to be held before the court of nisi prius; appeals to be filed with the high court of errors and appeals.

04/02/1804 Judge of the state supreme court, the circuit courts or the court of common pleas authorized to receive applications for divorce. Trials by jury to be held in the county or state court with appeals being allowed before the supreme court or court of errors and appeals.

06/03/1885 (PL 56) State Board of Health and Vital Statistics given responsibility for supervising the state system of registration of births, marriages and deaths. Central Bureau of Vital Statistics at Harrisburg, Pa. established.

04/27/1905 (PL 312) Department of Health created and given general responsibility for supervising 05/01/1905 (PL 330) registration of births, marriages and deaths throughout the state and having it recorded in a Central Bureau of Vital Statistics in Harrisburg, Pa. State divided into ten registration districts for the purpose of reporting births, deaths and burials (in cities or boroughs where health officers or secretaries, etc. were officiating as registrars of births and deaths they were to continue in office).

06/07/1915 (PL 900) Department of Health's duties and powers reiterated with provision that returns be made promptly and that no municipal system of registration of births and deaths existing in Commonwealth was to be continued or maintained thereafter. Supplemented or amended 04/20/1921 (PL 181); 05/24/1933 (PL 976); 05/24/1933 (PL 979).

05/09/1923 (PL 176) State registrar required to send a notice of registry of birth to the child's parents.

04/09/1929 (PL 177) "Reorganization Act of 1929" - Department of Health's duties and powers reiterated with emphasis made that the registration and prompt return of birth, death, marriage and disease records were to be uniformly and thoroughly enforced throughout the state.

05/24/1933 (PL 976) State registrar to maintain a file for receiving and registering birth certificates of children of citizens of Pennsylvania born beyond the limits of the United States. Adoption decrees also to be attached to the original birth certificate filed. Amended 04/22/1937 (PL 399); repealed 06/29/1953 (PL 304); and reinstated 07/03/1957 (PL 443).

07/02/1937 (PL 2719) Department of Health to inaugurate and maintain a special file for the records of births of veterans of the First World War.

07/16/1941 (PL 383) Bureau of Vital Statistics required to make delayed records of birth part of their files when sufficient evidence is available. In cases of dispute appeals were to be filed with, the orphans' court.

07/24/1941 (PL 497) Department of Health required to file and register every divorce, adoption and annulment of marriage or adoption received from county prothonotaries or clerks of court.

05/21/1943 (PL 414) "Uniform Vital Statistics Act of 1943" - Consolidated vital statistic laws and provided for special registration certificates for foundlings. Department of Health authorized to provide certified copies of its vital statistics to persons with a direct interest in the record only. Amended 03/11/1949 (PL 309) and repealed 06/29/1953 (PL 304).

04/09/1945 (PL 166) "Uniform Vital Statistics Act of 1943" – amended regarding the condition under which information on records could be furnished to applicants. United States and Commonwealth public agencies given access to complete certified copies of birth certificates while applicants with a direct interest could obtain only partial certified copies.

06/29/1953 (PL 304) "Vital Statistics Law of 1953" – General consolidation act relating to vital statistics with a description of the statewide administrative system of registering vital statistics by the Department of Health. Certified copies of vital statistics (marriage, divorce, adoption cases excepted) were to be furnished to applicants with a direct interest in the contents of the records upon request and payment of a fee. Supplemented 12/03/1975 (PL 468). 09/02/1961 (PL 1152; PL 1154) Department of Health rather than the local registrars of vital statistics to provide written reports to the registration commission of every city of the first class, second class, third class borough, town, and township.

11/17/1967 (PL 514) Dentists authorized in certain situations to issue certificates of death.

11/21/1967 (PL 67)

07/09/1971 (PL 213) Any local registrar of vital statistics authorized to issue certified copies of deaths.

10/18/1975 (PL 410) "Marriage Act of 1953" – amended to permit members of the Commonwealth court and full-time federal magistrates the right to solemnize marriages.

APPENDIX B

TOWNSHIP MAPS MADE AVAILABLE THROUGH THE LAND OFFICE'S WARRANT TRACT MAPPING PROGRAM, 1907-1995

ALLEGHENY COUNTY

Aleppo	Kennedy	Reserve
Baldwin	Kilbuck	Richland
Bethel	Leet	Robinson
Braddock	Lincoln	Ross
Chartiers	Lower St. Clair	Scott
Collier	Marshall	Sewickley
Crescent	McCandless	Sewickley Heights
East Deer	Mifflin	Shaler
Elizabeth	Moon	Snowden
Fawn	Neville	South Fayette
Findley	North Fayette	South Versailles
Forward	North Versailles	Springdale
Franklin	O'Hara	Stowe
Hampton	Ohio	Upper St. Clair
Harmar	Patton	Versailles
Harrison	Penn	West Deer
Indiana	Pine	Wilkins
Jefferson	Plum	

BEAVER COUNTY

Beaver (town plan; out lots and reserve tracts)	Franklin	North Sewickley
	Greene	Ohio
	Hanover	Patterson
Big Beaver	Harmony	Potter
Brighton	Hopewell	Pulaski
Brighton (Borough)	Independence	Raccoon
Center	Industry	Rochester
Chippewa	Marion	South Beaver
Darlington	Moon	White
Economy	New Sewickley	

339

BERKS COUNTY

Alsace
Bern
Bethel
Brecknock
Caernarvon
Cumru
Exeter
Heidelberg
Jefferson
Lower Heidelberg
Marion
Muhlenberg
North Heidelberg
Penn
Reading (City)
Robeson
South Heidelberg
Spring
Tilden
Tulpehocken
Upper Bern
Upper Tulpehocken
Union

BRADFORD COUNTY

Albany
Armenia
Asylum
Athens
Barclay
Burlington
Canton
Columbia
Franklin
Granville
Herrick
Leroy
Litchfield
Monroe
North Towanda
Towanda
Orwell
Overton
Pike
Ridgebury
Rome
Sheshequin
Smithfield
South Creek
Springfield
Standing Stone
Stevens
Terry
Troy
Tuscarora
Ulster
Warren
Wells
West Burlington
Wilmot
Windham
Wyalusing
Wysox

CAMERON COUNTY

Gibson
Grove
Lumber
Portage
Shippen

CUMBERLAND COUNTY

East Pennsboro

DAUPHIN COUNTY

Conewago
Derry
East Hanover
Halifax
Lower Paxton
Lower Swatara
Lykens
Middle Paxton
Susquehanna
Swatara
Upper Paxton
Washington

Harrisburg (City) Mifflin Wayne
Jackson Reed West Hanover
Jefferson Rush Williams
Londonderry South Hanover Wiconisco

ELK COUNTY

Benezette Highland Ridgway
Bensinger Horton Spring Creek
East Jones Jay West Jones
Fox Millstone

ERIE COUNTY

Amity Girard Springfield
Concord Greene Summit
Conneaut Greenfield Union
Elk Creek Harbor Creek Venango
Erie City Le Boeuf Washington
(out lots) Mill Creek Waterford
Fairview McKean Wayne
Franklin North East

FAYETTE COUNTY

Brownville Menallen Springhill
Bullskin Nicholson Steward
Connellsville North Union (northeast section)
Dunbar Perry Steward
Franklin Red Stone (southwest section)
Georges Salt Lick Upper Tyrone
German South Union Washington
Henry Clay Springfield Wharton
Jefferson (north section) (north section)
Lower Tyrone Springfield Wharton
Luzerne (south section)

FULTON COUNTY

Dublin Tod

GREENE COUNTY

Aleppo
Centre
Cumberland #1
Cumberland #2
Dunkard
Franklin
Greene

Gillmore
Jackson
Jefferson
Monongahela
Morgan
Morris
Perry

Richhill
Springhill
Washington
Wayne
Whiteley

HUNTINGDON COUNTY

Springfield

LACKAWANNA COUNTY

Abington
Benton
Blakely
Carbondale
Clifton
Covington
Elmhurst
Fell

Glenburn
Greenfield
Jefferson
Laplume
Lehigh
Madison
Newton
North Abington

Providence
Ranson
Roaring Brook
Scott
Scranton (city)
South Abington
Springbrook
West Abington

LANCASTER COUNTY

Bart
Brecknock
Caernarvon
Clay
Colerain
Conestoga
Conoy
Drumore
Earl
East Cocalico
East Donegal
East Drumore
East Earl
East Hempfield

East Lampeter
Eden
Elizabeth
Ephrata
Fulton
Leacock
Little Britain
Manheim
Manor
Martic
Mt. Joy
Paradise
Penn
Pequea

Providence
Rapho
Sadsbury
Salisbury
Strasburg
Upper Leacock
Warwick
West Cocalico
West Donegal
West Earl
West Hempfield
West Lampeter

LAWRENCE COUNTY

Big Beaver
Hickory
Little Beaver
Mahoning
Neshannock
New Castle (city)
North Beaver
Perry
Plain Grove
Pulaski
Scott
Shenango
Taylor
Union
Washington
Wayne
Wilmington

LUZERNE COUNTY

Bear Creek
Black Creek
Buck
Butler
Conyngham
Dallas
Dennison
Dorrance
Exeter
Fairmount
Fairview
Foster
Franklin
Hanover
Hazle
Hollenback
Huntingdon
Jackson
Jenkins
Kingston
Lake
Lehman
Marcy
Nescopeck
Newport
Pittston
Plains
Plymouth (north; northwest; south sections)
Rice
Ross
Salem
Slocum
Sugar Loaf
Union
Wilkes-Barre
Wilkes-Barre (city)
Wright

MERCER COUNTY

Coolspring
Deer Creek
Delaware
E. Lackawannock
Fairview
Findley
French Creek
Greene
Hempfield
Hickory
Jackson
Jefferson
Lackawannock
Lake
Liberty
Mill Creek
New Vernon
Otter Creek
Perry
Pine
Pymatuning
Salem
Sandy Creek
Sandy Lake
Shenango
South Pymatuning
Springfield
Sugar Grove
West Salem
Wilmington
Wolf Creek
Worth

343

MCKEAN COUNTY

Annin	Foster	Liberty
Bradford	Hamilton	Norwich
Ceres	Hamlin	Otto
Corydon	Keating	Sergeant
Eldred	Lafayette	Wetmore

MONROE COUNTY

Coolbaugh

NORTHUMBERLAND COUNTY

Coal	Mt. Carmel	Shamokin
Delaware	Ralpho	

PERRY

Buffalo	Juniata	Saville
Centre	Liverpool	Toboyne
Greenwood	Miller	Tuscarora
Howe	Oliver	Watts
Jackson (North;	Penn	Wheatfield
South Sections)	Rye	

PIKE COUNTY

Blooming Grove	Lackawaxen (north;	Palmyra
Delaware	south sections)	Porter
Dingham	Lehman	Shohola
Greene	Milford	Westfall

POTTER COUNTY

Abbott	Hebron	Sharon
Allegheny	Hector	Stewardson
Bingham	Homer	Summit
Clara	Keating	Sweden
East Fork	Oswayo	Sylvania
District	Pike	Ulysses
Eulalia	Pleasant Valley	West Branch
Genesee	Portage	Wharton
Harrison	Roulette	

SCHUYLKILL COUNTY

Blythe
Butler
Cass
Delano
East Brunswick
East Norwegian
East Union

Klein
Mahanoy
New Castle
North Union
Norwegian
Rahn
Rush

Ryan
Schuylkill
Union
Walker
West Brunswick
West Mahanoy
West Penn

SULLIVAN COUNTY

Cherry
Colley
Davidson

Elkland
Forks
Fox

Hillgrove
Laporte
Shrewsbury

SUSQUEHANNA COUNTY

Apolacon
Ararat
Auburn
Choconut
Clifford
Dimock
Forest Lake
Franklin

Gibson
Harford
Harmony
Herrick
Jackson
Jessup
Lathrop
Liberty

Middletown
New Milford
Oakland
Rush
Silver Lake
Springville

TIOGA COUNTY

Bloss
Brookfield
Charleston
Chatham
Clymer
Covington
Deerfield
Delmar
Dungan
Elk

Elkland
Farmington
Gaines
Hamilton
Jackson
Lawrence
Liberty
Middlebury
Morris
Nelson

Putnam
Richmond
Rutland
Shippen
Sullivan
Tioga
Union
Ward
Westfield

UNION COUNTY

White Deer

VENANGO COUNTY

Allegheny
Canal
Cherry Tree
Clinton
Cornplanter
Cranberry
French Creek

Irwin
Jackson
Mineral
Oakland
Oil Creek
Pine Grove
Plum

President
Richland
Rockland
Sandy Creek
Scrubgrass
Sugar Creek
Victory

WARREN COUNTY

Brokenstraw
Cherry Grove
Columbus
Conewango
Deerfield
Eldred
Elk
Farmington

Freehold
Glade
Limestone
Meade
Pine Grove
Pittsfield
Pleasant
Sheffield

Southwest
Spring Creek
Sugar Grove
Triumph
Warren (City)
Watson

WASHINGTON COUNTY

Allen
Amwell
Blaine
Buffalo
Canton
Carroll
Cecil
Chartiers
Cross Creek
Donegal
East Bethlehem
East Finley
East Pike Run

Fallowfield
Franklin
Hanover
Hopewell
Independence
Jefferson
Morris
Mt. Pleasant
North Franklin
North Strabane
Nottingham
Peters
Robinson

Smith
Somerset
South Strabane
South Washington
(borough)
Union
West Bethlehem
(Upper; Lower
Section)
West Finley
West Pike Run

WAYNE COUNTY

Berlin
Buckingham

Lake
Lebanon

Preston
Salem

Canaan	Lehigh	Scott
Cherry Ridge	Manchester	South Canaan
Clinton	Mt. Pleasant	Sterling
Damascus	Oregon	Texas
Dreher	Palmyra	
Dyberry	Paupack	

YORK COUNTY

Warrington

RECORD UNITS UTILIZED

The Division of Archives and Manuscripts uses the organizing units of Record Groups (RGs) and Manuscript Groups (MGs) for arranging its records. An appropriate group number appears in parentheses after the name of each series title that is found in this guide. Record units cited include these:

RECORD GROUPS

RG NO.	RG TITLE
1	Records of the Department of Agriculture
2	Records of the Department of Auditor General
4	Records of the Office of the Comptroller General
6	Records of the Department of Forests and Waters
7	Records of the General Assembly
8	Records of the General Loan Office and State Treas.
11	Records of the Department of Health
14	Records of the Department of Internal Affairs
15	Records of the Department of Justice
17	Records of the Land Office Records
19	Records of the Department of Military Affairs
21	Records of the Proprietary Government
22	Records of the Department of Education
23	Records of the Department of Public Welfare
24	Records of the Office of the Register General

26 Records of the Department of State
27 Records of the Penna.'s Revolutionary Governments
28 Records of the Treasury Department
30 Records of the Pennsylvania State Police
33 Records of the Supreme Court
38 Records of the Superior Court
41 Records of the Navigation Commission for the Delaware River and its Navigable Tributaries
42 Records of the Department of Revenue
45 Records of the Department of Mines and Mineral Industries
47 Records of County Governments
48 Records of Municipal Governments
50 Records of the Public School Employees Retirement System

MANUSCRIPT GROUPS

MG NO.   MG TITLE
2 Business Records Collection
3 Church and Cemetery Records Collection
4 County Records Collection
5 Deeds and Patents Collection
7 Military Manuscripts Collection
8 Pennsylvania Collection (miscellaneous)
4 J. Simpson Africa Collection
15 Hiram C. Alleman Papers
16 Francis Asbury Awl Papers
18 Battery B, First Pennsylvania Light Artillery Papers
21 John Bear Papers
25 Bloss Family Collection
26 Bodey-Cooper Collection
27 Bryant Family Papers
30 Burd-Shippen Family Collection
34 Campbell Family Papers
37 Conrad Family Papers
38 Cope Family Papers
43 Dock Family Papers
45 Elder Family Collection

A petiton submitted to the General Assembly by Jane Norton, a nurse during the American Revolution. From the HOUSE FILE, Militay Pensions, 49th Session, 1824-1825 (RG-7) PSA.

INDEX

attorneys, 39, 110-12, 131, 159, 160-
63, 167, 168, 225. *See also* students, law
auditor general, 120, 160, 331
Augusta and West Augusta districts.
See Virginia
autographs and signatures, 1, 6, 17,
22, 23, 36, 50, 63, 68, 71, 73, 76,
78, 82, 90, 92-94, 108, 110, 126,
127, 135, 148, 161, 167, 172, 173,
253-55, 263, 320, 321
Avery, Asahel, 312
Avoca, Pa., 299, 315

Baldwin family, 285
Baltimore, Md., 300
bankruptcies, 289
baptisms, 32, 202, 204-24, 241, 281,
304, 308
Barton family (Philadelphia), 284
Barton family (Robert R.), Lexington,
Va., 277
Bates, Samuel Penniman, 57
Bath, N.Y., 274
battalions, 49, 84, 92, 96, 97
batteries. *See* artillery batteries and
brigades
Baumann, Roland M., 115
Baynton, John, 193
Baynton, Wharton and Morgan, 33
Bear, John, 277
Beary, Gen. Frank D., 85
Beaver, James A., 277
Beaver, Pa., 193, 195, 199, 299
Beaver County, 51, 185, 200, 201,
225, 250, 284, 287, 288, 304, 339
Bedford, Pa., 196
Bedford County, 25, 43, 52-53, 55,
120, 133, 154, 173, 185, 225, 277,
281, 293, 296, 298, 308, 311, 326,
329
Bell, E. A.: Insurance Co., 277; family,
277
Bellamy family, 278
Belle Vernon, Pa., 60, 299
Bellwood, Pa., 299
Bender's Church (Lutheran),
Biglerville, 205

Bendersville, Pa., 205
beneficiaries, 317
Benjamin, Pa., 299
Bentel, Johann Georg, 288
Berks County, 43, 53, 107, 176, 223,
228, 278, 281, 282, 287, 293, 296,
304, 310, 326, 329, 340
Berlin, Pa., 299
Bernville, Pa., 299
Berrier family, 325
Berry family, 277
Bertillon Hand Books, 178, 183
Bertrand family, 300
Bethlehem, Pa., 61, 284, 288, 300
Bethlehem Lutheran Church,
Bendersville, 205
Bethlehem Steel Co., 117
Bevis, Sam, 29
Beyer family, 285
Bierer, Jacob J., 278
Big Spring, Pa., 51
Biglerville, Pa., 205, 206, 213
Binney family, 284
Birdsboro, Pa., 278, 299
Birdsboro Forge, Berks County, 25
birth, dates of, 8, 10, 13-16, 22, 26,
28, 30-32, 85, 87, 88, 90, 92, 109,
120, 124, 125, 127, 131, 132, 135,
149, 151, 155, 156, 166, 174, 178,
184, 188, 201, 202, 204-24, 253,
262, 299, 312, 322, 328, 329
birthplaces, 8, 10, 13, 15, 19-20, 22,
26-28, 30-32, 35, 85, 87, 88,
90, 92, 102, 109, 122, 132, 149,
151, 155, 161, 163, 166, 167, 172,
173, 181-84, 188, 202, 253, 254,
262, 271-74, 288, 301, 310
births, 8-10, 13, 15, 19-20, 22, 26-28,
30, 176, 178, 179, 205-26, 228-38,
240-47, 262, 302, 305, 309
Bishop, John, 194
blacks. *See* African Americans
Blackstone, H. Frank, 302
Blair County, 22, 53, 135, 278
Bliss family, 316
Bloomfield, Pa., 51
Bloss family, 278
Bodey family, 278

bonds, 155, 258, 260, 267, 288, 289, 304, 308, 316, 325
Bonneauville, Pa., 213
Boring family, 285
Boswell, Pa., 299
Bowerman, Solomon, 73-74, 77, 278
Bradford, Pa., 299
Bradford County, 122, 133, 136, 160, 169, 172, 176, 229, 252, 287, 340
Brady family, 78, 278
Bremer, Lewis, 285
brewing and bottling, 131, 167
bridges, 244, 247
Brooke family, 278
Brooklyn, Pa., 299
Brooks family, 285
Brotherhood of Railroad Trainmen, 158
Brownsville, Pa., 299
Brubaker, Francis L., 78
Bruner, Martin, 219
Bryant family, 278
Bryn Mawr, Pa., 61
Buchanan family, 278
Bucher family, 278, 290
Bucher, John Conrad, 290
Bucher-Hummel family, 33, 278, 290
Bucks County, 22, 43, 52-53, 176, 197, 229, 277, 279, 282, 283, 285, 293, 296, 298, 311, 326, 331
Bucktails, 42nd Regiment, Pennsylvania Volunteers, 56, 66, 76
Buffalo and Susquehanna Railroad, 306-308
Bulgarians, 299
Bull, Capt. John, 34
Burd family, 278, 287
Burd-Shippen family, 33, 278
burial(s), 23, 26-28, 30, 31, 119, 158, 201, 203, 205-22, 224, 226, 231-33, 235, 236, 238, 240, 244-46, 258, 308, 333, 336
Burn Brae, 305
Burnham, Pa., 109
Burrowes, Thomas H., 28
Butler, Ida, 317
Butler, Pa., 299
Butler County, 185, 230, 303
Butler family, 325

cadavers, 290
California, Pa., 299
Callahan, William A., 57
Cambria County, 51-52, 61, 185, 230
Cambria Iron Co., 291
Cambridgeboro, Pa., 299
Cameron County, 200, 306, 340
Camp Hill Prison, 190
Campbell family, 278
canals, 115-17, 153, 171, 257, 290, 294, 295, 309, 310, 315. *See also* names of individual canal companies
Canisteo, N.Y., 274
Canonsburg, Pa., 299
captains, ship. *See* ship captains
Carbon County, 18, 112, 132, 230, 253, 290, 320
Carbondale, Pa., 299, 315
Carlisle, Pa., 7, 51, 60, 196, 204, 220, 281, 284, 288
Carter, Lucius, 242
Carnegie, Pa., 299
Carr, Chapman, 312
Carter family, 278
Carter, John Joyce, 78
Carter, Lucius, 242
Casey family, 279
Cassatt, Alexander J., 142
casualties, 36, 38, 45, 48-91, 104, 149
Catawissa, Pa., 60
cavalry, 52, 58, 66, 78, 79, 104, 106
censuses, 268-76; decennial (federal), 106, 269-74; farm, 269, 274; register of inhabitants, 229, 243, 257; septennial (state), 268, 274, 275-76
Central Pennsylvania Quarry, Stripping, and Construction Co., 170
Centre County, 22, 51, 53, 176, 230, 277, 281, 287, 304
certified public accountants, 114
Chambersburg, Pa., 299, 324
chancery dockets, 306
Chandler family, 279
Chapel Cemetery, Monaca, Pa., 201
Charleroi, Pa., 299
Charming Forge, Berks County, 25
Chester County, 7, 22, 43, 52, 107, 176, 197, 230, 279, 280, 293, 296, 298, 311, 324, 326

Chestnut Grove Evangelical Lutheran Church, 206
chiropodists, 131
Chisuk Emuna Congregation, Harrisburg, 201
Christ Lutheran Church: Luzerne County, 202; Latimore Twp., 206; Gettysburg, 206
Christ Reformed Church, Littlestown, 202
church records, 201-24, 299
church charters, 312
cities and boroughs, panoramic views, 299
citizenship, 3-13, 16-18, 151, 230, 231, 272, 303. See also naturalizations
civil cases, 262
civil officers, 174
Civil War, 6, 51, 56-80, 232, 240, 272, 273, 301, 323; veterans' card file, 57; border raid claims, 323. See also military; regiments
Civilian Conservation Corps, 171
Claremont, Pa., 175
Clarion, Pa., 299
Clarion County, 22, 71, 231, 279, 287, 320
Clark, William S., 285
Claypoole family, 279
Clayton, Lt. Col. Asher, 290
Clearfield, Pa., 299
Clearfield County, 22, 185, 231, 306
clemency records, 292; petitions, 295
Clement, Martin W., 142
clerks, law office, 110-12, 161
Clinton County, 22, 232, 304, 306
coal mining, 133-34, 164, 170, 313, 315, 327; accidents, 164
Coaldale, Pa., 288
Coates, Abraham, 193
Codorus Forge, 119
Cohocton, N.Y., 274
Coleman family, 118, 279
Collegeville, Pa., 299
Columbia, Pa., 60, 237, 283, 299
Columbia and Philadelphia Railroad, 117
Columbia County, 22, 176, 232, 254, 263, 268

common pleas court, 3, 8, 10-11, 13-15, 111-13, 120, 124, 160, 228, 241, 246, 247, 255, 258, 259, 261, 333, 336
Concord Congregation, Pleasantville, Venango County, 202
condemnations, 264
Conewago Chapel (Catholic), 207
Confer, James, 57
Confluence, Pa., 299
Connecticut claimants, 193, 198
Connellsville, Pa., 60, 299
Conrad family, 279
conscientious objectors, 58, 71, 75
constables, 293
Cook, Caroline, 285
Cooper family, 278
Cope family, 279
Corbett family, 279
Cornwall, Pa., 117-19, 313
Cornwall Methodist Church, 202
Cornwall Ore Bank Co., 117-19
coroners' inquisitions, 20, 21, 238, 240, 244, 250, 253, 262, 267, 288, 293, 311, 312
corporations, 233
Corrections, Bureau of, 183, 190
Corry, Pa., 299
Coulter, Gen. Richard, 78
county commissions, 228, 231
county officers, 119
court: district, 247, 258; provincial, 231; Philadelphia City, 298; county, 44. See also names of courts
courts, U.S. circuit and district, 8, 228, 241, 247, 258, 264
Covert, Thomas M., 57
Cowperthwaite family, 316
Cox family, 284
Craven family, 316
Crawford County, 22, 185, 232, 267, 284, 315, 320
creditors, 264
Crees, Susannah E., 289
Croatians, 299, 313
Cromwell family, 284
Crum family, 278
Cumberland County, 7, 22, 43, 51, 71, 96, 107, 168, 170, 176, 220, 232, 255, 277-79, 280-83, 296, 327

Curtin Iron Works, Centre County, 25, 203

Cummings, Hubertis M., 309

Curwensville, Pa., 299

Dallas (Pa.) Prison, 190

damage claims, 323, 324

Dansville, N.Y., 274

Danville, Pa., 60

Danville State Hospital, 305

Dauphin County, 7, 43, 52-53, 72, 107, 115, 117, 120, 124, 131-33, 136, 152, 158, 160, 200, 201, 222, 233, 256 60, 200, 277-79, 283-85, 287, 297, 304, 326, 340

Davidson, Rev. Robert, 204

Davidson family, 285

Davis family, 302

Dawson, Pa., 299

death dates, 20, 22, 27, 28, 31, 48, 57, 63, 123, 131, 149, 158, 160, 161, 172, 189, 190, 201, 203-24, 251, 258, 259, 263, 264, 288, 291, 299, 319, 322, 332-38

death records, 12, 19-23, 25-28, 30, 31, 48, 51, 54, 59, 60, 119, 135, 181, 202, 233, 234, 237, 238, 240-47, 253, 262, 277, 288-90, 302, 309, 322

debtors, 289

decedents, 237

declarations of intention, 3-4, 6, 7, 9, 12-16. See also citizenship; naturalizations

deeds, 193, 194, 198, 200, 225-26, 228-38, 240-48, 251, 260, 277, 281, 284, 288, 289, 292, 296, 300, 303, 304, 306, 312, 315-17, 319, 325-29

Deemer, Henry L., 118

Delaware, 35, 196, 197, 306, 320

Delaware County, 22, 43, 52, 107, 176, 233, 297

Delaware, Lackawanna, and Western Railroad, 134-35

Delaware River, 195, 198

delinquent lists, military, 45

Delta, Pa., 313

Denison, Dr. Benjamin A., 312

Denison, Dr. Mason, 312

Dennis, John, 243

Denny family, 279

dental hygienists, 247

dentists, 120-22, 123, 159, 163, 174, 226, 229-30, 235-36, 238, 240, 247-48, 296, 338

depreciation lands, 37, 40, 194, 195; certificates, 37, 44; maps, 194

Derry Station, Pa., 299

diaries, 25

Diddy family, 278

Dietrich family, 280

Dimock, Elder Davis, 312

disease, 318, 324

District of Columbia courts, 18

Ditmer family, 279

divorce, 20, 23, 24, 27, 244, 252, 263, 289, 318, 333, 335-38

Dixmont State Hospital, 203

Dobbins, Alexander K., 296

Dobbins family, 279

Dock family, 279

Donation Lands, 36, 38-42, 194; New York, 38

Donora, Pa., 299

Downingtown, Pa., 299

Doylestown, Pa., 52

draft board records, 84

draftees and substitutes, 58, 71-73, 78. See also Selective Service

drunkards, 244, 256

DuBois, Pa., 299

Dunbar, Pa., 299

Dunmore, Pa., 315

Duquesne, Pa., 299

Duss, Caroline, 289

Duss, John, 289

Eagle Cemetery Association, 203

Earle, Gov. George H., 279, 317

East Springfield, Pa., 61

Eastern State Penitentiary, 175, 176-82, 190

Easton, Pa., 30, 52, 196, 288, 310

Eberhart, James W., 61

Eckley, Pa., 313

Economy, Pa., 282, 284, 302
Edwardsville, Pa., 299
ejectments, 252
Elder family, 279
electrical workers, 313
Elizabeth, Pa., 299
Elizabethtown, Pa., 299
Elk County, 15, 72, 200, 234, 300, 306, 315, 340
Ellwood City, Pa., 299
Emlenton, Pa., 299
Emmaus, Pa., 299
employees, 119, 125, 127, 128, 137, 139-57, 167, 170, 171; state, 148, 167
employers, 10, 25, 125
employment, 303
Endsley family, 279
engineers, military, 108
Engle family, 279
entertainers, actors, 304
Ephrata Cloister, 324
Eppeler family, 302
equity papers, 261-63
Erie, Pa., 195, 260
Erie County, 12, 13, 14, 17, 22, 121, 185, 194, 200, 234, 259-60, 279, 281, 282, 320, 340; naturalizations, 14
Erie Extension Canal, 117
Erie Railroad Co., 308
escheats, 20
Espionage Act, 301
Espy family, 277, 281
estates, 23, 41-42, 119, 231, 234, 235, 244, 246, 251, 260, 261, 303, 304, 312, 315, 317-19
estreat of fines, 25, 29
Evans, Samuel, 280
Evans City, Pa., 299
Evans family, 280
Everhart, Pa., 315
Ewing family, 285
Exchequer and Audit Department, British, 35
exemplifications, 243
exemptions, 243
Exeter, Pa., 315

exporters, 322
Eyre, John, 280
Eyre, Pamela, 280

Factoryville, Pa., 299
Fairfield, Pa., 212
Fall family, 280
familial relationships, 1, 7, 9, 10, 27, 32, 36, 42, 44, 45, 57, 58, 90, 115, 118, 119, 127, 129, 155, 158, 160, 161, 170, 178, 179, 181-84, 186, 187, 201-24, 257, 259, 262, 272-74, 288, 290-92, 328, 330
family Bibles, 19, 292
family papers, 277-87
Farley family, 280
farms, farmers, 291, 296, 325; Century Program, 291; ownership, 273
Fayette County, 7, 22, 43, 52-53, 107, 185, 200, 234, 297, 340
Feichtenberger, Maria Elisabeth, 285
Fencibles. See regiments
Fenn, George Washington, 66, 67, 280
Fenn family, 280
Ferree, Ozias, 280
Ferree family, 280
Feucht family, 284
fictitious names file, 262, 263
Fidelity Insurance, Trust, and Safe Deposit Co., 317
Filby, P. William, 7
fingerprints, 190
firemen, 135, 160
"First City Zouaves," 59, 78
First Lutheran Church, New Oxford, 207
First Presbyterian Church, Carlisle, 204
First Reformed Church, Lancaster, 219
Fischern, Hermann, 302
Fisher, Benjamin Franklin, 280
Fisher family, 281
Fleetwood, Pa., 299
Fleming, John, 78
Flickinger family, 280; Isaac, 285
Fliegel, Rev. Carl John, 218
Flohr's Lutheran Church, 208

Hall, Wilmer C., 79, 281
Hamburg, Pa., 299
Hamlin and Forest (land company), 306
handicapped persons, 268, 270-72
Hanover, Pa., 60
Harbaugh, Rev. M., 219
Harewood Hospital, 77
Harford, Pa., 61
Harmonsburg, Pa., 61
Harmony, Pa., 299, 303
Harmony Brickworks, 302
Harmony Society, 288-89, 301-304, 322. *See also* Economy Pa.; New Harmony, Ind.
Harper, John W., 281, 304
Harris family, 281, 316
Harrisburg, Pa., 31, 52, 60, 67, 112, 133, 135, 158, 159, 201, 216-17, 280-84, 290, 313, 325
Harrisburg and Pittsburgh Railroad, 117
Harrisburg City Grays, 78
Harrisburg *Home Star*, 304
Hartranft, John F., 79
Hartstown, Pa., 284, 286
Hastings family, 281
Haudenshield, John R., 281
Haverstick, Rudy, 57
Hawley, Pa., 315
Hazardville, Pa., 290
Hazen, Pa., 61
Hazleton, Pa., 170, 202, 285
health, 176, 180, 181, 183, 184, 186, 188, 270-73, 318, 324
Health, Department of, 31
Health, Board of, 19, 26, 30, 31
health officers, 1-2, 332-33, 335-38
Hecklebernie, Pa., 288
Heess, Albert F., 10
heirs and assigns, 38, 39, 46
Henrici, William T., 289
Henrici family, 302
Henry family, 278
Hershey family, 281
Hershey Museum, 304
Hessians, 36
Hetzel family, 302

Hickok, Ross A., 281
Hickok family, 281
Hiester family, 281
Highway Patrol, 155
Hill, Jacob R., 79
Hill Lutheran Church, Lebanon County, 217
Hillegas, Conrad, family, 281
Hines family, 281
Hinke, William John, 1
Hispanics, 313
History of Pennsylvania Volunteers, 1861-65, 57
Hocker family, 281
Hoffmeier, Johann Heinrich, 219
Holland Land Co., 195
Hollenbach family, 282; Mathias, 287
Holy Trinity Lutheran Church, York Springs, 209
home ownership, 273
Homestead, Pa., 61, 299
Honesdale, Pa., 299
Hoover family, 282
Hope Church, Mount Hope, 221
Hopper, Delphine T., 285
Houck, Henry, 193
Houghtelin, William Drayton, 79
household goods, 36
Houser, J. P., 304
Houston, Samuel, 79
Howard, David W., 79
Hoyt, Gov. Henry Martyn, 183
Hughes family, 280
Hughestown, Pa., 315
Hume family (Memphis, Tenn.), 277
Hummel family, 278, 290
Hummelstown, Pa., 285, 326
Hungarians, 299
Huntingdon, Pa., 182-85, 284
Huntingdon County, 43, 53, 107, 133, 172, 182, 185, 236, 277, 284, 297, 326, 340
Huntingdon Industrial Reformatory, 175, 182-85, 190

Immigration and Naturalization Service, U.S., 13, 15, 17, 18

Nicholson, John, 193, 197, 284
nisi prius, courts of, 6, 311, 336
nominations for public office, 135
Norfolk and Western Railroad, 145, 148
North East, Pa., 300
Northampton County, 25, 43, 107, 241, 290, 297, 298, 311, 312, 325, 326
Northumberland County, 7, 43, 52-53, 107, 176, 242, 265-66, 284, 293, 297, 316, 320, 329
Norton, Jane, 354
Norwood, Pa., 61
notarial dockets, 247
notary public, 117
nurses, 162, 174, 313, 354

Oakmont, Pa., 300
oaths of allegiance, 9, 13, 103, 293
occupational records, 109-174; data, 1, 7-10, 13, 15-17, 20, 22, 23, 25-28, 30-32, 41, 42, 49, 56-62, 65, 68, 71-73, 78, 80, 85, 89, 92-98, 101-105, 109, 122, 127, 128, 150, 160, 164, 165, 167, 170, 175, 176, 178-82, 187-89, 191, 203, 253, 254, 256, 258, 261, 262, 288, 289, 291, 292, 295, 296, 298, 301, 305, 312, 326
Odd Fellows, 258
O'Hara family, 279
Ohio, 280, 289, 308
Ohio River, 195
Oil City, Pa., 300
Old Economy Village, 322
Old Forge, Pa., 315
"Old Guard," 95
Olyphant, Pa., 315
optometrists, 135, 157, 229, 230, 235, 236, 238
oral history, 313
Orbison family, 284
Oregon Heights, Pa., 315
orphans, 57, 257
orphans' court, 19, 45, 47, 225-26, 228-238, 240-47, 260, 262, 263, 334-35
osteopaths, 120, 136, 158, 174, 229, 235, 238, 240, 248

Ott family, 284
Outman family, 285
Oxford, Pa., 52, 60
oyer and terminer, court of, 228, 230, 231, 247, 252, 258, 259, 265, 266, 293, 296, 298

Painted Post, N.Y., 274
Palmer, William Jackson, 79
pardons. See clemency records
Parker family, 284
parole data, 178-80, 185, 189
partitions, 264
passes, military, 35
passports and visas, 303
patents, land, 37, 38, 41, 42, 192, 194, 197-99, 243, 289, 292, 293, 296, 303, 304, 316, 325, 326
Path Valley and Falling Springs Church, Franklin County, 219
Patterson, Pa., 300
Patterson family, 287
Patton, Pa., 300
paupers, 183, 229, 233, 237, 241, 312. See also almshouses
Paupers Population Land Co., 198
payrolls, 25, 43, 117, 142, 167, 171, 230, 231, 302; Civil War, 232
Peckville, Pa., 300
peddlers and hawkers, 115, 123, 152, 160, 253. See also retailers; Indian traders
Peiffer family, 325
Pen Argyl, Pa., 300
penitentiaries, 175, 190; Eastern State, 175, 176-82, 190; Western State, 175, 185-90; Industrial Reformatory, Huntingdon, 175, 182-85, 190
Penn, R. W., 79
Penn Central Railroad, 137
Pennsylvania Archives, 6, 9, 33, 37, 42, 44, 50, 54
Pennsylvania Board of Pharmacy, 165-66
Pennsylvania Canal System, 115-16, 117, 257, 294, 295, 309; passenger lists, 315; Lehigh and Delaware division, 290

Pennsylvania claimants, 196
Pennsylvania Collection, 33
Pennsylvania Hospital for Insane,
    Philadelphia, 305
Pennsylvania Line, 38, 39, 41-43
Pennsylvania Nautical School, 109
Pennsylvania Railroad Co., 136-48,
    158, 257, 316, 317, 328; personnel,
    137, 158
Pennsylvania Reserve Militia, 105
Pennsylvania Reserve Volunteer Corps,
    58, 61, 65, 79
Pennsylvania Schuylkill Valley
    Railroad, 317
Pennsylvania Soldiers' and Sailors'
    Home, 68
Pennsylvania State Lunatic Hospital,
    Harrisburg, 305
Pennsylvania State Medical Boards, 69
Pennsylvania State Police, 122, 135,
    148-49, 155, 168, 296, 301, 312,
    320; personnel, 148-49, 155
Pennsylvania Veteran Volunteers, 59,
    66
Pennsylvania Volunteer Emergency
    Militia, 58, 61, 65
Pennsylvania Volunteers, 50, 51, 54,
    56, 57, 61, 66, 75, 76, 78-80, 94-95
Pennsylvania War History Commission.
    See War History Commission
Pennsylvania's Revolutionary
    Governments, records of, 35
Pennypacker, Gov. Samuel W., 284
Pennzoil Co., 315
pensioners, pensions, 44, 45, 47, 48,
    50, 54, 57, 75, 106, 129, 132, 134,
    230; bonus recipients, 87, 90;
    mothers, 312; Revolutionary War,
    230
Pepers, Capt. James, 290
Perkasie, Pa., 300
Perry County, 22, 51-53, 176, 200,
    242, 280, 282, 287, 296, 340
Peters, William, 192
pharmacists, 165; apprentices, 166;
    assistants, 165
Philadelphia, Pa., 7, 9, 14, 28, 43, 52,
    60, 68, 73, 95, 106-107, 120, 159,
    176, 195, 196, 198, 268, 278-81,
    283-85, 287, 290, 291, 293, 298,
    300, 309, 310-12, 316, 332, 333
Philadelphia, Port of, 1, 114, 155, 164,
    295, 310, 316, 322, 325
Philadelphia County, 7, 19, 22, 25, 43,
    51-53, 107-108, 119, 176, 193,
    196, 242, 243, 271, 293, 297, 311,
    312
Philadelphia Hospital, 305
Philadelphia and Reading Relief
    Association, 153; personnel, 154
Philippines' occupation, 81
Phillipsburg (Monaca), Beaver County,
    287
photographs, 80, 84-86, 120, 141,
    142, 182, 189, 190, 279, 282, 284,
    285, 286, 290, 292, 296, 299, 304,
    313, 314, 316, 325, 329, 330
physical descriptions, 1, 10, 11, 16,
    56-57, 59-61, 73-74, 78, 81-85, 94,
    96-99, 102-104, 127, 176, 181-83,
    186-88, 253, 296, 310
physical examinations, 88-89, 99, 128,
    184
physical therapists, 123
physicians, 26-28, 30-32, 112, 118,
    122, 124, 128, 132, 133, 149, 154,
    164, 167. *See also* surgeons, mili-
    tary; medical records
Pike County, 22, 176, 200, 285, 340
pilots, harbor and ship, 114, 155, 165,
    316
Pine Grove, Pa., 60
Pine Grove Furnace, Cumberland
    County, 25
Pitcairn, Pa., 300
Pithole City, Pa., 248
Pittsburgh, Pa., 7, 52, 53, 112, 185,
    248, 271, 279, 291, 300, 313, 321;
    riot claims, 250
Pittsburgh City Farm Insane Asylum,
    305
Pittston, Pa., 300, 315
Plains, Pa., 300, 315
Pleasantville, Pa., 61, 202
Polish, 299
politicians and candidates, 135, 304

poor, 241, 248; children, 229, 257; overseers of, 258, 266
poor houses. *See* almshouses
Port Griffith, Pa., 315
Potter County, 22, 185, 200, 243, 248, 283, 285, 306, 340
Potts family, 284
Pottstown, Pa., 300
Pottsville, Pa., 26, 30, 53, 60, 69, 290, 296, 300
power of attorney, 117, 260, 303, 308
Prattsburg, N.Y., 274
Preston, George L., 79
Preston family, 283
Priestley, Joseph, 284
Priestley, Joseph Jr., 316
prisons, 175-90, 198, 230; Camp Hill, 190; Dallas, 190; Graterford, 190; Greensburg, 190; Huntingdon, 190; Muncy, 190; Rockview, 190
prison population records, 175-90; indices to Eastern State Penitentiary, 175, and Western State Penitentiary, 189
prisoners of war, 48, 61, 63, 91
probate, 225, 245
property, personal, 323
Proprietary, Pennsylvania, 196-98, 242
Prospect, Pa., 61
Provincial Council, 33
Provost Marshall General Office, 75
public housekeepers, 298, 311
public officials, 174
Public School Employees Retirement System, 155-57
Pullman-Standard Car Co., Butler, Pa., 150-52
Pulteney, N.Y., 274
Punxsutawney, Pa., 300

quarter sessions, court of, 8, 120, 160, 228, 234, 244, 247, 258-60, 262, 265, 298

race, color or complexion, 1, 10, 13, 14, 16, 20, 22, 23, 26, 28, 31, 32, 56-57, 59-61, 73-74, 81-85, 87, 89, 94, 96-99, 102-104, 115, 124, 128, 149, 167, 170, 175, 178-81, 183-

89, 203, 253, 254, 262-64, 268, 296, 310, 312, 320. *See also* African Americans
Railroad Museum of Pennsylvania, 173
Railroad Trainmen, Brotherhood of, 158
railroads, 116, 117, 125-30, 134-48, 152, 158, 167, 173, 257, 290, 306-308, 316, 317, 319, 328, 329. *See also* names of individual railroad companies
Rall family, 302
Rapp, George, 288, 301; family, 302, 271-76, 291
Raynsford, Joshua W., 312
Rea, Samuel, 142
Read family, 325
Reading, Pa., 26, 31, 32, 53, 60, 196
Reading Furnace, Berks County, 25
real estate, 36, 263, 264, 288, 289, 295, 306-308, 310, 316-19, 323, 329
Real Estate Trust Co., Philadelphia, 317
Ream family, 284
Reamstown, Pa., 284
Receiver General, 197, 198
recognizance records, 231, 233
redemptioners, 243
Reed, Francis W., 79
Reem, Charles, 57
Reformed Church, Lancaster, 219
regiments, military, 34, 36, 38, 41-43, 48, 49, 50, 54, 56, 57-70, 73-76, 78-82, 87-88, 92-99, 101, 103, 106-108. *See also* artillery batteries and brigades; cavalry
Reichert, Johan Friedrich, 288
Reilly, James, 57
relief, 229, 237, 240
religious affiliation, 4, 179, 183, 184, 188
rent rolls and books, 198
residency, 3, 6, 8-10, 13-16, 18-20, 23, 26, 28, 30-32, 35, 36, 42, 43, 45, 49-51, 123, 131, 135, 152, 158-64, 167, 172, 173, 178, 179, 184, 185, 187, 188, 205, 208, 211-

17, 219, 251, 254, 259, 261, 263, 268, 295, 296, 298, 305, 311, 326, 328-30

retailers, 114, 115, 131. *See also* businessmen; peddlers and hawkers

revenue. *See* drawbacks or duties refunded; taxes

Revolutionary War: service, 34-49, 231; military abstract card file, 44; pensions, 230. *See also* Associators, accounts; Loyalists; oaths of allegiance; Sons of the American Revolution

Rex, Millicent Barton, 284

Reyle, John, 285

Rhode Island, 18

Rice, Samuel (farm), 296

Richardson, George A., 284

Ridgway, Pa., 300

Ritchie, Rosanna (Saltzman), 47

roads, 23, 141, 167, 226, 231, 236, 238

Roaring Brook, Pa., 315

Robbins, Lucy, 285

Roberts family, 280

Robeson, Brooke & Company, Berks County, 25

Robinson, W.D., 180

Rochester, Pa., 300

Rockport, Pa., 288

Rockview Prison, 190

Rohrer, Jeremiah, 79

Rohrigs, Wilhelm, 327

Roscoe, Pa., 300

Royersford, Pa., 300

Rupley family, 282

Russians, 299

Rutherford family, 282. *See also* Kunkel family

Rutz, John, 289

Sachs, Mary (Inc.), Harrisburg, Pa., 132

Sachse, Julius, 324

safety, 23

sailors, 248

St. Francis Hospital, Pittsburgh, 305

St. James Lutheran Church, Gettysburg, 211; Wenksville, 211

St. John's Episcopal Church, Carlisle, 220

St. John's Episcopal Church, Olympia, Washington Territory, 221

St. John's Evangelical and Reformed Church, Fairfield, 212

St. John's Lutheran Church, Abbottstown, 212, 213; Littlestown, 212

St. Luke's Lutheran Church, Bonneauville, 213

St. Luke's Episcopal Church, Lebanon, 220-21

St. Luke's Episcopal Church, New Tacoma, Washington Territory, 221

St. Mark's Episcopal Church, Jonestown, 221

St. Marys, Pa., 300

St. Patrick's Roman Catholic Burial Association, Lebanon County, 221

St. Paul's Lutheran Church, Biglerville, 213; Littlestown, 214; New Chester, 214; McSherrystown, 214

St. Peter's Episcopal Church, Tacoma, Washington territory, 221

St. Stephen's Episcopal Church, Thompsontown, 222

Salem German Reformed Church, Harrisburg, 216, 217

Salisbury, Pa., 300

Saltzman. *See* Ritchie, Rosanna

Sanderson, George, 28

Saulsburg, Pa., 61

Saylor, Livingston, 79

Sayre, Pa., 126

Schaffner family, 79, 285

Schilling, Edward, 80

Schlenker, Rev. J.O., 202

Schmidt, J. Augustus, 202, 285

Schrack, Samuel, 285

Schuylkill County, 22, 52-53, 121, 131, 136, 167, 176, 195, 243, 266, 280, 290, 310, 340

Schuylkill County Almshouse, 305

Schuylkill Navigation Co., 153, 171, 295, 310

Schuylkill River, 195, 310

Schuylkill Water Co., 310

Stewart, Thomas J., 80
Stine, Joseph S., 57
Stoey, William W., 325
Stofik, Harry, 11
Stover, Edward, 124, 285, 325
Stoystown, Pa., 76
Strasburg, Pa., 300
Strassburger, Ralph Beaver, 1
students: dental, 59; law 113, 123,
    125, 131, 159, 160, 162, 163, 166,
    168, 225; medical, 159
Sullenberger family, 325
Sullivan County, 10, 22, 200, 245, 340
Summers, William, 229
Summit Hill, Pa., 288
Sunbury, Pa., 7, 196, 199
Superior Court, state, 112, 124, 159;
    Eastern District, 112, 159; Middle
    District, 112, 159; Scranton
    District, 112, 159
Supreme Court of Pennsylvania, 3, 7-
    9, 13, 15, 25, 45, 124, 159, 293,
    296, 298, 330, 333, 336;
    Chambersburg (Southern) District,
    8; Eastern District, 4, 7, 9, 20, 21,
    25, 29, 36, 49, 166, 304, 312, 330;
    Middle District, 112, 123, 163, 166;
    Western District, 5, 8, 110, 125,
    160, 163
Supreme Executive Council, 35
Surgart, John W., 325
Surgeon General, 63, 69
surgeons, military, 69, 74, 76
Surveyor General, 39, 41, 69, 195,
    196, 329
Surveyor General, U.S., 58, 63
surveys, land, 37, 192-94, 196-99,
    226, 231, 242, 248, 281, 289, 304,
    306, 310
Susquehanna Company, 326
Susquehanna County, 176, 200, 245,
    246, 279, 326
Susquehanna River, 192, 194, 195,
    199
Swain family, 285
Swetland family, 285
Swope family, 285
Sybert, Henry, 289

Tabor First Reformed Church,
    Lebanon, 223
Tacony, Pa., 300
Taggert, Robert, 80
Tamaqua, Pa., 288
Tarentum, Pa., 300
Tate, Maj. Magnus (family), 287
tavern keepers, 119, 123, 168, 170.
    See also innkeepers
taverns, 123, 168, 169, 170, 233, 241,
    245, 298, 311. *See also* inns
tax: lists, 225, 228-29, 231-35, 241-
    42, 245, 248-51, 255; appeals, 266;
    assessments, 225, 228-29, 231-33,
    238-39, 242-44, 247-48, 252-54,
    267, 303; claims, 252; inheritance,
    318, 319; records, 264, 304, 328;
    returns, 256, 260; U.S. Direct Tax
    of 1798, 248
taxation, 23
taxpayers, 268
Taylor, William M., 80
Taylorsville, Pa., 288
teachers, 114, 155, 157, 158, 328, 329
Teiling, Carolina, 289
Telford, Pa., 300
Tennessee, 277
therapists, drugless, 132
Thomas family, 278
Thompson, E. O., 317
Thompson family, 33, 284; Edward
    Shippen, 33, 287
Thompson-Ullery, Kathleen, 287
Tidioute, Pa., 300
Tioga County, 22, 72, 176, 200, 245,
    267, 306, 340
Tionesta, Pa., 300
title briefs, 289
Titusville, Pa., 31, 300
town clerks, 332
transportation, public, 23
Trenton Cut Off Railroad Co., 317
Treziulny, Charles S., 327
Treziulny, Henry P., 327
Treziulny, Joseph Franklin P., 80
Treziulny family, 287, 327
Trimble, James, 39

Trinity (Episcopal) Church, Portland, Oregon Territory, 221
Trinity Lutheran Church, Arendtsville, 210
Troopers, State, 122
Troupsburg, N.Y., 274
Tulpehocken Church, Stouchsburg, Berks County, 223
Turtle Creek, Pa., 300
Tuscarora Old School Baptist Church, Juniata County, 223
Two Taverns, Pa., 208
Tyrone, Pa., 278, 300

Ukrainians, 299
Ullery, Kathleen Thompson, 287
Ullery family, 287
undertakers, funeral directors, 27, 30, 31, 109, 149, 203, 235
Union Canal Co., 295
Union City, Pa., 60, 300
Union County, 52, 267, 281, 285, 340
Uniontown, Pa., 7, 300
United Methodist Church, Gettysburg, 215
United Presbyterian Church, Mercersburg, 224
Upper Allen School District, 327

Van Booskirk, Mahlon, 229
Vauclain, S.M., 173
Venango County, 72, 185, 200, 202, 245, 248, 320, 340
Vensell family, 287
Verona, Pa., 300
veterans, military, 6, 39, 45, 48, 50, 54, 57, 60, 62, 70, 81-82, 87, 90, 94, 114, 226, 231, 238, 244, 248, 272, 301, 335, 337. See also military service
veterinarians, 172-74, 226, 229, 235, 236, 238, 240, 244, 248
Vietnam War, 90-91, 231; veterans' bonus, 91
Virginia, 248, 277, 287, 325; claims, 199; Yohogania County, 246; Augusta and West Augusta districts, 248
vital statistics, 19-32, 303, 332-38.

See also births; deaths; and marriages or marital status
Vital Statistics, Division of, New Castle, Pa., 22
voter registration, 253
voters, 254

Wagner, J. George, 285
Wagner, Oscar C., 57
Wahl, Elizabeth, 289
Wallis, J.T., 142
Wallis, Samuel, 329
War Department, U.S., 81, 89
War History Commission, Pennsylvania (World War I), 84, 87
War History Program (World War II), 89
War of 1812, 49-50; service index, 49
Warner, Samuel, 312
warrants: death, 295; land, 90, 94, 192-95, 198, 199, 231, 245, 289, 326; court, 293; bench, 298
Warren, Pa., 195, 199, 300
Warren County, 22, 185, 200, 245, 315
Washington, George, 194
Washington, Pa., 7, 300
Washington County, 7, 43, 52-53, 72, 107, 185, 200, 246, 285, 297, 313, 340
Waterford, Pa., 195, 199
Watrous family, 285
Watson family, 277, 280, 281
Wayne, Joseph, 285
Wayne, N.Y., 274
Wayne County, 176, 200, 246, 267, 283, 340
Waynesboro, Pa., 300
Waynesburg, Pa., 53, 300
Weaver family, 287
Weidner family, 287
Weingartner, Wallrath, 303
Weiser, Rev. Frederick S., 205
Weiser family, 287
Welles family, 287
Welsh, 299
Welsh Hill, Pa., 315
Wenksville, Pa., 211
Werner, William, 302

West Bethlehem, Pa., 300
West Elizabeth, Pa., 300
West Finley, Pa., 61
West Haven, Pa., 288
West Newton, Pa., 300
West Pittston, Pa., 300
West Virginia, 281
Western Correctional Diagnostic and
    Classification Center, 189
Western State Penitentiary, 175, 185-
    90
Westmoreland County, 7, 22, 24, 43,
    52-53, 107, 194, 247, 267, 278,
    297
Wharton, Samuel, 193
Whipkey, Harry E., 277
White Haven, 290
White, James, 284
Wiconisco Canal, 117
widows, 27-28, 45, 48, 50, 57, 171,
    203, 226, 231, 235, 253, 272, 312
Wilcox family, 316
Wilkes-Barre, Pa., 196, 287, 300, 326,
    327
Williams, Edward C., 50, 287; family,
    51
Williams family (Bucks County), 285
Williamsburg, Pa. 53
Williamsport, Pa., 28, 283
wills, 22, 225-26, 228-38, 240-47,
    251, 259, 277, 281, 289, 303, 304,
    312, 316-18, 332, 334
Wilmerding, Pa., 300
Wilson, Pa., 300
Wilson, James Harrison, 80
Wilson, Lucille, 329
Windber, Pa., 300
Wisconsin, 278
Wister family, 283
Wolfangel, Anna Catharina, 289
Wolfangel, Gottfrield, 289
women, 160, 313, 329; and law, 229
Woods family, 277, 281, 287
Woodville State Hospital, 201
workmen's compensation, 148, 170,
    171
Work Projects Administration (WPA), 7,
    313, 322

World War I, 84-88, 231, 301, 337
World War II, 88-90, 231, 321; veter-
    ans' bonus, 90
Worrelville, Pa., 61
Wrightsville, Pa., 300
writs, 312, 330
Wunder, Henry, 57
Wyalusing, Pa., 287
Wyoming County, 22, 247
Wyomissing Manufacturing Co., 229

Yatesville, Pa., 315
Yingst family, 325
Yohogania County, Va., 246
York, Pa., 196
York County, 25, 29, 43, 73, 107, 176,
    247, 279, 283, 293, 297, 298
York Springs, Pa., 209
Yorkville, Pa., 26

Zehner (Zaner) family, 287
Zelienople, Pa., 300
Zouaves: First City, 59; Penn Yan, 70
Zion Lutheran Church, Fairfield, 216
Zion United Church of Christ,
    Arendtsville, 210
Zundel family, 287